Social and Economic Studies within the Framework of Emerging Global Developments Volume 3

Muhammed Veysel Kaya and Seda Bayrakdar (eds.)

Social and Economic Studies within the Framework of Emerging Global Developments

Volume 3

PETER LANG

Lausanne - Berlin - Bruxelles - Chennai - New York - Oxford

Library of Congress Cataloging-in-Publication Data
A CIP catalog record for this book has been applied for at the Library of Congress.

Bibliographic information published by the Deutsche Nationalbibliothek.
The German National Library lists this publication in the German National Bibliography; detailed bibliographic data is available on the Internet at http://dnb.d-nb.de.

Cover illustration:
© gorodenkoff

ISBN 978-3-631-90121-2 (Print)
E-ISBN 978-3-631-90442-8 (E-PDF)
E-ISBN 978-3-631-90443-5 (E-PUB)
10.3726/b20968

Published by Peter Lang GmbH, Berlin, Deutschland

info@peterlang.com - www.peterlang.com

This publication has been peer reviewed.

Prof. Dr. Muhammed Veysel Kaya
Assoc. Prof. Seda Bayrakdar

Foreword

This book is the third series of the "Social and Economic Studies within the Framework of Emerging Global Developments." Second volume includes empirical and theoretical original papers written by researchers from different countries and universities. The target audience of this book is researchers, students and academics interested in business, economics and social sciences.

Challoumis examines the liability of the tax system. The analysis of the impact of liability on the tax system in combination with the impact factor of tax revenues is used from the Q.E. method. *Ribba* investigates the possible presence of fiscal dominance, that is, an explicit or implicit cooperation between federal government and central bank with monetary policy in a subordinate position. *Dat and Long* indicates the correlation between the established stock markets, such as the US and China, and the Vietnam stock market is altered during the COVID-19 pandemic. *Ghoneim* analysis, COVID-19 impact on "Decent Work and Economic Growth" goal in Africa through providing descriptive statistics of the situation before and after 2020. The paper highlighted unemployment changes after the pandemic as well as the highly affected sectors and groups in terms of job opportunities creation.

Alfoul investigates, the utility of natural language processing (NPL) and artificial intelligence (AI) in the context of improving research achievement in economics and finance. The research takes a case-study approach, using ChatGPT to illustrate an NLP tool with promising potential in the academic world. *Marcel, Diana and Yevheniy* examines socioeconomic indicators of Euroscepticism at the regional level in Slovakia and they differentiate three groups of regions: (1) weak regions (the Bratislava region exclusively), (2) moderate "transitive" regions, and (3) stable regions. *Ahmadov* examines in the form of group interviews to identify barriers that SMEs perceive on the adaptation and implementation of innovation for circular practices, and secondly, analyses the result of the survey that involved 190 companies operating in the Estonian computer, electric, chemical and metal industry. *Guzman, Tarapuez and Parra* try to identify the drivers of the future, recognize the scenario for nature tourism to the year 2035 in the context of the PCCC and propose strategies to achieve it. *Tsertseil* analysis of the activities of small and medium-sized businesses in the manufacturing sector of the Lipetsk region. *Ordov, Tsertseil and Zatsarnaya* identify the prerequisites for the successful development of the carbon units market in Russia as one of the tools for minimizing carbon emissions into the environment. *Dec and Wysocki* explores the issue of ecologically sound investments in Polish cities, which are part of the ongoing implementation of sustainable development goals, in the context of an increasingly noticeable limitation of financial resources available for these types of undertakings. *Rosyadi and Fitriadi* exhibits to remind and concentrate on the network in building SMEs. *Anunciacao and Petiz* exhibits to carried out through the focus group analysis aiming to reflect and consolidate the main dimensions and strategic subdimensions relevant to public local management authorities. The results show the importance of a collective vision of different stakeholders, and the process of change must be properly thought-out and prepared. *Anunciacao and Giroto* analysis, 20 years after its creation, the benefits of this legal change and the effects on the management of hospital institutions.

Anunciacao, Goncalves and Martins try to verify how the adoption of this tool requires a governance perspective on data/ information and information systems and what impacts it may have on the *modus operandi* of the largest cement companies in Portugal. *Anunciacao* et al. identify the main dimensions that should be considered in the scope of production management and to frame the critical factors in the management of equipment maintenance, in an industry 4.0 context. *Anunciacao* et al. analysis the information in the pandemic context management. *Koutroukis, Vlados and Chatzinikolaou* explore the implications of the COVID-19 pandemic on human resource management (HRM) and labor relations, specifically focusing on the role of social dialogue in the post-crisis era. *Birknerova and Zbihlejova* investigates the competencies of managers in the field of business. *Ross and Titov* describes the current and predicted trends in healthcare and leadership, connecting those to the authors' previous research and proposing an updated version of healthcare leadership competency model that will take into account the described trends and challenges. *Shoh* investigates to provide a scientific solution to a number of problems in achieving sustainable economic growth in the world. *Cercel* examines the competitive rural economy in the emerging countries of the European Union. *Nascimento and Correia* discuss the major changes that occurred in the higher education agents, including the expectations placed on their practices, teaching methodologies shifts, and pedagogical requirements needs, also shaped by the acceleration of education's digitalization. *Lesinskis* et al. explores the literature review on entrepreneurial intention and its influencing factors in a context of behavioral norms and regions, as well as on the peculiarities of the perception of generation Z in the age of digitalization. The empirical part of the article reflects, analyses, and discusses the results of the experimental research, where training sessions for the youth of generation Z in the countries of Central and Eastern Europe and Southern Europe were conducted. *Massari and Roversi* examines the potential of the traditional educational model that developed in time in the heart of Mediterranean culture and which has been implemented in the Paideia Campus Living Lab in Pollica (Southern Italy). *Antenoscu* analysis Romania's tourism in the period of the COVID-19 pandemic, in order to quantify the gaps compared to the highest performance achieved in 2019 and in what measure tourism started to resilience and recover. *Waqas* et al. investigates the effect of the global economic crisis on household food insecurity and coping strategies in Pakistan. The study shows that the quantity of coping does not matter for food security and identifies some prominent strategies to soften the effect of crises. *Hamburg and O Brien* examines that how digital entrepreneurship can support those from underrepresented and marginalized groups to engage in entrepreneurial activity. *Cho* investigates the relationship between economic inequality and a contraction in a supply of credit. Even though borrowers are willing to pay higher interest rates of loans, the lender may not offer loans simply by raising interest rates.

Contents

List of Contributers

Constantinos Challoumis

National and Kapodistrian University of Athens (N.K.U.A.), Greece

Antonio Ribba

University of Modena and Reggio Emilia, Italy

Nguyen Thanh Dat

Faculty of Banking, University of Economics, The University of Danang, Vietnam

Nguyen Ha Hoang Long

Faculty of Banking, University of Economics, The University of Danang, Vietnam

Hebatallah Ghoneim

Faculty of Management Technology, German University in Cairo, Egypt

Mohammed N. Abu-Alfoul

School of Business, Law, and Entrepreneurship, Swinburne University of Technology, Melbourne, Australia.

Martinkovic Marcel

The Faculty of Philosophy and Arts, Trnava University, the Slovak Republic

Haydanka Diana

The Faculty of Foreign Languages, Uzhhorod National University, Ukraine

Haydanka Yevheniy

The Faculty of Philosophy and Arts, Trnava University, the Slovak Republic

Tarlan Ahmadov

Department of Business Administration, Tallinn University of Technology, Tallinn, Estonia

Beatriz Elena Guzman-Diaz

Universidad del Quindio in Colombia

Edwin Tarapuez-Chamorro

Universidad del Quindio in Colombia

Ramiro Parra-Hernandez

Universidad del Quindio in Colombia

Juliya S. Tsertseil

Plekhanov Russian University of Economics, Russia

Konstantin V. Ordov

Plekhanov Russian University of Economics, Russia

Nadezhda A. Zatsarnaya

Plekhanov Russian University of Economics, Russia

Paweł Dec

Institute of Corporate Finance and Investment, SGH Warsaw School of Economics, Poland

Jacek Wysocki

Institute of Enterprise, Collegium of Business Administration, SGH Warsaw School of Economics, Poland

Rosyadi Rosyadi

Department of Economics and Development Studies, Faculty of Economics and Business, Universitas Tanjungpura, Indonesia

Fitriadi Fitriadi

Department of Economics, Faculty of Economics and Business, Universitas Mulawarman, East Borneo, Indonesia.

Pedro Fernandes da Anunciacao

CICE-ESCE/IPS (Research Centre in Business Sciences) - Polytechnic Institute of Setúbal, Setúbal, Portugal, Geicon (Research Group of Information and Knowledge Engineering) - University of Campinas, Campinas, Brasil,

Ricardo Daiel da Assuncao Pereira Petiz

Portuguese Sea and Atmosphere Institute, Lisbon, Portugal

Elisabete da Conceição Gandrita Giroto

Polytechnic Institute of Setubal, Setubal, Portugal

Fernando Miguel Goncalves

Polytechnic Institute of Setubal, Setubal, Portugal

Fabio Alexandre Chaves Martins

Polytechnic Institute of Setubal, Setubal, Portugal

Vitor Dinis

Cibersur, Palmela, Portugal

Antonio Briones Penalver

Polytechnic University of Cartagena, Cartagena, Spain

Francisco Joaquim Madeira Esteves

CICE-ESCE/IPS (Research Centre in Business Sciences) - Polytechnic Institute of Setubal, Setubal, Portugal

Rui Menezes Vaz

Polytechnic Institute of Setubal, Setubal, Portugal

Mario Vale

Polytechnic Institute of Setubal, Setubal, Portugal

Karollyne Cruvinel de Freitas

Polytechnic Institute of Setubal, Setubal, Portugal

Pedro Rosario da Costa

Polytechnic Institute of Setubal, Setubal, Portugal

Theodore Koutroukis

Department of Economics, Democritus University of Thrace, Komotini, Greece

Charis Vlados

School of Business, University of Nicosia, Nicosia, Cyprus

Dimos Chatzinikolaou

School of Social Sciences, Business & Organisation Administration, Hellenic Open University, Greece

Zuzana Birknerova

Faculty of Management and Business, University of Presov, Slovakia

Lucia Zbihlejova

Faculty of Management and Business, University of Presov, Slovakia

Mariken Ross

The North Estonia Medical Centre, Head of Haematology Centre, Estonia

Eneken Titov

Estonian Entrepreneurship University of Applied Sciences, Estonia

Khamdamov Shoh-Jakhon

Tashkent State University of Economics, Uzbekistan

Camelia Cercel (Zamfirache)

Faculty of Economics and Business Administration, University of Craiova, Romania

Maria Lígia Jardim do Nascimento Pires Bras

Universidade Lusíada de Lisboa and COMEGI Research Center, Portugal.

Maria Manuela Marques Faia Correia

Universidade Lusíada de Lisboa and COMEGI Research Center, Portugal.

Kristaps Lesinskis

BA School of Business and Finance, Riga, Latvia

Inese Mavlutova

BA School of Business and Finance, Riga, Latvia

Janis Hermanis

BA School of Business and Finance, Riga, Latvia

Aivars Spilbergs

BA School of Business and Finance, Riga, Latvia

Liga Peiseniece

BA School of Business and Finance, Riga, Latvia

Sara Roversi

Future Food Institute, Italy

Sonia Massari

University of Pisa, Italy

Daniela Antonescu

Center of Mountain Economy, Romanian Academy, Romania

Waqas Shair

Minhaj University Lahore, Pakistan

Saem Hussain

Technological University Dublin, University in Dublin, Ireland

Asma Halim

Department of Business Administration, Iqra University, Islamabad, Pakistan

Abdul Ghani

Independent Researcher

Ileana Hamburg

IAT, WH Gelsenkirchen, Germany

Emma O Brien

Mary Immaculate College, Limerick, Ireland

Hye-Jin Cho

Department of Economics, Durham University, United Kingdom

List of Figures and Graphs

List of Tables

Constantinos Challoumis

Impact Factor of Liability of Tax System According to the Theory of Cycle of Money

1. Introduction and Literature Review

The credibility of a tax system has to do with the stability of that tax system by generally influencing the behavior of businesses (Bhuiyan & Farazmand, 2020; Challoumis, 2019a; Cornelsen & Smith, 2018; Dollery & Worthington, 1996; Domingues & Pecorelli-Pere, 2013; Islam et al., 2020; Kroth et al., 2020; Mackean et al., 2020; McIsaac & Riley, 2020; Menguy, 2020; OECD, 2020; Silva et al., 2020). Companies involved in controlled transactions are encouraged for this activity, that is, an unreliable tax system favors companies carrying out controlled transactions to avoid being taxed. Unlike companies that are consistent and operate without carrying out controlled transactions to avoid being fully taxed (Challoumis, 2021d, 2021a, 2022c, 2022b, 2022a).

A business with a controlled transaction activity succeeds in avoiding its adequate taxation, unlike a business that is consistent and fully taxed by the tax authorities of its country. The consistent business usually also acts in favor of the domestic banking system, expanding the money cycle of the economy in question. Therefore, a stable tax system works not only in favor of consistent businesses but also in favor of the economy as a whole.

The quantification analysis of the sensitivity of the tax system to the liable tax system is done by the application of the Q.E. method. The background of this method stands on the behavior analysis of mathematical equations. Thus, there we determine two axes to the analysis of the Q.E. method which is:

- The analysis of the behavior of the model stands on the scrutiny of the structural characteristics of each model accordingly allowing with that way the extraction of general conclusions about the model which is under examination.
- The frequency analysis behavior scrutinizes the behavior of the dependent variables, but from the view of the number of appearances of a variable than another, estimating the impact that one independent variable has with one or more other independent variables.

Therefrom, using the prior two axes of methodology, is plausible to extract conclusions about the behavior of mathematical equations, and how some factors react to changes. Consequently, is plausible the transformation of quality data to quantity data. This method is applied for this study for controlled transactions and more precisely in the variables of the impact factor of the tax revenue (Bernasconi & Espinosa-Cristia, 2020; Biernaski & Silva, 2018; Blundell & Preston, 2019; Bowling et al., 2019; Castaño et al., 2016; Delgado Rodríguez & de Lucas Santos, 2018; dos Santos Benso Maciel et al., 2020; Russo Rafael et al., 2020; Tydir, 2019; Van de Vijver et al., 2020; Wright et al., 2017; Wu et al., 2019). The mechanism of Q.E. is based on the dependent variables which are modified for the generator. Thereupon, the generator produces values for the dependent variables. The extracted values of the generator permit the creation of magnitudes, which are the base for comparisons, and for the scrutiny of mathematical equations. Thus, it is plausible to quantify qualitative data. In our analysis, this method is used for clarification of the behavior of the impact factor of the global tax revenue.

2. Impact Factor of Tax Revenues

The impact factor of tax revenues of countries which are tax heaves, *s* according to the "Methods of controlled transactions and identifications of tax avoidance" is determined as that:

$$s = \frac{k+l}{r+c+t+i} \tag{1}$$

Therefore are countries that receive the products that are taxed in different countries. This allocation of profits between profits and losses permits the enterprises which participate in controlled transactions of the transfer pricing activities to maximize their utility. But, contemporaneously the tax revenue from a global view is declined. Then, the loss of tax income from some countries is more than the profits that make the countries which are tax havens. Thereupon, the symbol of *s* the impact factor of tax revenue from a global view, and there are some coefficients which are *k*, *l*, *r*, *t*, and *c*. Thus, the symbol of *k* is about the impact factor of capital, *l* is the impact factor about the liability of the authorities on the tax system. The symbol of *i* is about the intangibles. The parameter of r is about the risk, the *t* is about how much trustworthy is the tax system (Abdelkafi, 2018; Al-Ubaydli et al., 2021; Cascajo et al., 2018; Evans et al., 1999; Farah, 2011; Fernandez & Raine, 2019; Franko et al., 2013; Gilens & Page, 2014; Jomo & Wee, 2003; Lal et al., 2018; Limberg, 2020; Moreno-Jiménez et al., 2014; Stern, 2015;

Syukur, 2020). This means that *t* examines the case of liability of the tax system from the view of the bureaucracy. Additionally, the symbol of c is about the cost of enterprises. The symbols with the "~" are accordingly the same thing but from the view of uncontrolled transactions. Thus, the numerator is proportional to the income of taxes, as the investments and the stable tax environments, with tax liability, enhance the tax income. On the other hand, the denominator is inverted and proportional to the tax income, as the risk, the cost, and the unbalance of taxation cause less tax income (Challoumis, 2018a, 2019b, 2019c, 2020a, 2021a, 2021c, 2021e, 2021d, 2021b, 2022a, 2022c). Moreover, for $\tilde{s}$ we have that:

$$\tilde{s} = \frac{\tilde{k} + \tilde{i}}{\tilde{r} + \tilde{c} + \tilde{t} + \tilde{i}} \tag{2}$$

Since equation, equation (3) is determined the aggregate impact factor of tax revenues, which is symbolized by $\hat{s}$, and is defined by the next equation:

$$\breve{s} = s + \tilde{s} \tag{3}$$

Based on the prior equations we could proceed to the identification of the behavior of the impact factors of tax revenues in the case of tax heavens, and in the case of the non-tax heavens. Then, *s* is a factor that allows the comparison between the controlled the uncontrolled transactions. Thence is plausible to have a standalone behavior analysis of controlled transactions and a combined behavior analysis between the controlled transactions with the uncontrolled transactions. The next section is analyzed the impact factor of tax revenues with the rest impact factors.

3. Determination of Liability of Tax System

The determination of the stability of the tax system is established by the impact factor liability of the tax system (how stable is a tax system, with not many changes through some periods). To determine the way that liability affects global tax revenues, we proceed with the following diversion:

- In the first application of Q.E. methodology are applied all the factors of the global tax revenue, *s*. In that case, is plausible to obtain the behavior of the global tax revenue using the completed form of the equation (1) (Challoumis, 2018b, 2020b, 2022b).

- In the second application of the Q.E. methodology are applied all the factors are except the factor which is under review. Thereupon, in that case, is avoided the factor of liability of the tax system, *l*.

This methodology is illustrated below:

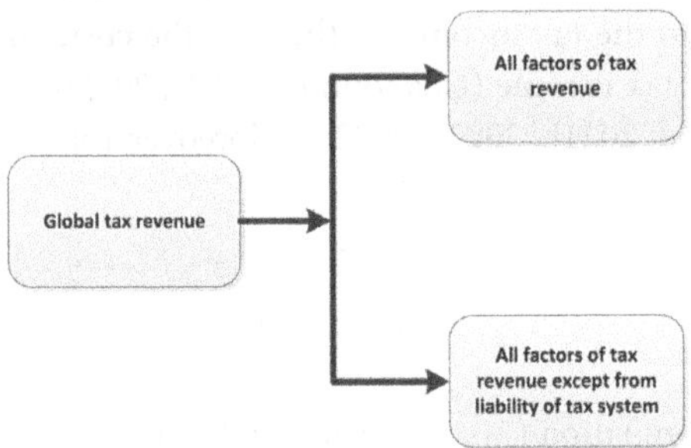

Figure 1. Steps of Q.E. application

The previous scheme is shown the methodology followed by the Q.E. method to determine the behavior of the global tax revenue in the case that there exists a liable tax system (ideal case) and the version in which we have an absence of this factor (figure 1).

4. Impact Factor of Tax Revenues on the Liability of the Tax System

The liability of the tax system is in a condition of interaction with the impact factor of tax revenues. In this behavioral analysis is determined the model which clarifies the behavior of the impact factor of tax revenues with the existence and with the avoidance of the impact factor of tax liability. All the necessary equations have been referred to in the previous sections, except for one condition. Then, for the application of the Q.E. method we use the following condition, which is:

$$t > l > i > k > c \tag{4}$$

Consequently, it is plausible to proceed to a quantitative analysis using equations (1), (2), and (4). Thence, applying the Q.E. method and choosing the appropriate magnitudes for the coefficients, we have that:

Table 1. Compiling coefficients

Factors	Values of s	Values of s′
k	0.4	0.4
i	0.6	0.6
l	0.7	–
r	0.5	0.5
c	0.3	0.3
t	0.8	0.8
fs	<0.3	<0.3
fsi	<0.3	<0.3

Based on the previous coefficients the generator formed the behavior of the model which is underdetermination. Thence should be noticed that the factors have an upper limit of 1, and a lower limit of 0. But, s and $\tilde{s}$ are plausible to receive values greater than one as their mathematical structure allows this. After 461 iterations extracted the next diagrams:

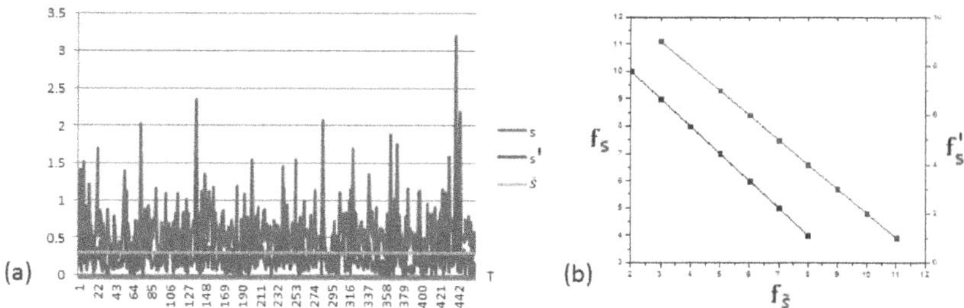

Figure 2. (a) Impact factors of S (series 1) and s′ (series 2), (b) frequencies of S and s′

In the previous figure, we used the $\tilde{s}$, which here is common for the tangibles and the intangibles. Then s (blue line) is symbolized the case that we have the impact factor of l which symbolizes the liability of the tax system (existence of a constant tax system). With s' (red line) it symbolized the case that we have the absence of the impact factor of liability of the tax system, l. In the case of s we have a constant and reliable system, and with s' we have an unstable tax system, with a low liability. In consequence, the global tax revenue is higher in the case that exists the impact factor of the liability (blue line) than in the case the impact factor of liability is not used (red line). We conclude as we expected that the existence of a tax system that has not to have many disturbances serves better the tax revenue from the global view. Additionally, from the diagram (b) of Figure 2, we obtain that the frequency of the f_s (black line) is lower than the frequency of f_s' (blue line). Thereupon, the companies which participate in controlled transactions of transfer pricing increased in the case where the liability of the tax system is low (blue line). Then, the number of uncontrolled transactions is declined when in an unreliable system, meaning the existence of tax systems with a lot of disturbances and changes to their tax policy (figure 3). Accordingly, when there exists a tax system that the companies can trust, then the number of controlled transactions is decreased and the number of uncontrolled transactions is increased (Figure 4). Thus, we obtain that reliable tax systems increase uncontrolled transactions and global tax revenue.

5. Conclusions

This paper examined the liability of the tax system. When there is an economic environment with an unreliable tax system the companies prefer to participate in controlled transactions activities. In contradiction when there exists a reliable tax system enterprises prefer to participate in uncontrolled transaction activities. Therefore, the companies design their business plans subject to the reliability of their economic environment. In general, we conclude that stable tax systems offer high global tax revenue and a lower number of controlled transactions of transfer pricing.

6. Appendix

Program of simulations © ® 2017 Constantinos Challoumis

```
%Q.E. method of Constantinos Challoumis for Transfer
Pricing

q=0;
while q<10
q=q+1;
count=0;
counts=1;
counts1=1;
while count<10
if rand()<9
      i=0.6*rand();
```

```
end
if rand()<9
      l=0.7*rand();
end
if rand()<9
      r=0.5*rand();
end
if rand()<9
      c=0.3*rand();
end
if rand()<9
      t=0.8*rand();
end
s=(k+l)/(r+c+t);
s_tilda=0.3;
      count=count+1
      if s<0.3
            counts=counts+1;
      else
            counts1=counts1+1;
      end
end
s1=(k)/(r+c+t);
s_tilda=0.3;
      count=count+1
      if s<0.3
            counts=counts+1;
      else
            counts1=counts1+1;
      end
end
vec=[c,count,counts,counts1,i,l,q,r,s,s1,s_
tilda,t;vec];
end
```

References

Abdelkafi, I. (2018). The relationship between public debt, economic growth, and monetary policy: Empirical evidence from Tunisia. *Journal of the Knowledge Economy*, *9*(4). https://doi.org/10.1007/s13132-016-0404-6

Al-Ubaydli, O., Lee, M. S., List, J. A., Mackevicius, C. L., & Suskind, D. (2021). How can experiments play a greater role in public policy? Twelve proposals from an economic model of scaling. *Behavioural Public Policy*, *5*(1). https://doi.org/10.1017/bpp.2020.17

Bernasconi, O., & Espinosa-Cristia, J. F. (2020). No politics, no society: Questioning the justification of entrepreneurship in chilean public policies. *RAE Revista de Administracao de Empresas*, *60*(2). https://doi.org/10.1590/S0034-759020200206

Bhuiyan, S., & Farazmand, A. (2020). Society and public policy in the Middle East and North Africa. *International Journal of Public Administration*, *43*(5). https://doi.org/10.1080/01900692.2019.1707353

Biernaski, I., & Silva, C. L. (2018). Main variables of Brazilian public policies on biomass use and energy. *Brazilian Archives of Biology and Technology*, *61*(Special issue). https://doi.org/10.1590/1678-4324-smart-2018000310

Blundell, R., & Preston, I. (2019). Principles of tax design, public policy and beyond: The ideas of James Mirrlees, 1936–2018. *Fiscal Studies*, *40*(1). https://doi.org/10.1111/1475-5890.12183

Bowling, S. J., Boyland, L. G., & Kirkeby, K. M. (2019). Property tax cap policy in Indiana and implications for public school funding equity. *International Journal of Education Policy and Leadership*, *15*(9). https://doi.org/10.22230/ijepl.2019v15n9a881

Cascajo, R., Diaz Olvera, L., Monzon, A., Plat, D., & Ray, J. B. (2018). Impacts of the economic crisis on household transport expenditure and public transport policy: Evidence from the Spanish case. *Transport Policy*, *65*. https://doi.org/10.1016/j.tranpol.2017.06.001

Castaño, M. S., Méndez, M. T., & Galindo, M. Á. (2016). The effect of public policies on entrepreneurial activity and economic growth. *Journal of Business Research*, *69*(11). https://doi.org/10.1016/j.jbusres.2016.04.125

Challoumis, C. (2018a). Analysis of the velocities of escaped savings with that of financial liquidity. *Ekonomski Signali*, *13*(2), 1–14. https://doi.org/10.5937/ekonsig1802001c

Challoumis, C. (2018b). Methods of controlled transactions and the behavior of companies according to the public and tax policy. *Economics*, *6*(1). https://doi.org/10.2478/eoik-2018-0003

Challoumis, C. (2019a). The impact factor of education on the public sector and international controlled transactions. *Complex System Research Centre, 2019*, 151–160. https://www.researchgate.net/publication/350453451_The_Impact_Factor_of_Education_on_the_Public_Sector_and_International_Controlled_Transactions

Challoumis, C. (2019b). Theoretical analysis of fuzzy logic and Q.E. method in economics. *IKBFU's Vestnik, 2019*(01), 59–68. https://doi.org/330.42

Challoumis, C. (2019c). Transfer pricing methods for services and the policy of fixed length principle. *Economics and Business, 33*(1), 222–232. https://doi.org/https://doi.org/10.2478/eb-2019-0016

Challoumis, C. (2020a). Analysis of the theory of cycle of money. *Acta Universitatis Bohemiae Meridionalis, 23*(2), 13–29. https://doi.org/https://doi.org/10.2478/acta-2020-0004

Challoumis, C. (2020b). The impact factor of education on the public sector—The case of the U.S. *International Journal of Business and Economic Sciences Applied Research, 13*(1), 69–78. https://doi.org/10.25103/ijbesar.131.07

Challoumis, C. (2021a). Chain of cycle of money. *Acta Universitatis Bohemiae Meridionalis, 24*(2).

Challoumis, C. (2021b). Index of the cycle of money—The case of Greece. *IJBESAR (International Journal of Business and Economic Sciences Applied Research), 14*(2).

Challoumis, C. (2021c). Index of the cycle of money—The case of Thailand. *Chiang Mai University Journal of Economics, 25*(2).

Challoumis, C. (2021d). Index of the cycle of money—The case of Ukraine. *Actual Problems of Economics, 243*(9).

Challoumis, C. (2021e). Index of the cycle of money—The case of Bulgaria. *Economic Alternatives, 27*(2). https://www.unwe.bg/eajournal/en

Challoumis, C. (2022a). Index of the cycle of money—The case of Greece. *Research Papers in Economics and Finance, 6.*

Challoumis, C. (2022b). Index of the cycle of money—The case of Poland. *Research Papers in Economics and Finance, 6*(1).

Challoumis, C. (2022c). Structure of the economy. *Actual Problems of Economics, 247*(1).

Cornelsen, L., & Smith, R. D. (2018). Viewpoint: Soda taxes—Four questions economists need to address. *Food Policy, 74.* https://doi.org/10.1016/j.foodpol.2017.12.003

Delgado Rodríguez, M. J., & de Lucas Santos, S. (2018). Speed of economic convergence and EU public policy. *Cuadernos de Economia, 41*(115). https://doi.org/10.1016/j.cesjef.2017.01.001

Dollery, B. E., & Worthington, A. C. (1996). The evaluation of public policy: Normative economic theories of government failure. *Journal of Interdisciplinary Economics, 7*(1). https://doi.org/10.1177/02601079x9600700103

Domingues, J. M., & Pecorelli-Pere, L. A. (2013). Electric vehicles, energy efficiency, taxes, and public policy in Brazil. *Law and Business Review of the Americas, 19*(55).

dos Santos Benso Maciel, L., Bonatto, B. D., Arango, H., & Arango, L. G. (2020). Evaluating public policies for fair social tariffs of electricity in Brazil by using an economic market model. *Energies, 13*(18). https://doi.org/10.3390/en13184811

Evans, W. N., Ringel, J. S., & Stech, D. (1999). Tobacco taxes and public policy to discourage smoking. *Tax Policy and the Economy, 13*. https://doi.org/10.1086/tpe.13.20061866

Farah, M. F. S. (2011). Public policy and public administration. *Revista de Administracao Publica, 45*(3). https://doi.org/10.1590/S0034-76122011000300011

Fernandez, M. A., & Raine, K. D. (2019). Insights on the influence of sugar taxes on obesity prevention efforts. *Current Nutrition Reports, 8*(4). https://doi.org/10.1007/s13668-019-00282-4

Franko, W., Tolbert, C. J., & Witko, C. (2013). Inequality, self-interest, and public support for "Robin Hood" tax policies. *Political Research Quarterly, 66*(4). https://doi.org/10.1177/1065912913485441

Gilens, M., & Page, B. I. (2014). Testing theories of American politics: Elites, interest groups, and average citizens. *Perspectives on Politics, 12*(3). https://doi.org/10.1017/S1537592714001595

Islam, A., Rashid, M. H. U., Hossain, S. Z., & Hashmi, R. (2020). Public policies and tax evasion: evidence from SAARC countries. *Heliyon, 6*(11). https://doi.org/10.1016/j.heliyon.2020.e05449

Jomo, K. S., & Wee, C. H. (2003). The political economy of Malaysian federalism: Economic development, public policy and conflict containment. *Journal of International Development, 15*(4). https://doi.org/10.1002/jid.995

Kroth, D. C., Geremia, D. S., & Mussio, B. R. (2020). National school feeding program: A healthy public policy. *Ciencia e Saude Coletiva, 25*(10). https://doi.org/10.1590/1413-812320202510.31762018

Lal, A., Moodie, M., Peeters, A., & Carter, R. (2018). Inclusion of equity in economic analyses of public health policies: systematic review and future directions. *Australian and New Zealand Journal of Public Health, 42*(2). https://doi.org/10.1111/1753-6405.12709

Limberg, J. (2020). What's fair? Preferences for tax progressivity in the wake of the financial crisis. *Journal of Public Policy, 40*(2). https://doi.org/10.1017/S0143814X18000430

Mackean, T., Fisher, M., Friel, S., & Baum, F. (2020). A framework to assess cultural safety in Australian public policy. *Health Promotion International, 35*(2). https://doi.org/10.1093/HEAPRO/DAZ011

McIsaac, J. L. D., & Riley, B. L. (2020). Engaged scholarship and public policy decision-making: A scoping review. *Health Research Policy and Systems, 18*(1). https://doi.org/10.1186/s12961-020-00613-w

Menguy, S. (2020). Tax competition, fiscal policy, and public debt levels in a monetary union. *Journal of Economic Integration, 35*(3). https://doi.org/10.11130/jei.2020.35.3.353

Moreno-Jiménez, J. M., Pérez-Espés, C., & Velázquez, M. (2014). E-Cognocracy and the design of public policies. *Government Information Quarterly, 31*(1). https://doi.org/10.1016/j.giq.2013.09.004

OECD. (2020). SME Policy Index—Eastern partner countries 2020. In *Assessing the Implementation of the Small Business Act for Europe.*

Russo Rafael, R. de M., Neto, M., de Carvalho, M. M. B., Leal David, H. M. S., Acioli, S., & de Araujo Faria, M. G. (2020). Epidemiology, public policies and COVID-19 pandemics in Brazil: What can we expect? *Revista Enfermagem, 28.* https://doi.org/10.12957/REUERJ.2020.49570

Silva, S. E., Venâncio, A., Silva, J. R., & Gonçalves, C. A. (2020). Open innovation in science parks: The role of public policies. *Technological Forecasting and Social Change, 151.* https://doi.org/10.1016/j.techfore.2019.119844

Stern, N. (2015). Economic development, climate and values: Making policy. *Proceedings of the Royal Society B: Biological Sciences, 282*(1812). https://doi.org/10.1098/rspb.2015.0820

Syukur, M. (2020). Insentif Pajak terhadap Sumbangan COVID-19 dari Perspektif Relasi Hukum Pajak Indonesia dengan Hak Asasi Manusia. *Jurnal Suara Hukum, 2*(2). https://doi.org/10.26740/jsh.v2n2.p184-214

Tydir, N. I. (2019). Conceptual issues of Ukraine's tax policy in the conditions of the forming a socially oriented market economy. *Actual Problems of Economics, 12*(222).

Van de Vijver, A., Cassimon, D., & Engelen, P. J. (2020). A real option approach to sustainable corporate tax behavior. *Sustainability (Switzerland)*, *12*(13). https://doi.org/10.3390/su12135406

Wright, A., Smith, K. E., & Hellowell, M. (2017). Policy lessons from health taxes: A systematic review of empirical studies. *BMC Public Health*, *17*(1). https://doi.org/10.1186/s12889-017-4497-z

Wu, J., Yu, Z., Wei, Y. D., & Yang, L. (2019). Changing distribution of migrant population and its influencing factors in urban China: Economic transition, public policy, and amenities. *Habitat International*, *94*. https://doi.org/10.1016/j.habitatint.2019.102063

Antonio Ribba

Fiscal Dominance in the US Economy Since the Great Recession

1. Introduction

In this chapter we want to investigate the presence of fiscal dominance in the US economy in the last 15 years, that is, since the Great Recession. In the context of the present study fiscal dominance can be characterized as an economic regime in which the central bank cannot conduct a completely independent monetary policy, finalized to price stability and smoothing of business cycle fluctuations, in light of concerns about the sustainability of public debt.

Indeed, in response to the deep recession triggered by the financial crisis that hit the United States and the world economy in 2008, President Obama signed the American Recovery and Reinvestment Act in February 2009, a sizable stimulus package estimated to be around 800 billion dollars. In more recent years, the COVID-19 pandemic exerted a significant and negative impact on the US economy. In response to the crisis the government provided further strong fiscal stimuli. For example, the American Rescue Plan Act, signed by President Biden in March 2021, was a 1.9 billion fiscal package.

Thus, as a result of two deep recessions experienced in the past 15 years and fiscal packages enacted in response, US public debt as a percentage of GDP peaked at 129 % in 2020.

Bordo and Levy (2021) have recently investigated the relation between enlarged fiscal deficits and inflation over two centuries. As far as the post-World War II era is concerned, the authors find that the Great Inflation in the 1960s and the 1970s is largely explained by the influence exerted by fiscal deficits on monetary policy.

Sargent and Wallace (1981) introduced the separate notions of monetary dominance and fiscal dominance, where the latter identifies a regime in which monetary policy is forced to accommodate fiscal policy in order to ensure solvency.

In the spirit of Sargent and Wallace, Martin (2020) has recently argued that if government sets debt, then the independence of the central bank becomes irrelevant.

Important studies in this area of research are, among others, Leeper (1991), Sims (2011) and Cochrane (2019). These authors develop the so-called Fiscal Theory of Price Level (FTPL). As stressed by Bordo and Levy (2021), the conclusion that fiscal deficits may exert inflationary effects is similar to the results presented in Sargent and Wallace (1981). Nevertheless, in the case of FTPL, the effects of fiscal policy on the price level do not necessarily require an increase in money supply.

Chen et al. (2022) investigate the strategic interaction between fiscal and monetary policy in the USA from 1955 to 2008. One of the main findings of the research is that fiscal targeting rules can mitigate the adverse effects of high debt on inflation.

Hodge et al. (2022) study the interaction between monetary and fiscal policy during the pandemic, by using a New Keynesian DSGE. Instead, as far as the Euro Area is concerned, Cavallo et al. (2018) investigate the dynamic effects exerted by an increase in government spending on output and inflation when the central bank implements an accommodative monetary policy (see also Dallari & Ribba, 2020).

In the present study we investigate the possible presence of fiscal dominance in a simple bivariate VAR model framework. In particular, we study the interaction between debt-to-GDP ratio and monetary base over the sample period 2008–2022. We find that an increase in the debt-to-GDP ratio causes an increase in the monetary base. Moreover, we also find evidence of unidirectional Granger causality running from debt to monetary base. These results seem to support the conclusion that the historical period under investigation may be characterized as a regime of fiscal dominance.

The rest of the chapter is organized as follows. In section 2 we test for Granger causality and find that there is evidence of unidirectional Granger causation running from debt-to-GDP ratio to monetary base in the US economy in the last 15 years. In section 3 we show the dynamic responses of the two variables to an increase in the debt-to-GDP ratio. The main finding is that there is a significant response of monetary base to public debt that lasts for around three years. In this section we also undertake a historical decomposition analysis, which allows us to separate the contribution of the orthogonal shocks to deviations of variables, in this case monetary base, from the forecasted path. The historical decomposition reveals that the influence of fiscal policy on monetary policy emerges more clearly from 2018 onward. Section 4 concludes.

2. The Interaction Between Debt-to-GDP Ratio and Monetary Base Over the Period 2008–2022

We start with a simple figure, showing the joint evolution of public debt and monetary base in the last 15 years in the US economy. Both series are taken from FRED at the St. Louis FED Web site. We use quarterly data.

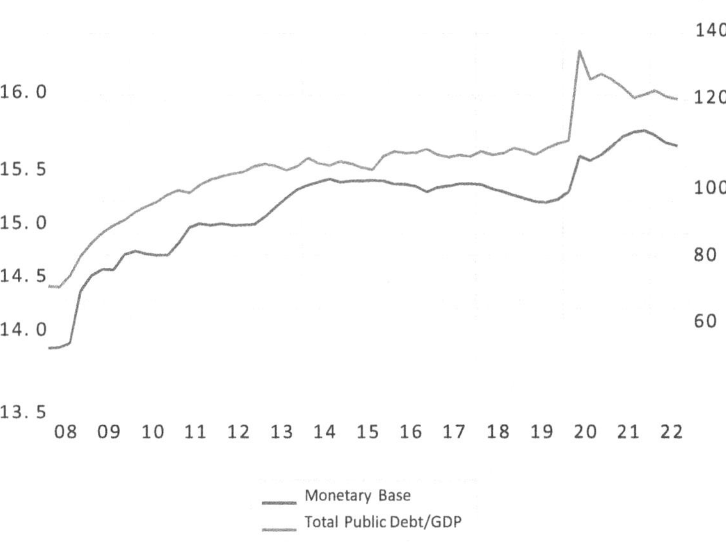

Figure 1. Evolution of Public Debt-to-GDP ratio and Monetary Base in the United States over the sample period 2008:1—2022:3

Values of total debt-to-GDP ratio are reported on the right-hand vertical axis, while on the left-hand vertical axis the (log) monetary base values are reported. Clearly, there is a strong co-movement between the two series and a significant increase in both total debt and monetary base is detected after 2008, as a consequence of The Great Recession, and after 2019, as a consequence of the COVID-19 pandemic. However, it would be important to establish possible causal relations characterizing their joint dynamics. Indeed, both government and central bank adopted expansionary policies in response to the strong adverse shocks that have hit the economic system. These policies have proved useful in mitigating recessions and it would be in principle possible that fiscal dominance has not materialized. For example, and with regard to the Euro Area,

Isabel Schnabel (2020) argues that in recent years the European Central Bank has undertaken aggressive expansionary policies pursuing the sole objective of price stability. In other words, according to Isabel Schnabel, the high level of public debt in the Eurozone has not exerted any influence on the conduct of monetary policy by the European Central Bank.

In Table 1 Granger causality tests are reported. There is strong evidence of unidirectional Granger causation: total debt Granger causes monetary base over the sample period under investigation. Instead, the null hypothesis of no Granger causality from monetary base to public debt is not rejected by data.

Table 1. Granger causality tests

Null Hypothesis	Obs	Chi-sq	Prob.
Public Debt does not Granger cause Monetary Base	57	9.914	0.007
Monetary Base does not Granger cause Public Debt	57	0.849	0.654

Notes: Sample 2008:1—2022:3; Lags 2.

3. The Response of the Monetary Base to an Increase in the Debt-to-GDP Ratio

We estimate a bivariate VAR model, including the debt-to-GDP ratio and the log of monetary base. The reduced-form, VAR model of order two, is given by:

$$X_t = \mu + A_1 X_{t-1} + A_2 X_{t-2} + e_t \tag{1}$$

μ is a vector of constant terms and e_t is the 2×1 vector of error terms, such that $E(e_t) = 0$

and $E(e_t e'_t) = \Sigma_e$. X_t is a 2×1 vector of macroeconomic variables, including the debt-to-GDP ratio and the log of monetary base.

It is worth stressing that if the variables are $I(1)$ and then behave as difference-stationary processes, and moreover exhibit long-run equilibrium relations, that is, the variables are cointegrated, the specification of the VAR model in levels is appropriate (see, e.g., Sims et al., 1990).

The reduced-form moving average representation of system (1) is given by:

$$X_t = \rho + C(L)e_t \tag{2}$$

Where L is the lag operator and $C(0) = I$.

Let us recall that in the previous section we have detected unidirectional Granger causality, since the debt-to-GDP ratio Granger causes the monetary base while the reverse causality does not hold. Thus, we recover orthogonal disturbances by imposing the following recursive structure:

$$X_t = \rho + B(L)\eta_t \tag{3}$$

Where $B(L) = C(L)P$ and $\eta_t = P^{-1}e_t$. The 2 × 1 vector η_t contains orthonormal disturbances, that is, $E(\eta_t\eta'_t) = I$ and P is such that $PP' = \Sigma_e$, where P is the Cholesky factor, that is, is the unique lower triangular matrix such that PP′ gives a factorization of the covariance matrix of error terms. Therefore, we impose a causal structure with the debt-to-GDP ratio ordered first in the causal ordering.

Figure 2 reports the dynamic responses of public debt and monetary base to unexpected increases in the two variables. Monetary base shows a significant increase in response to a positive public debt shock. This dynamic effect on monetary base lasts for around three years and thereafter becomes statistically non-significant. Conversely, a monetary base shock does not exert significant effect on public debt, more precisely on debt-to-GDP ratio, at all horizons.

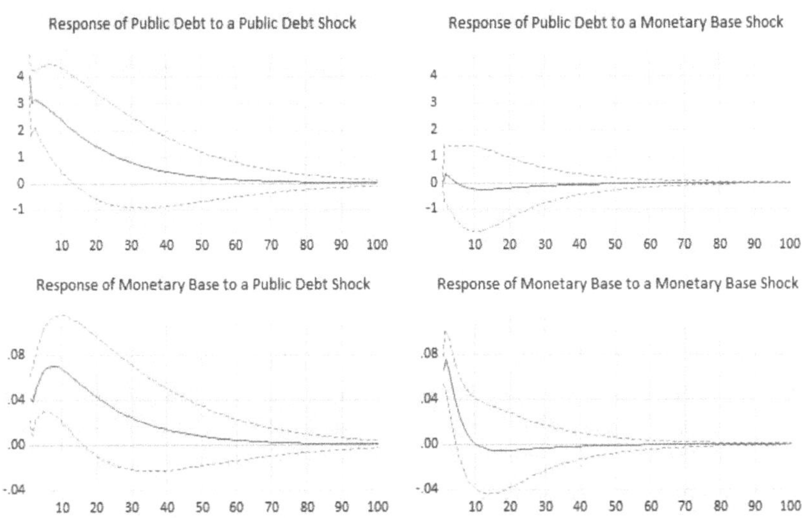

Figure 2. Responses of public debt and monetary base to the two orthogonal shocks

On the whole, we interpret these results as pointing to evidence of fiscal dominance in the sample period under consideration.

Figure 3 reports the contribution of the two shocks to deviations of monetary base from its forecasted path (cf. Canova, 2007, chap. 4). It is worth noting that the contribution of debt shocks to deviations of monetary base from the forecasted path becomes particularly significant after 2018. Therefore, it seems that the emergence of a significant fiscal influence on monetary policy is mainly related to reactions to the COVID-19 pandemic.

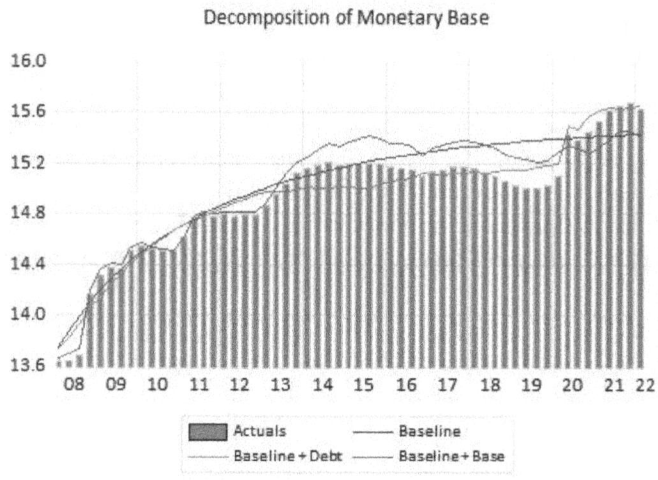

Figure 3. Contribution of public debt shocks and monetary base shocks to deviations from the baseline forecasted path of monetary base

Summing up the main findings of this section: our (relatively) simple analysis, based on a bivariate VAR model with causal structure, shows that the presence of fiscal dominance may have materialized in the US economy over the past 15 years, that is, since the global financial crisis. In other words, one cannot rule out the possibility that the central bank has followed the government and its fiscal policy, by ensuring fiscal solvency.

A further finding concerns the evidence of a central bank following the government's fiscal policy, especially in response to the crisis triggered by the COVID-19 pandemic. Instead, evidence of fiscal dominance is weaker in the first part of the sample, that is, in response to the global financial crisis.

4. Conclusion

In this chapter we have shown that there is some evidence of fiscal dominance in the USA over the period 2008–2022, since we find that an increase in public debt causes a positive response of monetary base. Another interesting result shown in the present study concerns the relative importance of shocks to public debt in explaining movements in the monetary base from 2018 onward. This last result seems to stress the important interaction between fiscal policy and monetary policy in response to the COVID-19 pandemic crisis.

In a very recent paper, Bianchi and Melosi (2022) have argued that an environment of stable and low inflation requires a stabilization of public debt and a consistent fiscal framework. In particular, they find that the fiscal response to the COVID pandemic has caused an increase in the inflation rate.

Indeed, in response to the two deep economic crisis that have affected the US economy in the last 15 years, there was a combination of expansionary fiscal policy and expansionary monetary policy. Sizable fiscal packages were, respectively, signed by Obama in 2009 and Biden in 2021. On the other hand, unconventional monetary policies, that is, quantitative easing and forward policy guidance, were adopted by the Federal Reserve after the financial crisis of 2007–2009 (see, e.g., Bernanke, 2020). Moreover, such aggressive expansionary monetary policy has also played an important role in response to the COVID-19 pandemic.

There are some important policy implications related to the findings of the present research. In fact, if the unprecedented level of public debt can actually condition the conduct of monetary policy, and according to the results presented in this paper it seems so, then a possible macroeconomic outcome will be the coexistence, at least in the coming years, between high public debt and an inflation rate higher than the targets usually set by the central bank. Another possible implication could be an increase in the volatility of the inflation rate.

One might conclude that, after all, an annual inflation rate say of 3 % or 4 % would not imply a drastic change in the macroeconomic scenario. Nevertheless, in this case, any new higher target should be clearly communicated by the central bank, in order to keep inflation expectations well anchored.

To the best of my knowledge, this is one of the first studies aiming to investigate the existence of fiscal dominance in the US economy, from the Great Recession to the COVID-19 pandemic. Therefore, and quite obviously, more research is needed to corroborate the findings presented in this paper for the US economy.

Possible extensions of this research might concern other countries and economic areas. For example, as far as the interaction of fiscal and monetary policy in the Eurozone is concerned, Buti and Messori (2022) suggest that an aggregate fiscal stance and fiscal capacity at the Euro Area level could counterbalance the ECB's role and thus avoid the risk of fiscal dominance. Indeed, it is well known that in the Eurozone a similar combination of aggressive fiscal policy and unconventional monetary policies has represented the policy response to the COVID pandemic. Furthermore, from 2019 onward, the European fiscal rules for the conduct of national fiscal policies have been suspended. Thus, one is naturally led to wonder whether in recent years a regime of fiscal dominance has also materialized in the Eurozone. This could, in fact, be the subject of future empirical investigations.

References

Bernanke, B. S. (2020). The new tools of monetary policy. *American Economic Review, 1110*(4), 943–983.

Bianchi, F., & Melosi, L. (2022). *Inflation as a fiscal limit* (Working Paper 2022-37). Federal Reserve Bank of Chicago.

Bordo, M. D., & Levy, M. D. (2021). Do enlarged fiscal deficits cause inflation? The historical record. *Economic Affairs, 41*, 1–25.

Buti, M., & Messori, M. (2022). The role of central fiscal capacity in connecting the EU's domestic and global agendas. *STG Policy Papers, 22*(13).

Canova, F. (2007). *Methods for applied macroeconomic research* (Chapter 4). Princeton University Press.

Cavallo, A., Dallari, P., & Ribba, A. (2018). *Fiscal policies in high debt Euro-Area countries.* Springer Books.

Chen, X., Leeper, E. M., & Campbell, L. (2022). Strategic interactions in U.S. monetary and fiscal policies. *Quantitative Economics, 13*, 593–628.

Cochrane, J. (2019). *The fiscal theory of the price level* [Mimeo]. Hoover Institution.

Dallari, P., & Ribba, A. (2020). The dynamic effects of monetary policy and government spending shocks on unemployment in the peripheral Euro area countries. *Economic Modelling, 85*, 218–232.

Hodge, A., Zoltan, J., Linde, J., & Nguyen, V. (2022). *U.S. and Euro Area monetary and fiscal interactions during the pandemic: A structural analysis* (IMF Working Paper 22).

Leeper, E. (1991). Equilibria under "active" and "passive" monetary and fiscal policy. *Journal of Monetary Economics, 27*, 129–147.

Martin, F. M. (2020). *Fiscal dominance* (Working Paper 2020-040). Federal Reserve Bank of ST. Louis.

Sargent, T., & Wallace, N. (1981). Some unpleasant monetarist arithmetic. *Federal Reserve Bank of Minneapolis Quarterly Review*, *5*(3), 1–17.

Schnabel, I. (2020). *The shadow of fiscal dominance: misconceptions, perceptions and perspectives* [Speech]. European Central Bank.

Sims, C. (2011). Stepping on a rake: The role of fiscal policy in the inflation of the 1970s. *European Economic Review*, *55*(1), 481–456.

Sims, C. A., Stock, J. H., & Watson, M. W. (1990). Inference in linear time series models with some unit roots. *Econometrica*, *58*, 113–144.

Dat Thanh Nguyen & Long Ha Hoang Nguyen

The Impact of Developed Stock Markets on Vietnam Stock Market During the COVID-19 Pandemic

1. Introduction

Market volatility refers to an unpredictably rising or falling stock price. At the time of COVID-19's global impact, the stock market was dropping every day. What then is the cause of this circumstance? Some investors claimed that this issue arose as a result of their fears over COVID-19's recent, rapid expansion and their worries about how it would affect the entire economy. Since the WHO brought up the possibility of an outbreak of the COVID-19 pandemic, stocks have plummeted continuously. Investors continuously sell off their stocks, and worries about the economy raise expectations that central banks will decrease interest rates to stimulate growth.

In 2020, concerns about a viral breakout in the US led to a significant loss in the US stock market on October 28, with the market's most significant indexes also declining. In both the US and Europe, the COVID-19 outbreak has infected more people in the previous week than ever before. Johns Hopkins University estimates that there are 71,832 new infections in the US on average per day.

The pandemic's risky development compelled numerous US states and European nations to enact new, stricter regulations. Following the negative global situation, stock prices in the Asia-Pacific region also decreased during the first session of trading on October 29. Besides, the Hang Seng Index fell by 1.37 % in Hong Kong. Shares in mainland China also fell as well. The Shanghai Composite Index and the Shenzhen Index both had declines in value of 0.7 % and 0.313 %, respectively.

In spite of the unfavorable facts about COVID-19 infections outside of the community, Vietnam's stock market continued to have thrilling momentum over many trading sessions. Most stocks experienced a great boost in market price compared to the beginning of the year, when the COVID-19 outbreak had not yet materialized. In actuality, the market has been in an upward trend for several weeks. In April 2020, Ho Chi Minh City officials announced a case of COVID-19 infection outside the neighborhood, but the market was still completely covered in green at the time. Translation COVID-19 has almost no effect on securities.

Numerous articles have examined the effects of COVID-19 and its stock market lockout (see Al-Awadhi et al., 2020; Alfaro et al., 2020; Eleftheriou & Patsoulis, 2020; He et al., 2020; Zhang et al., 2020). Nevertheless, a lot of research focuses on developed and rising markets, such as those in the US and Europe. Besides, few researches have examined how the spread of COVID-19 affects the stock returns in developing countries, like Vietnam. Even fewer studies have looked at how COVID-19 affected financial markets before and after the outbreak in nations that instituted a lockdown.

This paper will be examining the stock index returns of the Vietnamese market in parallel with the US and China markets. In addition, the results from this study aim to help to better understand the connection between the stock markets, helping policymakers, investors and companies better understand and be better prepared in the future when similar events occur.

In this study, Chinese and American stock markets are considered as the main conduits for the spread of contagious effects to the Vietnamese equity market. The United States was picked because it is the country that is most negatively affected by the COVID-19 pandemic. For instance, the S&P 500 Index experienced the quickest loss in American history, falling more than 30 % in just 22 trading days (Liu et al., 2020). Besides, in June 2020, the unemployment rate was estimated to be 11.1 %, up from 3.5 % in 2019 (Bureau Labor of Statistics). In addition, it is considered that the COVID-19 outbreak originated in China. Additionally, global supply chain management has been severely interrupted by China's two-month shutdown from January to March 2020 (Thomas, 2020). Finally, many previous studies have considered the stock markets in the US and China as the origin of equity market contagion (see Akhtaruzzaman et al., 2021; Mollah et al., 2016; Wang et al., 2017).

The paper proceeds as followed. In the second section, the backgrounds of the COVID-19 pandemic and its effects and the literature review are discussed. Section 3 describes the data and methodology. Chapter 4 analyses and discusses the empirical results. Chapter 5 concludes the paper.

2. Literature Review and Research Hypothesis

Our study complements to an emerging research strand that looks at how a health pandemic would affect stock markets. The aim of this study is to examine the effects of the US and China's stock markets on the Vietnam equity market prior to and during COVID-19.

The previous literature has discussed how the COVID-19 pandemic impacts financial markets around the globe and the interdependence between them. For example, Zaremba et al. (2020) explore that non-pharmaceutical treatments in reaction to COVID-19 considerably enhance equity market volatility in 67 different nations. De Vito and Gomez (2020) conduct an analysis of the impacts of the COVID-19 health issue on the liquidity of listed corporations in 26 different nations. In two simulated distressed circumstances, sales are predicted to fall by 50 % and 75 %, respectively. Eleftheriou and Patsoulis (2020) examine the impacts of social distancing policies on stock market indices using data from 45 different nations as their sample, and they discover indications of detrimental spillover (direct and indirect) effects during the initial phase of containment policies, such as a lockdown. He et al. (2020)'s empirical examination of daily return data from eight established stock markets shows that COVID-19 has a short-term negative impact on the examined stock markets and that there is bidirectional spillover across the countries in their sample data.

Fundamentally, in theory, the present literature suggests that there are two primary channels through which contagion effects are frequently spread throughout financial markets. Rebalancing portfolios is the main channel. In addition to having alarming effects on health, the exponential rise in COVID-19 infections also creates uncertainty in economic prospects and cash flows. The global lockdown has a severe impact on some key sectors, including airlines, tourism, services, and prolonged economic uncertainty. In the long run, firm values will decrease, which will eventually lead to decreased stock prices. As a result, portfolio managers have had to start sudden portfolio reconstructions in a variety of global financial markets, both within and beyond asset classes (Manela & Moreira, 2017). Because the US and Chinese economies accounted for more than 40 % of global GDP in 2018, the fact that the COVID-19-induced shutdown has harmed their economies only adds to their contagion risks and volatility (see Akhtaruzzaman et al., 2021; Zhang et al., 2020). Another possibility could be expressed by how reasonable investors behave in times of financial crises. When there is a financial distress, sensible investors are likely to substitute risky assets, like equities, for safer assets, like US Treasury Bills (Baele et al., 2020). This substitution leads to rapid portfolio withdrawals and erratic price volatility in international equity markets (Ji et al., 2020). Furthermore, the comparative significance of contagion sources (Baele et al., 2020; Zaremba et al., 2020), the interconnection of financial markets (Zhang et al., 2020), and technological progress (i.e., algorithmic trading) all contribute to the contagion effects under both channels (Bloom et al., 2018). Based on the above discussion, following research hypothesis is suggested:

H1: During the COVID-19 pandemic, there are contagion effects of the US and China equity markets on Vietnam equity markets.

3. Methodology

3.1. Data

In order to test the research hypothesis, we use stock index data from China (Shanghai SE A-Share), the United States (S&P500 Composite) and Vietnam (VN Index). The variables used in this research are listed in Table 1.

Table 1. List of variables

Variables	Definition
$Return_{China,t}$	The percentage returns of stock indexes from China (Shanghai SE A-Share)
$Return_{US,t}$	The percentage returns of stock indexes from the U.S. (S&P500 Composite)
$Return_{VN,t}$	The percentage returns of stock indexes from Vietnam (VN Index)

The returns of stock indexes, including China (Shanghai SE A-Share), the United States (S&P500 Composite) and Vietnam (VN Index), are calculated as followed:

$$Return_{i,t} = \frac{Stock\,index_{i,t} - Stock\,index_{i,t-1}}{Stock\,index_{i,t-1}} \times 100 \tag{1}$$

where *Stock index*$_{i,t}$ is the index value of country *i* in day *t*. The time index of S&P500 Composite is adjusted to take into account the different time zones of the US, China and Vietnam. All data of stock indexes from three countries are collected from investing.com database.

The sample period used in this study is from July 1 to December 31, 2021. The reason for using this data range is to have relatively equal subsample, namely pre-pandemic and during-pandemic periods. In the main test, the data set is divided on March 11, 2020, on which the World Health Organization (WHO) declared COVID-19 to be a worldwide pandemic. The pre-pandemic phase ranges from

July 1 to March 10, 2020, and the pandemic period ranges from March 11 to December 31, 2021.

3.2. Research Methodology

To investigate the impact of the US and China stock index returns on Vietnam stock return before and during the pandemic, we first run two regressions of $Return_{VN,t}$ against $Return_{US,t}$ and $Return_{ChinaN,t}$ respectively. The regression models are as follows:

$$Return_{VN,t} = \beta_0 + \beta_1 Return_{US,t} + \varepsilon_t \qquad (2)$$

$$Return_{VN,t} = \beta_0 + \beta_1 Return_{China,t} + \varepsilon_t \qquad (3)$$

As mentioned above, the existence of the contagion effects of the two influential markets on Vietnam stock market is claimed when β_1 has higher value during the pandemic than that before the pandemic.

In addition to the linear regressions, we also use VAR-Granger causality tests to examine the effect of the two big stock markets on Vietnam stock market. This approach is widely used by the previous study (see Andriosopoulos et al., 2017; Forbes & Rigobon, 2002; Hon et al., 2004; Mollah et al., 2016). The VAR model is specified as follows:

$$Return_{VN,t} = \alpha + \sum_{k=1}^{5} \beta_k Return_{VN,t-k} + \sum_{k=1}^{5} \gamma_k Return_{US,t-k} + \varepsilon_t \qquad (4)$$

$$Return_{VN,t} = \alpha + \sum_{k=1}^{5} \beta_k Return_{VN,t-k} + \sum_{k=1}^{5} \gamma_k Return_{China,t-k} + \varepsilon_t \qquad (5)$$

In order to capture the possible autocorrelation in the trading pattern, we choose five lags that corresponding to five business days of the week. In term of Granger causality, we implement the Wald test that the coefficients on the five lags of $Return_{US,t-k}$ and $Return_{China,t-k}$ that appear in the equations (4) and (5) are jointly zero. The null hypothesis of these tests is $Return_{US,t}$ ($Return_{China,t}$) does not Granger-cause $Return_{VN,t}$ If the during-pandemic null hypothesis is found to be rejected, hence we can conclude that the US and/or China stock market Granger causes the Vietnam stock market and there may be a contagion effect due to the COVID-19 pandemic's spread.

4. Results

4.1. Summary Statistics

Table 2 presents the descriptive statistics of the index returns from three markets in our data set. The full sample, before the pandemic and during the pandemic periods are reported in three separate panels.

Table 2. Descriptive statistics

Variables	Observations	Mean	Standard deviation	Min	Max
Full sample period					
$Return_{VN,t}$	914	0.0005368	0.010469	-0.0667	0.0498
$Return_{US,t}$	914	0.0006096	0.0125379	-0.1198	0.0938
$Return_{China,t}$	914	0.0002333	0.0086089	-0.0772	0.0571
Pre-pandemic period					
$Return_{VN,t}$	253	-0.0005379	0.0070749	-0.0628	0.0168
$Return_{US,t}$	253	-0.0002206	0.0100826	-0.076	0.046
$Return_{China,t}$	253	-0.0000198	0.0091104	-0.0772	0.0315
During-pandemic period					
$Return_{VN,t}$	661	0.0009481	0.0114843	-0.0667	0.0498
$Return_{US,t}$	661	0.0009274	0.013352	-0.1198	0.0938
$Return_{China,t}$	661	0.0003301	0.0084142	-0.045	0.0571

Source: Authors' calculations

As can be seen from Table 2, the US stock percentage returns before the pandemic ranges from a minimum value of -0.076 to a maximum value 0.046 with the mean value equals to -0.0002206 and a standard deviation of 0.0100826. The China stock return ranges from a minimum value of -0.0772 to a maximum value of 0.0315 with a mean equal to -0.0000198 and a 0.0091104 standard deviation. The Vietnam stock index return ranges from a minimum value of -0.0628 to a maximum value 0.0168 with a -0.0005379 mean value and a standard deviation of 0.0070749.

Looking at the during the pandemic panel, the US stock index return ranges from a minimum value of -0.1198 to a maximum value 0.0938 with a mean equal to 0.0009274 and a standard deviation of 0.013352. The China stock return ranges from a minimum value of -0.045 to a maximum value of 0.0571 with a mean equal to 0.0003301 and a standard deviation of 0.0084142. The Vietnam stock index return ranges from a minimum value of -0.0667 to a maximum value 0.0498 with a mean equal to and 0.0009481 and a standard deviation of 0.0114843.

Through the descriptive statistics, the standard deviation of the US and Vietnam increased while China received an inconsiderable decline which supposes that the return of the US and Vietnam stock markets' volatility is stronger during the COVID-19 period. The same is also true for the US' while the volatility of China stock return seems to decline faintly during this period. The results indicate that there might be a change that had a statistically significant effect on Vietnam stock market from the US and Chinese stock markets prior to and during the pandemic periods.

4.2. Linear Regression Results

Contagion is characterized as a large increase in correlations prior to and during a crisis. Hence, in this section we investigate the contagion effects from stock markets in the US and China on Vietnam stock market by comparing the coefficients from the linear regressions of (2) and (3) from pre-pandemic and during-pandemic subsamples.

Table 3. The coefficients of the impacts of the US and China stock markets on Vietnam stock market

Variables	Coefficients	p value
Pre-pandemic period		
$Return_{US,t}$	0.1745077	0.000
$Return_{China,t}$	0.2532348	0.000
During-pandemic period		
$Return_{US,t}$	0.2027822	0.000
$Return_{China,t}$	0.3398672	0.000

Source: Authors' calculations

Table 3 shows the regression results of (2) and (3) which are corresponding to the before and during the COVID-19 pandemic periods. Looking at the first panel of Table 3, the coefficient value of $Return_{US,t}$ is 0.1745077 and statistically significant at 1 % level. This means if the SP500 index return increases by one percentage point, the VN index return increases by 0.1745077 percentage point. Similarly, there is a statistically significant positive effect of the Shanghai SE A-Share index return on the VN index return. The coefficient value is 0.2532348 and significant at 1 % confident level. In other words, one percentage point increase in China stock market index returns leads to a 0.2532348 percentage point increase in VN index return.

Next, we examine the impacts of the US and China stock markets on Vietnam stock market during the pandemic subsample. Similar to those in the pre-pandemic panel, the two coefficients are statistically significant at 1 % level. The value of $Return_{US,t}$ coefficient is 0.2027822 which means when the US stock market index increase by one percentage point the VN index return increases by 0.2027822 percentage point. In addition, the value of $Return_{China,t}$ coefficient is 0.3398672 which means when the China stock market index increase by one percentage point the VN index return increases by 0.3398672 percentage point.

Several interesting results can be spotted via these regression results. First, the correlation of the US and China stock market indices is consistently positive and statistically significant in both panels, namely pre-pandemic and during-pandemic. Second, the correlation coefficients of the two big markets with Vietnam stock market are stronger during the pandemic than those before the WHO marked COVID-19 as a pandemic. This evidence seems to suggest health crisis, such as COVID-19 pandemic, can be a source of a global financial contagion.

4.2. VAR-Granger Causality Test

Following previous literature, for example, Andriosopoulos et al. (2017), Forbes and Rigobon (2002), Hon et al. (2004), Mollah et al. (2016), and Nguyen et al. (2021), the examination of the contagion effect is proceeded by testing the VAR-Granger causality between the three stock markets in pre-pandemic and during-pandemic periods. To capture the possible autocorrelation in the trading pattern, 05 lags are selected for the VAR specified in (4) and (5). As mentioned above, we use five lags, which are corresponding to five business days of the week, in order to capture the possibility of autocorrelation in the trading pattern. Table 4 summarizes the findings of the Granger causality tests.

Table 4. Granger causality test results

Equation	**Excluded**	**Chi²**	**p value**
Pre-pandemic period			
$Return_{VN,t}$	$Return_{US,t}$	22.614	0.000
$Return_{VN,t}$	$Return_{China,t}$	6.4303	0.267
During-pandemic period			
$Return_{VN,t}$	$Return_{US,t}$	2.4056	0.791
$Return_{VN,t}$	$Return_{China,t}$	9.6592	0.085

Source: Authors' calculations

Table 4 presents the Chi^2 value and p value from the test with the null hypothesis of no causation from the two big stock markets to Vietnam market. The first panel provides the results for pre-pandemic period and the second one provides the results for during-pandemic period. Some interesting observations standouts. The Granger causality test suggests that, before the COVID-19 pandemic there is a causation relation from the US stock market to Vietnam stock market. Besides, the findings indicate that prior to the pandemic, China stock market does not Granger cause Vietnam stock market. However, these relations are reversed during the pandemic sample period. The US stock market causes Granger for the Chinese stock market, but the Vietnamese stock market does not. These findings suggest that the COVID-19 pandemic may cause a financial contagion between China and Vietnam.

The contagion effect generated by COVID-19 pandemic spread from China to Vietnam can be explained by the fact that China is one of Vietnam's main and largest export markets for electronic components, textiles, but especially agricultural products since Vietnam is one of the most agricultural nations in the world which annually produces and provides a large amount of agricultural product. As a country of billions of people with the most developed economy, when the COVID-19 epidemic broke out, China was extremely severely affected and so were other countries, especially Vietnam in exports and followed by its stock market.

5. Conclusion

Our research results contribute to the emerging literature about how a health pandemic would affect equity markets. Different from some earlier studies in which the source of contagion is a financial crisis, the findings point out that a health pandemic like COVID-19 can also become a cause of financial contagion to not only worldwide stock markets but also other developing ones like Vietnam stock market. Thus, our findings support demands made by the BIS (Aldasoro et al., 2020) and IMF (Bloom et al., 2018) to bank regulators, banks, and fund managers to include health hazards in their risk management procedures.

Our analysis suggests that new controlling capital regulations on bank capital should be imposed to ensure that they can withstand large unanticipated shocks brought on by an epidemic. As a result, the bank's stress testing approach should account for the possibility of another health pandemic. The volatility of the stock index and its impacts, among other factors, influence investment firms' portfolio hedging, and optimization. Furthermore, those countries whose financial economies have been heavily affected by COVID-19 should also consider referring to and learning from Vietnam's pandemic control method in limiting infections while promoting economic development.

References

Akhtaruzzaman, M., Abdel-Qader, W., Hammami, H., & Shams, S. (2021). Is China a source of financial contagion?. *Finance Research Letters*, *38*, 101393.

Al-Awadhi, A. M., Alsaifi, K., Al-Awadhi, A., & Alhammadi, S. (2020). Death and contagious infectious diseases: Impact of the COVID-19 virus on stock market returns. *Journal of behavioral and experimental finance*, *27*, 100326.

Aldasoro, I., Fender, I., Hardy, B., & Tarashev, N. (2020). *Effects of COVID-19 on the banking sector: The market's assessment* (No. 12). Bank for International Settlements.

Alfaro, L., Chari, A., Greenland, A. N., & Schott, P. K. (2020). Aggregate and firm-level stock returns during pandemics. *Real Time*, p. 1050.

Andriosopoulos, K., Galariotis, E., & Spyrou, S. (2017). Contagion, volatility persistence and volatility spill-overs: The case of energy markets during the European financial crisis. *Energy Economics*, *66*, 217–227.

Baele, L., Bekaert, G., Inghelbrecht, K., & Wei, M. (2020). Flights to safety. *The Review of Financial Studies*, *33*(2), 689–746.

Bloom, D. E., Cadarette, D., & Sevilla, J. P. (2018). Epidemics and economics. *Finance & Development*, *55*(2), 46–49.

De Vito, A., & Gómez, J. P. (2020). Estimating the COVID-19 cash crunch: Global evidence and policy. *Journal of Accounting and Public Policy, 39*(2), 1–14.

Eleftheriou, K., & Patsoulis, P. (2020). *COVID-19 lockdown intensity and stock market returns: A spatial econometrics approach* (MPRA Paper 100662). University Library of Munich.

Forbes, K. J., & Rigobon, R. (2002). No contagion, only interdependence: measuring stock market comovements. *The Journal of Finance, 57*(5), 2223–2261.

He, Q., Liu, J., Wang, S., & Yu, J. (2020). The impact of COVID-19 on stock markets. *Economic and Political Studies, 8*(3), 275–288.

Hon, M. T., Strauss, J., & Yong, S. K. (2004). Contagion in financial markets after September 11: Myth or reality?. *Journal of Financial Research, 27*(1), 95–114.

Ji, Q., Zhang, D., & Zhao, Y. (2020). Searching for safe-haven assets during the COVID-19 pandemic. *International Review of Financial Analysis, 71*, 101526.

Liu, H., Manzoor, A., Wang, C., Zhang, L., & Manzoor, Z. (2020). The COVID-19 outbreak and affected countries stock markets response. *International Journal of Environmental Research and Public Health, 17*(8), 2800.

Manela, A., & Moreira, A. (2017). News implied volatility and disaster concerns. *Journal of Financial Economics, 123*(1), 137–162.

Mollah, S., Quoreshi, A. S., & Zafirov, G. (2016). Equity market contagion during global financial and Eurozone crises: Evidence from a dynamic correlation analysis. *Journal of International Financial Markets, Institutions and Money, 41*, 151–167.

Nguyen, D. T., Phan, D. H. B., & Ming, T. C. (2021). An assessment of how COVID-19 changed the global equity market. *Economic Analysis and Policy, 69*, 480–491.

Thomas, L. (2020). *Coronavirus wreaks havoc on retail supply chains globally, even as China's factories come back online*. CNBC.

Wang, G. J., Xie, C., Lin, M., & Stanley, H. E. (2017). Stock market contagion during the global financial crisis: A multiscale approach. *Finance Research Letters, 22*, 163–168.

Zaremba, A., Kizys, R., Aharon, D. Y., & Demir, E. (2020). Infected markets: Novel coronavirus, government interventions, and stock return volatility around the globe. *Finance Research Letters, 35*, 101597.

Zhang, D., Hu, M., & Ji, Q. (2020). Financial markets under the global pandemic of COVID-19. *Finance Research Letters, 36*, 101528.

Hebatallah Ghoneim

COVID-19 Impact on Decent Work: Overview of Africa

1. Introduction

COVID-19 went beyond being a pandemic situation to a global economic crisis. The pandemic is affecting the working hours, place and productivity of most workers. Moreover, number of firms had to cut down the level of employment or at least decrease wages. Those employment categories that depend on irregular job vacancies are currently depending on social transfer from the government. Besides, most of the families are facing major disturbance due to working at home and dispense of schools. These variables: employment, productivity, income, social insurance and balanced income-family relation, are components of the eighth Sustainable development goal "Decent work and Economic Growth."

The African continent statistics are lower in terms of Corona Virus infection and death during the last two years. While deaths in Europe due to the Corona virus are approaching two million, the African share does not exceed a quarter of a million. Where 40 % of the death is concentrated in South Africa, followed by Tunisia and Egypt (both 20 %). Most of the countries in the continent recorded less than 1,000 people died due to COVID-19 (World-meters, 2022). The continent that includes more than 17 % of world population has nearly 3 % of world infection and 5 % share in mortality level. Bamgboye et al. (2021) explained that African countries exposure to other diseases such as Malaria or previous waves of corona viruses might have contributed in gaining immunity against COVID-19; besides, the more abundance of sunlight that helps in production of Vitamin D which is believed to contribute in faster recovery of the infection. Bamgboye et al. (2021) have also highlighted the larger number of Youth in African continents living in heat and humidity; in comparison to other continents such as Europe. They also explained that most African countries have low capacity of rt-PCR tests that is used to positively ensure the disease; which have led to misleading results.

Nevertheless, the African countries have faced less mild pandemic waves in comparison to other continents. This raised the research interest to evaluate whether the economic slowdown is also less mild. Based on World Bank data, the world economic growth recorded -3.3 % in 2020. This is even higher adverse effect than the period following 2007 financial crises; during which the economic growth reached -1.9 % in 2009. The slowdown was the cost of lockdown that kept individuals at home and led to disclosure to number of industries; besides, social distancing practices that increased the cost of production. How far economic growth in Africa is affected and is the economy still capable of creating job opportunity or spread of unemployment expanded due to global slow down.

COVID-19 economic shock was accompanied with major changes in life of every family routine which were not experienced before; such as school closure, e-learning and remote working. Recession conditions together with having children at home would derive women out of the working market. Especially that service sector; which is the main absorbent of female employment, was the most affected (Zamarro et al., 2020). Zahed et al. (2020) raised the fear that with children out of school and parents at edge of losing their job opportunity; there would be exposure of more children into work. How far these two hypotheses are true in the African continent is another target of this paper.

Respectively, the paper will give an overview of the main changes in unemployment as well as major affected labor groups, gender changes in labor market for African countries as well as highlight on work-life balance.

2. Unemployment: Before vs. After COVID

During the pandemic, the governments imposed non-pharmaceutical interventions (NPIs) that all target keeping social distance in attempt to decrease the virus spread. NPIs included lockdown of restaurants, closing of schools, banning of gatherings, travel bans, curfews and remote working (Kong & Prinz, 2020; Perra, 2021). These measures had led to closure of some workplaces for more than six months which cost the loss of jobs for number of labors. Moreover, demand of households changed toward more online purchase, conference software, computer hardware and medical essential goods such as gloves and masks (Kampf et al., 2020; Sarkis et al., 2020). Change in households demand implies shift of expenditures from sector to another respectively would change employment structure.

Table 1. Unemployment for selected regions (% of total labor force–ILO estimate)

Country name	YR2019	YR2020
Africa (53 countries)	6.42	7.89
Asia[1]	5.89	6.92
Australia	5.16	6.46
European Union	6.7	7.0
Latin America and the Caribbean	7.9	10.1
North America	3.89	8.21
World	5.36	6.57

Source: World Bank Data Bank

Based on World Bank data (see Table 1), It can be documented that the COVID-19 pandemic has resulted in nearly 1.5 % increase of unemployment in the African continent.[2] Unemployment rate (% of labor force—based on ILO estimates) increased from an average 6.42 % for 53 African countries[3] to 7.89 %. This implies that about 916.23 thousands lost job in only one year as a result of COVID-19 economy slow down. Africa is no different than the rest of the world, where unemployment rates increased dramatically in North America in specific and the whole world in general as indicated in Table 1.

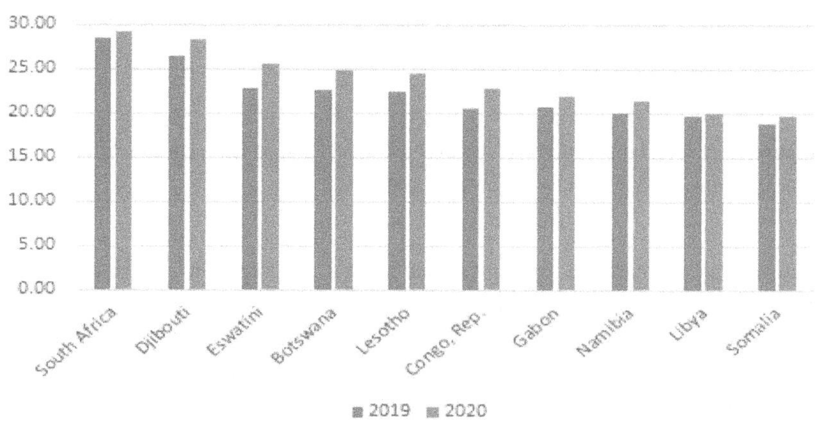

Figure 1. Unemployment (% of total labor force–ILO estimate): Highest ten record in Africa
Source: Constructed by author based on World Bank Data Bank

1 Calculated by author for 46 countries based on World Bank data bank.
2 Calculated by author based on Data provided by World Bank Data Bank.
3 No data was available for Seychelles.

Nevertheless, in 2020 highest level of unemployment all over the world were recorded in African countries; South Africa (29.2 %) and Djibouti (28.4 %), while eight other African countries recorded unemployment rates higher than or equal 20 % (see Figure 1). Nevertheless, during 2020 increase in unemployment in these ten countries ranged between 0.41 (Libya) and 2.67 (Eswatini), in comparison to a range of change -0.007 to 1.6 in 2019[4] (see Figure 2). In general, these ten countries have suffered of high rate of unemployment in the last decade and their unemployment rates have always been higher than world average unemployment rate. These countries suffer of unemployment either due to few availability of natural resources, less dependence on manufactured sector, expansion of informal sector and inadequate education sector.

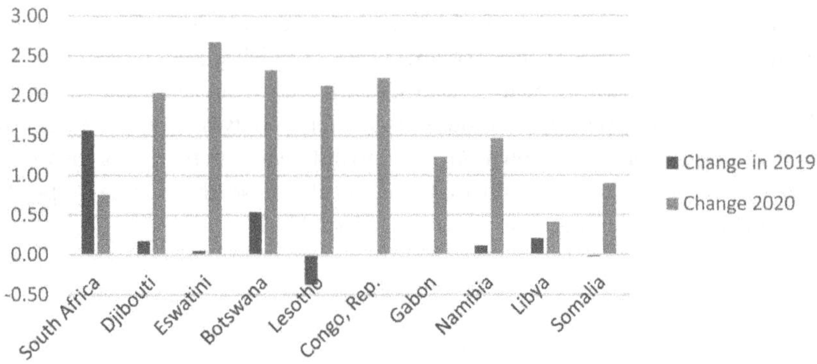

Figure 2. Changes in unemployment 2019 vs. 2020: Highest ten record in Africa
Source: Constructed by author based on World Bank Data Bank

Substantial increase in unemployment rates are reported in Cabo Verde, Eswatini, Botswana, Republic of Congo, Morocco and Lesotho. In these countries, the increase in unemployment rates ranged between 2.12 and 3.09 (see Table 2). The most common feature of these economies is the dependence on service sector to create job opportunities. Employment in service sector for male ranged from 42.39 % of male employment to 67.6 % (see Table 2). While, Botswana and Lesotho in particular are two out of the 11 richest countries in producing Diamond (The Global Economy.com, 2022b). Demand on diamond has decreased massively specially with the closure of most Diamond selling shops

4 Calculated by author based on world bank data.

all over the world and difficulty of exporting. Respectively, diamond mining companies had to consider temporary closure and reduce some of its workers. In Botswana, Diamond production fell by 29 % during the first 9 months of the pandemic (Analytica, 2021) and there was a 54.5 % decrease in Lesotho during the year 2020 (Statista.com, 2022a).

Table 2. Unemployment (% of total labor force) and employment for selected countries

Country	2019	2020	Change in unemployment rate	Employment in services, male (% of male employment) 2019
Cabo Verde	12.22	15.31	3.09	67.6
Eswatini	22.84	25.51	2.67	64.6
Botswana	22.61	24.93	2.32	62.49
Congo, Rep.	20.62	22.84	2.22	44.99
Morocco	9.28	11.45	2.17	43.66
Lesotho	22.44	24.56	2.12	42.39

Source: Constructed by author based on World Bank Databank (2022)

Nevertheless, governments in Africa have been depending on tourism in accelerating growth and creating employment (Christie & Cromption, 2001). Africa known to be the second growing tourism sector in the world; with its large-scale beaches and wild-life as well as rich culture and historical monuments. Cabo verde; for example which is an island in the Atlantic known for its beautiful beaches, depends mainly on tourism as main instrument for job creation and gaining foreign currency, where in 2019 more than 56 % of exports revenue gained from tourism (Word Bank Databank, 2022) and the country witnessed 39 % decline in tourism expenditures in 2020 in comparison to previous year. Tourism sector is a labor-intensive sector that can create job for both skilled and unskilled labor. Also, it's a key sector that has impact on the income and employment of other services and manufacturing sector; such as food, transportation, cloth and crafts.

Other African countries with high dependence on tourism are: Sao Tome and Principe with 73.19 % of exports revenues in 2018, Eritrea with 36.84 % of exports revenues in 2018, Ethiopia with 29.58 % of exports revenues in 2018 and Comoros with 26.9 % of exports revenues in 2018 (Word Bank Databank, 2022). Moreover, based on the Global Economy (.com, 2022a) Seychelles, Cape

Verde and Mauritius are three African countries ranked as 5th, 7th and 19th (respectively) out of 135 countries worldwide in terms of international tourism revenue as percentage of GDP.

In 2020, flights stopped, gatherings were prohibited and people were advised to stay at home. These strict social distancing measures led to closure of restaurants, hotels, resorts, travel agencies and open door entertainment activities (Nhamo et al., 2020). In 2020, massive decrease in number of international tourists arrivals to Africa were witnessed, for example number of arrivals in December 2020 is 1,603 thousands in comparison to 6,310 thousands in 2019 (Statista.com, 2022). African Union estimated that nearly $55 million lost their jobs in the first three months of the pandemic (Monnier, 2021).

Even in 2021 after the vaccine campaigns, international tourists' arrivals to Africa decreased by 74 % in comparison to 2019 in comparison to 63 % decline in Europe and 62 % in the Americas (UNWTO, 2022). Decrease of revenue and job opportunities affect other sectors such as private transportation services, food and beverages and even cloth sector. Employment recap in the tourism sector depends on the country ability of creating a competitive edge; ensuring for international tourists the safety measures applied, technology facilities provided and social distance granted. In order for the continent to create more job opportunities and depend on tourism as a pillar for decent job opportunities; the countries should gain world confidence through expanding vaccination and ensuring hygiene precautions.

3. Highly Affected Labor Groups

No one escaped from the social and economic impact of the pandemic, however some groups were affected more. With massive closures in sectors that substantial percentage of the youth labor force, such as retail, tourism and consumer services, youth faced more loss in jobs. Youth Unemployment (% of total labor force age 15–24) exceeded 50 % in some countries such as Djibouti, South Africa and Eswatini. Major changes exceeding 3 % change in your unemployment from year 2019 to 2020 occurred in number of African countries such as; Botswana, Cabo Verde, Djibouti, Eswatini, Morocco and Algeria (see Figure 3). In earlier financial crises, young workers were more vulnerable to employment shocks, never the less they get highly hired after the economic recap (Verick, 2009).

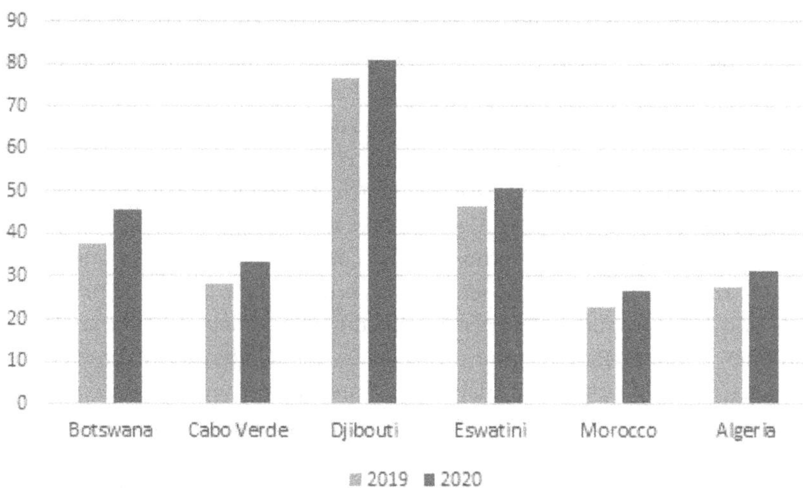

Figure 3. Changes in unemployment, youth total (% of total labor force ages 15–24)
Source: Constructed by author based on World Bank Data Bank

COVID-19 has decelerated the economy ability to create job. Although the informal sector is unmeasurable, but it can be confirmed that many informal workers and enterprises went out of business cycle. Specially that highly affected sectors; such as tourism and retail sales; heavily includes on casual and partly contracts as well as self-employed sellers (ILO, 2020). Drop in the tourism sector had led to closure of many informal business unites; such as informal vending of crafts, cloth and beverages in the touristic areas (Makoni & Tichaawa, 2021). Africa with an average 71.9 % informal employment as percentage of non-manufacturing sector (Narula, 2020; p. 304); compared to 50 % in the European Union and 60 % in the United States, workers faced double stress between losing jobs; due banning street vending in a number of countries as part of social distance policies, and working under condition that put them under risk of infection and death without health insurance opportunity. Moreover, some countries have followed a night-time curfew; such as Cameroon, which made it difficult for vendors and informal workers to move from city to another fulfilling their daily business (Schwettmann, 2020)

Another dimension that worth examining is the impact of COVID-19 on gender equality. Casale and Posel (2020, p. 3) has demonstrated that gender gap as increased dramatically in South Africa. Out of 2.9 million job losses occurred in the first two months after announcing the pandemic by WHO organization;

women share was two third. Previous recessions and financial crises would usually hit women employment strongly; specially in developing countries, due to male dominance in the manufacturing, better education received by male, the existing gender inequalities and women's dependence on informal start-ups activities to fill employment gap (Madgavkar et al., 2020; Mehra, 1997). Based on World Bank data, a number of African countries faced more than 2 % increase in female unemployment; such as Algeria, Botswana, Cabo Verde, Congo Republic, Djibouti, Egypt, Eswatini, Lesotho, Morocco, Sao Tome and Principe and Sudan.

COVID-19 by all means has set more stress on women, the pandemic did not only slowdown production but also reshaped working environment transferring most jobs remotely. Based on statistical data, men might be more exposed to risk of infection and death (Carli, 2020), but women are definitely more exposed to physiological stress and anxiety. Women are working from home; which have been seen by some scholars as a method to ensure decent work with life balance (Crosbie & Moore, 2004; Ghoneim, 2021); turned into a nightmare. Each mother has been working for nearly a year under the stress of losing job, handling online schooling and seeking methods to improve internet connection. Moreover, women; who should be physically, at work faced problem of school and day care closure (Alon et al., 2020; Goldstein et al., 2022). It was not preferred to leave children with grandparents to avoid the probability to transfer the infection. Simply some mothers would have to leave work to take care of the children. In general, those who have the talent, skills and resources are those who managed to keep their jobs and survive the pandemic. Nevertheless, COVID has affected the ability of many to achieve work-life balance.

4. Work-Life Balance

One dimension of evaluating decent work is securing significant time for family and leisure (Ghoneim, 2021; Nam & Kim, 2019). Decent work implies a working atmosphere that facilitate work-life balance; ensuring family time, leisure time and self-time. Hjálmsdóttir and Bjarnadóttir (2021) have defined Work-life balance as a situation in which worker are able to manage family and work obligations simultaneously; respectively gain better mental and physical health.

COVID-19 has encouraged remote working and working at home. However, this did not contribute to less tension or more life balance. During the pandemic, especially the lockdown time, parents were overwhelmed with several tasks (Hjálmsdóttir & Bjarnadóttir, 2021). Since our houses turned into working places, backyard, clubs and schools, parents acted as workers, coaches, friends and teachers. With working from home, parents were not able to separate working time from family time and personal life time (Irawanto et al., 2021). Moreover, teleworking or remote working made it adjusted for employer to reach employee at any time regardless of weekends or official holiday. Parents gained flexibility with working from home but paid price less life balance. Mostafa (2021) showed based on structured interviews held in Egypt that employees would stay longer hours working during remote working in comparison to office hours. The same was supported by Workers can often overwork themselves.

Moreover, COVID-19 lockdown had crashed leisure industry. With restricted access to beaches and gardens, closed clubs and fitness centers, banning travel and limited social visits, people had no choice but to move into more online meetings and online entertainment (Amin et al., 2022; Young, 2020). Being house bounded and with limited leisure activities, online games became a preferred activity. Online games have been a method to escape reality and socialize at a time where socialization is prohibited (Zhu, 2021). Communications' application and smart phones expanded the dependence on online activities for leisure and work break.

Harding and Noorbhai (2021) analysis of a sample in South Africa during the Pandemic, showed that more than 40 % of the sample play video games in the pandemic on daily basis and more than 69 % of the population would spend three hours a day playing. Harding and Noorbhai (2021) added that nearly 69.1 % of the population would prefer being seated rather than active games.

5. Conclusion

COVID-19 did not infect all human on earth but for certain affected the life of all human. It reshaped our consumption habits, gatherings, working environment and learning systems. If one is not affected of either these conditions, he would be affected by the economic slowdown accompanied the social distaining procedures set by all governorates. In this paper, the unemployment in Africa accompanying the decrease in economic growth was highlighted. The paper also, shed the light on the changes in youth, informal sector, female unemployment and work-life balance. Many questions are raised post-COVID-19 concerning decent work, how fast will African economies recap, how can tourism be backed up from shocks, how can worker benefit from the tele-communication expansion and will remote working last.

References

Alon, T., Doepke, M., Olmstead-Rumsey, J., & Tertilt, M. (2020). *This time it's different: The role of women's employment in a pandemic recession* (No. w27660). National Bureau of Economic Research.

Amin, K. P., Griffiths, M. D., & Dsouza, D. D. (2022). Online gaming during the COVID-19 pandemic in India: strategies for work-life balance. *International Journal of Mental Health and Addiction*, *20*(1), 296–302.

Analytica, O. (2021). Botswana's Masisi faces growing political challenges. *Emerald Insights: Expert Briefings*. https://doi.org/10.1108/OXAN-DB258515

Bamgboye, E. L., Omiye, J. A., Afolaranmi, O. J., Davids, M. R., Tannor, E. K., Wadee, S., Niang, A., Were, A., & Naicker, S. (2021). COVID-19 pandemic: Is Africa different?. *Journal of the National Medical Association*, *113*(3), 324–335.

Carli, L. L. (2020). Women, gender equality and COVID-19. *Gender in Management: An International Journal*, *35*(7/8), 647–655.

Casale, D., & Posel, D. (2020). *Gender and the early effects of the COVID-19 crisis in the paid and unpaid economies in South Africa* (NIDS-CRAM Policy Paper Recuperado el, 18).

Christie, I., & Cromption, D. E. (2001). *Tourism in Africa. Africa region findings & good practice* (Infobriefs; No. 187, License: CC BY 3.0 IGO). World Bank. https://openknowledge.worldbank.org/handle/10986/9804

Crosbie, T., & Moore, J. (2004). Work-life balance and working from home. *Social Policy and Society*, *3*(3), 223–233.

Ghoneim, H. (2021) Decent work for women through digital social network. In W. Leal Filho, A. M. Azul, L. Brandli, A. Lange Salvia, & T. Wall (Eds.), *Decent work and economic growth. Encyclopedia of the UN sustainable development goals*. Springer.

Global Economy.Com, The (2022a). Diamond production, carats—Country rankings. Retrieved April 2022, from https://www.theglobaleconomy.com/rankings/international_tourism_revenue_to_GDP/

Global Economy.Com, The (2022b). International tourism revenue, percent of GDP—Country rankings. Retrieved April 2022, from https://www.theglobaleconomy.com/rankings/diamond_production_carats/

Goldstein, M., Gonzalez, P., Papineni, S., & Wimpey, J. (2022). *Childcare, COVID-19 and female firm exit: Impact of COVID-19 school closure policies on global gender gaps in business outcomes* (Policy Research Working Paper no. 10012). World Bank Group: Africa Gender Innovation Lab & Development Research Group.

Harding, N., & Noorbhai, H. (2021). Physical activity levels, lifestyle behaviour and musculoskeletal health profiles among seated video gamers during COVID-19. *BMJ Open Sport & Exercise Medicine*, *7*(3), Article e001194.

Hjálmsdóttir, A., & Bjarnadóttir, V. S. (2021). "I have turned into a foreman here at home": Families and work-life balance in times of COVID-19 in a gender equality paradise. *Gender, Work & Organization*, *28*(1), 268–283.

ILO. (2020). *COVID-19 crisis and the informal economy: Immediate responses and policy challenges* (ILO Brief). International Labour Organisation.

Irawanto, D. W., Novianti, K. R., & Roz, K. (2021). Work from home: Measuring satisfaction between work-life balance and work stress during the COVID-19 pandemic in Indonesia. *Economies*, *9*(3), 96.

Kampf, G., Scheithauer, S., Lemmen, S., Saliou, P., & Suchomel, M. (2020). COVID-19-associated shortage of alcohol-based hand rubs, face masks, medical gloves, and gowns: Proposal for a risk-adapted approach to ensure patient and healthcare worker safety. *Journal of Hospital Infection, 105*(3), 424–427.

Kong, E., & Prinz, D. (2020). The impact of shutdown policies on unemployment during a pandemic. *COVID Economics*, *17*(13), 24–72.

Madgavkar, A., White, O., Krishnan, M., Mahajan, D., & Azcue, X. (2020). COVID-19 and gender equality: Countering the regressive effects. *McKinsey Global Institute, 15.*

Makoni, L., & Tichaawa, T. M. (2021). Impact analysis of the COVID-19 pandemic on the informal sector business tourism economy in Zimbabwe. *African Journal of Hospitality, Tourism and Leisure*, *10*(1), 165–178.

Matli, W. (2020). The changing work landscape as a result of the COVID-19 pandemic: Insights from remote workers life situations in South Africa. *International Journal of Sociology and Social Policy*, *40*(9/10), 1237–1256.

Mehra, R. (1997). Women, empowerment, and economic development. *The Annals of the American Academy of Political and Social Science*, *554*(1), 136–149.

Monnier, O. (2021). A ticket to recovery: Reinventing Africa's tourism industry. World Bank Group: International Finance Corporations. Retrieved April 2022, from https://www.ifc.org/wps/wcm/connect/news_ext_content/ifc_external_corporate_site/news+and+events/news/reinventing-africa-tourism

Mostafa, B. A. (2021). The effect of remote working on employees wellbeing and work-life integration during pandemic in Egypt. *International Business Research*, *14*(3), 41–52. https://doi.org/10.5539/ibr.v14n3p41

Nam, J. S., & Kim, S. Y. (2019). Decent work in South Korea: Context, conceptualization, and assessment. *Journal of Vocational Behavior, 115*, 103309.

Narula, R. (2020). Policy opportunities and challenges from the COVID-19 pandemic for economies with large informal sectors. *Journal of International Business Policy, 3*(3), 302–310.

Nhamo, G., Dube, K., & Chikodzi, D. (2020). Restaurants and COVID-19: A focus on sustainability and recovery pathways. In *Counting the cost of COVID-19 on the global tourism industry* (pp. 205–224). Springer.

Perra, N. (2021). Non-pharmaceutical interventions during the COVID-19 pandemic: A review. *Physics Reports, 913*, 1–52.

Sarkis, J., Cohen, M. J., Dewick, P., & Schröder, P. (2020). A brave new world: Lessons from the COVID-19 pandemic for transitioning to sustainable supply and production. *Resources, Conservation and Recycling, 159*, 104894.

Schwettmann, J. (2020, April). *COVID-19 and the informal economy. Impact and response strategies in Sub-Saharan Africa.* Friedrich Ebert Stiftung (FES). https://library.fes.de/pdf-files/iez/16414.pdf

Statista.com. (2022, January). *Monthly international tourist arrivals in Africa during the coronavirus (COVID-19) pandemic from 2019 to 2021.* https://www.statista.com/statistics/1193505/monthly-international-tourist-arrivals-in-africa/

Statista.com. (2022a, April). *Production of diamonds in Lesotho from 2004 to 2020.* https://www.statista.com/statistics/964880/lesotho-diamond-production-volume/

UNWTO. (2022). *Tourism dashboard.* United Nations: World Tourism Organization.

Verick, S. (2009). *Who is hit hardest during a financial crisis? The vulnerability of young men and women to unemployment in an economic downturn* (Discussion Paper No. 4359). IZA: Institute of Labor Economics.

World Bank Databank. (2022, January). *World development indicators.* World Bank. https://databank.worldbank.org/source/world-development-indicators

Worldometer. (2022, January). *COVID-19 live: Reported cases and deaths by country or territory.* https://www.worldometers.info/coronavirus/

Young, M. E. (2020). Leisure pursuits in South Africa as observed during the COVID-19 pandemic. *World Leisure Journal, 62*(4), 331–335.

Zahed, G., Chehrehrazi, N., & Nouri Talemi, A. (2020). How does COVID-19 affect child labor?. *Archives of Pediatric Infectious Diseases, 8*(3).

Zamarro, G., Perez-Arce, F., & Prados, M. J. (2020). *Gender differences in the impact of COVID-19* (Working Paper). Centre for Economic and Social Research, University of Southern California. https://tinyurl.com/CESRGenderDiffs

Zhu, L. (2021). The psychology behind video games during COVID-19 pandemic: A case study of Animal Crossing: New Horizons. *Human Behavior and Emerging Technologies*, *3*(1), 157–159.

Mohammed N. Abu-Alfoul

Unlocking the Potential of ChatGPT in Economic and Finance Studies: A Game-Changing Case Study

1. Introduction

Recent years have seen a surge in interest in artificial intelligence (AI) (Science Daily, 2022). The potential effects of AI on everything from the military to the entertainment industry have sparked much discussion. Concerns have been raised regarding whether AI will replace humans in the workforce or if it will be used to supplement human abilities. This essay explores the potential effects of generative AI, a subfield of AI, on the fields of Economic and Finance studies. Journalism and media professors are delving into the effects of technology like AI (Luttrell et al., 2020).

What is the ChatGPT? ChatGPT is a language model based on OpenAI's GPT-3 (Generative Pre-trained Transformer 3, 2020; Brown et al., 2020). It was designed to produce natural language conversation and has received attention in the media and tech industries. The Transformer architecture used by GPT-3 was introduced by Vaswani et al. (2017) and is widely used in NLP. GPT-3 is one of the largest language models with 175 billion parameters and can perform various tasks such as translation, summarization, question answering, and text generation with little task-specific training.

GPT-3 has taken the world by storm since its grand entrance, showcasing its versatility across translation, content creation, and language modeling. This AI has proven its linguistic prowess by delivering virtually flawless translations and easily summarizing lengthy documents. GPT-3 has even wowed us with its chatbot capabilities, engaging in natural conversations and answering queries with remarkable acumen. However, its ability to generate text that is both convincing and coherent has sparked both admiration and concern, igniting discussions about the potential and ramifications of AI in language processing.

GPT-3 has a myriad of applications, including content creation. Some users of GPT-3 have reported that the generated text is indistinguishable from text written by humans, and GPT-3 has been used to generate articles (Elkins & Chun, 2020; GPT-3 et al., 2022; Lucy & Bamman, 2021). This has sparked concerns that GPT-3 could be misused to spread misinformation or manipulate public perception

(Floridi & Chiriatti, 2020). But, the AI giant also holds promise, offering to streamline repetitive content production tasks (Jaimovitch-López et al., 2022) and of assisting writers and content creators in generating ideas and overcoming writer's block (Duval et al., 2020).

Everything you have read was written by the author. The following text was written in collaboration between the author and the machine. It may make you wonder if we've finally arrived at artificial intelligence when machines like ChatGPT can pass the Turing test. In other words, computer scientist Alan Turing (1950)[1] proposed a game in which players try to determine whether they are conversing with a machine or another human. Readers will decide if ChatGPT is up to snuff in this regard. In this case, the author asked some queries and prompts, and ChatGPT gave its answers. The dates of the query and the response are recorded in the ChatGPT statement. No portion of ChatGPT has been revised by the human author of this article. The conclusions were written by a human author.

2. Explain How Scientific Papers Works?

Scientific papers are the primary means by which scientists communicate their research findings and ideas to the wider scientific community. The process of writing a scientific paper typically involves the following steps:

1. Conducting research: This involves collecting data, analyzing it, and interpreting the results.
2. Writing an abstract: This is a brief summary of the research, including the main findings and conclusions.
3. Creating an introduction: This provides background information on the topic and outlines the research question being addressed.
4. Presenting the methods: This section describes the methods used to collect and analyze the data, including any experimental designs or statistical methods.
5. Reporting the results: This section presents the data and results of the analysis, including tables, graphs, and statistical tests.
6. Discussing the results: This section interprets the results and discusses their implications in the context of previous research and theories.
7. Drawing conclusions: This section summarizes the main findings and draws conclusions based on the research results.

---

1 Turing, A.M., 1950. Mind. Mind, 59(236), pp. 433–460.

8. Writing the references: This section lists all of the sources used in the paper, including books, articles, and other sources.
9. Submitting the paper: The completed paper is submitted to a scientific journal for peer review.
10. Peer review: The paper is reviewed by other experts in the field, who provide feedback on the methodology, results, and conclusions. Based on their feedback, the authors may revise the paper.
11. Final publication: If the paper is accepted, it is published in the journal and becomes part of the scientific literature.

The purpose of this process is to ensure that the results of scientific research are rigorously scrutinized and validated, and to promote transparency and reproducibility in the scientific process.

(By ChatGPT February 3, 2023)

3. What Does the Nature of AI?

The nature of AI, or artificial intelligence, refers to the inherent characteristics and qualities of AI systems and technologies. AI is the simulation of human intelligence in machines that are designed to think and act like humans.

The nature of AI can be described as follows:

1. Intelligent: AI systems can analyze, reason, and make data-based decisions.
2. Automated: AI systems are designed to perform tasks without human intervention, although some AI systems may require human supervision.
3. Adaptive: AI systems have the ability to learn and improve over time through exposure to new data and experience.
4. Interdisciplinary: AI involves a combination of disciplines, including computer science, mathematics, engineering, and psychology.
5. Data-driven: AI relies on large amounts of data to train and improve its performance.
6. Dual use: AI has both positive and negative applications, including uses in fields such as healthcare, finance, and military.

The nature of AI is constantly evolving as new developments and breakthroughs occur, and as society continues to grapple with the implications of this technology.

(By ChatGPT February 3, 2023)

4. Can a ChatGPT Have Creativity? What Does It Mean to Be Creative?

As an AI language model, ChatGPT does not have consciousness or emotions and therefore cannot be creative in the sense that humans can be creative.

Creativity is often defined as the ability to produce novel and valuable ideas or concepts. It can refer to the ability to think outside the box and come up with innovative solutions, or to the ability to create art or music that is original and inspiring. Creativity involves both imagination and the ability to take action on those imaginative ideas.

While ChatGPT can generate original text and complete tasks that might require some degree of imagination or problem-solving, it is ultimately limited by its programming and training data, and does not have the subjective experience of being creative.

(By ChatGPT February 3, 2023)

5. When It Comes to Scientific Writing, How Useful Is Generative AI?

Generative AI can be useful in scientific writing in certain ways. For example, AI language models like ChatGPT can assist with generating text and completing tasks such as writing summaries or composing research papers with a certain degree of accuracy and speed. However, it's important to note that AI models do not have a deep understanding of the scientific concepts they are writing about and are limited by their training data. Therefore, the quality of their output may not always be on par with that of a human expert in the field.

Additionally, scientific writing often requires critical thinking, logical reasoning, and the ability to interpret and analyze data, which are tasks that are still beyond the capabilities of AI language models. Therefore, while AI can be a useful tool for some aspects of scientific writing, it is not a replacement for human judgment and expertise.

(By ChatGPT February 3, 2023)

6. What Is the Role of ChatGPT in Academic Research? What Are the Advantages and Implications?

The role of ChatGPT in academic research is to assist researchers in various tasks, such as data analysis, literature review, and paper writing. Some of the advantages of using ChatGPT in academic research include:

1. Increased Efficiency: ChatGPT can automate certain tasks, such as data analysis and literature review, freeing up time for researchers to focus on other aspects of their work.
2. Improved Data Analysis: ChatGPT can analyze large amounts of data, identify patterns, and generate insights that might not be easily noticed by human researchers.
3. Streamlined Writing Process: ChatGPT can be used to generate a draft of a research paper, allowing researchers to focus on refining and editing the content, rather than starting from scratch.
4. Enhanced Collaboration: ChatGPT can assist researchers in different locations to work together on a project, even if they are not physically in the same place.

However, it is important to note that there are also implications to consider when using ChatGPT in academic research. Some of these include:

1. Bias in Data: If the data used to train ChatGPT is biased, this bias will be reflected in the outputs generated by the model.
2. Reliance on Technology: Relying on AI systems like ChatGPT can reduce the critical thinking skills and creativity of researchers.
3. Quality of Outputs: The quality of outputs generated by ChatGPT will depend on the quality and accuracy of the data it was trained on, as well as the algorithms used to analyze that data.

In conclusion, while ChatGPT has the potential to be a useful tool in academic research, it is important to use it responsibly and to consider both the advantages and implications of using AI in research. Researchers should strive to ensure the quality and accuracy of the data used to train AI systems and to use their outputs in conjunction with their own expertise and critical thinking skills to produce high-quality research.

(By ChatGPT February 3, 2023)

7. What Is the ChatGPT Cannot Do for Academic Researchers?

ChatGPT, like any other AI system, has limitations and cannot do certain things for academic researchers. Here are some of the things that ChatGPT cannot do:

1. Replace Human Expertise: ChatGPT is trained on a large dataset and can generate outputs based on that data, but it cannot replace human expertise and judgment. Researchers must still verify and validate the outputs generated by ChatGPT and must use their own knowledge and experience to interpret and understand these outputs.
2. Handle Complex Problems: While ChatGPT is a powerful tool, it may not be able to handle complex problems that require a deep understanding of a particular field or domain. Researchers must still use their own expertise and knowledge to tackle complex problems.
3. Make Ethical Decisions: ChatGPT is a machine and does not have the ability to make ethical decisions or understand the social and moral implications of its outputs. Researchers must take responsibility for the ethical use of AI systems like ChatGPT and must ensure that the outputs generated by these systems are used responsibly.
4. Ensure Data Privacy: While ChatGPT can generate outputs based on data, it cannot ensure data privacy. Researchers must still take steps to protect personal data and comply with data privacy laws and regulations.
5. Avoid Bias: ChatGPT is trained on data and can reflect the biases in that data in its outputs. Researchers must be aware of the potential for bias in AI systems and must take steps to minimize and address these biases.

In conclusion, while ChatGPT is a powerful tool that can help academic researchers generate outputs, it cannot replace human expertise, handle complex problems, make ethical decisions, ensure data privacy, or avoid bias. Researchers must still use their own expertise and knowledge to tackle complex problems and must be responsible for the ethical and responsible use of AI systems like ChatGPT.

(By ChatGPT February 3, 2023)

8. Are There Ethical Considerations or Legal Restrictions Regarding the Use of ChatGPT in Academic Research?

Yes, there are ethical considerations and legal restrictions regarding using ChatGPT in academic research. Some of these include:

1. Data Privacy: The use of personal data in academic research must comply with data privacy laws, such as the General Data Protection Regulation (GDPR) in the European Union and the California Consumer Privacy Act (CCPA) in the United States. Researchers must ensure that they have obtained the necessary permissions to use personal data in their research and that they are using it in a manner that is compliant with privacy laws.
2. Intellectual Property: The use of third-party data, such as academic papers and articles, in academic research must comply with intellectual property laws.

Researchers must ensure that they have obtained the necessary permissions to use this data and that they are giving proper credit to the original authors.

3. Bias and Discrimination: The use of AI systems like ChatGPT in academic research must be free from bias and discrimination. If the data used to train ChatGPT is biased, this bias will be reflected in the outputs generated by the model, which can potentially have negative consequences for certain groups of people.
4. Responsibility for Outputs: Researchers must be aware of the limitations of AI systems like ChatGPT and must ensure that the outputs generated by these systems are used responsibly. They must also be aware of the potential for errors and inaccuracies in the outputs and take steps to verify and validate them.

In conclusion, while ChatGPT has the potential to be a useful tool in academic research, it is important to use it responsibly and in compliance with ethical considerations and legal restrictions. Researchers must ensure that they are using personal data, third-party data, and AI systems in a manner that is compliant with privacy laws, intellectual property laws, and anti-discrimination laws. They must also be aware of the limitations and potential errors in the outputs generated by ChatGPT and take steps to verify and validate them.

(By ChatGPT February 3, 2023)

9. Does Using ChatGPT Infringe on Any Copyrights?

The use of ChatGPT in academic research or any other context may infringe on copyrights if it involves the unauthorized use of third-party content, such as text, images, or other forms of creative expression.

Copyright law generally gives the creators of original works, such as books, articles, and music, the exclusive right to control the use of their works, including the right to reproduce, distribute, and create derivative works.

If a researcher or any other user of ChatGPT uses text or other content generated by the model that is based on or substantially like copyrighted works, without obtaining the necessary permissions or licenses, this could be considered an infringement of copyright.

It is the responsibility of the user of ChatGPT to ensure that the use of the model complies with copyright law and to obtain the necessary permissions or licenses for the use of any third-party content.

In conclusion, using ChatGPT does not automatically infringe on copyrights, but it is important to use the model responsibly and comply with copyright law to avoid potential legal issues.

(By ChatGPT February 3, 2023)

10. Is AI a Danger to Human Scientific Writing and Academics? Explain Why?

AI is not inherently a danger to human scientific writing and academics, but it can pose some challenges and risks that need to be carefully considered.

On the one hand, AI can automate certain aspects of scientific writing and academic work, such as data analysis or text generation, freeing up time and resources for researchers to focus on more high-level tasks. On the other hand, there are concerns about the quality and accuracy of AI-generated content, as AI models are only as good as the data they are trained on and can sometimes produce results that are biased or inconsistent with reality.

Another risk is that AI may eventually replace human writers and researchers in certain tasks, leading to job loss and reduced opportunities for human workers. This could negatively affect the scientific community and academia, as human expertise and creativity are often crucial for generating new ideas and advancing knowledge.

In conclusion, AI has the potential to both benefit and challenge the field of scientific writing and academia, and it is important to approach its use with caution and carefully consider its potential impacts.

(By ChatGPT February 3, 2023)

11. What Should Authors and Academics Researchers Teach Students About AI?

Authors and academic researchers play a crucial role in teaching students about AI and its impact on society. Here are some key topics they should cover:

1. Understanding AI: Students should have a basic understanding of what AI is and how it works, including the different types of AI systems, such as machine learning, deep learning, and natural language processing.
2. Ethics and Bias: Students should learn about the ethical and social implications of AI, including issues of bias and discrimination in AI systems and the potential for AI to reinforce existing social inequalities.
3. Data Privacy: Students should learn about the importance of data privacy and the impact that AI can have on privacy rights. This includes understanding data protection laws and regulations and the ethical considerations surrounding using personal data in AI systems.
4. Interdisciplinary Study: Students should understand that AI is a complex and multi-disciplinary field that requires knowledge from multiple domains, including computer science, mathematics, and psychology.

5. Real-World Applications: Students should learn about the real-world applications of AI and its impact on various sectors, such as healthcare, finance, and education.
6. Limitations of AI: Students should understand the limitations of AI and its potential for errors, including the need for human oversight and verification of AI outputs.

In conclusion, authors and academic researchers play a crucial role in educating students about AI and its impact on society. By covering these key topics, they can help students develop a well-rounded understanding of AI and its potential for both good and harm.

(By ChatGPT February 3, 2023)

12. Where Can We See ChatGPT Being Used in The Financial and Economic Sectors?

ChatGPT has the potential to be used in a variety of applications in the financial and economic sectors, including:

1. Banking and Financial Institutions: ChatGPT can be used by banks and other financial institutions to provide customer service, answer questions, and provide personalized financial advice to their clients.
2. Investment Management: ChatGPT can be used by investment management firms to analyze financial data, make predictions, and provide investment advice to clients.
3. Stock Trading: ChatGPT can be used by stock traders to analyze financial data and provide insights into market trends, helping them to make informed investment decisions.
4. Insurance: ChatGPT can be used by insurance companies to process claims, answer customer questions, and provide personalized insurance recommendations to clients.
5. Economic Research: ChatGPT can be used by economists to analyze large amounts of economic data, make predictions, and provide insights into economic trends and patterns.

These are just a few examples of how ChatGPT can be used in the financial and economic sectors. It is important to note that while ChatGPT has the potential to be a useful tool, it is only as reliable as the data it is trained on and the algorithms used to analyze that data. It is important to ensure the quality and accuracy of the data used to train AI systems to ensure the reliability of their outputs.

(By ChatGPT February 3, 2023)

13. Does the ChatGPT Able to Build the Econometrics Model?

No, ChatGPT is not capable of building econometric models. ChatGPT is a language model designed for text generation and can generate text-based answers to questions, but it does not have the capability to perform data analysis or build econometric models. These tasks typically require specialized software and advanced mathematical and statistical knowledge.

(By ChatGPT February 3, 2023)

14. How Can ChatGPT Help Economic Policymakers?

ChatGPT can assist economic policymakers in several ways, including:

1. Data analysis: ChatGPT can help policymakers analyze large datasets and provide insights into key economic indicators, such as GDP growth, inflation, unemployment, and trade balances.
2. Scenario analysis: ChatGPT can be used to simulate various economic scenarios and assess the potential outcomes of different policy decisions.
3. Forecasting: ChatGPT can help policymakers make more accurate forecasts of key economic indicators, such as GDP growth, inflation, and employment, by leveraging historical data and machine learning algorithms.
4. Text analysis: ChatGPT can be used to analyze large volumes of text data, such as news articles and reports, and provide insights into economic trends and public sentiment.
5. International comparisons: ChatGPT can be used to compare economic data across countries and help policymakers assess the competitiveness of different economies.

In conclusion, ChatGPT has the potential to significantly assist economic policymakers by providing valuable insights into key economic indicators, simulating policy scenarios, making more accurate forecasts, analyzing large volumes of text data, and comparing economic data across countries. By leveraging the capabilities of AI, policymakers can make more informed decisions that can drive economic growth and improve living standards for citizens.

(By ChatGPT February 3, 2023)

15. Conclusion

AI, specifically ChatGPT, can improve academic research in economics and finance by speeding up the research process, improving data accuracy, and enhancing writing quality. However, its use should be managed carefully with human oversight to ensure the validity and reliability of results. While AI has limitations in critical thinking and creativity, it can still be a valuable tool in scientific writing. The use of generative AI systems like ChatGPT needs to be investigated and assessed, and academic institutions should consider its inclusion in curricula and teach students about its risks, ethics, and biases. The rapid change in the human-computer interface requires careful consideration of its impact on the economy and finance.

References

Brown, T., Mann, B., Ryder, N., Subbiah, M., Kaplan, J. D., Dhariwal, P., et al. (2020). Language models are few-shot learners. *Advances in Neural Information Processing Systems*, *33*, 1877–1901.

Duval, A., Lamson, T., de Kérouara, G. D. L., & Gallé, M. (2020). Breaking writer's block: Low-cost finetuning of natural language generation models. *arXiv preprint arXiv*:2101.

Elkins, K., & Chun, J. (2020). Can GPT-3 pass a writer's turing test?. *Journal of Cultural Analytics*, *5*(2), 17212.

Floridi, L., & Chiriatti, M. (2020). GPT-3: Its nature, scope, limits, and consequences. *Minds and Machines*, *30*(4), 681–694.

Generative Pre-trained Transformer 3. (2020, September 8). A robot wrote this entire article. Are you scared yet, human? *The Guardian*. https://www.theguardian.com/commentisfree/2020/sep/08/robot-wrote-this-article-gpt-3

GPT-3, Osmanovic Thunström, A., & Steingrimsson, S. (2022). *Can GPT-3 write an academic paper on itself, with minimal human input?* https://hal.archives-ouvertes.fr/hal-03701250/document

Jaimovitch-López, G., Ferri, C., Hernández-Orallo, J., Martínez-Plumed, F., & Ramírez-Quintana, M. J. (2022). Can language models automate data wrangling? *Machine Learning*, 1–30. https://doi.org/10.1007/s10994-022-06259-9

Lucy, L., & Bamman, D. (2021). Gender and representation bias in GPT-3 generated stories. In *Proceedings of the Third Workshop on Narrative Understanding*, pp. 48–55.

Luttrell, R., Wallace, A., McCollough, C., & Lee, J. (2020). The digital divide: Addressing artificial intelligence in communication education. *Journalism & Mass Communication Educator*, *75*(4), 470–482.

Science Daily. (2022). https://www.sciencedaily.com/news/computers_math/artificial_intelligence/

Vaswani, A., Shazeer, N., Parmar, N., Uszkoreit, J., Jones, L., Gomez, A. N., Kaiser, L., & Polosukhin, I. (2017). Attention is all you need. *Proceedings of NeurIPS*, *2017*, 5998–6008.

Martinkovic Marcel, Haydanka Diana, & Haydanka Yevheniy

Socioeconomic Indicators of Euroscepticism at the Regional Level in Slovakia (2020–2022)

1. Introduction

Paradoxically, since 2004, various populist movements have come to the fore in Central European countries, and as a result, openly conservative politicians frequently come to power. Although only right-wing radicals have recently tackled the membership issue, or precisely, "-exit" from the European Union, the relations between the Central European Governments and Brussels can sometimes be quite strenuous. Suffice it to mention decade-long "Orbanism" in Hungary, the monopole leadership of "Law and Justice" in Poland, and the rise of the right-wing Eurosceptic movement in the present-day Czech Republic. In this regard, Slovakia is no exception. However, the tension between Slovak Eurooptimists and Eurosceptics has regional specificities. For their part, the peculiarities of European pessimism in the eight regions of the Slovak Republic[1] are determined by the respective socioeconomic structures.

Comparative political and economic sciences typically relate Euroscepticism to residents of economically depressed regions without college degrees (Anderson & Reichert, 1995; Hakhverdian et al., 2013; Kunst et al., 2020). However, this is ever a stereotypical image of a Eurosceptic who does not envisage their future as an EU citizen and repeatedly confirms their political views in elections (Hooghe & Marks, 2018). Given the socioeconomic differentiation in the regions of the Slovak Republic, we will attempt to confirm or refute the correlation of electoral orientations (Eurooptimists ↔ Europessimists) with the essential socioeconomic indicators, like (a) unemployment rate, (b) gross average monthly salary, (c) poverty risk, and (d) the number of region's residents with a college degree.

1 The administrative-territorial division of the Slovak Republic on the eve of its EU accession in 2004 includes eight self-governing regions at the NUTS-3 level.

2. Eurobarometer in the Slovak Style: Vices and Virtues of the European Union

The summer 2022 Standard Eurobarometer survey shows up-to-date information on Eurosceptic sentiments among the Slovak general public. Notably, when discussing particular facets of the Slovak attitude toward the EU (economic, political, etc.) or overall, the survey already considers the European community's reaction to the Russian military intervention in Ukraine and its consequences for the European Union (particularly in the energy sector). Rather than security risks for their country, Slovaks express grave concern over the severe economic consequences of the Russian-Ukrainian war. Among the most anticipated negative war consequences, Slovaks articulate *Problems in the supply of energy or goods* and *Inflation/rising prices*. Then follows the threat of a nuclear war or the deployment of military operations directly in Slovakia (European Union, n.d.). In general, Slovaks' expectations of a Russian military invasion of Ukraine contradict the official position of the EU superpowers and the relatively new post-communist members.[2]

The current assessment of the economic situation in the country (79 % of disapproval rates) signals crisis phenomena in the socioeconomic plane. Moreover, the prospects for economic improvement in Slovakia after one calendar year look bleak: 70 % of Slovaks speak of deteriorating processes. The situation with the EU economic potential looks slightly better. However, over half of Slovaks (51 %) are pessimistic about the state of the economy. What they are increasingly concerned about is *Rising prices, inflation, cost of living* and *Energy supply* (European Union, n.d.). We refer primarily to economic problems in the EU energy sector, having followed the sanctions imposed on Russia after the military invasion of Ukraine. The traditional indicator of the Euroscepticism level in the country, citizens' trust in specific institutions, displays a high level of the Slovak Government delegitimation. Ultimately, 80 % of Slovaks distrust the Government,[3] while 44 % continuously trust the EU. Thirty-nine percent of Slovaks are positive toward the EU image, while a quarter of the Slovak citizens rate it negatively (European Union, n.d.).

2 In Germany—*The war spreading to more countries in Europe*, in France—also *The war spreading to more countries in Europe*, and *Inflation/rising price*; in Estonia—*The war spreading to our own country*, in the Czech Republic—*The war spreading to more countries in Europe*.

3 Figures are similar regarding the national Parliament (82 %).

Public opinion polls display moderate levels of Euroscepticism in this Central European country. However, the negative economic consequences following Russia's military aggression in Ukraine led to a decline in Eurooptimistic sentiments in the EU and Slovak Republic. However, Slovak citizens tend to widely support Eurosceptic parties, which has become more of a tradition than a deviation. Based on the 2020 parliamentary elections, we will try to determine the differentiation in the electoral support of Eurosceptic political forces by the region.

3. Slovak Eurosceptics: Who Are They?

The political arena of today's Slovakia is quite diversified, with ideologies ranging from neoliberal progressive parties to right-wing extremists. Eurosceptic parties, occupying a significant segment of Slovak politics, are tentatively classified into two general groups: (1) Moderate Eurosceptics and (2) Europessimists.[4] But this distinction does not entirely reflect the peculiarities of Slovak party Euroscepticism. The Moderate Eurosceptics include Soft Eurosceptics who support renewing relations with the EU by strengthening the foundations of national sovereignty. An overwhelming majority of them are center-right or conservative political parties that frequently get to the Government or in the parliamentary opposition, for example, SaS and SME RODINA.[5] Unlike Moderate Eurosceptics, Euro-pessimist parties do not enjoy such substantial electoral support and are more varied. The oldest is the nationalist SNS, balancing between Moderate Eurosceptics and Europessimism. The party gravitates toward hard Euroscepticism, for SNS politicians were the first from the Slovak political community to get into populist games and flirt with the EU exit (Gyarfášová, 2015, p. 38). Marian Kotleba, with his "Ľudová strana naše Slovensko," exemplifies modern radical right-wing extremism. Radical REPUBLIKA, led by

4 The classification of Eurosceptic parties is the prerogative of modern comparative political science research (see Kaniok, 2009). We rely on the views of Paul Taggart and Aleks Szczerbiak by dividing the parties into Soft Eurosceptics ("revision" of the country's membership in the European Union) and Hard Eurosceptics (the country's likelihood of leaving the European Union) (Taggart & Szczerbiak, 2002).

5 We could also mention *Kresťansko demokraticke hnutie (KDH)*, which ideologically evolved from Euro-optimism in 1998 to cautious Euroscepticism on the eve of joining the European Union. The main reason for the party's joining Eurosceptics is its conservative Christian-democratic ideology, which contradicts EU values according to the most conservative KDH politicians (Kopecký & Mudde, 2002). Currently, the party should be classified as Euro positive.

Milan Uhrík, was founded within the ĽSNS environment. The party is heading to its first parliamentary elections and is likely to succeed. Eventually, "VLASŤ," led by Štefan Harabin, tends to resort to populist rather than radical electoral strategies and can also be referred to as Europessimistic. Europessimists criticize European politics, emphasizing the priority of Slovakia's national interests. They interpret anti-Russian sanctions following the military invasion of Ukraine as unnecessary and harmful to the domestic economy. Hard Euroscepticism is frequently reinforced by anti-NATO rhetoric (anti-Americanism) and a pro-Russian position.

4. The Peculiarities of the Slovak Socioeconomic Determinants of Euroscepticism in the Regions

As the most recent parliamentary elections show (the National Council of the Slovak Republic elections in 2020), we observe considerable support for Eurosceptic parties, which is the joint result of Moderate Eurosceptics and Europessimists (see Table 1).

Table 1. The electoral support for Eurosceptics in the regions of the Slovak Republic (the 2020 Parliamentary Elections)

Region	Europessimists	Moderate Eurosceptic	Score
Bratislava region	9.11 %	18.68 %	27.79 %
Trnava region	10.98 %	12.72 %	23.7 %
Nitra region	12.64 %	13.23 %	25.87 %
Košice region	13.5 %	13.55 %	27.05 %
Prešov region	15.7 %	12.47 %	28.17 %
Banská Bystrica region	16.38 %	14.72 %	31.1 %
Žilina region	17.95 %	14.11 %	32.06 %
Trenčin region	16.7 %	15.46 %	32.16 %

Source: The authors' calculations are based on the results of the Statistical Office of the Slovak Republic (Voľby a referenda, n.d.)

Based on the electoral support level, we differentiate three groups of regions in Slovakia: (1) *weak regions*[6]—the Bratislava region, (2) *moderate ("transitive")*

6 Only the capital belongs to this group, hence, it is an exception.

regions (< 30 %)—Trnava, Nitra, Prešov and Košice regions, and (3) *stable regions (> 30 %)*—Trenčin, Žilina, and Banská-Bistrica regions (see Figure 1). Bratislava region-wise is where the most reactionary Europessimists have won less than 10 %, which is the lowest figure throughout the country. Given the socioeconomic dynamics in the Bratislava region, we have allocated it into a separate group.

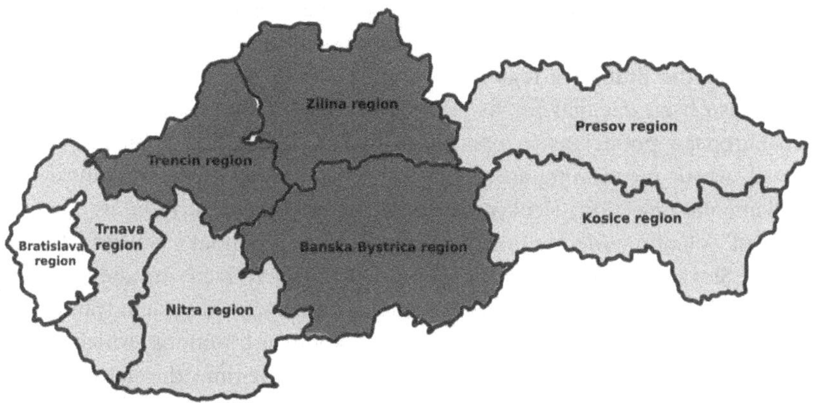

Figure 1. Fragmentation of the Slovak Regions by the Support for Eurosceptic parties (According to the 2020 National Council Elections)

Source: The authors' calculations are based on the results of the Statistical Office of the Slovak Republic (Voľby a referenda, n.d.)

Among the Slovak regions, the pro-European *Bratislava region* has stood out for showing consistently high support for progressive political forces, for example, "soft" populist OĽaNO or "presidential" Progressive Slovakia. Europessimists in the region have repeatedly lost from election to election. In 2020, they similarly failed to pass the 5 % barrier. Kotleba's ĽSNS's best result was 4.62 %, but even this was insufficient to obtain the necessary 5 %. Voting preferences in Bratislava often contradict those in the east of the country. Several decades of election campaigns in independent Slovakia have led to the formation of a sociopolitical cleavage of "West VS East" (Haydanka, 2021). Sociopolitical cleavages in the former transitory CEE countries[7] deepen the electoral differentiation between the capital and peripheral regions.

7 We cannot but mention the seminal study on the nature of sociopolitical cleavages in the post-communist countries of Central and Eastern Europe by Stephen Whitefield (2002).

Regarding its socioeconomic condition, the capital region stands out noticeably from the rest of the regions in Slovakia. Moreover, its GDP per capita approximates that of the highest indicators among the EU NUTS 2 (≥120) (Eurostat, n.d.) and the best economic indicators throughout the country. In the region, the minimum unemployment rate is slightly over 2 %, the average gross wages are 22 % higher than the national average, and the threat of poverty is in the marginal range of over 6 %. The capital is also the undisputed leader regarding the residents' educational qualifications. Almost every third resident of the Bratislava region has a university degree. Since independence, it has also been peculiar for its "European" history and electoral support for pro-European politicians in opposition to reactionary conservatives. In this regard, worth mentioning are the fateful for Slovakia's European future 1998 parliamentary elections ("collective democrat" Mikuláš Dzurinda[8] vs. "people's populist" Vladimír Mečiar[9]) or the recent 2019 presidential elections (the new face of Slovak politics Zuzana Čaputová[10] vs. Robert Fico's candidate Maroš Šefčovič[11]). Therefore, the Bratislava region is characterized by an advantageous socioeconomic situation and pro-European political traditions, which lay the foundations for tenacious Euro-optimism. At the same time, the status of Euro-pessimist parties, primarily right-wing ones, is still marginalized.

The second group includes *four "moderate" regions*: two from the West and two from the East. Paradoxically, the group combines regions that not only come from the most polar parts of the country but stereotypically consolidate the most opposite, for example, liberally oriented West and conservative East. Let's analyze the history of elections in post-socialist Slovakia. Notably, ideologically-liberal pro-European politicians get more support in the West of the country.

---

8 Mikuláš Dzurinda headed the anti-Mečiar coalition SDK (slov.—*Slovenská demokratická koalícia*) to change the foreign policy course and deepen the Euro-Atlantic integration of the post-communist Slovak Republic.

9 Vladimír Mečiar is the most outstanding Slovak politician of the 1990s, having implemented conservative politics through populist methods. He positioned himself as a "people's populist" because of his never-ending concern for the Slovak people (Kevin Deegan-Krause 2012).

10 Zuzana Čaputová's political image strongly resonates with mainstream Slovak politicians, frequently accused of corruption (Haydanka & Haydanka, 2022, p. 213). She is a well-known public activist who managed to become the first female President of the Slovak Republic.

11 After the deep 2018 political crisis, the notorious Robert Fico sought to maintain his political influence in Slovakia. In the presidential elections, Fico supported the diplomat Maroš Šefčovič (Haydanka & Haydanka, 2022, p. 213).

On the other hand, in the eastern regions, conservatives or populists more often get elected to the Parliament and win in the presidential elections (Haydanka, 2021). As we can see, the sociopolitical cleavage "West VS East" is not relatable when dividing the electoral sympathies between "Moderate Eurosceptics and Europessimism." Eurosceptic parties have a pronounced electoral advantage in the eastern Prešov and Košice regions (fluctuating at 27–28 %). In the Trnava and Nitra regions, Eurosceptics get somewhat less—23 % and 25 %, respectively. The level of support for Europessimists is yet another distinctive feature within this group. In the Trnava region, they got a cumulative result of 10 % of the votes,[12] whereas, in the Prešov region, the right-wing radicals-Eurosceptics appeared quite competitive.[13] Despite the comparable level of support for Eurosceptics, this group of four Slovak regions is quite fragmented and transitive.

Regarding socioeconomic indicators, regions differ considerably. According to the Regional Development Strategy of the Slovak Republic, the Trnava Region is the second most competitive region in terms of its potential (Metodika tvorby PHRSR, 2020). The promising regions also include Nitra and Košice, with high indicators of gross wages, approaching the national level of 1,211 euros. The Nitra region is the second best after Bratislava, with unemployment of only 4.5 %. The neighboring Trnava region has a similarly low unemployment rate (6 %). Worse is the situation in the Košice region, with unemployment exceeding 10 % and one of the highest in the country numbers of people at risk of poverty (every fifth resident). However, the worst indicators are in the Prešov region, not only in this group but throughout the country, with gross wages lower than a thousand euros, the highest unemployment rate (11.4 %) in the country, and over 20 % of people at risk of poverty. The West Slovak regions are characterized by their proximity to the capital, which fully meets European socioeconomic standards. Also, closeness to the borders with Austria and the Czech Republic increase employment opportunities. Based on the statistics, the level of foreign investments in the Trnava and Nitra regions has significantly grown in recent years (Priame zahraničné investície, n.d.). In the Košice region, there is a disparity in the socioeconomic development of the regional center of Košice and the periphery. With a population of 250,000, Košice is the second most populated city in Slovakia, concentrating the country's multiple industrial facilities. In the Prešov region, socioeconomic prospects are associated with the

12 The most influential ĽSNS was only fifth.

13 ĽSNS was third, receiving 8.5 % of the votes.

"green economy" and the development of the agricultural sector. However, it is characterized by a significant outflow of labor (economically active persons).

In each of the four regions, the number of people with university degrees ranges from 15 % to 16 %. Four large university centers,[14] which can compete with Bratislava universities, successfully operate in the west and provide training for students from non-European countries in the east. According to the number of university graduates, the regions of the "transitive" group are stable and correspond to national indicators.

The last group, or *stable regions*, is the geographical core of Slovakia. The Žilina, Trenčin, and Banská Bystrica regions are located at the intersection of the country's pro-European West and the conservative East. The parliamentary and regional elections confirm the high level of conservatism of Slovak voters in these regions. Conservatives and populists traditionally stand firm there. In particular, in the last elections to the National Council in 2020, Robert Fico's SMER-SD arrived second in all three regions. Slovak social populists conceded only to their biggest competitor, Igor Matovic's OĽANO. At the same time, the elections occurred during a deep political crisis and Robert Fico's delegitimization as a politician. Moreover, one of the most notorious Slovak politicians, Marian Kotleba, was elected the president (slov.—*Župan*) of the Banská Bystrica region in 2013.

The 2020 parliamentary elections confirmed that every third voter is Euroscepticaly-minded. Notably, well known for their radical political position, Europessimists obtained significant electoral support. Eventually, having received 9 %–10 % of the votes, ĽSNS lost only to the two leaders, OĽANO and SMER-SD. In the Žilina region, the right-wing radical SNS was only a few hundred votes short of passing the voting barrier (4.73 %), whereas Moderate Eurosceptics of SME RODINA and SaS have successfully overcome it. The results of the 2020 parliamentary elections only confirmed persistent Eurosceptic sentiments in the three central Slovak regions.

In general, socioeconomic determinants in the Žilina, Trenčin, and Banská Bystrica regions create a heterogeneous environment for Eurosceptic parties. Foremost, the Banská Bystrica region demonstrates the worst economic indicators throughout the country, for example, the risk of poverty, according to which every fourth of its residents is in this group. Over 10 % of the unemployed and a gross monthly salary of slightly over a thousand Euros led to a stable social

14 Trnava University in Trnava, Constantine the Philosopher University in Nitra, Pavol Jozef Šafárik University in Košice and University of Prešov.

stratum dissatisfied with the actions of the pro-European authorities and the European Union in general. On the other hand, the level of electoral support for right-wing populists is growing. Compared to Banská Bystrica, the economic indicators in Žilina and Trenčin regions make them stand out. Both are in a good position regarding unemployment, gross wages, and the number of people at risk of poverty. According to these, the Žilina and Trenčin regions correlate with the "transitive" group and run after the capital. Therefore, based on economic indicators, these Central Slovak regions can hardly be considered "persistently Eurosceptic." Regarding the number of university graduates, all three in the stable group show fair indicators, the situation being slightly worse in the Banská Bystrica region.[15] In each region, large state universities operate, with Banská Bystrica university having over 10.000 students (slov.—*Univerzita Mateja Bela v Banskej Bystrici*), which is a high indicator for Slovakia.

5. Conclusion

We argue that the relationship between the principal socioeconomic indicators and the level of electoral support for Eurosceptic parties touches on specific elections and regional development features and requires more in-depth insight. To conclude, we argue that the relationship between the principal socioeconomic indicators and the level of electoral support for Eurosceptic parties touches on specific elections and regional development features and requires more in-depth insight. As the most recent parliamentary elections in the Slovak Republic show, we can outline three groups of regions based on the level of electoral support for Eurosceptic parties: the Bratislava region, the group "West-East," and the Central Slovak group. Only the Prešov and partly Banská Bystrica regions show low (insignificant) indicators of socioeconomic development as a prerequisite for growing electoral support for Eurosceptics. In the Bratislava region, high socioeconomic indicators sustain the pro-European orientations of residents. The "West-East" group, which united as many as four areas, looks contradictory. Thus, we can call into question the long-standing Slovak sociopolitical cleavage of "West VS East." Despite the high socioeconomic level, the central Slovak regions of Žilina and Trenčin, with considerable support for Eurosceptics, remain a mystery. This way or another, we should redirect research into socioeconomic determinants of Euroscepticism from the national to the regional level.

15 Žilina region—17.6 %, Trenčin region—16.7 %, Banská-Bystrica region—15.8 % of people with university degrees.

References

Anderson, C. J., & Reichert, M. S. (1995). Economic benefits and support for membership in the EU: A cross-national analysis. *Journal of Public Policy, 15*(3), 231–249.

Deegan-Krause, K. (2012). Populism, democracy, and nationalism in Slovakia. In C. Mudde & C. R. Kaltwasser (Eds.), *Populism in Europe and the Americas. Threat or corrective for democracy?* (pp. 182–204). Cambridge University Press.

European Union. (n.d.). *Standard Eurobarometer 97—Summer 2022.* https://europa.eu/eurobarometer/surveys/detail/2693

Eurostat. (n.d.). *Regional GDP per capita ranged from 32% to 260% of the EU average in 2019.* https://ec.europa.eu/eurostat/web/products-eurostat-news/-/ddn-20210303-1

Gyarfasova, O. (2015). Euroscepticism: A mobilising appeal? Not for everyone! *Politics in Central Europe, 11*(1), 31–50.

Hakhverdian, A., van Elsas, E., van der Brug, W., & Kuhn, T. (2013). Euroscepticism and education: A longitudinal study of 12 EU member states, 1973–2010. *European Union Politics, 14*(4), 522–541.

Haydanka, Y. (2021). Electoral cleavages and fragmentation of regions in the Slovak Republic: A case study of the parliamentary elections held in 1990–2020. *Regionology, 29*(2), 230–249.

Haydanka, Y., & Haydanka, D. (2022). Notable presidential elections of 1999 and 2019 in the Slovak Republic: Communicative markers and electoral cleavages. *Agathos, 13*(2/25), 207–220.

Hooghe, L., & Marks, G. (2018). Cleavage theory meets Europe's crises: Lipset, Rokkan, and the transnational cleavage. *Journal of European Public Policy, 25*(1), 109–135.

Kaniok, P. (2009). Party based Euroscepticism: Opposing the Commission or the European integration? *Contemporary European Studies, 2*, 25–45.

Kopecký, P., & Mudde, C. (2002). The two sides of Euroscepticism: Party positions on European integration in East Central Europe. *European Union Politics, 3*(3), 297–326.

Kunst, S., Kuhn, T., & van de Werfhorst, H. G. (2020). Does education decrease Euroscepticism? A regression discontinuity design using compulsory schooling reforms in four European countries. *European Union Politics, 21*(1), 24–42.

Metodika tvorby PHRSR. (2020). Ministerstva investícií, regionálneho rozvoja a informatizácie Slovenskej republiky. https://www.nro.vicepremier.gov.sk/site/assets/files/1140/metodika_phrsr2020_verzia_1_0_4.pdf

Priame zahraničné investície. (n.d.). Národná banka Slovenska. https://nbs.sk/statisticke-udaje/statistika-platobnej-bilancie/priame-zahranicne-investicie/

Taggart, P., & Szczerbiak, A. (2002). Crossing Europe: Patterns of contemporary party-based Euroscepticism in EU member states and the candidate states of Central and Eastern Europe. In *European Consortium for Political Research Joint Workshops, Turin, March 21–27, 2002*. https://sro.sussex.ac.uk/id/eprint/29357/

Univerzita Mateja Bela v Banskej Bystrici. https://www.umb.sk/

Voľby a referenda. (n.d.). Štatistický úrad Slovenskej republiky. https://volby.statistics.sk/

Whitefield, S. (2002). Political cleavages and post-communist politics. *Annual Review of Political Science*, *5*, 181–200.

Tarlan Ahmadov

Innovation for Circular Economy: Overview of Estonian Enterprises' Transition Journey

1. Introduction

The concept of circular economy (CE) is viewed as an economic system that can contribute to the sustainability of organizations and challenges the prevailing idea of sustaining linear model growth (Kirchherr et al., 2017; Korhonen et al., 2018; Lieder & Rashid, 2016). It is argued that the transition to CE results in a win-win situation for organizations, the economy, and the environment (Barreiro-Gen & Lozano, 2020; Korhonen et al., 2018).

Although there seems to be an appreciable awareness of the benefits of the CE and substantial public support, implementation remains in its early stages with progress being slow and neither widespread nor uniform (Kirchherr et al., 2018). The adoption of CE practices means having to overcome a variety of barriers and challenges in line, that is, with each firm's strategy, resources, and capabilities. This is especially true of small and medium-sized firms (SMEs), given that they typically face greater constraints regarding the availability of resources (Ormazabal et al., 2018). The role of innovation for CE in the development of SMEs has begun to attract research attention (Iqbal et al., 2021; Jahanshahi et al., 2020). The OECD (2011) proposes that sustainable growth is an inevitable trend in future development and that sustainable development is driven by innovation (Fernández Fernández et al., 2018).

However, to date, data constraints have substantially limited empirical analyses of the barriers to the CE to theoretical and conceptual frameworks and case studies (Govindan & Hasanagic, 2018) and, as De Jesus and Mendonça (2018) have highlighted, more empirical evidence concerning these barriers is still required. In addition, current studies ignore the perspectives from Central and Eastern Europe (Mazur-Wierzbicka, 2021) where enterprise transition to CE comes with a certain delay.

According to the literature, Estonia has acknowledged the importance of implementing CE practices within SMEs. In this context, the government has introduced several initiatives and reforms such as fiscal incentives to accelerate the implementation of digitalization and improvement of resource and energy efficiency (Ahmadov et al., 2022). Also, a recent study by the Tallinn University of Technology (TalTech, 2022) shows that there is some level of awareness about CE applications in organizations. These findings from Estonia show that although there are policies and initiatives to build a sustainable and low-carbon economy, their uptake by the business organizations is questionable, which warrants further empirical investigation, making the country a suitable candidate for the study.

To fill this gap, in the present study, the author seeks to provide an empirical answer to the following research question: What is the proportion of Estonian firms undertaking technical innovation for circular practices and the difference between industries? and, How Estonian SMEs have encountered with regard to undertaking technical innovations for circular practices? To do so, the author carried out mixed method research, which provides the opportunity to study a set of barriers related to the innovation implementation for circular practices at five phases of the product life cycle.

2. Literature Review

The circular economy reduces the extraction of raw materials from nature and the heap of waste in landfills by extending the useful life of materials and goods already in circulation. Since the CE strategy is founded on claims of saving the environment and increasing GDP, it has garnered a lot of interest from industry and policymakers alike (Ghisellini et al., 2016). Firms must embrace CE principles and make linear models circular and resource-efficient.

Special attention should be given to SMEs, as they represent about 90 % of businesses and more than 50 % of employment worldwide (World Bank Finance, 2021). Manufacturing SMEs are reported to account for 64 % of air pollution, whereas only a small proportion of 0.4 % of these SMEs comply with an environmental management program (Bonner, 2019). This can be attributed to the fact that a manufacturer spends more than 60 % of its income on materials and services (Krajewski et al., 2010). In order for a product, process or service to be more efficient and circular, there is a context of innovation (Neder et al., 2019).

Innovation, in turn, introduces new routines, new procedures and new practices into the production chains that choose to make the transition to the CE (Scarpellini et al., 2020). They range from eco-innovation to the introduction of new business models, environmental accounting, application of the principles of the 3Rs and management of the flow of materials so that they can be reintroduced into new production chains, reused, recycled or remanufactured, thus closing the loop of the material processes.

There are several barriers to adopt advanced environmental measures within SMEs' such as a lack of financial support, inadequate information management system, lack of proper technology, technical and financial resources, lack of consumer interest in the environment, lack of support from public institutions, lack of access to qualified professionals in environmental management, and lack of senior management commitment, which collectively lead to slower and/or unsuccessful uptake of circular economy within these organizations (Ormazabal et al., 2016; Prieto-Sandoval et al., 2018; Ritzén & Sandström, 2017; Rizos et al., 2016).

3. Methodology

The author implemented a mixed methodology, starting with qualitative (group interviews) and quantitative (survey) methods and descriptive in nature.

For the qualitative part of the study, four group interviews were conducted with a heterogeneous sample of SMEs (9 SMEs and 4 industry associations) (Table 1) to explore key themes and develop deeper understandings. These interviews, which comprised a semi-structured interview schedule with follow-up, probing questions around emerging themes, were approximately one hour in length. With the permission of all respondents, these were audio recorded for subsequent transcription for data analysis.

Table 1. Group interview sample structure

Industry	Participants
Manufacture of computers, electronic and optical equipment	2 SMEs
Production of electrical equipment	3 SMEs and 1 industry association
Manufacture of chemicals and chemical products, except plastics industry	2 SMEs and 1 industry association
Production of metal products	2 SMEs and 2 industry associations

For the quantitative part, an online survey questionnaire was set up digitally by the author and distributed in Estonia (October 2021–December 2021). The total number of SMEs targeted was 2,211 from four industries and a total of 440 (≈20 %) responses were received, and based on the screening (removing the partly filled responses) 190 were deemed as useful (complete). All the responses were considered complete to undertake the analysis without missing values. The demographics of the sample obtained are shown in Table 2.

Table 2. Survey sample structure

Industry	**Number**	**Percentage (%)**
Manufacture of computers, electronic and optical equipment	24	13
Production of electrical equipment	27	14
Manufacture of chemicals and chemical products, except plastics industry	34	18
Production of metal products	105	55
Total	*190*	*100*
Number of employees		
0–9	143	75
10–49	26	14
50–249	21	11
Total	*190*	*100*
Year of establishment		
≤3	33	17
4–9	49	26
≥10	108	57
Total	*190*	*100*

4. Results Analysis and Discussion

4.1. Group Interview

Before exploring the main motivation behind the involvement in CE and the potential challenges that they face, circular initiatives have been a topic of discussion to find out if the participant of the group interview is aware of the CE and if they implement it to some degree. There have been several initiatives already taking place in those firms that participated in the qualitative part of the study. An example from the computer industry, firm A: "running a campaign to buy back lighting from our customers. Because we can recycle all expensive mechanical parts and even electronics." Meanwhile, firm B: "recycling of cable waste so that it can be measured back" and firm C from the electric industry: "waste, e.g. the packaging materials, the raw material of the cable is taken away—it is then sold back to the manufacturer." There are also some initiatives in the participant from the chemical and metal industry: "we started to pick up the packaging back through the co-network and gave the customer a choice in the e-shop, with or without an outer package"—firm B from the chemical industry; "We do the same packaging, but we put less metal in … makes the material thinner"—firm A from the metal industry. Those mentioned initiatives are examples of circular practices that cover recycling, recovering and redesigning. But the question is what drives those companies to engage in circular activities? To answer the question, group interview participants were asked about their main motivation for the implementation of innovation for circular practices.

Participants also underlined the importance of customer engagement as their driver: "more and more customers are making a much more informed choice and a cleaner / more sustainable choice"—firm A from the chemical industry; "The main motive is efficiency … If you don't think about it (innovation for CE), there's nothing to do with Scandinavia"—firm A from the metal industry. Moreover, improvement in product design toward circularity leads to motivating consumers to opt for such products (Cui et al., 2017). In the case of group interview participants, the Ecodesign directive by European Commissions motivate them to develop more efficient products: "The Ecodesign Directive (Ecodesign and Energy Labelling—2009/125/EC) also points in the direction of developing more efficient products"—firm A from the electric industry.

A company's policies and strategies are considered a significant cornerstone for the successful implementation of circular practices (Ferasso et al., 2020). However, when these policies are not devised appropriately in coherence with other sectors, such as service providers, governing bodies and stakeholders, they become a salient restraint (Kumar et al., 2019). In the case of firm B from the computer industry, they see company strategy as a barrier to innovation: "As part of big company …. we are developing the printed circuit board here (Estonia). There is no other innovation." In this case, they are not fully involved in the product life cycle and are limited to a single phase where they cannot innovate toward CE.

The extant literature has recognized financial and cost barriers as significant hindrances to circularity implementation (Kirchherr et al., 2018). A firm's transition to CE requires massive investments in technological ventures, employee training for new operations and the production and sale of circular products. Similar to the literature, the participant in the group interview sees finance as one of the main barriers. Participant C from the electric industry put financial barriers as: "Upgrading the equipment is certainly necessary, but it is lagging behind the finances" and "Cooperation with science is a painful issue."

Meanwhile, an industry association from the chemical industry confirm firm C by adding: "A company does not digitize if the process is expensive." The financial barrier exists in the electric industry as firm B states: "Everything is still behind the finances."

The lack of knowledge regarding the circular practices among participants was considered a barrier. An example of firm B from the metal industry: "we still have no knowledge" and this statement was confirmed by the industry association in the same industry: "It (innovation abilities and skills) is not particularly available in Estonia and there is no competence" and "human resources are the biggest problem." However, in addition to knowledge as a barrier, collaboration between partners is also seen as the main barrier in the case of group interview participants. Bocken et al. (2016) indicated social relationships and collaboration as crucial components of the closed-loop supply chain and in the case of the chemical industry in Estonia: "most partners did not find it worthwhile to start cooperating"—association from the chemical industry. Also, the lack of knowledge regarding collaborations continues to impede firms' efforts to adopt circular practices (Jabbour et al., 2019) and this is relevant for firm A from the electric industry: "it's hard to find a partner to practice."

4.2. Questionnaire

This section presents the results of the survey study which will provide a broader understanding of the results. To investigate survey responses, the Statistical Product and Service Solutions (SPSS) software version 27 was used to sort, code and analyze using descriptive statistics such as percentage and frequency distribution. Analysis of variance was used to measure constraints hindering technical innovation implementation for circular practices by Estonian SMEs.

According to the participants' answers, 42 % of the participants had been engaged in an innovation implementation for circular practices in some way, which was done in the phase of product design (Figure 1). The results presented in Figure 1 demonstrated the application of innovation for circularity along the life cycle of the product. Most of the participants have not implemented any innovation at the end-of-life phase and material phase which accounts for 89 % and 82 %, respectively.

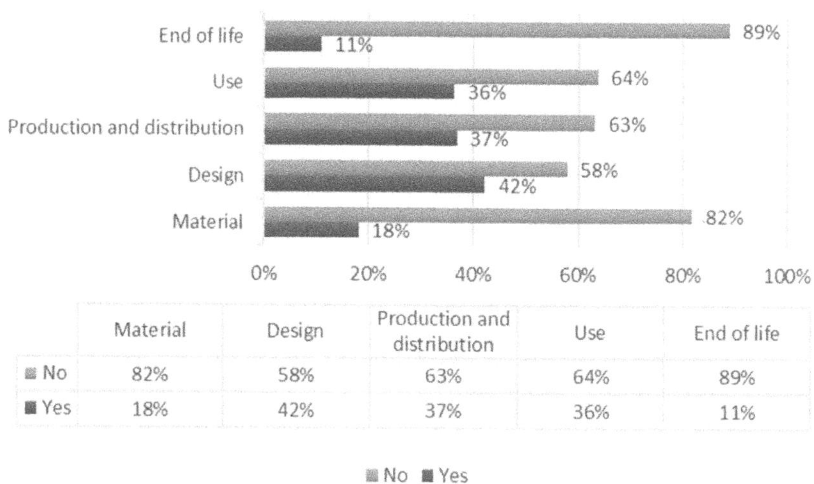

Figure 1. The proportion of implementation of innovation for circular practices
Source: Author's own, N = 190 firms

The SME's involvement in innovation for circular practices in Estonia varies based on the industry. Figure 2 demonstrates the share of innovation implementation for circular practices within industries. In the computer industry, technical innovation is implemented mostly in the use phase and followed by the design phase. The production and distribution phase also innovated in the computer industry compared to the material and end-of-life phases where the innovation is only 17 % and 15 %, respectively. Meanwhile, data from the electric industry demonstrate that most innovation for circular practices takes place in the design phase at 42 % and follows by the production and distribution as well as use phase (31 % and 30 %). End-of-life phase is the least innovative phase in the electric industry in Estonia, where only 6 % of participants are involved in innovation for circular practices. The chemical industry, on the other side, is mostly involved in production and distribution as well as the use phase with 29 % and 24 %, respectively. The other three phases, share a similar result for innovation implementation, between 13–16 %. Results from the metal industry demonstrate the current involvement in innovation for circularity takes place in the design, production and distribution and use phases with 47 %, 36 % and 33 %, respectively. Also, some technical innovation is implemented in the material phase, as 20 % of respondents from the Estonian metal industry confirm their engagement with technical innovation for circular practices. End-of-life phase of metal products comes as the least innovative phase, only 10 %.

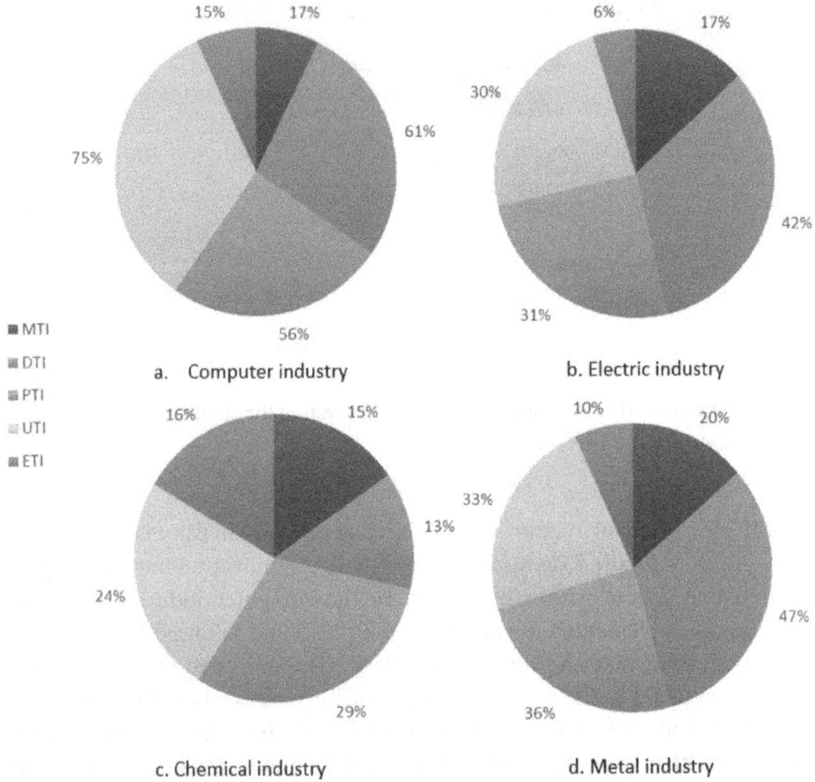

Figure 2. Share of innovation implementation for circular practices in each phase of a product life cycle in four industries. Shares as a percentage of each industry's innovative activities in the relevant phase

Source: Author's own, N = 190 firms

The questionnaire also covers the aspect of why technical innovation is not implemented in each phase of the product life cycle of Estonian SMEs. To uncover the reasons, a set of options is developed based on the literature and provided: (1) We lack necessary knowledge; (2) There is a lack of trust; (3) Our current financial situation does not allow it; (4) It is hard to get a loan; (5) It is not a priority; (6) Lack of potential cooperation partners; (7) It is not applicable to us; (8) Other. Questionnaire participants also could specify other reasons in each section of the above-listed options did not cover the barrier that they face.

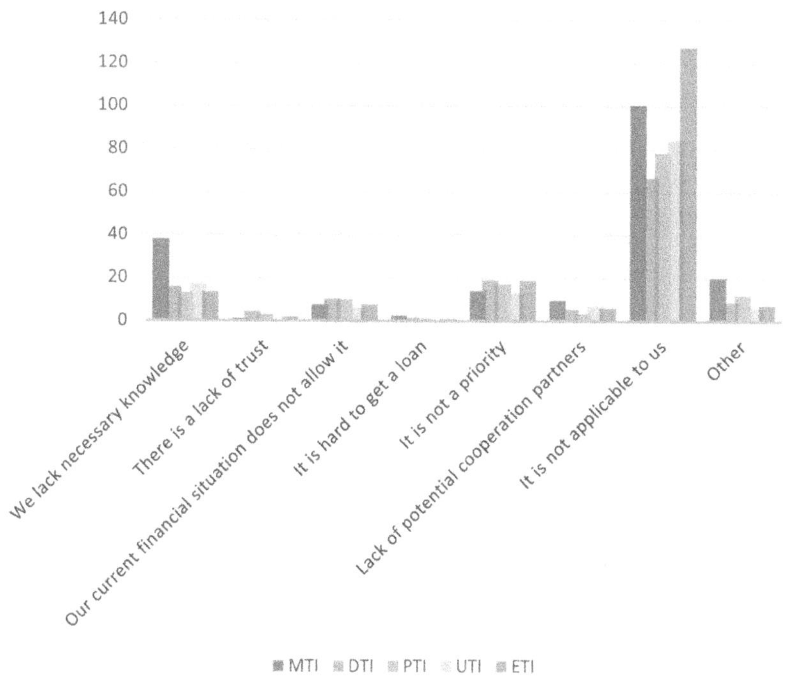

Figure 3. Share of SMEs that encountered any of the following issues when undertaking innovation for circular practices

Source: Author's own, N = 190 firms

Figure 3 shows the reasons Estonian SMEs for not implement technical innovation for circular practices. The majority of the respondents selected the "it is not applicable to us." The reason for SMEs to select "it is not applicable to us" or "it is not a priority" can be as a barrier to the implementation of innovation for CE, either due to the unfamiliarity of the concept of CE (Ormazabal et al., 2018) or due to the non-existent exchange of information among companies (Piñeiro-Chousa et al., 2019). The majority of firms selected this reason for not implementing innovation for circular practices the reason for this is probably that the sample includes all SMEs, regardless of their knowledge of CE. To dive more into the reasons, the author excluded the option of "it is not applicable to us" in Figure 4 to show the details of what Estonian SMEs perceive as a barrier to innovation implementation.

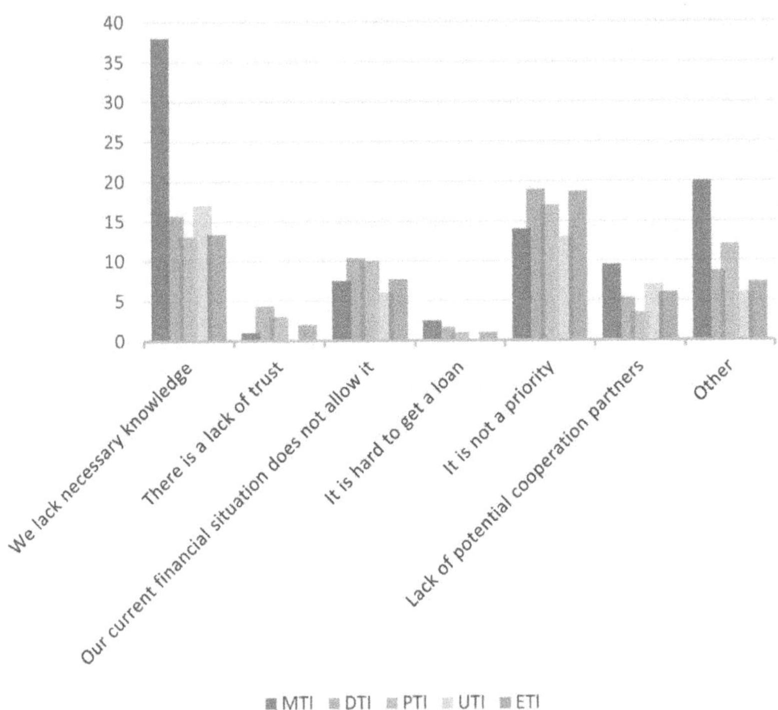

Figure 4. Share of SMEs that encountered any of the following issues, excluding the "it is not applicable to us" option when undertaking innovation for circular practices
Source: Author's own, N = 190 firms

Figure 4 shows the survey respondents lack the necessary knowledge to implement technical innovation for circular practices. One of the barriers that empirical investigation brought is collaboration. CE implementation involves complexity and interdependence between the actors that no company can achieve alone, so joint action by an entire ecosystem is necessary (Parida et al., 2019). Gregory et al. (2020) also concluded that the transition to CE depends on the recognition by stakeholders that no single actor can address the core issue alone. Respondents also could specify their reason why they are not engaged with innovation. Among the answers, some SMEs respond as: "We do not engage in production ourselves" "the final product is 95 % completed by a subcontractor" where they outsource the production part or "we are not product owners and what is left from our facility, does not come back" or "our production is handicraft, there is no such technology" which is not applicable to them or "there are no technologies used in our field" which might be based on the lack of awareness and knowledge in the field or "small business, not so financially reasonable" which the financial aspect seen as the barrier or "we deal with very old designs. … as a result, the design does not allow for change" or "we are subcontractors" where they do not involve in the product design phase of the product life cycle. Similar to the findings from the literature, SMEs in Estonia see finance as the barrier to the innovation implementation for CE and it is followed by a lack of potential cooperation partners. Lack of trust and access to a loan for innovation implementation is not considered an important barrier in the case of Estonia.

5. Conclusion

The results have shown that Estonian SMEs' involvement in innovation for circular practices is uneven across the product life cycle. The most interest is given to the product design phase, while the material and end-of-life phases are neglected. This result can be explained by the firms' perceived barriers on their journey for innovation which are lack of knowledge, missing technological know-how, and lack of awareness that leads them to not prioritize sustainability. The innovation is necessary to leave behind the traditional business practices and commit to new circular practices and new ways of operating in the supply chains that allow the circle to be closed and all the waste to be taken advantage of.

Based on the results of the empirical investigation of Estonian SMEs' involvement in innovation for circular practices, some recommendations are drawn to policymakers to accelerate the transition of SMEs in Estonia toward CE. To foster the transition toward a CE, a policy framework needs to be developed and strengthened; there must be diverse support mechanisms in addition to institutional support; implementation support programs need to be developed for companies to help them engage with partners to straighten collaboration. Finally, end consumers and citizens should be educated on the environmental, economic and social advantages of purchasing close-the-loop products. This would lead to support for CE-oriented companies that have undertaken a strategic path to sustainability, generating a positive return on their investment.

To conclude, some future research directions are suggested that emerge from the findings. Future research could investigate organizational factors to map more in detail the human aspect of the challenges that Estonian SMEs face. In addition, explore the impact of public incentives on the uptake of CE among businesses of different sizes and sectors. Finally, researchers could also examine the extent to which a company's inclination toward the CE effectively affects its creditworthiness.

Acknowledgment

The author is thankful to Wolfgang Dieter Gerstlberger, Tarvo Niine, Merle Küttim, Tarmo Kalvet, Tarmo Tuisk and Ulrika Hurt for data collection.

References

Ahmadov, T., Gerstlberger, W., & Prause, G. K. (2022). Fiscal incentives for Circular Economy: Insights from the Baltic States. *Business Models for the Circular Economy*, 219–239.

Barreiro-Gen, M., Lozano, R., & Zafar, A. (2020). Changes in sustainability priorities in organisations due to the COVID-19 outbreak: Averting environmental rebound effects on society. *Sustainability*, *12*(12), 5031.

Bocken, N., de Pauw, I., Bakker, C., & van der Grinten, B. (2016). Product design and business model strategies for a circular economy. *Journal of Industrial and Production Engineering*, *33*(5), 308–320.

Bonner, J., (2019). SMEs and environmental/social impacts, ACCA Think ahead. Available at: https://blogs.accaglobal.com/2012/09/27/smes-and-environmentalsocialimpacts/ (Accessed: 14 June 2022).

Cui, L., Wu, K., & Tseng, M. (2017). Selecting a remanufacturing quality strategy based on consumer preferences. *Journal Of Cleaner Production*, *161*, 1308–1316.

de Jesus, A., & Mendonça, S. (2018). Lost in transition? drivers and barriers in the eco-innovation road to the circular economy. *Ecological Economics*, *145*, 75–89.

Ferasso, M., Beliaeva, T., Kraus, S., Clauss, T., & Ribeiro-Soriano, D. (2020). Circular economy business models: The state of research and avenues ahead. *Business Strategy and the Environment*, *29*(8), 3006–3024.

Fernández Fernández, Y., Fernández López, M., & Olmedillas Blanco, B. (2018). Innovation for sustainability: The impact of spending on CO_2 emissions. *Journal of Cleaner Production*, *172*, 3459–3467.

Ghisellini, P., Cialani, C., & Ulgiati, S. (2016). A review on Circular Economy: The expected transition to a balanced interplay of environmental and economic systems. *Journal of Cleaner Production*, *114*, 11–32.

Govindan, K., & Hasanagic, M. (2018). A systematic review on drivers, barriers, and practices towards circular economy: A supply chain perspective. *International Journal of Production Research, 56*(1–2), 278–311.

Gregory, A., Atkins, J., Midgley, G., & Hodgson, A. (2020). Stakeholder identification and engagement in problem structuring interventions. *European Journal of Operational Research, 283*(1), 321–340.

Iqbal, Q., Ahmad, N.H. & Li, Z. (2021). Frugal-based innovation model for Sustainable Development: Technological and Market Turbulence. *Leadership & Organization Development Journal*, 42(3), 396–407.

Jabbour, C., Jabbour, A., Sarkis, J., & Filho, M. (2019). Unlocking the circular economy through new business models based on large-scale data: An integrative framework and research agenda. *Technological Forecasting and Social Change, 144*, 546–552.

Jahanshahi, A., Al-Gamrh, B. & Gharleghi, B. (2019). Sustainable development in Iran post-sanction: Embracing green innovation by small and medium-sized enterprises. *Sustainable Development*, 28(4), 781–790.

Kirchherr, J., Reike, D., & Hekkert, M. (2017). Conceptualizing the circular economy: An analysis of 114 definitions. *Resources, Conservation and Recycling, 127*, 221–232.

Kirchherr, J., Piscicelli, L., Bour, R., Kostense-Smit, E., Muller, J., Huibrechtse-Truijens, A., & Hekkert, M. (2018). Barriers to the Circular Economy: Evidence from the European Union (EU). *Ecological Economics, 150*, 264–272.

Korhonen, J., Honkasalo, A., & Seppälä, J. (2018). Circular Economy: The Concept and its Limitations. *Ecological Economics, 143*, 37–46.

Kumar, V., Sezersan, I., Garza-Reyes, J. A., Gonzalez, E. D., & AL-Shboul, M. A. (2019). Circular economy in the manufacturing sector: Benefits, opportunities and barriers. *Management Decision, 57*(4), 1067–1086.

Krajewski, L. J., Ritzman, B., & Malhotra, M. (2010). *Operations Management Processes and supply chains* (9th ed.). Pearson.

Lieder, M., & Rashid, A. (2016). Towards circular economy implementation: a comprehensive review in context of manufacturing industry. *Journal of Cleaner Production, 115*, 36–51.

Mazur-Wierzbicka, E. (2021). Circular economy: Advancement of european union countries. *Environmental Sciences Europe, 33*(1).

Neder, R., da Silva Rabêlo, O., Passos Honda, D., & Augusto Ramalho de Souza, P. (2019). Relações Entre Inovação e Sustentabilidade: Termos e tendências na Produção científica mundial. *Gestão & Regionalidade, 35*(104).

Organisation for Economic Co-operation and Development (OECD) (2011). Towards Green Growth: Monitoring Progress. OECD Indicators. Paris, France: Organisation for Economic Co-operation and Development.

Ormazabal, M., Prieto-Sandoval, V., Jaca, C., & Santos, J. (2016). An overview of the circular economy among smes in the Basque Country: A multiple case study. *Journal of Industrial Engineering and Management*, *9*(5), 1047.

Ormazabal, M., Prieto-Sandoval, V., Puga-Leal, R., & Jaca, C. (2018). Circular economy in Spanish SMEs: Challenges and opportunities. *Journal of Cleaner Production*, *185*, 157–167.

Parida, V., Burström, T., Visnjic, I., & Wincent, J. (2019). Orchestrating industrial ecosystem in circular economy: A two-stage transformation model for large manufacturing companies. *Journal of Business Research*, *101*, 715–725.

Piñeiro-Chousa, J., Vizcaíno-González, M., & Caby, J. (2019). Financial development and standardized reporting: A comparison among developed, emerging, and frontier markets. *Journal of Business Research*, *101*, 797–802.

Prieto-Sandoval, V., Ormazabal, M., Jaca, C., & Viles, E. (2018). Key elements in assessing circular economy implementation in small and medium-sized enterprises. *Business Strategy and the Environment*, *27*(8), 1525–1534.

Ritzén, S., & Sandström, G. Ö. (2017). Barriers to the circular economy – integration of perspectives and domains. *Procedia CIRP*, *64*, 7–12.

Rizos, V., Behrens, A., van der Gaast, W., Hofman, E., Ioannou, A., Kafyeke, T., Flamos, A., Rinaldi, R., Papadelis, S., Hirschnitz-Garbers, M., & Topi, C. (2016). Implementation of circular economy business models by small and medium-sized enterprises (smes): Barriers and enablers. *Sustainability*, *8*(11), 1212.

Scarpellini, S., Valero-Gil, J., Moneva, J. M., & Andreaus, M. (2020). Environmental management capabilities for a "circular eco-innovation." *Business Strategy and the Environment*, *29*(5), 1850–1864.

TalTech (2022). *A study on circular economy application completed by Taltech Department of Business Administration Taltech*, Available at: https://taltech.ee/en/news/study-circular-economy-application-completed-taltech-department-business-administration (Accessed: 14 June 2022).

World Bank Finance (2021). *Improving SMEs' access to finance and finding innovative solutions to unlock sources of capital.* Available at: https://www.worldbank.org/en/topic/smefinance (Accessed: 14 June 2022).

Beatriz Elena Guzman-Diaz, Edwin Tarapuez-Chamorro, &
Ramiro Parra-Hernandez

Prospective and Strategy in Tourism Businesses in the Coffee Region of Colombia

1. Introduction

The tourism as a sector that generates important income worldwide was significantly affected by the appearance of COVID-19, which forced to rethink the new business models in this economic activity. According to the World Tourism Organization, the pandemic reaffirmed the tendency to value more and more the attributes of the landscape and the interaction with nature.

The Colombian coffee region includes the departments of Caldas, Risaralda, Quindío and northern Valle del Cauca. Quindío is the second smallest department in Colombia (Figure 1). It has an area of 1.845 km^2 and 12 municipalities, an exceptional natural and cultural wealth that has become a touristic attraction for national and foreign visitors. The tourism is an economic activity that was not planned, on the contrary, it arose as a consequence of the coffee crisis of the eighties. Since the beginning of the century, initiatives have been generated to promote the sector from an economic point of view, considering several lines such as rural, landscape and cultural tourism, among others.

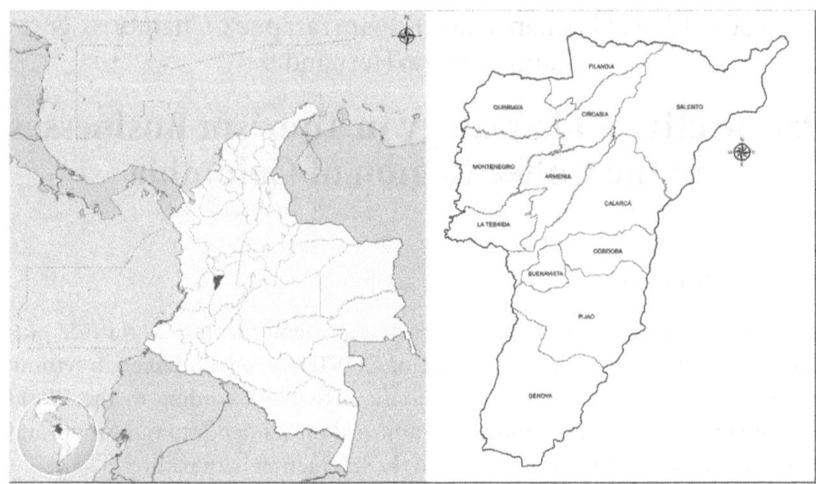

Figure 1. Location and administrative division of Quindío in Colombia
Source: Government of Quindío and DANE

In June 2011, UNESCO inscribed the Colombian Coffee Cultural Landscape (PCCC) on the World Heritage List, recognizing 47 municipalities of the Coffee Region (Caldas, Risaralda, Quindío and north of Valle del Cauca), a region characterized by the production of coffee, with a set of attributes, relationships between its inhabitants and cultural heritage (Conpes, 2014), which represent the material expressions of the coffee culture and demonstrate the exceptional and universal values of the PCCC (Universidad Tecnológica de Pereira, Red Alma Mater, Universidad del Quindío, Centro de Estudios e Investigaciones Regionales, 2010).

Different local actors have made an effort to contribute to the growth of the sector at a general level. Thus, this has allowed the generation of significant income for some tourism operators. However, there have been some phenomena that have limited its consolidation, such as, the prevalence of particular interests, the absence of leadership, associativity and political will to strengthen the sector through the development of specialized lines and the generation of differentiated products and services with sustainability criteria. That is to say, surpassing a purely commercial approach and promoting the improvement of the quality of life of the inhabitants, the protection of natural resources and the preservation of the Coffee Cultural Landscape of Colombia. Indeed, 11 of 12 municipalities of the department are part of the list of 47 municipalities included in the UNESCO declaration granted in 2011 as World Heritage of Humanity.

In the same way, and taking into account the post-pandemic trends. Tourism must be on the same wavelength with the Sustainable Development Goals (SDGs), there is a need to achieve convergence among local actors for the collective construction of the future. It is based on the recognition of the particular characteristics of Quindío, which is part of the coffee-growing region of Colombia, and whose natural and cultural attributes are recognized in the national and international context. Therefore, the objective of the research is to generate a prospective vision of tourism in the department of Quindío, which allows a strategic direction and becomes a navigation route for the development of plans, programs and projects to be implemented in the short, medium and long term.

It is important to recognize that, future study is a thematic that has generated interest in different areas of knowledge and has become a tool for the strategic direction of companies, industries and territories. According to Mojica (2005), perspective is a technique for visualizing the future, choosing the desirable future and designing strategies to achieving it, recognizing the changes in the environment and its complexity. In this sense, Godet (2007) affirms that preparing for the expected changes should not become a limitation to promote the desired changes.

Prospective is a useful tool for strategic management because it provides alternatives to present and unsatisfactory past (Medina, 2003). It gives meaning to visions of the future through quality information (Trujillo, 2008). Thus, making it possible to create the best decisions in the present in order to build the future (Mojica, 2005). Therefore, it is necessary to achieve the convergence of actors that allows awareness and synergy in the face of a problem in order to work collectively in decision-making and the generation of actions that are consistent with the future to be achieved.

Strategy is directly related to the direction of organizations, sectors and territories. In the first place, it consists of the formulation of development plans by governmental entities and strategic plans in the business and trade sector (long term in both cases). This must be materialized through the definition and implementation of plans, programs and projects in the short, medium and long term. At the same time, effective follow-up monitoring mechanisms and control must be included. From this perspective, the strategy or strategic process is recognized as a set of sequential stages that make it possible to establish long-term objectives and then assign resources and responsible parties to carry out specific actions in a given period (Pérez, 2012).

In the international context, there exist different research that shows the tourism potential worldwide. Especially, nature tourism, the preference of tourists for natural and cultural attractions is reaffirmed. However, the need for governmental entities to be more connected and committed to planning processes is also evident (Carrillo et al., 2021; Cornejo et al., 2019; Salsona, 2014). Regarding the national context, studies were identified that seek to boost this subsector by leveraging comparative advantages in comparative regions (García et al., 2020; Leguizamón et al., 2020; Plata, 2013; Quintana, 2018; Serrano et al., 2018).

A qualitative and quantitative methodology was used for the development of the research. And then, a series of workshops were conducted on November 2021 and June 2022. Furter, 40 local stakeholders acted as representatives of the university, the company, the State and society. Furthermore, union was achieved for the collective construction of the future. For this purpose, strategic prospective techniques were used, such as the change factors questionnaire, structural analysis, morphological analysis, Peter Schwartz's axes, Regnier's Abacus, brainstorming and Importance and Governance (IGO). The document is structured as follows: first the introduction, then the methodological aspects, followed by the results and discussion, then the conclusions and bibliographical references.

2. Methodology

The methodology used for this research is qualitative and quantitative. Also, it is descriptive because it takes into account a set of variables particular to the object of study, such as: future leaders, future scenarios and strategies aimed at achieving the chosen stage. Additionally, it is a correlational study because it analyzes the relationships of mobility and dependence between variables, which allows describing the phenomenon studied and provides possibilities of predicting the behavior of the object of study.

The research is of a factual or empirical nature because it implies the use of operations based on objective experience, from the collection of data to their analysis and interpretation. In addition, it is based on concepts and theoretical schemes proposed by internationally recognized authors. Above all, the study is of an applied nature because it seeks to solve practical problems that present themselves with concrete characteristics. And then, it is exploratory because it aims at analyzing a topic that has not been investigated in the department in particular circumstances originated by COVID-19. Notably, the research is flexible in its methodology, it allows the collection of relevant and updated information and its objective is fundamentally to discover.

The prospective study counted on 40 Quindío tourism experts' participation. Moreover, local actors representing four sectors: University—Business—State—Society (Figure 2). During November 2021 and June 2022 workshops were held through the use of strategic prospective techniques. The research determined the future leaders, the future scenarios and the chosen one, and the strategies to achieve it.

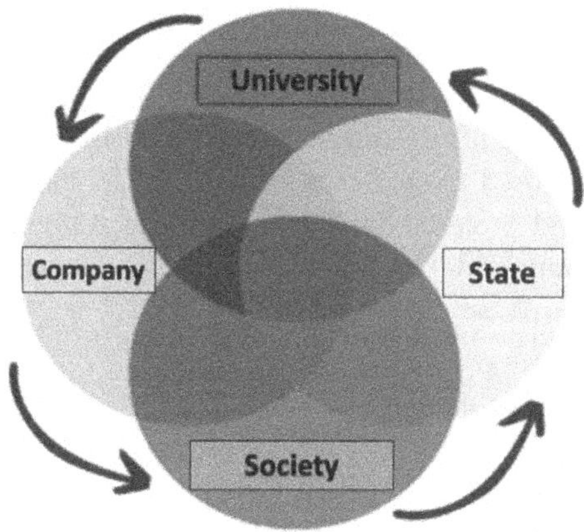

Figure 2. Convergence of strategic stakeholders
Source: Own elaboration

The secondary sources used for the research corresponded to documentary information from studies and statistics of national, departmental and municipal governmental entities as well as research in the international, national and local context on prospective and nature tourism and cultural identity. Also, books and documents on economics and prospective. The information from primary sources was obtained directly from the actors in Quindío tourism, who acted as thematic experts and represented the different stakeholders.

The development of the study had a special emphasis on the strengthening of nature tourism and was structured in two major phases. First, consist of identifying future leaders, and the second in recognizing the scenario and proposing key strategies and actions to achieve it.

Phase 1: Future leaders

In this phase, the experts selected the most important change-generating factors or phenomena related to the development of nature tourism in Quindío, which were prioritized to select the strategic variables. It means, those with the greatest impact on the subsector. Finally, these were gathered into two major vectors for the future. Consequently, the following techniques were used: questionnaire of change factors, structural analysis and Peter Schwartz's axes.

Phase 2: Scenario Change and Strategies

In this phase, the experts proposed the most likely future stages and subsequently chose the most relevant scenario. Thus, it was constituted as the change that Quindío wants to make for the development of tourism. Subsequently, a set of strategies were proposed around this scenario for its materialization through plans, programs and projects. The Peter Schwartz Axes technique, Regnier's Abacus, brainstorming and IGO (Importance and Governance) were once again used to advance this phase.

3. Results and Discussion

3.1. Future Leaders

The factors generating change for the development of nature tourism in Quindío were identified through workshops conducted with experts. These phenomena were grouped by economic, sociocultural, environmental and organizational factors (Table 1).

Table 1. Change source factors

Economic factors	Sociocultural factors
Sustainable Intelligent Territory Strategic and Attractive Tourist Territory Innovation in the Tourism Offer Tourism and Support Infrastructure Productive Linkages	Experienced Tourism Human Capital Formation in Tourism Corporate Social Responsibility Regional Community Empowerment Cultural Identity
Environmental factors	**Organizational factors**
Land Use Planning Environmental and Landscape Protection Tourist Carrying Capacity	Tourist Planning Public-Private Articulation Normativity and Tourism Offer Standardization

Source: Own elaboration

As shown in Table 1, the phenomena identified are oriented toward the development of sustainable tourism that seeks a balance between the economic, social and environmental dimensions. This approach, is articulated with the sustainable tourism policy defined by the national government (Mincit, 2021). From a systemic perspective, the factors of change were subsequently analyzed in order to establish causal relationships. Therefore, through structural analysis the variables are classified, and the motricity and dependence of each one of them is determined. In such a way, this allows them to be located in a Cartesian plane and classified in different zones (Figure 3).

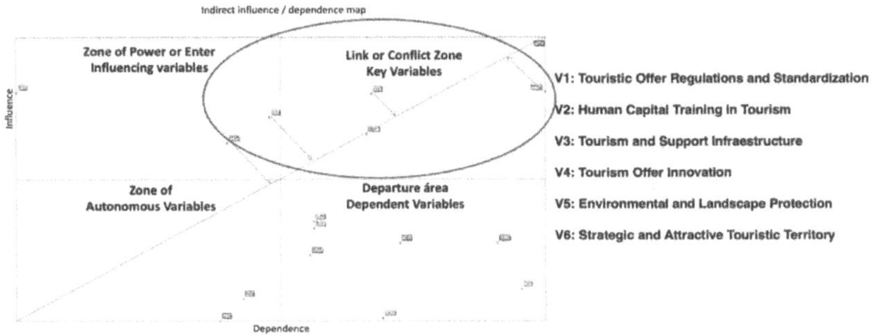

Figure 3. Indirect Influence Matrix
Source: Own elaboration

Figure 3 classifies the variables by zones, recognizing the variables in the upper right quadrant with the greatest influence and dependence on the system. That is why, they have a high impact on the others. According to the results obtained, the strategic variables are the following: (1) Touristic Offer Regulations and Standardization, (2) Human Capital Training in Tourism, (3) Tourism and Support Infrastructure, (4) Tourism Offer Innovation, (5) Environmental and Landscape Protection, and (6) Strategic and Attractive Touristic Territory.

Finally, the Peter Schwartz Axes technique was used to identify future leaders. Whereby, the strategic variables were gathered into two major vectors: (1) Public-private management, and (2) Tourism development (Figure 4).

Figure 4. Future leaders in the touristic sector
Source: Own elaboration

The causal relationship between management and development of the sector is possible to determine by grouping vectors. Also, through the decisions and actions of public entities as well as the business sector, trade unions and society. Moreover, through regulations structure around tourism, the protection of ecosystems and the improvement of training processes for innovation. This process should have an impact on the strengthening of infrastructure around tourism and the generation of a tourist territory that is attractive; based on strategic development.

3.2. Change Scenario and Strategies

Taking into account strategic variables and future leaders, the experts proposed four possible scenarios for nature tourism in Quindío for 2035. In order to do that, the Morphological Analysis technique was used and three future hypotheses were proposed for each variable, with the following scale: H1: rupture hypothesis, implies important challenges and demands. H2: transformational hypothesis, requires significant changes. H3: trend hypothesis, it means continuing as we are going. According to these hypotheses, the experts proposed four possible scenarios, as follows: E1: "We win the lottery without buying it," E2: "No hurry, but no pause," E3: "Where there is a will there is a way," and, E4: "We go all in." Table 2 presents the hypotheses selected for each proposed scenario.

Table 2. Scenarios and future hypotheses

Variable	Stage 1	Stage 2	Stage 3	Stage 4
Normativity and Tourism Offer Standardization	H3	H2	H1	H1
Human Capital Formation in Tourism	H3	H2	H2	H1
Tourism and Support Infrastructure	H3	H2	H2	H1
Innovation in the Tourism Offer	H2	H2	H1	H1
Environmental and Landscape Protection	H3	H2	H2	H1
Strategic and Attractive Tourist Territory	H1	H2	H1	H1

Source: Own elaboration

The proposed scenarios have marked differences in regards to the future hypotheses. As follows: stage 1 "We win the lottery without buying it." It requires few efforts, but seeks an optimal result in the strategic and attractive tourist territory variable. Stage 2 "Without haste but without pause." It is more conservative in all its future hypotheses and therefore, visualizes Quindío as a tourist attraction with little competitiveness progress. Stage 3 "Where there is a will there is a way." It implies significant efforts in regulations and innovation and seeks optimal results in terms of territory, however it is conservative in the other future hypotheses. Finally, stage 4 "Let's go all out." It is challenging in five future hypotheses, which demands great challenges. Also, it is conservative only in the training variable, and therefore focuses on having optimal results to achieve a competitive territory with great effort from different angles.

Therefore, Figure 5 shows the current situation of Quindío and visualizes the proposed scenarios using the Schwartz Axes technique that identified the future leaders (public-private management and tourism development).

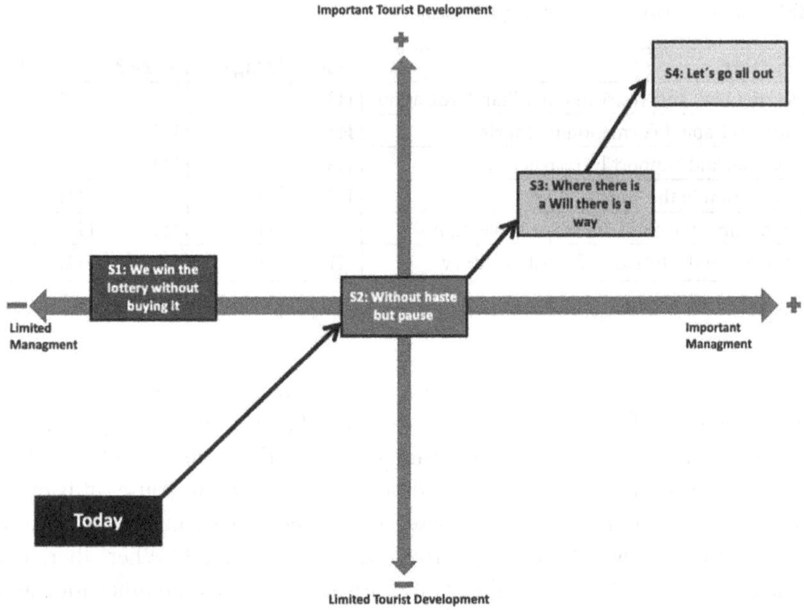

Figure 5. Future tourism scenarios
Source: Own elaboration

As shown in Figure 5, the scenarios are located in the Cartesian plane according to the level of public-private management and tourism development, which allows the identification and selection of the best scenario for the department of Quindío. According to Godet, a scenario is relevant when it meets five fundamental conditions: importance, plausibility, relevance, transparency and coherence (Mojica, 2005). In accordance with the above, the prioritization was carried out using the Regnier Abacus technique, which allows determining the most relevant scenario for the future of Quindío using the following scale: 1 (very relevant), 2 (relevant), 3 (doubt), 4 (not very relevant), 5 (no relevance at all), and B (no answer).

	Scenarios	Results											
4	*"Let's go all out"*	1	1	1	2	2	2	2	3	3	3	4	4	5
3	*"Where there is a will there is a way"*	2	2	2	2	2	2	2	3	4	4	4	4	4
2	*"Without haste but without pause"*	2	3	3	3	3	3	3	3	4	4	4	4	4
1	*"We win the lottery without buying it"*	3	4	4	4	4	4	4	4	4	4	5	5	5

Figure 6. Level of relevance for proposed stages
Source: Own elaboration

Figure 6 shows that the scenario chosen by the experts as a change is "Let's go all out", as it is considered the most relevant. Subsequently, the brainstorming technique was used to propose actions for each strategic variable in order to achieve the desired scenario. A total of 56 actions were proposed. These initiatives were then prioritized using the IGO technique (importance and governance), which made it possible to classify them into four groups: key actions, challenges, less urgent actions and unnecessary actions. Figure 7 shows the first two categories, which require implementation in the short term. Meanwhile, the key actions have high importance and governance (upper right quadrant). The challenges, despite being very significant, have less governance (upper left quadrant), that is why they require a more in-depth analysis.

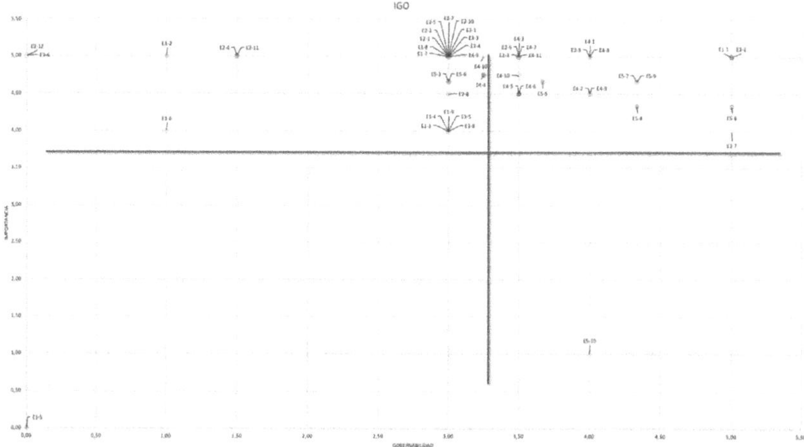

Figure 7. Importance and governance of proposed actions plane
Source: Own elaboration

Table 3 shows the most relevant key actions identified. These should be prioritized through the formulation and implementation of plans, programs and projects.

Table 3. Key actions proposed to achieve the change scenario

Strategies		Key actions
Normativity and Tourism Offer Standardization	E1–3	Articulation of initiatives in the sectoral tourism plan 2022–2032
	E1–8	Project management for the financing of the implementation of the NTS-TS
Human Capital Formation in Tourism	E2–3	Identification of the educational offer in nature tourism and gaps in levels
	E2–6	Design and implementation of training programs for tourism service providers
	E2–9	Tourism and environmental training programs for complementary tourism personnel
Tourism and Support Infrastructure	E3–2	Classification, categorization and strengthening of the supply of rural lodgings
	E3–7	Public-private management to strengthen air and land connectivity
Innovation in the Tourism Offer	E4–1	Diagnosis of research needs in nature tourism
	E4–8	Strengthening of productive linkage networks for innovation
Environmental and Landscape Protection	E5–4	Monitoring and controlling mechanisms of compliance with current legislation
	E5–5	Outreach and awareness-raising programs for businessmen related to the care of the natural environment
	E5–9	Strengthening of cultural heritage watch and forest ranger programs
Strategic and Attractive Tourist Territory	E6–3	Generation of rhetoric on cultural identity for territorial brand positioning
	E6–6	Service delivery model oriented to territorial sustainability

Note: Technical Standards for Sustainable Tourism.
Source: Own elaboration

The proposed actions should be aligned with the strategic tourism plan of Quindío (Secretariat of Tourism, Industry and Commerce, 2022). From this position, Carrillo et al. (2021) highlight the importance of tourism development plans that integrate the different actors for the development of differentiated products and the consolidation of strategic alliances. Cornejo et al. (2019) affirm that nature tourism is a very valuable alternative for both local development and territorial conservation with sustainability criteria.

4. Conclusion

Tourism is an economic activity with an important potential for Quindío. Its natural and cultural wealth has characterized it. For that reason, special emphasis on the development of nature tourism should be done. From this perspective, it is essential to promote public-private management processes for the development of tourism in the department. In this order of ideas, the scenario chosen like a change represents great challenges for the region.

The chosen scenario "let's go all out" implies a series of challenges. Hence, the proposed actions should be incorporated in the strategic plans of governmental entities and other public and private institutions. The resources allocation should be used to strengthen the sector like a modifying factor for the socioeconomic development of the region with sustainability criteria.

References

Carrillo, A., Ávalos, D., Aguilar, L., Juárez, J., & García, C. (2021). Turismo Rural y Turismo de Naturaleza en la Región de las grandes montañas de Veracruz. *Revista Rosa dos Ventos—Turismo e Hospitalidade*, *13*(3), 662–680. https://www.researchgate.net/publication/354673486_Turismo_Rural_y_Turismo_de_Naturaleza_en_la_Region_de_las_Grandes_Montanas_de_Veracruz

Consejo Nacional de Política Económica y Social, Conpes. (2014). *Política para la preservación del Paisaje Cultural Cafetero de Colombia* (Documento No. 3803). https://colaboracion.dnp.gov.co/CDT/Conpes/Econ%C3%B3micos/3803.pdf

Cornejo, J., Chávez, R., & Espinoza, R. (2019). Prospectiva del turismo de naturaleza en la costa de Jalisco. *Revista Investigaciones Turísticas*, *17*, 189–212. https://rua.ua.es/dspace/bitstream/10045/92932/1/Investigaciones-Turisticas_17_09.pdf

García, D., Vargas, H., & Restrepo, J. (2020). El turismo de naturaleza: educación ambiental y beneficios tributarios para el desarrollo del Caquetá. *Revista Aglala*, *11*(1), 107–132. https://revistas.curn.edu.co/index.php/aglala/article/view/1568

Godet, M. (2007). *Prospectiva Estratégica: Problemas y métodos* (Cuadernos de LIPSOR, No. 20, Ed. 2ª). Laboratoire d´Investigation et Stratégique. https://archivo.cepal.org/pdfs/GuiaProspectiva/Godet2007.pdf

Leguizamón, L., Mora, N., Pabón, W., & Marulanda, A. (2020). Identificación de estrategias de gestión pública para el fomento del turismo sostenible en Chinácota, Norte de Santander. *Revista Reflexiones Contables, UFPS, 3*(2), 29–39. https://doi.org/10.22463/26655543.2973

Medina, J. (2003). *Visión Compartida de Futuro.* Universidad del Valle.

Ministerio de Comercio, Industria y Turismo, Mincit. (2021). *Política de Turismo Sostenible: Unidos por la naturaleza.* https://www.mincit.gov.co/minturismo/calidad-y-desarrollo-sostenible/politicas-del-sector-turismo/politica-de-turismo-sostenible/politica-de-turismo-sostenible-9.aspx

Mojica, F. (2005). *La Construcción del Futuro, Concepto y modelo de prospectiva estratégica, territorial y tecnológica.* Convenio Andrés Bello, Universidad Externado de Colombia.

Plata, B. (2013). *Santa Rosa de Cabal, Risaralda: Un modelo prospectivo estratégico territorial para el sector turístico* (Tesis de maestría). Universidad Externado de Colombia.

Perez, R. (2012). *Pensar la estrategia.* La Crujia.

Quintana, V. (2018). *Análisis prospectivo del turismo para la construcción de paz en el municipio de San Jacinto, Bolívar* (Trabajo de pregrado). Universidad Externado de Colombia.

Salsona, J. (2014). Análisis prospectivo del turismo rural: El caso de la comunidad Valenciana. *Revista Cuadernos de Turismo, 34*, 313–334.

Secretaría de Turismo, Industria y Comercio. (2022). *Plan estratégico de turismo 2022–2032—Departamento del Quindío.* Documento Técnico. Gobernación del Quindío. https://www.quindio.gov.co/home/docs/items/item_109/DOCUMENTO_TECNICO.pdf

Serrano, A., Montoya, L., & Cazares, I. (2018). Análisis de la sostenibilidad y competitividad turística en Colombia. *Revista Gestión y Ambiente, 21*, 99–109. https://dialnet.unirioja.es/servlet/articulo?codigo=6687502

Trujillo, R. (2008). *El campo de los estudios de futuro, Análisis de Foresight y prospectiva.*

Universidad Tecnológica de Pereira, Red Alma Mater, Universidad del Quindío, Centro de Estudios e Investigaciones Regionales. (2010). *Paisaje Cultural Cafetero Colombiano.* Universidad Tecnológica de Pereira, UTP.

Tsertseil Juliya Sergeevna

Key Trends in the Clustering of Small and Medium-Sized Businesses in the Manufacturing Sector on the Example of the Region

1. Introduction

Abyazova Yu. A., Antonova M. P. and others (2020), Boldyrev S. N., Bykovskaya Yu. V. and others (2018), Vilensky A. V. and others (2018), Gleb O. V. (2017), Ilyukhina I. B., Ilminskaya S. A. (2016), Kireev N. N., Ksenofontova E. A., Tolmachev D. E. and others (2015), and many others.

Theoretical aspects of the innovative development of small and medium-sized businesses are reflected in the works of Abdurazakova A.Sh. (2010), Zimin D. P. (2013), Kurilo A. K. (2018), Kookueva V. V. and Tsertseil J. S. (2020), Leonov E. F. (2017) and other authors.

Currently, scientists around the world are devoting a large amount of research to the development of territories. The works of Bernard Pecqueur (2013), Cielo Morales, Ricardo Pérez, Eduardo Medeiros, Marjan van Herwijnen, Sandra Di Biaggio, Bernice den Brok, Zintis Hermansons, Laurent Frideres, Ilona Raugze, Torre A., Beibei Guo, Xiaobin Jin, Yelin Fang and Yinkang Zhou (2020), Eeva Furman, Jean-Pascal van Ypersele, Reter Messerli (2019), Jackson, R., J. D. Hewings, S. Rey, and N. Lozano-Garcia (2019), Charlie Karlsson, Börje Johansson, and others are devoted to this topic.

Currently, there are quite a large number of sources of information about the processes of formation of small and medium-sized businesses in the Russian Federation. With all the variety of ongoing initiatives, both from government agencies and the private sector, the issues of successful development of small and medium-sized businesses, especially the manufacturing sector, are not sufficiently developed in the scientific literature.

2. Discussion

The legal regulation of the activities of small and medium-sized businesses is carried out in accordance with Federal Law № 209 "On the development of small and medium-sized businesses in the Russian Federation" dated July 24,

2007 (as amended on November 04, 2022).[1] The Federal Law introduces the concept of "subjects of small and medium-sized businesses" as business entities (legal entities and individual entrepreneurs), classified in accordance with the conditions established by this Federal Law, to small enterprises, including micro-enterprises, and medium-sized enterprises. Information about them is included in the unified register of small and medium-sized businesses.

In accordance with Article 4[2] of this Law, small and medium-sized businesses include those registered in accordance with the legislation of the Russian Federation and meeting the conditions established by Part 1.1 of this Article, business companies, business partnerships, business partnerships, production cooperatives, consumer cooperatives, peasant farms and individual entrepreneurs.

The proposed clustering algorithm for small and medium-sized businesses in the manufacturing sector lists the main groups of participants, which is shown in Figure 1:

- state programs for the development of territories,
- industrial (public) enterprises—anchor participants,
- subjects of small and medium business;
- special economic zone of industrial-production type (SEZ IPT) or technology-innovative type (SEZ TIT),
- the sphere of professional training and retraining of personnel,
- innovative infrastructure.

1 The document was provided by ConsultantPlus: information and legal portal. Access mode: by subscription.

2 The document was provided by ConsultantPlus: information and legal portal. Access mode: by subscription.

Table 1. Algorithm for clustering small and medium-sized businesses in the manufacturing sector

State programs for the development of the territory, the implementation of cluster policy, strategies for innovative development, etc.			
Special economic zone of industrial-production type or technology-innovative type, administrative resource			
Participant group 1	Participant group 2	Participant group 3	Participant group 4
Production (public) corporations of the real sector of the economy	Educational sector in the field of vocational training and retraining of personnel	Innovation infrastructure: business incubators, manufacturers' associations, technology parks, technopolises: "innovation block"	Small and medium-sized enterprises in the manufacturing sector

Source: Compiled by the author

Today, special economic zones are one of the tools for the development of territories. Together with them, this function is performed by zones of territorial development and territories of advanced socioeconomic development. This is reflected in Table 1. The activities of small and medium-sized businesses cannot be considered in isolation from the general strategy for the development of the national economy. Thus, at the state level, an approach is currently being implemented to form individual plans for the development of territories in order to equalize the pace of development of territories characterized by a low level of a number of indicators. The following indicators are analyzed: average per capita cash income of the population, adjusted for the ratio of the cost of a fixed set of consumer goods; the proportion of the population with monetary incomes below the regional subsistence level in the total population of a constituent entity of the Russian Federation; unemployment rate; investment in fixed capital (excluding budget investments) per capita. In accordance with the federal law of the Russian Federation of December 3, 2011, № 392-FZ (as amended on December 28, 2013), territorial development zones include a part of the territory of a constituent entity of the Russian Federation, where, through the provision of state support measures, favorable conditions for attracting investments are created. The state does this in order to accelerate its socioeconomic development.

Table 2. Characteristics of the territories of development of the Russian Federation

Territory type	Key characteristics
Special economic zone	Focused on the development of manufacturing sectors of the economy, high-tech sectors of the economy, the development of technologies and the commercialization of their results, the production of new types of products
Territorial development zones	Focused on reducing differences in the level of socioeconomic development of the constituent entities of the Russian Federation by creating favorable conditions for attracting investment in their economy
Territories of advanced socioeconomic development	Focused on the territory of the Far East in order to organize non-primary production-oriented export capacities to the countries of the Asia-Pacific region. A favorable investment climate is formed as a result of the implementation of state support measures

Source: Retrieved from http://legalacts.ru/doc/federalnyi-zakon-ot-03122011-n-392-fz-o/

In the general approach, the balanced territorial development of the Russian Federation is carried out within the framework of the "Strategy for the Spatial Development of the Russian Federation for the period up to 2025." This strategy was approved by the Decree of the Government of the Russian Federation dated February 13, 2019, No. 207-r. Its main provisions involve the elimination of infrastructural restrictions within the territories. As one of the tools for the development of the territories of the Russian Federation, special economic zones (SEZs) can be distinguished. According to the official website of the Ministry of Economic Development of the Russian Federation, there are currently 43 SEZs operating in the country, including 24 industrial and production SEZs, 7 technological innovation SEZs, 10 tourist and recreational SEZs, and 2 port SEZs. Each of them involves the formation of the investment potential of a particular territory. The main share of SEZ participants are small and medium-sized businesses. According to the Ministry of Economic Development of the Russian Federation, the total number of SEZ residents, some of which belong to small and medium-sized businesses, is more than 967 participants.

As an example of building a cluster, we considered the Lipetsk region.

Table 3. Algorithm for clustering small and medium-sized businesses in the manufacturing sector of the Lipetsk region

State programs for the metallurgical and machine-building industries, the implementation of cluster policy, innovative development strategies, etc.			
Special economic zone of industrial-production type (SEZ IPT) "Lipetsk" was created in accordance with the Federal Law "On Special Economic Zones in the Russian Federation" dated July 22, 2005, № 116-FZ			
Participant group 1	**Participant group 2**	**Participant group 3**	**Participant group 4**
Production enterprises of the real sector of the economy	Educational sector in the field of vocational training and retraining of personnel	Innovation infrastructure: business incubators, manufacturers' associations, technology parks, technopolises: "innovation block"	Subjects of small and medium business
PJSC Novolipetsk Iron and Steel Works (PJSC NLMK) OJSC Studenovsk Joint-Stock Mining Company (JSC STAGDOK) JSC Indesit International LLC LPO "Electroapparat"	– Lipetsk branch of the federal state budgetary educational institution of higher professional education "Russian Academy of National Economy and Public Administration under the President of the Russian Federation"; – Branch of the Federal State Budgetary Educational Institution of Higher Professional Education "Moscow State University of Technology and Management named after K.G. Razumovsky" in Lipetsk;	Sodruzhestvo business incubator business incubators (Yelets, Chaplygin, Lipetsk, Dobrink, Terbuny, Usman and Khlevny); information and consultation centers in municipalities; Small and Medium Business Support Fund; Center for Innovative Youth Creativity; Regional engineering center; Regional integrated center based on the Lipetsk Chamber of Commerce and Industry; Industrial Technopark "Millennium"; MBU "Technopark—Lipetsk"; Industrial technopark "Sokol."	LLC "ABB ELECTRIC EQUIPMENT," AVION LLC, LLC "AUTONOE" ALTAIR LLC, ART-PRINT LLC, LLC "BEKART LIPETSK," BIPLAST LLC, BS Processing LLC, LLC "Lipetsk Machine Tool Enterprise," Lipetsk Experimental Plant "Gidromash" LLC (LOEZ "Gidromash" LLC), CJSC Lipetsk Machine Tool Plant Vozrozhdenie, JSC "Polymer," etc.

(*continued on next page*)

Table 3. Continued

State programs for the metallurgical and machine-building industries, the implementation of cluster policy, innovative development strategies, etc.			
Special economic zone of industrial-production type (SEZ IPT) "Lipetsk" was created in accordance with the Federal Law "On Special Economic Zones in the Russian Federation" dated July 22, 2005, № 116-FZ			
Participant group 1	**Participant group 2**	**Participant group 3**	**Participant group 4**
	– Lipetsk branch of the Federal State Educational Budgetary Institution of Higher Professional Education "Financial University under the Government of the Russian Federation"; – Federal State Budgetary Educational Institution of Higher Professional Education "Lipetsk State Technical University."		

Source: Compiled by the author based on data posted on the official websites of companies: http://admlip.ru/economy/industry/promyshlennost/perechen-predpriyatiy-promyshlennosti-lipetskoy-oblasti/, http://vuz.edunetwork.ru, https://map.cluster.hse.ru/cluster/385

The dynamics of profitability indicators of medium-sized enterprises of the Lipetsk region, operating in the field of mechanical engineering, is shown in Figures 1–3.

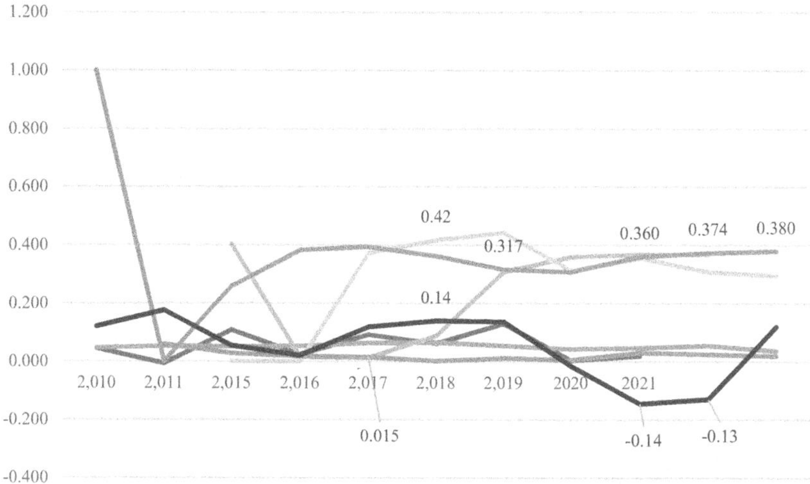

Figure 1. Dynamics of gross profitability indicators of medium-sized enterprises of the Lipetsk region, employed in the engineering industry, for the period 2010–2021, shares of units

Source: Compiled by the author based on data posted on the official website https://www.list-org.com

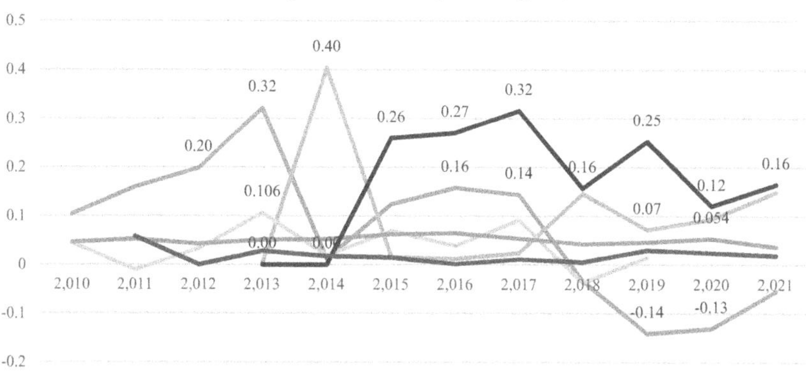

Figure 2. Dynamics of indicators of profitability of operating profit of medium-sized enterprises of the Lipetsk region for the period 2010–2021, shares of units

Source: Compiled by the author based on data posted on the official website https://www.list-org.com

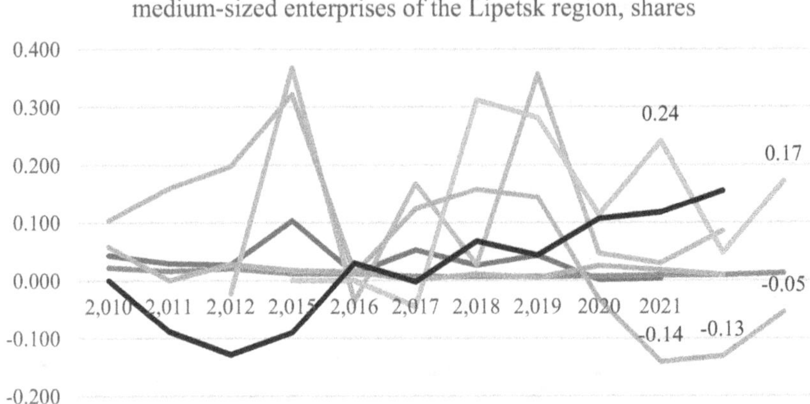

Figure 3. Dynamics of indicators of profitability and profit before taxation of medium-sized enterprises of the Lipetsk region operating in the engineering industry for the period 2010–2021, shares of units

Source: Compiled by the author based on data posted on the official website https://www.list-org.com

According to the data in Figures 1–3, there is a progressive decrease in the value of profitability of profits of medium-sized enterprises.

The dynamics of the indicator of profitability of operating profit of small enterprises in the Lipetsk region for the period 2010–2021, operating in the engineering industry, is shown in Figure 4.

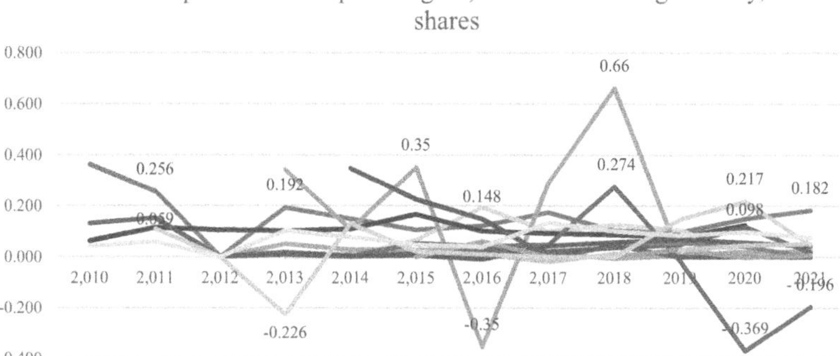

Figure 4. Dynamics of indicators of profitability of operating profit of small enterprises in the engineering industry operating in the Lipetsk region for the period 2010–2021, shares of units

Source: Compiled by the author based on data posted on the official website https://www.list-org.com

According to Figure 4, the operating profit margin of small enterprises in the Lipetsk region operating in the engineering industry did not exceed 18.2 % in 2021.

3. Conclusion

Among the main groups of participants that ensure the clustering of small and medium-sized businesses in the manufacturing sector, there are anchor public companies operating in the industry of the same name. When considering the cluster of the Lipetsk region, the activities of PJSC Novolipetsk Iron and Steel Works are singled out. The dynamics of NLMK's profitability indicators is shown in Figure 5.

Figure 5. Dynamics of profitability indicators of PJSC Novolipetsk Iron and Steel Works for the period 2010–2021

Source: Compiled by the author based on data posted on the official website https://www.list-org.com

According to Figure 5, the maximum value of the company's profitability indicator is 27 % for the period 2010–2021.

When forming key profitability indicators, the starting point is the "sales proceeds" indicator, the absolute value of which directly depends on the range of products sold, which is reflected in Table, in relation to PJSC Novolipetsk Iron and Steel Works.

Table 4. NLMK's product range

Application industry	Name of product
Oil and gas infrastructure	Hot-rolled steel
Cars	Hot-rolled steel, cold-rolled steel, wire
Trucks	Hot rolled, cold rolled, Quard, Quend
Railway transport	Hot-rolled steel, cold-rolled steel, galvanized steel, Quard, Quend
Construction and mining machinery	Hot-rolled steel, cold-rolled steel, Quend
Agricultural machinery	Hot-rolled steel, cold-rolled steel, galvanized steel, Quard, Quend
Shipbuilding	Hot-rolled steel

Table 4. Continued

Application industry	Name of product
Construction, renovation and decoration	Hot-rolled steel, cold-rolled steel, galvanized steel, pre-painted steel, fittings, shaped steel, hardware products, blast-furnace slag, steel-smelting slag, granulated slag
Household appliances	Hot-rolled steel, cold-rolled steel, galvanized steel, color-coated steel, dynamic steel
Energy equipment	Transformer rolling steel, dynamic rolling steel
Special equipment	Hot-rolled steel
Steel production	Pig iron, coke, iron ore, slabs

Source: Compiled by the author based on data from an official source: NLMK's official website https://nlmk.com

As we can see, the degree of conversion of raw materials by a key participant is limited to rolled products.

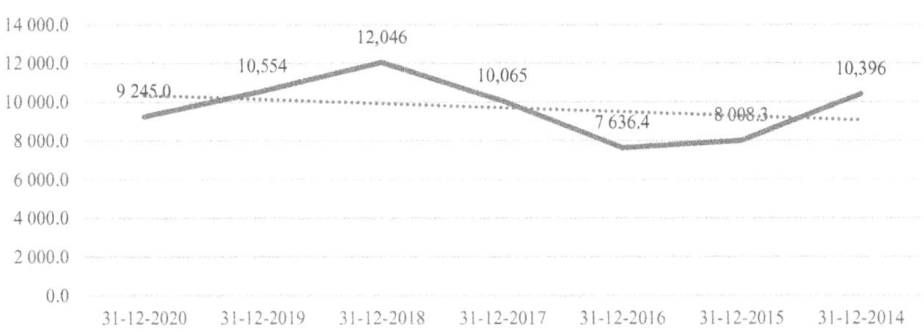

Figure 6. Dynamics of the indicator "revenue from sales" of PJSC "Novolipetsk Iron and Steel Works" for the period 2014–2020

Source: Compiled on the basis of data provided by the information and analytical terminal Refinitive

The dynamics of changes in the indicator of economic value added of the anchor enterprise of the territorial cluster PJSC Novolipetsk Iron and Steel Works is shown in Figure 7.

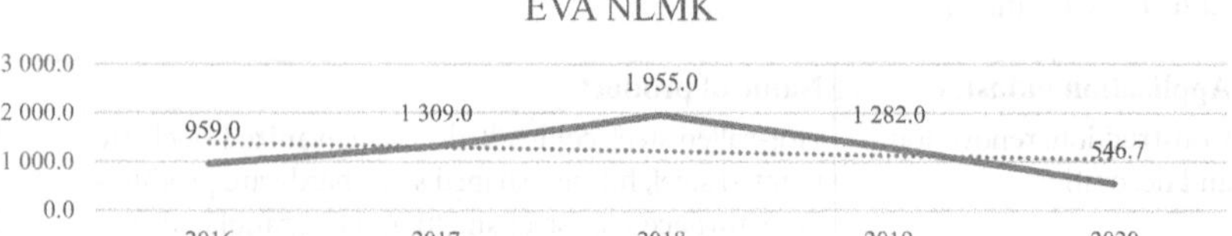

Figure 7. Dynamics of changes in the indicator of economic value added of PJSC Novolipetsk Iron and Steel Works for the period 2016–2020, million US dollars

Source: Compiled on the basis of data provided by the information and analytical terminal Refinitive

According to Figures 6 and 7, it can be said that in the presence of a fairly developed metallurgical and machine-building cluster of the Lipetsk region, the indicators of the anchor enterprise PJSC Novolipetsk Iron and Steel Works do not have a stable progressive dynamics in relation to the formation of an indicator of economic value added (EVA). At the same time, the indicator of the average cost of capital of PJSC NLMK is quite low among the companies of this group: Basic materials, which is shown in Figure 8. It is 4.9 %.

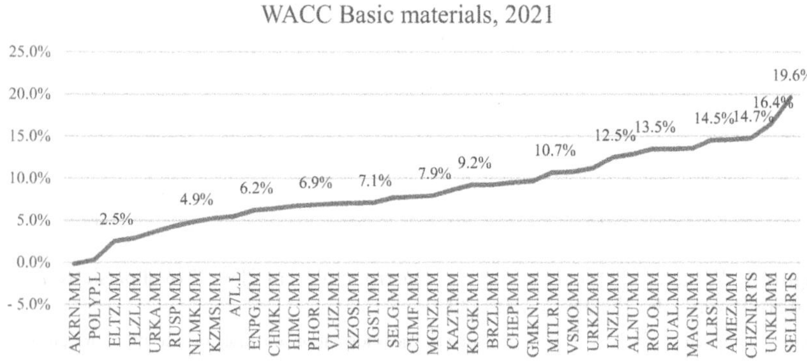

Figure 8. Indicators of the average cost of capital of Russian public companies in the Basic materials industry, 2021

Source: Compiled on the basis of data provided by the information and analytical terminal Refinitive

In this case, we can say that profit indicators should be formed at a higher level. This can be facilitated by expanding the circle of potential consumers formed by small and medium-sized businesses in the manufacturing sector of the Lipetsk region. At present, the introduction of coordinating measures of state support and development of small and medium-sized businesses is required. The purpose of these measures should be targeted impact in the branches of specialization of geographical territories, mainly in the manufacturing sector. This is due to the fact that today the proportion of small and medium-sized enterprises engaged in production activities identified with the specialization of the territorial cluster is extremely low. According to the data of the statistical collection of the Federal State Statistics Service, when evaluating the activities of small enterprises, certain characteristics were identified as important factors limiting the development potential. These factors include lack of own financial resources, high cost of debt financing. These shortcomings can be minimized as a result of the formation of cooperative relationships with large public companies.

References

Abdurazakova, A. Sh. (2010). *Malyj biznes kak faktor innovacionnogo razvitiya* (Cand, Abstr of Diss.). [Small business as a factor of innovative development. Ph.D. Abstr of Diss.]. 21 p.

Antonova, M. P., Barinova, V. A., Gromov, V. V., Zemtsov, S. P., Krasnoselskikh, A. N., Milogolov, N. S., Potapova, A. A., & Tsareva, Yu. V. (2020). *Razvitie malogo i srednego predprinimatel'stva v Rossii v kontekste realizacii nacional'nogo proekta [Development of small and medium-sized businesses in Russia in the context of the implementation of the national project]* (88 p.). Publishing house "Delo" RANEPA.

Beibei Guo, Xiaobin Jin, Yelin Fang, & Yinkang Zhou (2020). Evaluation of sustainable regional development combining remote sensing data and ecological constraints: A case study of Chaohu Basin, China. d: 21 October 2020; Accepted: 23 November 2020; Published: 25 November 2020. *Sustainability, 12*, 9836. https://doi.org/10.3390/su12239836

Bernard, P. (2013). Territorial development. A new approach to development processes for the economies of the developing countries. *Revista Internacional Interdisciplinar INTERthesis, Florianópolis, 10*(2), 8–32.

Bykovskaya, Yu. V., Ivanova, L. N., & Safokhina, E. A. (2018). Small and medium business in modern Russia: state, problems and directions of development. *Bulletin of Eurasian Science, 5*, 16.

Furman, E., van Ypersele, J.-P., & Messerli, P. (2019). Draft Global Sustainable Development Report 2019: messages for the globe, insights for the EU. European Parliament Public Hearing "The remaining 12 years: EU action towards achieving the 2030 Agenda for Sustainable Development" 7.2.2019.

Gleba, O. V., & Aseeva, M. A. (2017). The main problems and prospects for the development of small and medium-sized businesses in the Moscow region. *Economy and Entrepreneurship*, 9(part 4), 451–456.

Ilminskaya, S. A., & Ilyukhina, I. B. (2016). Analysis of the state and prospects for the development of small business. *Vestnik Orel GIET*, *1*(35), 46–54.

Jackson, R., Hewings, J. D., Rey, S., & Lozano-Garcia, N. (2019). Regional development: Challenges, methods, and models. In R. Jackson (Ed.), *Web Book of Regional Science*. Regional Research Institute, West Virginia University.

Kookueva, V. V., & Tsertseil, J. S. (2020). The role of state support for small and medium-sized businesses in the context of innovative economic development. *Sustainable Energy Systems: Innovative Perspectives (SES-2020)*, *220*, 7 p.

Kurilo, A. K. (2018). *Razvitie malogo i srednego predprinimatel'stva v usloviyah formirovaniya novoj tekhnologicheskoj bazy promyshlennosti* (Cand, Abstr of Diss.). [The development of small and medium-sized businesses in the context of the formation of a new technological base for industry. Ph.D. Abstr of Diss.]. 23 p.

Leonov, E. F. (2017). *Povyshenie konkurentosposobnosti malyh i srednih predpriyatij sfery uslug na osnove formirovaniya institucional'nogo prostranstva* (Cand, Abstr of Diss.). [Increasing the competitiveness of small and medium-sized enterprises in the service sector based on the formation of an institutional space. Ph.D. Abstr of Diss.]. 25 p.

Tolmachev, D. E., Ulyanova, E. A., & Pliner, L. M. (2015). Development of small and medium-sized businesses in the region: the formation of priority areas on the example of the Sverdlovsk region. *Economy of the Region*, *1*.

Torre, A. (2019). Territorial development and proximity relationships. In R. Capello & P. Nijkamp (Eds.), *Handbook of regional and development theories* (2nd ed., 674 p.). Edward Elgar.

Vilensky, A. V., Domnina, I. N., & Maevskaya, L. I. (2018). *Vozdejstvie nekrupnogo predprinimatel'stva na social'no-ekonomicheskoe razvitie regionov Rossijskoj Federacii* [The impact of small business on the socio-economic development of the regions of the Russian Federation] [Report] (39 p.). Institute of Economics of the Russian Academy of Sciences.

Zimin, D. P. (2013). *Razvitie malogo innovacionnogo predprinimatel'stva v regione (na primere Moskovskoj oblasti)* (Cand, Abstr of Diss.). [Development of small innovative entrepreneurship in the region (on the example of the Moscow region). Ph.D. Abstr of Diss.]. 27 p.

Konstantin V. Ordov, Juliya S. Tsertseil, &
Nadezhda A. Zatsarnaya

Prospects for the Development of the Market of Carbon Units within the Framework of the ESG Orientation and the Possibility of Using Green Bonds for Its Development

1. Introduction

To date, a fairly large number of authors are developing issues of ESG orientation, in particular: Jean-Florent Helfre and Elise Depetiteville (2022), Xiaohang Rena et al. (2022), Marín-Rodríguez et al. (2022), Zasarnaya (2022), and Yves Rannou et al. (2020).

Successful experience in the implementation of Russian natural and climatic projects and the activities of carbon landfills has made it possible to form a significant scientific and statistical knowledge and data base. The next step toward the development of the climate regulation system in Russia should be the replication of the accumulated experience in the functioning of carbon landfills, the transition to monetization of the sequestration of greenhouse gas emissions as the national market for carbon units and the quota trading system are formed, and a significant increase in private investment in natural and climatic projects. In this regard, the problems of creating conditions for attracting private investment, developing financial instruments and mechanisms for investing in natural and climate projects, methods for financial and economic evaluation of such projects, creating a convenient digital platform that unites the main participants in the greenhouse gas emission regulation system become relevant.

The value of the global carbon market in 2021 increased by 164 %. As a result, the market volume reached a record level of 760 billion euros (Statista, 2023). This growth was mainly due to increased demand for carbon emission rights, culminating in rising prices. Carbon trading is the buying and selling of credits that allow a company or organization, such as a power plant, to emit a certain amount of carbon dioxide. The European Union Emissions Trading System is the largest carbon market by value and accounted for approximately 90 % of the global market in 2021, as shown in Figure 1.

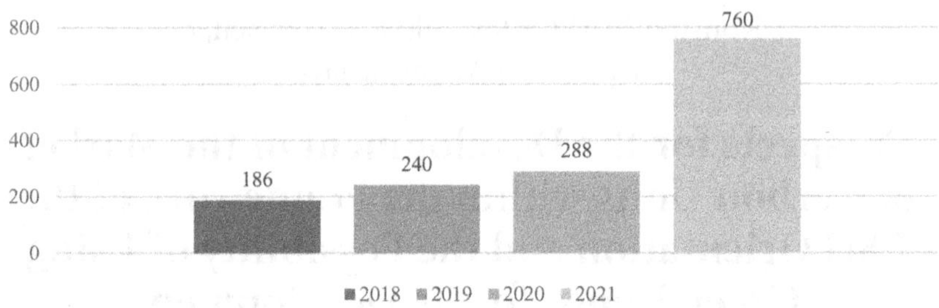

Figure 1. Dynamics of the volume of the carbon market in the world for the period 2018–2021, billion euros

Source: Compiled by the authors based on site data https://www.statista.com/statistics/1334848/global-carbon-market-size-value/

As part of the methodological and methodological support for the greenhouse gas market in Russia, it is necessary to develop:

- methodology for estimating carbon credits;
- new financial instruments based on carbon credits;
- methods for assessing the economic efficiency of natural and climatic projects;
- rules regarding the process of issuing, trading and financial evaluation of carbon credits and climate projects;
- digital financial assets based on a carbon unit.

One of the promising tools to achieve these goals is the issuance of green bonds.

2. Discussion

Simultaneously with the market for carbon credits, the green bond market is currently emerging, which is also considered as a tool for minimizing carbon dioxide emissions. These categories pursue the same goal, but from different positions. While the carbon credit market aims to reduce the carbon footprint of existing businesses, green bonds act as a source of funding for projects with environmental benefits that avoid carbon footprint.

The green bond market is actively developing, as can be seen in Figures 2 and 3.

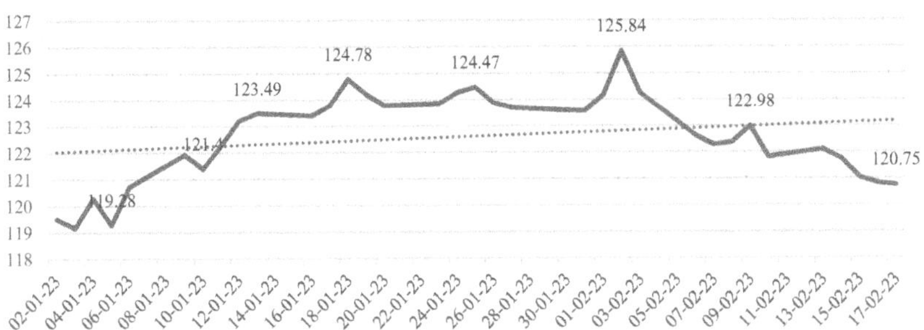

Figure 2. Dynamics of the Green Bonds Index S&P, 2023

Source: Compiled by the authors based on site data https://www.spglobal.com/spdji/en/indices/esg/sp-green-bond-index/#overview

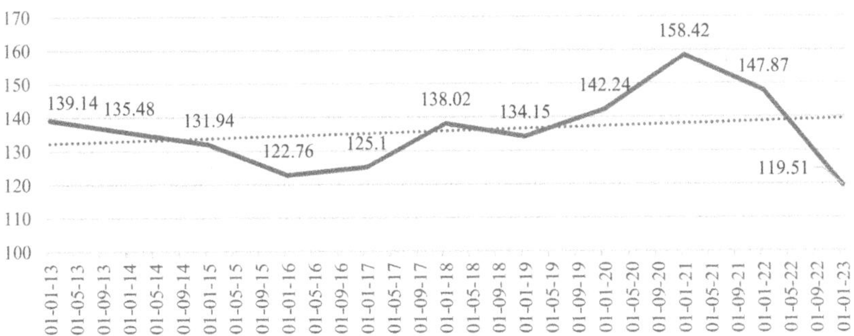

Figure 3. Dynamics of the Green Bonds Index S&P for the period from 2013 to 2023

Source: Compiled by the authors based on site data https://www.spglobal.com/spdji/en/indices/esg/sp-green-bond-index/#overview

In this regard, various authors are conducting research to identify the interdependence and influence of the green bond market and the carbon unit market. Xiaohang Rena et al. (2022) consider the prospects for building investment portfolios involving both green bonds and derivatives traded on the carbon market, focusing on the S&P Green Bond Index. Marín-Rodríguez et al. (2022) introduce the notion that green bonds play a key role in financing sustainable infrastructure systems. At the same time, the authors introduce both the volume of carbon dioxide emissions and oil prices as factors influencing the development of the green bond market.

It is interesting to note that the main difference between this type of bonds and traditional ones is that the funds received from the issue will be used to implement new or existing projects to reduce emissions into the atmosphere, renewable energy sources, and the like (Lysenko, 2019).

The OECD Report (2015) identifies several forms of green bonds:

- Corporate bond
- Project bond
- Asset-backed security (ABS)
- Supranational, sub-sovereign and agency (SSA) bond
- Municipal bond
- Financial sector bond.

Also, the OECD Report (2015) presents a complete matrix of green bond issuance areas by industry, which is reflected in Table 1.

Table 1. Matrix of directions for issuing green bonds in different sectors of the economy

Energy	**Low-carbon buildings**	**Industry& energy intensive commercial**	**Waste & pollution control**	**Transport**	**Information technology & communications**	**Agriculture forestry & land use**	**Adaption**
Solar	New residential	Manufacturing	Recycling facilities	Low-carbon transport	Power management	AFOLU mitigation	Water
Wind	New commercial	Energy efficiency processes	Recycling products & circular economy	Vehides	Tele-conferencing	AFOLU adaptation	Energy
Bioenergy	Retrofit	Energy efficiency products	Waste to energy	Public transport	Resource efficiency	Agricultural products	Industry & waste
Geothermal	Products for building carbon efficiency	Retail & wholesale	Geo-sequestration	Bus rapid transport			Transport
Marine		Data centers		Alternative fuel infrastructure			ICT
Dedicated transmission		Process & fugitive emissions		Water-borne			Building
Energy distribution & management		Energy efficient appliance					Food supply
		Combined heat & power					Coastal

Source: Retrieved from https://www.oecd.org/environment/cc/Green%20bonds%20PP%20%5Bf3%5D%20%5Blr%5D.pdf

Issuing green bonds has a number of advantages:

- opportunity to attract new investors;
- investor confidence, especially since the implementation of a green bond issue has higher reporting and disclosure requirements than traditional bonds;
- brand awareness and value: the prospect of introducing more innovative methods and sustainability to investors.

"Green" bonds can be issued not only by corporate companies, but also by the government of the country. The funds received can be invested in the development of innovative infrastructure through "long" money. It is assumed that environmental projects could be financed through the issuance of "green" bonds, which could be bought by the Bank of Russia, domestic and foreign investors. With this model, debt sources of financing develop, and part of the funds remains in the real sector of the economy (Lysenko, 2021). At the same time, this contributes to the active reduction of carbon emissions.

In 2018, the first issue of green bonds in Russia in the amount of 1.1 billion rubles. carried out by a regional company. In 2019 and 2020, the average green bond issue amounted to RUB 12.2 billion. and 10.5 billion rubles, respectively. In 2021, larger issuers entered the Russian market, which was reflected in the growth of the average amount of funds raised to RUB 16.3 billion (ESG and Russia's Green Finance 2018–2022 Report, 2022).

Today in the Russian Federation there is a steady trend toward reducing carbon emissions. This is facilitated by the provisions of the Federal Law of July 2, 2021, No. 296FZ "On Limiting Greenhouse Gas Emissions." This document establishes the legal basis for mandatory carbon reporting, due to start in 2023 for the most polluting companies, and carbon offset schemes. This is an integral element in resolving issues of ESG orientation, which is reflected in Figure 4.

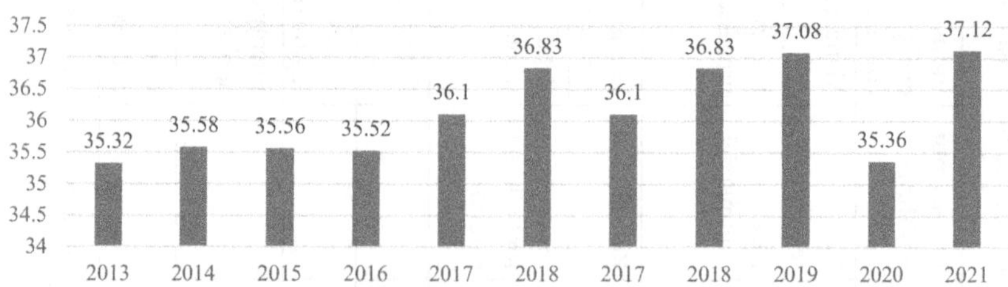

Figure 4. Dynamics of global carbon dioxide (CO_2) emissions for the period 2013–2021, billion tons

Source: Compiled by the authors based on site data https://www.statista.com/statistics/1334848/global-carbon-market-size-value/

In Figure 5, these data for different countries are presented for 2021.

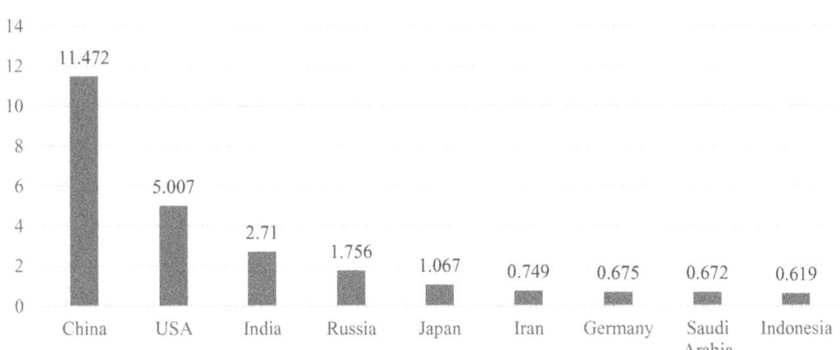

Figure 5. Volumes of carbon dioxide emissions in different countries in 2021, billion tons

Source: Compiled by the authors based on site data https://www.statista.com/statistics/1334848/global-carbon-market-size-value/

It should be noted that the volumes of carbon dioxide emissions in different countries are directly related to the development of the market for green financial instruments in these countries. For example, in 2020, the bulk of the issue was placed by issuers from the Asia-Pacific region—$1.7 billion. Issuers from China—$786 million, Japan—$714 million, USA—$489 million were the largest issuers. Major issues were made by the Japanese company JRTT in the amount of $388 million and the Russian company RZD Capital Plc, which is part of the Russian Railways group of companies, in the amount of $257 million.

According to statistics in Jean-Florent Helfre and Elise Depetiteville (2022), the largest volume of green bond issuance is registered in the Renewable electricity and heat production sector, followed by the Transport sector by a fairly large margin, followed by the Building sector.

Consider the dynamics of the development of the green bond market in the world in the context of industries. To this end, we will single out groups: leading industries, medium industries and outsider industries. Figures 6–8 show the dynamics of green bond issues by industry in the world in 2021.

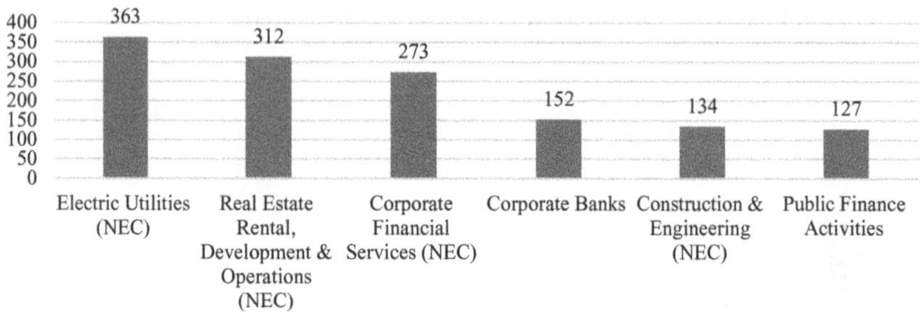

Figure 6. Number of green bond issues by leading industries in 2021, number of issues
Source: Compiled by the authors based on data from the Refinitive information and analytical terminal

As we can see, in the context of the leading industries, there is a fairly large spread in the volume of green bond issues in the world, according to Figure 6. The range of variation in the number of issues in the leading industries is from 127 to 363 issues in 2021. The largest number of green bond issues in 2021 was recorded in the electric power industry (363 issues), the rental, development and operation of real estate industry (312 issues), as well as corporate financial services (273 issues). The remaining leading industries are characterized by almost the same distribution of green bond issuance volumes: the corporate banking sector (152 issues), construction and design (134 issues) and public finance activities (127 issues).

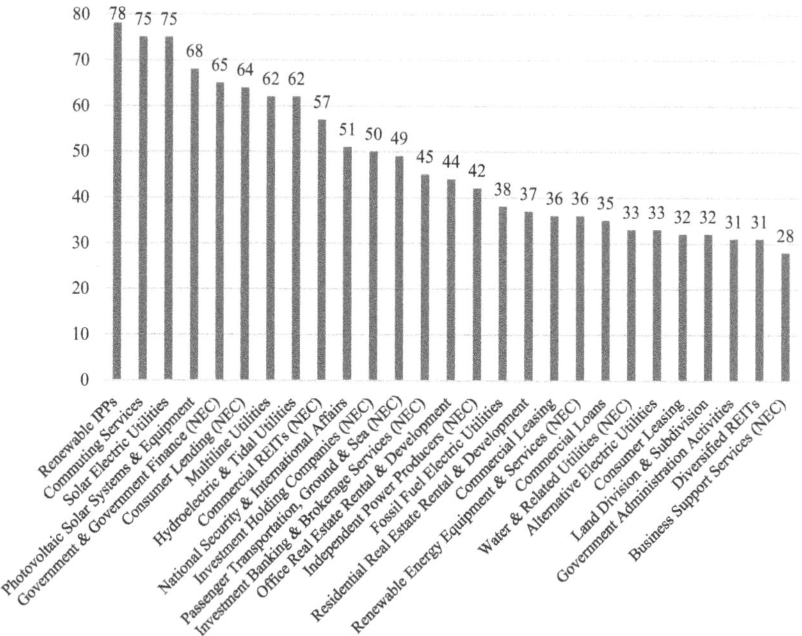

Figure 7. Number of green bond issues by "medium" industries in 2021, number of issues

Source: Compiled by the authors based on data from the Refinitive information and analytical terminal

The second group, which forms the "medium" industries, according to Figure 7, includes industries of alternative forms of energy: solar power plants (75 outputs), photovoltaic solar systems (68 outputs), hydropower and tidal energy (62 outputs).

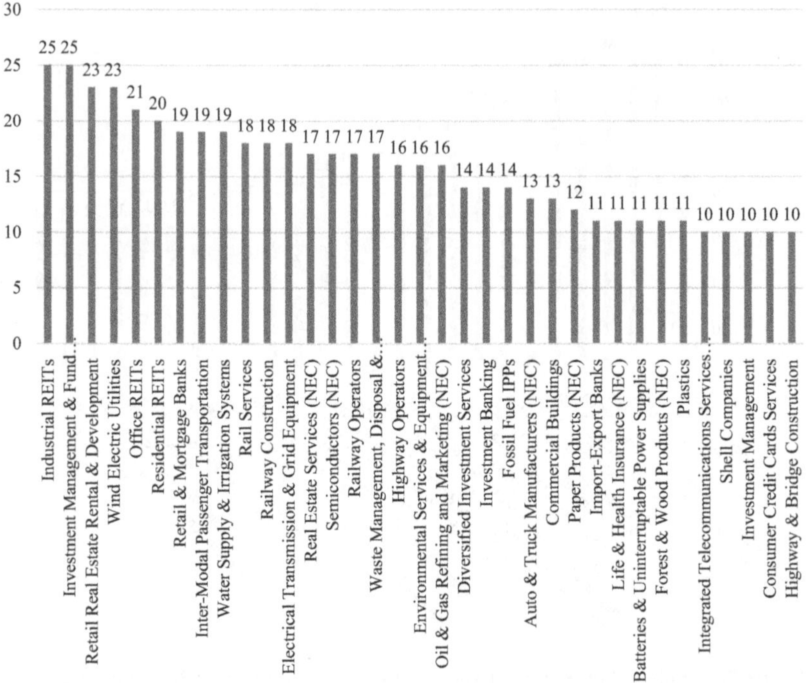

Figure 8. Number of green bond issues by outsider industries in 2021, number of issues
Source: Compiled by the authors based on data from the Refinitive information and analytical terminal

According to Figure 8, the range of variation in the number of issues in outsider industries is from 10 to 25 issues in 2021. Ordov et al. (2022) also wrote about this in their study.

As an example, we also considered the dynamics of a decrease in the volume of electricity use in the economy of the Russian Federation for the period 2012–2021 (Figure 9).

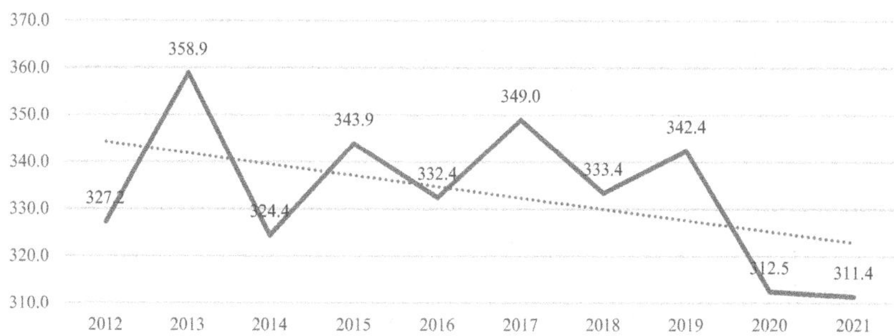

Figure 9. Dynamics of the actual consumption of electricity supplied by diesel power plants (powered by internal combustion engines) per unit of certain types of manufactured products and services in the Russian Federation for the period 2012–2021, thousand kWh

Source: Compiled by the authors based on site data https://rosstat.gov.ru/statistics/accounts

The rate of reduction in the consumption of electricity supplied by diesel power plants (operated by internal combustion engines) per unit of certain types of manufactured products and services in the Russian Federation for the period 2012–2021 is shown in Figure 10.

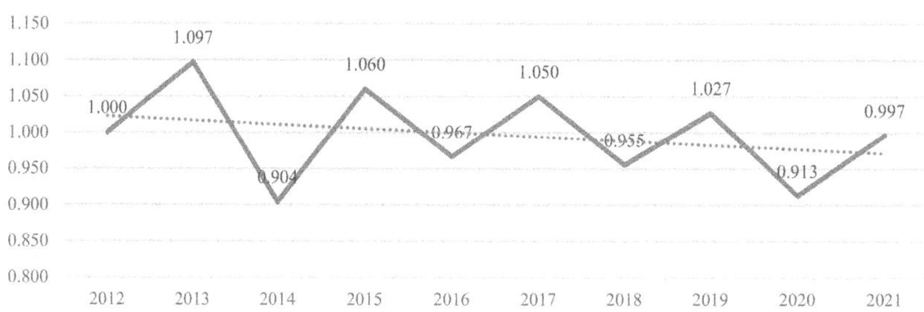

Figure 10. The rate of decrease in the volume of electricity consumption supplied by diesel power plants (powered by internal combustion engines) per unit of certain types of manufactured products and services in the Russian Federation for the period 2012–2021, shares of units

Source: Compiled by the authors based on site data https://rosstat.gov.ru/statistics/accounts

In Figure 10, we see that, in general, in the economy of the Russian Federation, there is a decrease in actual fuel consumption per unit of certain types of products or services produced, which, in general, can be considered as a positive prerequisite for the development of the green bond market and an increase in their efficiency as a result of their use as sources financing of project activities by business entities.

It is worth noting that through the issuance of green bonds, issuers attracted financing for the implementation of projects in the energy sector, real estate, waste management, engineering, as well as in the financial and transport sectors. Among issuers of green bonds there are companies of both federal and regional levels. Projects financed through the issuance of green bonds are implemented both in the Russian Federation (e.g., PJSC Russian Railways) and in the territories of individual constituent entities of the Russian Federation, including the Khanty-Mansiysk Autonomous Okrug—Yugra, Moscow, St. Petersburg, the Republic of Adygea, Stavropol Territory, as well as Astrakhan, Rostov and Moscow regions. At the beginning of 2022, the leading industry segment among issuers of bonds in the format of sustainable development was transport sector (ESG and Russia's Green Finance 2018–2022 Report, 2022).

Despite the fact that green bonds are a fairly new tool, they have a number of significant advantages, in addition to those already mentioned in this scientific article. Additionally, the following advantages of green bonds can be distinguished:

- they can be classified as cheap "long" money;
- governments of countries can act as issuers;
- they can be considered as a tool for financing the fight against environmental threats;
- they can be seen as a tool for shaping investors' perceptions of responsible behavior;
- they can be seen as a tool for diversifying funding sources.

These advantages contribute to their rapid spread and development, expansion of the scope and market of their circulation. There is a clear trend toward support for green investment in the Russian market, and in the future there may be new incentives for issuers and more attractive green bonds for investors. To actively develop this product in Russia, there are several ways. First, it is necessary to reduce the tax burden on investors who buy green bonds. Secondly, large funds should dedicate part of their assets to green bonds (Morozova et al., 2021).

The development of this instrument in Russia makes it possible to stand on a par with leading countries, attract new investors to the market, which can reverse the negative trend in the outflow of capital from the country, and also solve environmental problems, which is in line with the provisions of the Kyoto and Paris agreements.

3. Conclusion

At the end of the study, we can say that when considering the level of development of the most involved industry in the field of issuing green bonds—the electric power industry of the Russian Federation, we can note the positive dynamics of its development.

At the same time, according to the official website of the Federal State Statistics Service of the Russian Federation, the share of renewable sources in electricity generation is constantly increasing. In 2020, this figure was 19.8 %. For the period from 2012 to 2020, there is a steady forward movement in the change in this indicator from 15.3 % to 19.8 %, respectively.

These results can be viewed as positive regarding the prospects for the development of the industry, taking into account the ESG orientation.

References

ESG and Russia's Green Finance 2018–2022 Report. (2022). *Expert-analytical platform "Infrastructure and Finance for Sustainable Development."* https://esg-consulting.ru/wp-content/uploads/2022/03/infragreen_green_finance_esg_in_russia_2018-2022.pdf

Global Carbon Market Size 2018–2021. (2023). *Statista. A provider of market and consumer data.* https://www.statista.com/statistics/1334848/global-carbon-market-size-value/

Helfre, J.-F., & Depetiteville, E. (2022). Measuring the impact of green bonds. https://www.spglobal.com/esg/insights/blog/measuring-the-impact-of-green-bonds#:~:text=Green%20bonds%20fund%20projects%20with,compared%20with%20a%20conventional%20approach

Lysenko, D. O. (2019). Green bonds: A tool for managing environmental risks. In *Financial literacy—a guarantee of the well-being of the population: Proceedings of the All-Russian Scientific and Practical Conference* (pp. 313–314). St. Petersburg State University of Industrial Technologies and Design.

Lysenko, D. O. (2021). *Prospects for "green" bonds in the Russian financial market. Financial Management, 1*, 54–64.

Marín-Rodríguez, N. J., González-Ruiz, J. D., & Botero, S. (2022). Dynamic relationships among green bonds, CO_2 emissions, and oil prices. *Frontiers of Environmental Science & Engineering, 10*, 992726. https://doi.org/10.3389/fenvs.2022.992726. https://www.frontiersin.org/articles/10.3389/fenvs.2022.992726/full

Morozova, G. V., Filichkina, Yu. Yu., & Eremina, O. I. (2021). Green bonds as a responsible investment tool: International experience and Russian practice.

Contentus, 3. https://cyberleninka.ru/article/n/zelenye-obligatsii-kak-instrument-response-investirovaniya-mezhdunarodnyy-opyt-i-rossiyskaya-praktika

Ordov, K. V., Tserceil, Yu. S., & Lysenko, D. O. (2022). Trends in the development of the green bond market: Prospects for development in the electric power industry of the Russian Federation. *Financial Life, 2*, 10–16.

Refinitive information and analytical terminal Reports. Official website. https://ir.thomsonreuters.com/financial-information/annual-reports

Report OECD. (2015). *Green bonds Mobilising the debt capital markets for a low-carbon transition.* https://www.oecd.org/environment/cc/Green%20bonds%20PP%20%5Bf3%5D%20%5Blr%5D.pdf

Reports of Federal State Statistics Service of the Russian Federation. Official website. https://rosstat.gov.ru/statistics/accounts

Rannou, Y., Barneto, P., & Boutabba, M. A. (2020). *Green bond market vs. carbon market in Europe: Two different trajectories but some complementarities.* https://hal.uca.fr/hal-02981422/document

Xiaohang Rena, Yiying Lia, Cheng Yanb, Fenghua Wena, & Luc (2022). *The interrelationship between the carbon market and the green bonds market: Evidence from wavelet quantile-on-quantile method.* https://www.researchgate.net/publication/359274702_The_interrelationship_between_the_carbon_market_and_the_green_bonds_market_Evidence_from_wavelet_quantile-on-quantile_method

Zatsarnaya, N. A. (2022). Evaluation of the efficiency of ESG-transformation of Russian companies for sustainable spatial development of the country. In *Global uncertainty. Development or degradation of the world economy?* Collection of articles of the XI International scientific conference. In 2 volumes (Volume 2, pp. 103–109). Plekhanov Russian University of Economics. https://www.elibrary.ru/download/elibrary_49590229_86744668.pdf

Paweł Dec & Jacek Wysocki

Threats to the Financing of Eco-Investments in Polish Cities and Towns

1. Introduction

At present, it has become increasingly popular to discuss the need to transform existing cities and towns into "green (that is, ecological) cities" that would be oriented toward coexistence with the surrounding nature and whose further development would be guided by the concept of sustainable development. The discussion on the "green transformation" of urban areas is gaining importance, as this is a consequence of the unfolding global environmental crisis.

It seems, therefore, that in the near future the managers and administrators of urban settlements will have to pay attention to the development of projects, that will be environmentally friendly and will allow their urban centers to transform into "green cities" that operate according to the principles of eco-development (Grzymała, 2016a). It is also important for urban communities to play an active part in these plans and feel responsible for co-creating environmentally friendly cities and towns. However, to meet this challenge, three key issues need to be taken into consideration: the willingness to undertake eco-investments (and preferably eco-innovations), social acceptance of such environmental investments (resulting from environmental awareness) and the availability of funds for these projects (along with the ability to effectively apply for financing).

The latter of these three issues seems to be a particularly important one, as the lack of possibilities to obtain financing for eco-investments (also referred to later in this chapter as "pro-ecological investments," "pro-environmental investments" or "green investments") will constitute a severe obstacle for the efforts to make Polish cities and towns more environmentally friendly, especially in the context where prospects of increased revenue inflows to city budgets are limited. Thus, the main objective of this article will be to assess the risks to the financing of pro-environmental investments in urban settings, arising as an adverse effect of the COVID-19 pandemic or the war in Ukraine (as direct causes of the current economic crisis).

2. Directions of Changes in the Development of Cities in Poland

A city should develop so that this will bring benefits to its residents and the communities living in the surrounding area and, perhaps above all, to the natural environment around it. It can therefore be assumed that the need to protect the environment, on which every city has an impact, was what advanced the concept of "green cities," that is, cities that will develop sustainably and therefore, not pose a threat to nature. One should remember that the concept of green cities emerged as early as in the late 1960s and early 1970s (Rapoport, 2014), to be later partly identified with either the concept of sustainable cities (Jenks & Jones, 2010) or the concept of smart cities (Cavada et al., 2014). At present, no green city in its pure form exists, although some examples of eco-cities can be found, such as the zero-emission Masdar City in the UAE (Dziedzic, 2015), or the cities ranked according to various "eco" solutions, as described by Z. Grzymała (2016b).

Difficulties in defining a "green" or "eco" city are also a result of differing approaches to the concept itself. For example, an eco-city would be defined as offering its inhabitants a clean environment, self-sufficient, based on renewable resources, responsibly disposing of or recycling the waste it generates and not causing pollution to harm its inhabitants and the environment (Brodowicz et al., 2015). In the context of modern circumstances, it is worth extending this definition to include the aspect of so-called sustainability, by adding that such a city should also be a location that strikes a balance between economic, social and environmental issues, as it is in the case of corporate sustainability (Wysocki, 2021). In other words, it is about incorporating the principles of sustainable development into the concept of ecological cities. This is particularly important as the concept of sustainable development itself has been incorporated into the economic policies of various countries for quite a long time. Apart from this, it forms the basis for the identification of the 17 Sustainable Development Goals of the 2030 Agenda. One of these is Goal 11, which is about sustainable cities and communities, emphasizing that a key objective is to "Make cities and human settlements inclusive, safe, resilient and sustainable" (United Nations, 2021). This is compounded by excessive consumerism, overproduction of waste, and climate changes resulting from the deterioration of the natural environment (Ripple et al., 2020).

Analyzing the views and aspects presented above, one can accept that " 'green' cities" in Poland should be defined at least by the following characteristics: rational use of energy and water resources, proper waste management, low-emission transport, a high proportion of green areas, and that—at the same time—they should aim at the application of eco-innovations and smart IT solutions (Dziedzic, 2015).

While the proposed direction of changes in urban development should be considered appropriate, we should remember that ecological cities are still a matter of the future which will not come into existence overnight, especially in Poland. Cities representing larger or smaller concentrations of people who work and live there should, therefore, provide these people, in first order, with appropriate conditions for functioning and living. This, however, is not only about the construction of functional housing estates, but above all, about the availability of public services: that is, access to educational, cultural, social welfare and health care facilities, essential administrative services, means of transportation, and also about access to green spaces for active outdoor recreation and contact with nature. This is all the more important as Polish cities and towns are among the most polluted in Europe in terms of dust particles (e.g., Opoczno, Żywiec, Rybnik), although there are also exceptions that can boast clean air or a friendly attitude toward the environment (Suwałki, Słupsk, Zielona Góra) (Statistics Poland, 2021). In the next step, the aim could be to carry out extensive pro-ecological investment projects in key areas that determine the smooth functioning of the urban structure, but also generate significant risks for residents and the natural environment. Key issues here appear to be pro-ecological actions with regard to electricity, heat and water supply services, sewage treatment, landfilling, disposal and recycling of waste, and the development of green areas.

3. Eco-Investments in Cities and Threats to Their Implementation

Cities are today the primary place to live for the majority of people around the world. This situation is not expected to change and by 2050, more than 66 % of the world's population will live in them as a result of the greater opportunities that cities offer in terms of finding work, self-development or improving the quality of life (Szymańska et al., 2016). Unfortunately, the urban future does not only involve benefits and also has its dark sides. Cities that do not develop sustainably generate numerous hazards for their residents and the natural environment. This situation is influenced by the rapid growth of urban populations, resulting from the global demographic explosion that has continued since the beginning of the previous century (Lin et al., 2018) or from urbanization in the broader sense (Henzelmann et al., 2011). In effect, there is a congestion of living space, overcrowding, lack of accessibility to municipal services, increasing crime rates, and the generation of large amounts of various types of pollution. The latter affect not only human health, but also pose a gigantic threat to the natural environment in and around cities, also spreading to a global scale (Dec & Wysocki, 2022).

Answers or solutions to environmental problems can be found in any eco-friendly initiatives, but in particular in pro-environmental investments that would gradually eliminate the threats to the environment present in cities and/or caused by them. It makes sense to undertake these investments, as they have long been a leading theme in the activities of many countries and NGOs at a global level (Korzeniowski, 2012). At this point, however, one should emphasize the importance of ecological innovations, also known as eco-innovations, which are perceived as a fundamental element of sustainable development which simultaneously contributes to it (Rennings, 2000). The main objective of implementing eco-innovations is environmental considerations (European Commission, 2011), and the common feature of all definitions of eco-innovation is the environmental aspect and the ecological benefits that accrue to all beneficiaries of such innovations (Wysocki, 2021), and thus also to the cities represented by their authorities.

Key eco-investments in cities include those that will be innovative (or will ft the typical eco-innovation models), will be based on or use modern information technologies and will be implemented across different areas of urban infrastructure covering various aspects of life (housing, services, transport, roads, social and environmental infrastructure). At the same time, their scope should include (Brodowicz et al., 2015; Grzymała, 2016b; Leźnicki & Lewandowska, 2016; Szymańska et al., 2016). A strategic approach and the creation of so-called green urban development strategies can be extremely helpful in the implementation of these eco-investments (Szelągowska & Bryx, 2016); these strategies should preferably be modeled on plans implemented in companies, but with a focus on smart and sustainable growth conducive to social inclusion.

As a result, the problem of financing eco-investments from the budgets of Polish cities poses a real threat to the execution of these projects, as cities lack sufficient own or external capital (e.g., in the form of loans, credit facilities, bond issues or EU grants). In addition, many Polish cities are still under severe budgetary pressure as a result of declining and reduced revenues, slim prospects for future tax revenue growth, and because of their relatively high levels of debt (PWC, 2012). This time it is a result of the crisis caused by the COVID-19 pandemic (Geels et al., 2022; Griffiths et al., 2021; Kunzmann, 2020), the war in Ukraine (Kuzemko et al., 2022), and the absence of funds from the National Recovery Plan (Kozlowski, 2022; Sgambati, 2022).

The private sector's role in financing urban infrastructure appears to be a foregone conclusion and is rather not to be replaced, although cities may also obtain subsidies for public green investments from the state budget. While the opportunities are out there, yet given the state's growing budget deficit and numerous interested parties, acquiring these funds is no easy task. Still, cities in Poland may apply for funds from the Strategic Investment Program, the Government's Local Investment Fund (RFIL), where support is non-repayable and comes from the COVID-19 Countermeasure Fund, and the National Recovery and Resilience Plan (NRP)—aimed at rebuilding the economy and minimizing the impact of the crisis caused by the COVID-19 pandemic.

4. Analysis of the Problems of Financing Pro-Ecological Investments in Cities: Case Studies

This section will discuss a selection of examples of cities which have won awards for eco-investments and which are currently experiencing severe problems in maintaining balanced budgets.

In Krakow, a local government unit, under the name Climate-Energy-Water Management (KEGW), was set up with the aim of being one of the first in Poland to adapt the city to climate change (11). KEGW has been operating since January 1, 2020, and is engaged primarily in the construction and maintenance of the city's drainage system, flood protection, as well as investments in renewable energy sources. The most important of investments of KEGW are: the improvement of the rainwater management system through an inventory of the network of ditches and canals carrying rainwater, their modernization and construction, the design and creation of retention reservoirs of various sizes, rain gardens and other elements of green-blue infrastructure aimed at more efficient rainwater management in the city of Krakow. Another action is to reduce atmospheric greenhouse gas emissions through a program to improve the energy efficiency of public buildings. To achieve this, an energy and utility management system for municipal buildings has been developed, and investments are being prepared for the thermo-modernization of buildings and their adaptation to modern technical and environmental requirements. Further plans include electricity generation from renewable sources (including the construction of high-power photovoltaic farms on brownfield and degraded land) and intensifying the development of distributed electricity generation based on individual rooftop photovoltaic installations or energy production systems within energy clusters and cooperatives. All these developments require substantial financial support and, in the face of the energy crisis, rising inflation, or the continuing uncertainty related to the armed conflict in Ukraine. Such support may be scaled back or even temporarily suspended and postponed. In addition, an important threat is the rising cost of debt servicing and the search for new sources of funding. City budget deficits confirm this—for Krakow, the 2023 deficit has been planned at more than PLN 1.082 billion (12). As a result, the eco-investments that are carried out are mostly those initiated in previous years, and among them mainly those for new road investments and repairs to the most dilapidated infrastructure. In addition to this, the city has had to significantly increase its funding for educational facilities as the current government has shifted this responsibility to local authorities.

In Szczecin, pro-ecological investments focus on the expansion and modernization of the water supply and sewage infrastructure (through the use of the latest water production and sewage treatment technology) at an estimated cost of a quarter of a billion zlotys (13). Thanks to this, city residents will not only receive a continuous supply of clean and safe water, but the problem of the efficient collection and treatment of wastewater will also disappear. The main water pipeline and the water production plant will be modernized, and asbestos cement will also be removed from the water network. In addition, renovation work will be carried out at the wastewater treatment plant so that it will meet the highest possible environmental standards. Further green investments in renewable energy sources are planned, namely the construction of new photovoltaic farms to provide cheaper energy for water supply facilities. Given the fact that city's own sources already provide more than 25 % of the energy required by Szczecin's waterworks, these are tangible and quantifiable savings. The structure of financing eco-investments in these urban areas in Szczecin is based on the use of own funds as well as available subsidies and preferential loans. This is intended to keep the cost of debt servicing relatively low, yet has unfortunately proved extremely difficult from 2022 onward due to galloping inflation (16). However, Szczecin's administrators are consistently focusing on pro-environmental measures, guided by the idea of Floating Garden 2050, which means promoting a responsible approach to the management of natural resources, the city's return to the waterfront, care for the environment and investments that enhance the quality of life. An example of a specific action of this kind was the construction and commissioning of the Eco Generator waste incineration plant. The difficult year of 2022 (already mentioned) also caused financial problems in Szczecin, with the consequence that a significant budget deficit (PLN 165 million) has been planned for 2023 and many previously planned investments were downsized or postponed.

In the city of Wrocław, which experienced a major flood in 1997 (which the recent hit Netflix "High Water" is based on), four retention reservoirs with a total capacity of more than 60,000 m^3 (the capacity of 19 Olympic-sized swimming pools) were built as part of environmentally friendly investments (18). Each reservoir has a capacity of over 15,000 cubic meters and is 15 meters high. In addition, pumping stations, an air deodorization station, a transformer station, a network of pipelines and technical chambers have also been built. All this is designed to minimize the effects of climate change and unforeseen weather phenomena. The difficult budget period in 2023 (planned deficit of PLN 667 million) resulted in the reduction of planned investment projects to only key infrastructural ones (construction of roads, bridges, a tram line). At the same time, the typically eco-investments were reduced to those related to the replacement of heating equipment with environmentally friendly solutions (resulting in the reduction of air emissions of substances such as PM2.5, PM10, carbon dioxide, and benzo-a-pyrene). The main threat to the financing of investments by the city, including pro-ecological investments, is the freeze of Personal Income Tax (PIT), inflation and the high cost of services (primarily fuel costs). The structure of the city's revenues is as follows: own income accounts for 72 %, grants and funds from the state budget—6 %, general subsidy (including education)—19 %, and subsidies for the implementation of tasks with the participation of EU funds—3 %. Thus, efforts to increase the share of own income must come first.

One Polish city that stands out for its efficient waste management is Gdynia. It is here that soft funding, that is, increasing the level of education of residents on waste management, should be particularly emphasized (14). In addition to this, a second distinctive feature of the city is the establishment of the first electric vehicle charging station in Poland, using electricity recovered from trolleybuses (in the process of decelerating these vehicles). It was implemented as part of two EU projects (EfficienCE and CAR). A mobile charging station of this type offers significant advantages over traditional solutions, as the connection of such a station does not require additional installation costs and cuts investment time. In addition, it offers the possibility to increase the time of use of the available overhead power line infrastructure to a full twenty-four-hour period at no additional cost. The station could potentially be upgraded in the future with an intelligent energy monitoring system to control the level of energy consumption in the overhead line and detect which one is not being used. Thanks to the energy storage reservoir in the charger's battery (lithium-ion battery), the requirements for connecting it to the public electricity grid are minimal and do not require the involvement of significant financial and technical resources. Gdynia's planned budget deficit for 2023 is PLN 194 million, so the number of investment projects will mostly include road infrastructure, communication and education (17). Projects in the field of eco-investments—energy modernization of public buildings in Gdynia—will be negligible, which again confirms that there is a financing barrier to these types of projects if no sufficient revenues flow to the municipal budget. These units have suffered the greatest losses from the changes in personal taxes, and Gdynia alone will receive more than PLN 57 million less from this source.

5. Conclusion

The examples of cities and towns analyzed in this paper illustrate different types of pro-ecological (eco, green) investments initiated and implemented by these entities. Their scale, scope or duration vary and are determined by the specific characteristics and needs of individual cities and towns. However, all these cases reveal a clearly noticeable obstacle impeding the progress of such projects—namely, the lack of assured funding sources. City authorities have given priority to investments in infrastructure associated with the construction of roads, the development of urban transport systems or the construction of public buildings and facilities. pro-ecological investments, although present in urban plans, did not constitute major items in their budgets. Still, the efforts toward the continuation of these projects, aimed above all at reducing the most polluting heating sources, must be appreciated. There is a need for long-term governmental support for cities and towns in their environmental aspirations, as these are directly linked to the residents' health. Hence, ensuring stable funding for these types of projects cannot be left solely to the discretion of municipal authorities, as it has been shown to be case studies in the research to date, but it should be included in strategic programs of a nationwide reach and, above all, in the state government environmental policies, which—with regard to the natural environment—must be guided by the principle: *Primum non nocere, secundum cavere, tertium sanare* [First do no harm, then prevent and finally heal].

References

Brodowicz, D. P., Pospieszny, P., & Grzymała, Z. (2015). *Eco Cities*. CeDeWu.

Cavada, M., Hunt, D. V. L., & Rogers, Ch. D. F. (2014). *Smart cities: Contradicting definitions and unclear measures.* World Sustainability Forum—Conference Proceedings Paper.

Dec, P., & Wysocki, J. (2022). In search of non-obvious relationships between greenhouse gas or particulate matter emissions, renewable energy and corruption. *Energies*, *15*, 1347. https://doi.org/10.3390/en15041347

Dziedzic, S. (2015) Ekologiczne miasta przyszłości. Masdar City - studium przypadku. *Prace Naukowe Uniwersytetu Ekonomicznego we Wrocławiu, 409.*

European Commission. (2011). *Innovation for a sustainable future—The eco-innovation action plan (Eco-AP).* http://eur-lex.europa.eu/legal-content/EN/TXT/?uri=CELEX%3A52011DC0899

Geels, F. W., Pereira, G. I., & Pinkse, J. (2022). Moving beyond opportunity narratives in COVID-19 green recoveries: A comparative analysis of public investment plans in France, Germany, and the United Kingdom. *Energy Research & Social Science*, *84*, 102368.

Griffiths, S., Del Rio, D. F., & Sovacool, B. (2021). Policy mixes to achieve sustainable mobility after the COVID-19 crisis. *Renewable and Sustainable Energy Reviews*, *143*, 110919.

Grzymała, Z. (2016a). Ekoinnowacje w miastach. *Kwartalnik Nauk o Przedsiębiorstwie*, *38*(1), 103–104.

Grzymała, Z. (2016b). Miasta ekologiczne—studia przypadków i perspektywy rozwoju. *Prace Naukowe Uniwersytetu Ekonomicznego we Wrocławiu*, *432*, 61–66.

Henzelmann, T., Schaible, S., Stoever, M., Meditz, H. (2011). *Geneza zielonej rewolucji ekonomicznej i spodziewane korzyści*, in: *Zielony wzrost, zielony zysk.* A Wolters Kluwer Business.

Herbuś, I. (2015). Innowacje w miastach jako wyznacznik sukcesu współczesnych samorządów. *Zeszyty Naukowe Politechniki Częstochowskiej*, *19*, 35–43. https://kegw.krakow.pl/o-nas/ [15.01.2023].

https://krakow.wyborcza.pl/krakow/7,44425,29288840,budzet-krakowa-na-2023-rok-przyjety-rekordowy-deficyt-ponad.html?disableRedirects=true [15.01.2023].

https://wiadomosci.szczecin.eu/artykul/mieszkancy/cwierc-miliarda-na-inwestycje-w-ekologie-w-szczecinie [15.01.2023].

https://www.gdynia.pl/co-nowego,2774/gdynskie-innowacje-wsrod-najlepszych-w-polsce,565890 [15.01.2023].

https://www.portalsamorzadowy.pl/finanse/5-56-mld-zl-dochodow-w-przyszlorocznym-budzecie-wroclawia-deficyt-667-mln-zl,417639.html [15.01.2023].

https://www.rmf24.pl/regiony/szczecin/news-prawie-20-inwestycji-na-wylocie-szczecin-ma-projekt-budzetu,nId,6412536#crp_state=1 [15.01.2023].

https://www.trojmiasto.pl/wiadomosci/Budzet-Gdyni-przeglosowany-Beda-inwestycje-i-deficyt-n173859.html [15.01.2023].

https://www.wroclaw.pl/dla-mieszkanca/najwazniejsze-inwestycje-we-wroclawiu-w-2023-roku-co-gdzie-i-kiedy-szczegoly-daty [15.01.2023].

Jenks, M., & Jones, C., (2010). *Dimensions of the sustainable city*. Springer Science + Business Media B.V. http://www.mopt.org.pt/uploads/1/8/5/5/1855409/mikejenks.pdf

Korzeniowski, P. (2012). *Bezpieczeństwo Ekologiczne Jako Instytucja Prawna Ochrony Środowiska*. Wyd. Uniwersytetu Łódzkiego.

Kozłowski, J. (2022). Difficult road to decarbonize economy. *Nauka*, *4*, 7–35.

Kunzmann, K. R. (2020). Smart cities after COVID-19: Ten narratives. *disP-The Planning Review*, *56*(2), 20–31.

Kuzemko, C., Blondeel, M., Dupont, C., & Brisbois, M. C. (2022). Russia's war on Ukraine, European energy policy responses & implications for sustainable transformations. *Energy Research & Social Science*, *93*, 102842.

Leźnicki, M., & Lewandowska, A. (2016). Contemporary concepts of a city in the context of sustainable development: Perspective of humanities and natural sciences. *Problemy Ekorozwoju*, *11*(2), 45–54.

Lin, D., Hanscom, L., Murthy, A., Galli, A., Evans, M., Neil, E. and others. (2018). Ecological footprint accounting for countries: updates and results of the National Footprint Accounts, 2012–2018. *Resources, 7, 58.*

PWC. (2012). *Wyzwania inwestycyjne głównych miast Polski—perspektywa 2035.* Raport, www.pwc.pl/miasta

Rapoport, E., (2014). Utopian visions and real estate dreams: The eco-city past, present and future. *Geography Compass*, *8*(2).

Rennings, K. (2000). Redefining innovation, eco-innovation research and contribution from ecological economics. *Ecological Economics*, *32*, 319–322.

Ripple, W. J., Wolf, C., Newsome, T. M., Barnard, P., & Moomaw, W. R. (2020). World scientists' warning of a climate emergency. *BioScience*, *70*, 1, 8–12. https://doi.org/10.1093/biosci/biz088

Sgambati, S. (2022). The interventions of the Italian Recovery and Resilience Plan: Energy efficiency in urban areas. *TeMA-Journal of Land Use, Mobility and Environment*, *15*(2), 345–351.

Szelągowska, A., & Bryx, M. (red.). (2016). *Eco-innovations in cities*. CeDeWu.

Szymańska, D., Korolko, M., Grzelak-Kostulska, E., & Lewandowska, A. (2016). *Ekoinnowacje w miastach*. Wydawnictwo Naukowe Uniwersytetu Mikołaja Kopernika.

United Nations. (2021). *The Sustainable Development Goals Report 2021*. https://unstats.un.org/sdgs/report/2021/, https://www.unep.org/resources/making-peace-nature. [5.03.2023].

Wysocki, J. (2021). Innovative green initiatives in the manufacturing SME sector in Poland. *Sustainability*, *13*, 2386.

Rosyadi Rosyadi & Fitriadi Fitriadi

Rethinking and Design Facilitating Pillars SME Performance: An Illustration for Indonesia

1. Introduction

From the macroeconomic context, small and medium enterprises or what are often called "SMEs" are proven to have a strong level of resilience. Since the era of the monetary crash, in 1997 to be precise, SMEs in Indonesia have avoided financial shocks and have instead controlled the national economy without colliding with the banking sector (Wijaya et al., 2022). In fact, Aktürk (2014), Bourletidis and Triantafyllopoulos (2014), Soininen (2012) and Tambunan (2019) argued that many business people and workers under SMEs survived the global economic recession in 2008. For example, the advantage of SMEs in Turkey, Greece, Finland and Indonesia compared to other industries lies in their independence, the majority of which do not always depend on external factors. Surprisingly, even though the increase in Indonesian SME members over the past two decades has been quite expansive, reforms to improving the "status" of small to medium units have been quite difficult (e.g., Gunawan et al., 2022; Panjaitan et al., 2021). Several layers of business in the manufacturing and provision of food and beverage accommodation, for example, have stagnant phases that have not evolved toward relying on internet access such as: digital payments, promotional tactics, sales formats, and distribution variations, or switching to services.

The principles contained in the Law of the Republic of Indonesia Number: 20 of 2008 imply that SMEs are productive business incubators owned by individuals or business materials under individuals who have small and medium scale criteria. In a more detailed explanation stated in "article 1" of the regulation, it also defines SMEs into two parts. First, small business is a type of business from the economic sector that was established independently, either by an individual or a business entity, where this small scale does not include branches of large and medium businesses based on ownership, power, and shares according to the criteria for small businesses regulated in regulations. Second, the concentration of medium-scale businesses is bridged by certain individuals or business entities that are not included in the small and large business branches from the aspect of ownership and involvement of power.

The characteristics of SMEs and their criteria are implied in Indonesian Government Regulation Number: 7 (articles 35–36) of 2021 on the convenience, protection and empowerment of cooperatives and SMEs which are contained in the Law of the Republic of Indonesia Number: 11 of 2020 concerning job creation. From several SMEs, there were still mistakes in studying the new regulations, some of them even admitted that they had not received this information. In this new regulation, there are striking differences from the previous ones, which are summarized in Table 1.

Table 1. SME specifications regarding legality

Portion	Class	
	Small	**Medium**
Capital (excluding buildings/business premises and land)	Business nominal in the range of IDR 1 billion–IDR 5 billion	Business nominal in the range of IDR 15 billion–IDR 50 billion
Sale	Every year a maximum of IDR 2 billion–IDR 15 billion	Every year a maximum of IDR 15 billion–IDR 50 billion

Source: Muhammad (2021) and Wijaya dan Kurniawan (2022)

Actually, there are extra criteria in the regulations governing technical SMEs, including: implementation of environmentally friendly technology, local content, incentives and incentives, quantity of labor, investment value, net worth, and accumulated turnover. However, any institution may formulate criteria and modify them for certain interests, even though it is conditional. In terms of explanation, there is no difference between the new version and the old version, that is, Law Number: 20 of 2008 of SMEs, where the net worth of SMEs was originally defined according to the results of annual sales or receipt of net profits after deducting all tax obligations, now transforming and switching to SME capital originating from loans and personal assets.

Table 2. Profile of Indonesian SMEs

Scope	2017	2018	2019	2020
Total of SMEs (units)	62.9 million	64.2 million	65.46 million	46.6 million
Transaction (IDR)	7,820 trillion	8,573 trillion	8,400 trillion	4,235 trillion
GDP (%)	5.71	5.1	5.54	6.20
Labor (%)	97	91	96	73

Source: Ministry of Cooperatives and SMEs–Indonesia (2022)

Table 2 displays the trend of SMEs in Indonesia from 2017 to 2020. The annual publication by the Ministry of Cooperatives and SMEs–Indonesia (2022) reports that there was an increase in the number of SMEs during three periods detected from 2017: 62.9 million to 2018: 64.2 million (2.07 %), then in 2019: 65.46 million (1.96 %). The success of SMEs did not last long. After the SARS-CoV-2 attack, Indonesian SME units decreased dramatically from 2019: 65.46 million to 2020: 46.6 million, or around -28.82 %. This bad effect also affects the transaction value, for example, from 2019: 8,400 trillion to 2020: 4,235 trillion or in other words the transaction decreased by 49.58 %. In particular, there is an increase in the contribution of SMEs to the constant Gross Domestic Product (GDP) in 2020 reaching 6.20 % compared to 2018: 5.54 %, where growth has increased 11.91 % from the previous period. Uniquely, this positive achievement was not matched by growth in the workforce, whose absorption decreased by 23.96 %. What is crucial is that when the pandemic polemic in early 2020 also hit Indonesia, there was a large reduction in skilled workers in the SME sector, such as from 2019: 96 % to 2020: 73 %. At the employment level, the percentage of SME workers in the overall workforce is more dominant than other sectors. Another anomaly is shown by the picture of labor absorption in 2018, which grew -6.19 %. Comparatively, considering that in 2017 SME workers were 97 %, but not for 2018 which illustrates that labor absorption in SMEs is 91 %. Thus, it is also connected to GDP growth reaching -10.68 % or a decrease of 0.61 % from 2017 to 2018.

On the micro perspective, there are serious dynamics that impede the development of SMEs, which are sometimes overlooked by intellectuals. In detail, studies from various multidisciplinary relatively highlight entrepreneurial talent referring to organizational structure (Cunningham et al., 2022), HR recruitment (Hu et al., 2022), technology adoption (van der Westhuizen & Goyayi, 2020; Zenebe et al., 2018), managerial skills (Petríková & Soroková, 2016), interest in participation (García-Rodríguez et al., 2019; Nguyen et al., 2021), training (Ho et al., 2018), and business networking (Fernández-Pérez et al., 2014). In fact, an academic paper that discusses or evaluates the performance of SMEs is inseparable from the concrete foundation that forms the ability of SMEs. Ideally, the success of a business is determined by two specifications: internal–external.

In operating SMEs, at first glance, there are no significant obstacles. In practice, this business intensity looks normal and in their manifestation when encountered, at first glance it does not require careful planning, elaboration, monitoring. Interestingly, the general situation is not a priority, but the entrepreneurial spirit has been running naturally since the past decade. The realization is, although creativity and innovation are born from the talents of personnel or groups of entrepreneurs without a comprehensive understanding, it actually triggers a fatal construct of thinking and actualization. Surprisingly, SMEs activists who are involved in various clusters often ignore adaptive business principles. Take, for example, how is the strategy toward sustainable business performance? Then, what pillars are highlighted? And from that condition, which one needs to be addressed so that it is not misinterpreted? Of course, this is the basis that must be observed by every businessman. Simply put, the fundamental dimension in generating business is examined the quality of the actors, including the capabilities of human resources (HR).

2. Basic Concepts

2.1. Input Attribute

Some research explains that HR strategy determines competitive advantage. Inan and Bititci (2015) conclude that competitive advantage is highly dependent on the HR quality. Meanwhile, Strandskov (2006) focuses on the sources and processes of generating competitive advantage. Rehman et al. (2019) actually emphasizes the importance of the strategic role of organizational capability to create, maintain, and expand competitive advantage. This is an accumulation of resources that are expected to have the potential to strengthen competitive advantage (Holdford, 2018; Omerzel & Gulev, 2011). Othman et al. (2015) and Srivastava et al. (2013) argue that managing resources, skills and competencies is the key to achieving a competitive advantage.

Capital budgeting focuses on financial work plans for investment projects. Because the time span is long, the risk is high (AlKulaib et al., 2016). Business capital planning is required to predict future income and costs. Five universal principles for capital budgeting include friendly investment, net cash flow, weighted average cost of capital, investment value and sources of financing, and finally market share (Dangol, 2011). By learning that, businesses are able to optimally control working capital, enabling their organizations to gain market share and sustain success. Given that managing working capital can act as a safeguard against the power of access to capital, tactically maintaining operational excellence (de Souza Michelon et al., 2021).

When a business has been operating for a long time, it gains more experience to put its customers first. The length of business has a systematic effect on increasing turnover (Ivanova, 2019; Vizano et al., 2021).

2.2. Process Attribute

From a broad angle, turnover is an element that influences business performance (Ali Qalati et al., 2020; Popa & Ciobanu, 2014). The progress of a business depends on business flexibility and excellence. Knowing the first advantage is marketing, then this will facilitate market penetration and have implications for sales levels. The more superior the marketing staff, the more directly proportional to the acquisition of turnover. The strength of the business network has a positive effect on turnover (Newbery et al., 2016).

A business needs to include the size of the influence of labor costs on production results. Siregar and Mahardika (2019) studied if wage recapitulation is related to production volume, so that it will adjust labor performance. All wage payments are limited by the volume of production and the skills of the workers (e.g., Deming, 2017; Lollo & O'Rourke, 2020). Control motivation and proper accounting for labor costs is an active concern by businesses (Hopper & Armstrong, 1991). A reliable, cooperative, loyal and wise workforce is a significant contribution to the operations of a business entity.

2.3. Output Attribute

Market share is central to entering into market competition. How good is an SME that outperforms its competitors, it must follow the desired market share (Išoraitė, 2018). Fundamental changes are worth considering quite significant costs, where there is a need for labor costs, overhead costs, promotion costs, transportation costs, and other items highlighted.

In this era of intense competition, profit is truly the standard for business growth. Claro et al. (2016), Joshi (2021), and Kouakou et al. (2019) analyzed mindset changes that move to understand profit and not make turnover in assessing business progress. In fact, the current business challenges highlight how costs incurred in production are smaller and running a business to exceed the greatest profit (Wulandari et al., 2018).

3. Conclusions

There is an imbalance in the premise that overrides the essence of input: governance and HR, process: finance, and output: product and profit goals, makes us aware to provide a simple understanding, clarify, and review the urgency of these three components in the "SME landscape." The next session is a description of the aspects that stimulate the existence of SMEs including: capital, business experience, turnover, workers' wages, market share, and profit.

The point, there are three hierarchies that are mutually bound in the business framework, including: input–process–output. All three are attached to each other to determine the prospects of a business (see Figure 1). In the business stage, the first instrument is determined by HR. Business management is always dealing with HR, where the management will form or form healthy business behavior. Not only does he control his employees, but the owner is also motivated to correct mistakes in running the business, improve services, boost productivity, to a more explicit "upgrading mindset" as the era changes. Besides the level of formal education, efforts to absorb business knowledge are also inspired by soft skill courses and certain business programs.

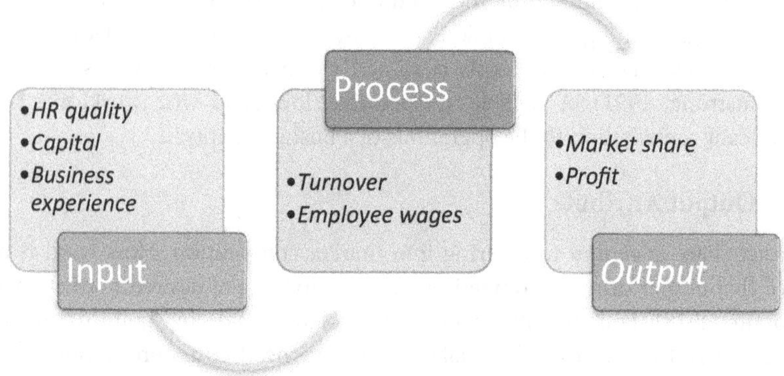

Figure 1. Three key elements of doing business
Source: Created by Authors

Equally important is capital. The element of capital is the initial driver of a business. Broadly speaking, capital can be obtained from trade/credit loans, personal assets, or from partnerships such as: government grants, corporate social responsibility (CSR) assistance, and other types of support. After gaining actual insight, conducive safeguards should be able to guarantee future business. Business experience does not automatically reduce business risk, but through examination and correction of business problems. Related to this, the accuracy of professional information and communication about business certainly facilitates business instincts. To maintain business, closely related to turnover. Normatively, turnover is often considered a business motive that must be prioritized. In fact, there are differences in the literature between turnover and profit. Turnover or gross profit is measured by adding up all income. On the one hand, profit is calculated as all revenue minus the cost of goods sold or the cost of production. Our opinion focuses that business profit is net income, while turnover is gross income apart from employee wages, fixed capital, current capital, commercial forest installments or credit, land leases or business premises leases for those who contract, business entity tax payments, land property tax only for those who have permanent buildings, employee income tax, and other business expenses.

The position of the workforce in business is not only limited to the capacity of the production process, but also plays a role in pioneering, making, popularizing, up to marketing a service or product that creates new business networks. In the SME procedure, business schemes are empowered independently/individually or in groups. In other words, the SMEs wheel is dominated by household groups. Facts on the ground, found the mobility of SMEs that are vulnerable to being affected due to the "family bond" system. Mechanisms for business collaboration that involve the family, or what is abbreviated as "family business," tend to cause many and complicated internal rifts, for example the reality in campus environments and small traders.

From an employment perspective, nominal wages are not separated by a "portrait of demand–supply." If the wage standard is disproportionate according to the work load at the lower–middle–upper level or employees who are selected based on business decision-making control, high work motives and involvement, loyalty, employment contracts, the principle of fairness, or a particular job desk, then there is a wage gap. Not to mention talking about financial regulatory conflicts and disparities in profit sharing, also weakening design and business obsession, which in turn breaks emotional ties. With family conditions that are not harmonious, it can damage business methods and disrupt profitability segmentation. From a sustainability perspective, poor competence prevents entrepreneurship from entering a competitive market. At the same time, business habitat, which is the opposite of market penetration, can trigger uncertainty, one of which is losses in a certain period. Holistically, profit symbolizes achievement in business progress. But, the orientation is not only to pursue profit and return ability ratios, but also how to creating sustainable SMEs.

References

Aktürk, O. (2014). Impact of the economic crisis on SMEs (small and medium-sized enterprises): A general evaluation on SMEs in Turkey. *European Journal of Social Science Education and Research, 1*(1), 169–173.

Ali Qalati, S., Li, W., Ahmed, N., Ali Mirani, M., & Khan, A. (2020). Examining the factors affecting SME performance: The mediating role of social media adoption. *Sustainability, 13*(1), 75.

AlKulaib, Y. A., Al-Jassar, S. A., & Al-Saad, K. (2016). Theory and practice in capital budgeting: Evidence from Kuwait. *Journal of Applied Business Research, 32*(4), 1273–1286.

Bourletidis, K., & Triantafyllopoulos, Y. (2014). SMEs survival in time of crisis: Strategies, tactics and commercial success stories. *Procedia—Social and Behavioral Sciences, 148*, 639–644.

Claro, S., Paunesku, D., & Dweck, C. S. (2016). Growth mindset tempers the effects of poverty on academic achievement. *PNAS Proceedings of the National Academy of Sciences of the United States of America, 113*(31), 8664–8668.

Cunningham, J. A., Lehmann, E. E., & Menter, M. (2022). The organizational architecture of entrepreneurial universities across the stages of entrepreneurship: A conceptual framework. *Small Business Economics, 59*(4), 11–27.

Dangol, J., Sthapit, A., & Rajbhandari, R. (2011). Capital budgeting practices in Nepali manufacturing companies. *PYC Nepal Journal of Management, IV*(1), 5–20.

de Souza Michelon, P., Lunkes, R. J., & Bornia, A. C. (2021). Use of capital budgeting practices: An integrative review. *Enfoque Reflexão Contábil, 40*(3), 139–157.

Deming, D. J. (2017). The growing importance of social skills in the labor market. *The Quarterly Journal of Economics, 132*(4), 1593–1640.

Fernández-Pérez, V., Esther Alonso-Galicia, P., del Mar Fuentes-Fuentes, M., & Rodriguez-Ariza, L. (2014). Business social networks and academics' entrepreneurial intentions. *Industrial Management & Data Systems, 114*(2), 292–320.

García-Rodríguez, F., Gutiérrez-Taño, D., & Ruiz-Rosa, I. (2019). Analysis of the potential of entrepreneurship education in young children. *Entrepreneurship Research Journal, 9*(1), 20170064.

Gunawan, A. A., Bloemer, J., van Riel, A. C. R., & Essers, C. (2022). Institutional barriers and facilitators of sustainability for Indonesian batik SMEs: A policy agenda. *Sustainability, 14*(14), 8772.

Ho, R. M.-H., Uy, M. A., Kang, B. N. Y., & Chan, K. Y. (2018). Impact of entrepreneurship training on entrepreneurial efficacy and alertness among adolescent youth. *Frontiers in Education*, *3*, 13.

Holdford, D. A. (2018). Resource-based theory of competitive advantage—A framework for pharmacy practice innovation research. *Pharmacy Practice*, *16*(3), 1351.

Hopper, T., & Armstrong, P. (1991). Cost accounting, controlling labour and the rise of conglomerates. *Accounting Organizations and Society*, *16*(5–6), 405–438.

Hu, W., Liu, H., Tian, Y., Zhang, X., & Mao, Y. (2022). Entrepreneurial capability, career development, and entrepreneurial intention: Evidence from China's HR survey data. *Frontiers in Psychology*, *13*, 870706.

Inan, G. G., & Bititci, U. S. (2015). Understanding organizational capabilities and dynamic capabilities in the context of micro enterprises: A research agenda. *Procedia—Social and Behavioral Sciences*, *210*, 310–319.

Išoraitė, M. (2018). The competitive advantages theoretical aspects. *EcoForum*, *7*(1), 1–6.

Ivanova, M. (2019). Main factors of turnover and minimization of turnover rate within business organization. *Open Journal for Research in Economics*, *2*(2), 73–84.

Joshi, P. L. (2021). Change management and management of mindset. *Asian Journal of Management and Commerce*, *2*(1), 83–86.

Kouakou, K. K. E., Li, C., Akolgo, I. G., & Tchamekwen, A. M. (2019). Evolution view of entrepreneurial mindset theory. *International Journal of Business and Social Science*, *10*(6), 116–129.

Lollo, N., & O'Rourke, D. (2020). Factory benefits to paying workers more: The critical role of compensation systems in apparel manufacturing. *PloS One*, *15*(2), e0227510.

Ministry of Cooperatives and SMEs–Indonesia. (2022). *Snapshot of cooperatives and SMEs in numbers*. https://kemenkopukm.go.id/kumkm-dalam-angka/?IB8Z3ncCNetVUlXj8FqDS14nrFMp9T09eYQtUhamysFr8Y9hXI [Accessed on January 6, 2022].

Muhammad, F. (2021). Enforcing omnibus law: Formalizing micro, small, and medium enterprises in Indonesia using behavioural science. *Indonesian Law Journal*, *14*(2), 95–118.

Newbery, R., Gorton, M., Phillipson, J., & Atterton, J. (2016). Sustaining business networks: Understanding the benefit bundles sought by members of local business associations. *Environment and Planning C: Government and Policy*, *34*(7), 1267–1283.

Nguyen, T. T., Nguyen, L. T. P., Phan, H. T. T., & Vu, A. T. (2021). Impact of entrepreneurship extracurricular activities and inspiration on entrepreneurial intention: Mediator and moderator effect. *SAGE Open*, *11*(3), 21582440211.

Omerzel, D. G., & Gulev, R. E. (2011). Knowledge resources and competitive advantage. *Managing Global Transitions*, *9*(4), 335–354.

Othman, R., Arshad, R., Aris, N. A., & Arif, S. M. M. (2015). Organizational resources and sustained competitive advantage of cooperative organizations in Malaysia. *Procedia—Social and Behavioral Sciences*, *170*, 120–127.

Panjaitan, J. M., Timur, R. P., & Sumiyana, S. (2021). How does the Government of Indonesia empower SMEs? An analysis of the social cognition found in newspapers. *Journal of Entrepreneurship in Emerging Economies*, *13*(5), 765–790.

Petríková, D., & Soroková, T. (2016). Managerial and entrepreneurial skills as determinants of business. *Polish Journal of Management Studies*, *14*(1), 184–194.

Popa, A.-E., & Ciobanu, R. (2014). The financial factors that influence the profitability of SMEs. *International Journal of Academic Research in Economics and Management Sciences*, *3*(4), 177–185.

Rehman, Su., Mohamed, R., & Ayoup, H. (2019). The mediating role of organizational capabilities between organizational performance and its determinants. *Journal of Global Entrepreneurship Research*, *9*(30), 1–23.

Siregar, M. U., & Mahardika, D. E. K. (2019). An implementation of web-based payroll information system in Universitas Proklamasi 45 Yogyakarta. *International Journal on Informatics for Development*, *7*(2), 48–53.

Soininen, J., Puumalainen, K., Sjögrén, H., & Syrjä, P. (2012). The impact of global economic crisis on SMEs: Does entrepreneurial orientation matter?. *Management Research Review*, *35*(10), 927–944.

Srivastava, M., Franklin, A., & Martinette, L. (2013). Building a sustainable competitive advantage. *Journal of Technology Management and Innovation*, *8*(2), 47–60.

Strandskov, J. (2006). Sources of competitive advantages and business performance. *Journal of Business Economics and Management*, *7*(3), 119–129.

Tambunan, T. T. H. (2019). The impact of the economic crisis on micro, small, and medium enterprises and their crisis mitigation measures in Southeast Asia with reference to Indonesia. *Asia & the Pacific Policy Studies*, *6*(1), 19–39.

van der Westhuizen, T., & Goyayi, M. J. (2020). The influence of technology on entrepreneurial self-efficacy development for online business start-up in developing nations. *The International Journal of Entrepreneurship and Innovation*, *21*(3), 168–177.

Vizano, N. A., Sutawidjaya, A. H., & Endri, E. (2021). The effect of compensation and career on turnover intention: Evidence from Indonesia. *The Journal of Asian Finance, Economics and Business*, *8*(1), 471–478.

Wijaya, A., Awaluddin, M., & Kurniawan, A. E. (2022). The essence of fuel and energy consumptions to stimulate MSMEs industries and exports: An empirical story for Indonesia. *International Journal of Energy Economics and Policy*, *12*(2), 386–393.

Wijaya, A., & Kurniawan, A. (2022). *Ekonomi koperasi: Ekspedisi, dinamika dan tinjauan di Indonesia*. Madza Media.

Wulandari, M., Abror, A., & Inggita, M. (2018). The effect of production cost to net profit: A case study of PT. Indorama Synthetics Tbk. *Emerging Markets: Business and Management Studies Journal*, *4*(1), 54–64.

Zenebe, A., Alsaaty, F. M., & Anyiwo, D. (2018). Relationship between individual's entrepreneurship intention, and adoption and knowledge of information technology and its applications: An empirical study. *Journal of Small Business & Entrepreneurship*, *30*(3), 215–232.

Pedro Fernandes da Anunciação &
Ricardo Daniel da Assuncao Pereira Petiz

Governance to Digital Transformation in Portuguese Public Local Authorities

1. Introduction

The emergence of powerful digital technologies, digital platforms, and digital infrastructures has transformed economic organizations (Baiyere et al., 2020). Modern organizations are increasingly served by information systems and technology (IST) (Filet et al., 2020). The alignment between business and IST increases organizational performance (Gerow et al., 2015), offers economic value, and contributes to the enterprise success (Castellanos & Correal, 2013). So, digital transformation (DT) represents a strategic challenge and constitutes a critical success factor for an organization's sustainability.

The reality of DT is not the same in all economic sectors. Strategies for DT development of the public sector are limited to Portuguese Government initiatives and are mainly reflected in their ministries. The remaining public sector, particularly the public local authorities, faces greater difficulties with technological development. Technologies such as Internet-of-Things (IoT), Artificial Intelligence (AI), and Analytics have several associated challenges and offer some opportunities that must be identified and globally understood by the public institutions.

The easy adoption of technological innovation by consumers pressures organizations to consider technologies as a competitive market driver factor (Anunciação, 2012). According to the IDC (2019), in 2023, 75 % of all information technologies expenses will be related to third-platform technologies and more than 90 % of all companies will create digital native environments to thrive in the digital economy. Regarding this macro-trend, managers should understand the direction of development and prepare their organizations to act in a strong digital context of operation.

Digital skills are not only technological and demand Governance and management capabilities (Anunciação, 2012). Modern societies are organizational economies, based on the sharing of operational activities, and IST dependence generates significant economic vulnerability. Some dimensions have become critical, such as architecture, security, privacy, etc. (Anunciação et al., 2014). Economic relations are increasingly dependent on the IST availability.

The integration of the digital dimension into people's lives and organizations' activities will increase the collective responsibility of the various stakeholders to ensure the availability and operation of the technological infrastructure (Bounfour, 2016).

DT at the public level can be a harder process (breaking information silos, overcoming legal barriers, mindsets, and rooted culture) (Gray & Parce, 2017). However, public institutions have to respond in short timeframes, making their *modus operandi* more flexible according to the demands of society. The integration of a multiplicity of devices, systems, requirements, activities, processes, and users, among others, challenges the mastery of architecture and demands a new urbanistic approach to organizations, economy, and society (Anunciação, 2015, 2016).

The impact of new IST, such as AI, for example, requires a more aggressive approach concerning DT (Tiersky, 2017) and represents an opportunity for human beings to rethink the economy and society. In the economic field, AI allows smarter choices and offers the possibility of developing predictive analyses, linking work environments, personal life, leisure, health, etc. But what will be the frontier? Will we have technologies to decide for humans? What will be the economic impact?

Most business leaders agree that digital transformation is disrupting their business or soon will be, but fewer than half have enacted a digital strategy (Olavsrud, 2017). According to Westerman (2018), technology does not provide value to a business. Instead, the value of technology comes from doing business differently. For example, e-commerce is not about the Internet; it is about selling differently. Analytics is not about databases and machine language algorithms, it is about understanding customers better (Westerman, 2018).

Technologies will continue to dictate the vision and managers need to understand changes. DT stimulates traditional organizations to become "Exponential Organizations" (Ismail, 2014). The economy demands better, faster, and cheaper organizations. So, the ability to provide digital products and services will be an economic critical factor and demands the greatest challenge to organizational digital change. Making digital transformation a business strategy is a management imperative (Albanese & Manning, 2016), but it depends on the managers' ability and vision.

2. What Is Digital Transformation?

DT is seen as changes in a company's business model, products, or organizational structures or in the automation of processes as a result of digital technologies (Hess et al., 2016); changes induced by digital technologies throughout an organization (Chanias & Hess, 2016); realignment of technology and new business models to engage digital customers (Schuchmann & Seufert, 2015); use of new digital technologies to enable significant business improvements (Piccinini et al., 2015); or business models driven by the changes associated with the application of digital technology in all aspects of human society (Henriette et al., 2015). DT presupposes business change (Weill & Woerner, 2018); new business models (Verhoefa et al., 2021); business and economic value creation (Nambisan et al., 2019); business transformation (Vial, 2019); customer's experience (Weill & Woerner, 2018); data asset (Rogers, 2016); digital capabilities (Evans, 2017); digital governance (Evans, 2017); digital infrastructure (de Reuver et al., 2018); digital innovation (de Reuver et al., 2018); digital platform (Nambisan et al., 2019); digital strategies and vision (Evans, 2017); digital Technologies (Evans, 2017); organizational capabilities (Li et al., 2018); organizational change (Nambisan et al., 2019); organizational culture (Tronvoll et al., 2020); organizational transformation (Warner & Wager, 2019); people and culture (Verhoefa et al., 2021); speed of change (Tiersky, 2017).

We can consider DT as a set of disruptive changes that institutions must make in business, organizations, structures, and forms of operation and development of several activities based on the digital paradigm. It must be understood as a strategic decision and a management process of immersion in the technological potential and inclusion (Hess et al., 2016).

3. Digital Transformation in Portuguese Public Administration

Digital technologies are transforming the public sector by affecting applications, processes, culture, structure, and civil servants' responsibilities and tasks (Tangi et al., 2020). The new way of working needs proactivity, real-time service, and contextual adaptation (Jassens, 2021). In the Portuguese case, IoT, Cloud, and AI have accelerated the opportunity for public service DT and forced public institutions to the opening of new dynamic operations. Through the approval of the Information and Communication Technology (ICT) Strategy 2020, by the Council of Ministers Resolution number 108/2017 (RD, 2017), a project was born to provide the Central Public Administration with a comprehensive strategy for the promotion and improvement of ICT to support administrative simplification, and providing citizens with better quality in public services. The measures/actions predicted under the ICT 2020 Strategy are based on three specific axes: integration and interoperability; innovation, and competitiveness;

and sharing of resources. This strategy aimed to make digital services more straightforward, more accessible, and inclusive; enhance the uptake of digital services by citizens and businesses; and ensure sustainable development in the field of DT. The challenge was to provide information, products, and services in digital support by public institutions, to any citizen at any time and place, and generate value for all agents and sectors.

In this sense, the decisive role of ICT in the evolution and modernization of the public sector still has a long way to go when compared to the level of innovation of private institutions. The strategy for DT in Portugal has been focused only on technologies, seeking to achieve from them the simplification of services.

4. Objectives and Methodology

The main objective of this work was to analyze the general understanding of the relevant governance dimensions associated with the digital transformation of Portuguese local authorities.

So, the general managers and the IST managers of Portuguese local authorities responded to a survey classifying the relevance of a set of dimensions proposed for a DT process governance, considering the importance of IST innovation in local public administration digital development.

In this sense, four nuclear areas have been proposed to frame the digital transformation process: business (impact of digital transformation on activities carried out—sustainability perspective); organizational (needs for adjustment in the architecture and operating dynamics—efficiency perspective); IST (specification of various conditions to provide services in a digital context—effectiveness perspective); and Client/Citizens (client services—economic value generation perspective). The study covers three geographical axes: the interior of the country, traditionally less developed and with an older population, the coast of Portugal, more developed and with more significant economic resources, and the metropolitan area of the Portuguese capital with a higher population index, development, and more cosmopolitan characteristics.

5. Results and Analysis

The study was funded in nine municipalities: three on the coast, three in the interior, and three around the capital (Lisbon). This distribution allows general coverage of the national territory, including regions with different levels of development. Regarding the area/function performed, 33 % have management/administration responsibilities while 78 % have intermediate IST management responsibilities. This result emphasizes the participation of management with responsibility for defining digital service strategies and the IST area that is responsible for the systems' designing and administration to support the digital operation.

Regarding the hierarchical level, the results show that those surveyed perform intermediate organizational functions (22 % as top management; 67 % as intermediate management; and 11 % do not know/do not answer).

All the surveyed consider relevant the DT theme. However, they attributed more relevance to the "Information Systems and Technologies" and "Clients/Citizens." If we consider the "very relevant" as a closer management position to the inclusion of these areas in organizational strategies, it seems contradictory that "Business" and "Organizational" have not recorded a higher level of relevance in the context of the DT opportunities. In this sense, it can be considered that there is a weak strategic acuity in terms of economic value generation in the digital context as well as a weak commitment to change the organizational dynamics associated with digital process transformation. The percentage of Dk/Da responses reinforces this analysis.

Table 1. Domain relevance in the digital transformation process

Domains	1	2	3	4	Dk/Da
Business	–	–	78 %	11 %	11 %
Organization	–	–	67 %	33 %	–
IST	–	–	33 %	67 %	–
Clients/Citizens	–	–	33 %	56 %	11 %

The results show an inverted positioning of the synergistic effects that IST can have in business as well as the role of organizational dynamics and capabilities in meeting the needs of clients/citizens. Eventually, the relevance of these two areas is due to the predominant role that IST plays, not only in the organizational perspective but also in the daily lives of people's needs.

A more detailed analysis needs to be done to better understand the results obtained. Thus, starting with the domain of "Business," it is possible to see, as shown in Table 2, that all dimensions are relevant. However, the dimensions of "Vision/Strategy" and "Communication" stand out for their response expressiveness.

It would be expected that the dimension of "Products/Services" would have a more relevant expression as one of the traditional axes associated with these transformation processes associated with the limited development and availability of digital products and services. On the other hand, "Vision/Strategy" is very relevant. Still, it does not seem to make much sense that there is a significant difference between the two, as both the vision and strategy focus on the market and, consequently, on products and services.

It is also interesting to note that the high relevance given to these dimensions ("Vision/Strategy," "Innovation," and "Communication"), in the process of digital business transformation, does not match the relevance previously attributed to the domain itself, as shown in Table 1. It would make perfect sense, by most of the answers given to these three dimensions, that the domain was also relevant to respondents, which is not the case. However, despite this apparent incoherence, it is possible to infer that these dimensions may be the focus of management in future digital transformation processes.

Table 2. Business dimensions relevance in digital transformation process

"Business" dimensions	1	2	3	4	Dk/Da
Vision/Strategy	–	–	11 %	89 %	–
Innovation	–	–	44 %	56 %	–
Products/Services	–	–	67 %	33 %	–
Communication	–	–	22 %	78 %	–

In the analysis of the dimensions associated with the organization domain, Table 3 shows that "Operation" and "Skills" are assumed to be the most important. The most considerable relevance of operations in the organizational field may correspond to their centrality in supporting activities, products, and services through digital platforms. Some of the respondents underestimate the need for skills in a digital context. They are also assuming that the impacts on the structure are insignificant.

Table 3. Organization dimensions relevance in digital transformation process

"Organization" dimensions	1	2	3	4	Dk/Da
Digital Capability	–	–	67 %	33 %	–
Structure	–	11 %	44 %	44 %	–
Operation	–	–	22 %	78 %	–
Skills	–	11 %	33 %	56 %	–

Although the "Organization" domain has been classified as relevant, as shown through Table 1, only 50 % of its dimensions ("Operation" and "Skills") stands out as very significant, which appears to be incoherent.

In the analysis of the dimensions associated with the "IST" domain, it appears, through Table 4, that the dimensions of "Governance," "Integration" and "Safety" stand out in the classification assigned. Among these three dimensions, "Integration" takes higher expression, possibly justified by the critical role that IST assume in the provision of global information services to citizens and the presence of legacy systems that traditionally characterize Public Administration.

Table 4. IST dimensions relevance in digital transformation process

"Information Systems and Technologies" dimensions	1	2	3	4	Dk/Da
IST Governance	–	–	33 %	67 %	–
Integration	–	–	22 %	78 %	–
Digital platform	–	–	56 %	44 %	–
Safety	–	–	33 %	67 %	–

The relevance of most dimensions associated with IST follows the relevance of the domain itself, all being considered very relevant. Interestingly, this is the first domain where there is a general agreement between the domain and its dimensions.

Regarding "Clients/Citizens" it is possible to see, through Table 5, the most relevant dimensions are "Knowledge" and "Value." "Value" is the most expressive dimension indicated and corresponds to the need to generate economic and social value in relations with public local authorities. Since they are public entities and there is no competition, this dimension does not assume cultural relevance among professionals. Since it's based on the relationship between citizens and local public authorities, there is an obligation of legal involvement in many matters of citizenship, such as building permits, residence certificates, etc. For this reason, the result of the responses associated with this dimension is surprising.

Table 5. Client/Citizen dimension relevance in digital transformation process

"Clients/Citizens" dimensions	1	2	3	4	Dk/Da
Value	–	11 %	22 %	67 %	–
Knowledge	–	–	44 %	56 %	–
Service levels	–	11 %	44 %	44 %	–
Digital interaction	–	–	56 %	44 %	–

It is also noteworthy that the dimensions associated with the "Clients/Citizens" domain do not follow the significant relevance previously attributed to the domain itself, which can be seen in Table 1.

Generally, the analysis of the results allows us to witness a general awareness of the relevance of the domains and dimensions associated with digital transformation.

Still, within the scope of the first research objective, a comparative analysis was carried out between the various geographical regions studied to verify the result's confluence or divergence. Thus, concerning the domains, as shown in Table 6, in the Lisbon area there is relevant unanimity regarding the impact of digital transformation on the activities and services (Business) provided by public local authorities. The reasons for these results were probably associated with higher population pressure, and levels of knowledge, and a different culture regarding technology adoption. This evidence can be understood as a strategic need for new ways of providing public services.

The public local authorities in the Portugal's coastline considered the IST context important in the digital transformation process. It is possible that this evidence was associated with the many organizational legacy systems that can condition the feasibility and success of a digital transformation process.

Table 6. Relevance domains of digital transformation by geographical area

Domains	Greater Lisbon Area					Interior of Portugal					Coast of Portugal				
	1	2	3	4	Dk/Da	1	2	3	4	Dk/Da	1	2	3	4	Dk/Da
Business	–	–	100 %	–	–	–	–	67 %	33 %	–	–	–	67 %	0 %	33 %
Organization	–	–	67 %	33 %	–	–	–	67 %	33 %	–	–	–	67 %	33 %	–
Information Systems	–	–	67 %	33 %	–	–	–	33 %	67 %	–	–	–	–	100 %	–
Customers/ Citizens	–	–	33 %	67 %	–	–	–	67 %	33 %	–	–	–	–	67 %	33 %

Concerning the dimensions of "Business," as shown in Table 7, the "Greater Lisbon Area" is unanimous in the relevance of the "Vision/Strategy" dimension in the digital transformation process. Interestingly, the dimension of "Products/Services" in all regions does not have a relevant expression, which appears to be a contradiction in the sense that digital transformation aims at the provision of products and services in a digital environment. The local authorities from the coast also stand out by highlighting the dimensions of "Vision/Strategy" and "Communication" as the most decisive in the process of digital transformation.

Table 7. Business dimensions relevance in digital transformation process by geographical area

Business Dimensions	Greater Lisbon Area					Interior of Portugal					Coast of Portugal				
	1	2	3	4	Dk/Da	1	2	3	4	Dk/Da	1	2	3	4	Dk/Da
Vision/Strategy	–	–	–	100 %	–	–	–	33 %	67 %	–	–	–	–	100 %	–
Innovation	–	–	33 %	67 %	–	–	–	67 %	33 %	–	–	–	33 %	67 %	–
Products/Services	–	–	67 %	33 %	–	–	–	67 %	33 %	–	–	–	67 %	33 %	–
Communication	–	–	33 %	67 %	–	–	–	33 %	67 %	–	–	–	–	100 %	–

Regarding the dimensions of the "Organization" area, as shown in Table 8, it stands out in the "Greater Lisbon Area," a reference to the impact of "Operation" in the context of digital transformation, with unanimity regarding its importance. Concerning "digital capacities," the public local authorities from the interior of the country consider it unanimously relevant. Still, its consideration is not imperative in the context of the impacts of digital transformation strategies. It should also be noted that the dimensions of "Skills" and "Structure," in the field of "Organization," has little relevance in inland public local authorities.

Table 8. Organization dimensions relevance in digital transformation process by geographical area

Dimensions of the Organization	Greater Lisbon Area					Interior of Portugal					Coast of Portugal				
	1	2	3	4	Dk/Da	1	2	3	4	Dk/Da	1	2	3	4	Dk/Da
Digital Capability	–	–	67 %	33 %	–	–	–	100 %	–	–	–	–	33 %	67 %	–
Structure	–	–	33 %	67 %	–	–	–	67 %	33 %	–	–	33 %	33 %	33 %	–
Operation	–	–	–	100 %	–	–	–	33 %	67 %	–	–	–	33 %	67 %	–
Skills	–	–	33 %	67 %	–	–	–	67 %	33 %	–	–	33 %	–	67 %	–

As far as the dimensions of the "Information Systems and Technologies" domain are concerned, as shown in Table 9, the "Greater Lisbon Area" stands out again by agreeing with the responses in most dimensions. There is consensus on the relevance about the "IST Governance," "Integration" and "Security" dimensions in the digital transformation process. In this sense too, most coastal public local authorities accept the high importance of these dimensions. Regarding the interior of Portugal, it is possible to note that the majority only stress the perspective of integration as being relevant.

Table 9. IST dimension relevance in digital transformation process by geographical area

Dimensions of IST	**Greater Lisbon Area**					**Interior of Portugal**					**Coast of Portugal**				
	1	**2**	**3**	**4**	**Dk/ Da**	**1**	**2**	**3**	**4**	**Dk/ Da**	**1**	**2**	**3**	**4**	**Dk/ Da**
IST Governance	–	–	–	100 %	–	–	–	67 %	33 %	–	–		33 %	67 %	–
Integration	–	–	–	100 %	–	–	–	33 %	67 %	–	–	–	33 %	67 %	–
Digital platform	–	–	33 %	67 %	–	–	–	67 %	33 %	–	–	–	67 %	33 %	–
Safety	–	–	–	100 %	–	–	–	67 %	33 %	–	–	–	33 %	67 %	–

The last domain "Clients/Citizens" stands out for the dispersion of the valuations attributed. There is no evidence of unanimity in the valorization of some dimensions. However, there is only consensus on the "Value" dimension.

Table 10. Clients/citizens dimension relevance in digital transformation process by geographical area

Clients/ Citizens Dimension	**Greater Lisbon Area**					**Interior of Portugal**					**Coast of Portugal**				
	1	**2**	**3**	**4**	**Dk/ Da**	**1**	**2**	**3**	**4**	**Dk/ Da**	**1**	**2**	**3**	**4**	**Dk/ Da**
Digital interaction	–	–	67 %	33 %	–	–	–	33 %	67 %	–	–	–	67 %	33 %	–
Service levels	–	–	33 %	67 %	–	–	–	67 %	33 %	–	–	33 %	33 %	33 %	–
Knowledge	–	–	67 %	33 %	–	–	–	33 %	67 %	–	–	–	33 %	67 %	–
Value	–	–	33 %	67 %	–	–	–	33 %	67 %	–	–	33 %	–	67 %	–

6. Conclusions

The results of this study allow concluding that the dimensions proposed to combine and complement the dimensions identified by the academic authors in the literature review. This work sought a logical sequencing of the dimensions and subdimensions to serve the DT management of public institutions. With this objective, it is possible to verify a significant concordance with the proposed dimensions and subdimensions. In the study carried out, the greatest preponderance is centered on technologies and on people/citizens.

It should be noted that respondents assume the relevance of DT. However, this does not mean that there is a clear strategy for it. Any DT strategy can be compromised when there are different perceptions about the relevance of the different dimensions between the different decision levels. So, business, organizational, IST, and clients/citizens' perspectives should have an umbilical relationship. Businesses and customers are at the beginning and the end of the value chain, and the organization and IST support them.

The differences in the relevance of the dimensions are even more clear when the analysis focuses on the geographical areas of the country. This evidence can only be contradicted by a governance perspective developed by the country's governments.

As Evans (2017) points out that DT must be a journey. It should aim at continuous improvement or permanent adaptation and should not be a destination. It is a journey that begins with market listening. The challenge includes the provision of instruments, means, and services that meet the needs, and expectations. Also, with DT, management must create knowledge about the organization and clients/citizens, through the identification of their expectations, adjustment of operations, development of new products and services in digital support, and generation of value for the different stakeholders, to allow a better understanding of the mission of local authorities.

Limitations and future research work:

Although the survey only covers a sample of public local authorities in Portugal, it would be interesting to extend this study to other authorities to obtain a better understanding of the reality of the country. As future work, it is expected to develop a model that facilitates the management of the change inherent in DT. After identifying the most relevant dimensions, it would be interesting to increase the degree of detail associated with the reorganization of public institutions.

References

Albanese, J., & Manning, B. (2016). *REVIVE: How to transform traditional businesses into digital leaders*. Pearson Education.

Anunciação, P. F. (2012). *Ethics, society and information systems, new realities in information management and management*. Sílabo Publishing (in Portuguese).

Anunciação, P. F. (2015). Organizational change through information systems: Metavision-project management model in internet banking. In *Handbook of research on effective project management through the integration of knowledge and innovation* (Chapter 23, pp. 450–465). IGI Global.

Anunciação, P. F. (2016). Organizational urbanism: A value proposal for the generation of organizational intelligence to healthcare institutions—The case of a Portuguese hospital center. In *Handbook of research on information architecture and management in modern organizations* (Chapter 21, pp. 458–486). IGI Global.

Anunciação, P. F., Esteves, F. J. M., & Santos, J. R. (2014). Some information systems requirements in view of organizational sustainability in an information society. *Information Resource Management Journal*, *27*(1), 21–35.

Baiyere, A., Hannu, S., & Tommi, T. (2020). Digital transformation and the new logics of business process management. *European Journal of Information Systems*, *29*(3), 238–259. https://doi.org/10.1080/0960085X.2020.1718007

Bounfour, A. (2016). *Digital futures, digital transformation—From lean production to acceluction*. Springer.

Castellanos, C., & Correal, D. (2013). A framework for alignment of data and processes architectures applied in a government institution. *Journal on Data Semantics*, *2*(2–3), 61–74. https://doi.org/10.1007/s13740-013-0021-5

Chanias, S., & Hess, T., (2016). Understanding digital transformation strategy formation: Insights from Europe's automotive industry. In *PACIS 2016 Proceedings, Chiayi*.

de Reuver, M., Sorensen, C., & Basole, R. C. (2018). The digital platform: A research agenda. *Journal of Information Technology*, *33*(2), 124–135, https://doi.org/10.1057/s41265-016-0033-3

Evans, N. D. (2017). *Assessing your organization's digital transformation maturity*. CIO.

Filet, P., Van de Wetering, R., & Joosten, S. (2020). Enterprise architecture alignment. In Sorensen, F. L. (Ed.), *Enterprise architecture and service-oriented architecture* (Chapter 1, pp. 13–52). Nova Science Publishers.

Gerow, J. E., Grover, V., & Thatcher, J. (2015). Alignment's nomological network: Theory and evaluation. *Information & Management*. https://doi.org/10.1016/j.im.2015.12.006

Gray, J., & Pearce, C. (2017, 10 March). Canberra hack digital transformation: Digital transformation. *The Australian Financial Review*, p. 28.

Henriette, E., Feki, M., & Boughzala, I. (2015). The shape of digital transformation: A systematic literature review. *MCIS 2015 Proceedings*, Paper 10, pp. 1–19.

Hess, T., Matt, C., Benlian, A., & Wiesbock, F. (2016). Options for formulating a digital transformation strategy. *MIS Quarterly Executive*, *15*(2), 123–139.

IDC. (2019). ICT directory—Enterprises and professionals 2019–2020. In *The essential guide to digital transformation* (in Portuguese).

Ismail, S. (2014). *Exponential organizations—Why new organizations are ten times better, faster, and cheaper than yours (and what go do about it).* DIVERSIONBOOKS.

Jassens, J. (2021). Digital transformation journeys: The future is now. In *Encyclopedia of organizational knowledge, administration, and technology* (Chapter 176, pp. 2533–2550). IGI Global.

Li, L., Su, F., Zhang, W., & Mao, J. Y. (2018). Digital transformation by SME entrepreneurs: A capability perspective. *Information Systems Journal* (Special Issue), *28*(6), 1129–1157. http://doi.org/10.1111/isj.12153

Nambisan, S., Wright, M., & Feldman, M. (2019). The digital transformation of innovation and entrepreneurship: Progress, challenges and key themes. *Research Policy* (Special Issue), *48*(8), Article 103773. http://doi.org/10.1016/j.respol.2019.03.018

Olavsrud, T. (2017). *Digital disruption is coming but most businesses don't have a plan*. CIO.

Piccinini, E., Hanelt, A., Gregory, R., & Kolbe, L. (2015). Transforming industrial business: The impact of digital transformation on automotive organizations. In *36th International Conference on Information Systems, Fort Worth*.

RD. (2017). Republic Diary n.º 143/2017, Série I of 2017-07-26. https://data.dre.pt/eli/resolconsmin/108/2017/07/26/p/dre/pt/html (in Portuguese).

Rogers, D. L. (2016). *The digital transformation playbook—Rethink your business for the digital age*. Columbia Business School Publishing.

Schuchmann, D., & Seufert, S. (2015). Corporate learning in times of digital transformation: A conceptual framework and service portfolio for the learning function in banking organizations. *iJAC*, *8*(1), 31–39.

Tangi, L., Janssen, M., Benedetti, M., & Noci, G. (2020). 19th IFIP WG 8.5 International conference on electronic government, EGOV 2020, held in conjunction with the IFIP WG 8.5 International Conference on Electronic Participation, ePart 2020, and the International Conference for E-Democracy and Open Government Conference, CeDEM 2020, Linkoping, August 31, 2020–September 2, 2020.

Tiersky, H. (2017). *The 5 key drivers of digital transformation today*. CIO.

Tronvoll, B., Sklyar, A., Sorhammar, D., & Kowalkowski, C. (2020). Transformational shifts through digital servitization. *Industrial Marketing Management*, *89*, 293–305. http://doi.org/10.1016/j.indmarman.2020.02.005

Verhoefa P. C., Broekhuizena, T., Bart, Y., Bhattacharya, A., Dong, J. Q., Fabian, N., & Haenlein, M. (2021). Digital transformation: A multidisciplinary reflection and research agenda. *Journal of Business Research*, *122*, 889–901.

Vial, G. (2019). Understanding digital transformation: A review and a research agenda. *The Journal of Strategic Information Systems*, *28*(2), 118–144.

Warner, K. S. R., & Wager, M. (2019). Building dynamic capabilities for digital transformation: An ongoing process of strategic renewal. *Long Range Planning*, *52*(3), 326–349. http://doi.org/10.1016/j.lrp.2018.12.001

Weill, P., & Woerner, S. L. (2018). Is your company ready for a digital future?. *MIT Sloan Management Review, Cambridge*, *59*(2), 21–25.

Westerman, G. (2018). Your company doesn't need a digital strategy. *MIT Sloan Management Review; Cambridge*, *59*(3), 1–5.

Pedro Fernandes da Anunciação &
Elisabete da Conceição Gandrita Giroto

Integrated Responsibility Center as a New Organizational Model of Health Institutions in Portugal: The Case of a Central Portuguese Hospital

1. Introduction

Economic organizations have been experiencing significant pressures over the last decades. The economic and financial instabilities associated with the markets and society and, finally, the COVID-19 pandemic are some examples of the need to adapt to change that have challenged the management from a sustainability perspective (Anunciação & Geada, 2021). Health institutions have been no exception to these challenges. Being highly dependent on governmental policies, Health institutions have been subject to frequent political and governmental changes in many countries (Mikkola & Stormi, 2020; Saltman & Duran, 2016). Pressure from government budget constraints, population aging, and growth, the increase in private competition in the sector, or the effects of the pandemic, among other factors, have forced the search for better efficiency and management indices for their performance (CAHS, 2023; Harfouche, 2008).

One of the main focuses of government intervention in these institutions has been the need to reduce costs. This reduction has been reflected in the frequent adjustment of the national health system and in the organizational structures of hospitals, seeking to lighten them and thus reduce fixed costs. This reduction in structural weight has been balanced through investment in new information and communication technologies (ICT), to reduce the bureaucratic and administrative burden associated with health records and, consequently, the weight of human resources in the respective institutions. In addition to investment in ICT, other more structural strategies have been adopted, with a broader scope, which includes the splitting up of services and competencies between Hospitals and Health Centers in an attempt to respond to the demands of the population.

In addition to the strategies, whose results emerge over a longer period of time, other solutions have also been developed, some as extreme solutions and with the aim of obtaining immediate results given the scarcity of resources and organizational inability to respond, and which even include the temporary closure of services or emergency rooms, forcing patients to travel hundreds of kilometers to other hospitals outside their area of residence. In addition to this reality, guardianship requires health professionals to adopt an *open-minded* posture that makes the new and dynamic operating strategy feasible.

In the various organizational restructurings that have been carried out, the centrality of the role of information systems (IS) stands out. Besides the fact that hospital activity is Information-based and emphasizes the high importance of IS, investments in ICT always imply adjustments at the IS level. Most of the investments have been aimed at improving IS and decision-making performance. However, the respective decision-makers do not always take into account that, conceptually, besides ICT, IS also includes data/information, people/users, and defined procedures/rules. This means that the introduction of ICTs alone does not allow for obtaining advantages or benefits if the remaining elements of the systems are not reorganized or re-architected. The improvement in performance or organizational performance does not result solely from technologies, but from the information they produce, the decisions they provide, and the way they are included in organizational dynamics.

In the health sector, information represents a critical organizational asset. To have adequate and quality information it is important to have good IS. It is through the information that organizational performance is improved, and strategy is made fully meaningful, making the core processes of decision and action dynamic. To this end, there is a pressing need to identify the types of information, the processing required by IS, and the required flows, to operationalize the organizational and economic dynamics (Oliveira & Anunciação, 2023). In this logic, it is necessary to find models that value an intrinsic relationship between information, knowledge, and intelligence (Vaz, 2020), defining a strategy for generating economic value in this way.

Thus, the need for intelligent management is perceived which, based on the organizational reality, the respective characteristics, and resources, allows for the creation of value and economic and social advantages, leveraging productivity, efficiency, effectiveness, and the promotion of sustainability, through the change of the existing dynamics and processes. Management controls should be associated with strategic management, simultaneously enabling an assessment of the institution's performance in an appropriate, transparent, and timely manner (Jordan et al., 2015). Similarly, the respective management should ensure the operationalization of the organizational strategy, through the alignment with the objectives and goals to be achieved, exercising close surveillance of the processes and support systems in order to ensure consistent results with the defined sustainability policies (Jordan et al., 2015).

This is a change that is not easy or immediate in health institutions, to the extent that, as Silva (2021) states, it depends on the knowledge and analysis of the organization and its culture since this domain allows for the adaptation and adequacy of measures that help strategic planning and decision-making.

The difficulties of managing information in the public sector and non-profit organizations have long been recognized, seriously limiting the respective strategies (Kaplan & Norton, 2001). In contrast to the private sector organizations, in the public sector, it is not the financial indicators that reveal the fulfillment of the organization's mission. In this sense, it is vital for the public sector to implement objectives that are representative of its mission in the long term, which, in the case of public health, translates into ensuring timely access, quality, and effectiveness of healthcare.

2. Organizational Urbanism as a Reorganization Factor

Organizational and information systems Urbanization seeks the definition of a conceptual, coherent, integrated, and modular framework for the steering of organizational change, through the identification and framing of the various organizational systems or subsystems (functional, informational, and technological), in a relational context (Anunciação & Zorrinho, 2006). Urbanizing is in fact designing, organizing, arranging, ordering, and optimizing, that is, finding organizational solutions for a set of needs felt in the various domains. The UO aims to ensure, in a relational context, the organizational flexibility to, from activity referential and anchor points, articulate the various elements of a given system.

The vision inherent in the urbanistic approach extends far beyond organizations, businesses, departments, or the technical specifications of activities or products. Urbanism allows the creation of a larger ecosystem that facilitates the management of the multidimensional complexity of a system capable of integrating a diversity of subsystems, resources, and responsibilities within a broader scope. To this end, an approach to this domain should take into account the following dimensions (Anunciação & Zorrinho, 2006):

- Vision: expressed in a development direction and strategy through the definition and implementation of guidelines determining the development and objectives to be achieved by the organization;

- Planning: expressed in the architecture(s) that enhance the conceptualization and construction of the different aspects and respective components and systems that make up the organizational reality;
- Urban Planning: expresses the contextualization, articulation, and contribution, between the various areas or systems, aimed at ensuring a coherent and integrated operation of the overall system and, simultaneously, of each of the subsystems;
- Governance: expresses the definition of management policies and models that ensure the operation, maintenance, and coordination of the defined structure, as well as its development.

Organizational restructuring should be carried out according to a functional, informational, and technological reference framework to ensure that current and future business needs are met. The UO objective focuses on the global alignment of the organization and IS among the various intervening parties, based on the identification of the mission and global objectives. It should enable the articulation of systems, the coherent regrouping of organizational components, and the identification and closing of gaps in strict accordance with business dynamics, with a view to a quick organizational response capacity to the economy and society's demands.

3. Integrated Responsibility Centers in the Health Sector in Portugal

Hospital institutions are characterized by their high management complexity, heavy organizational structure, and high social relevance and sensitivity. Traditionally, they are structured by specialty areas, representing a significant diversity of systems, equipment, data/information, and stakeholders (health professionals and others), among other aspects.

In Portugal, the growing trend of increasing healthcare costs has raised questions related to the sustainability of hospital systems. Particularly in the public sector, this concern has been reflected in management efforts aimed at optimizing hospital systems, making them more efficient, without compromising their quality and performance. This need has been present in the various management policies that the various governments have been implementing in the area of Health, embodied in the sector reforms, with a view to improving the levels of efficiency and effectiveness (Alves, 2014; Fernandes, 2014; Harfouche, 2008).

Considering that hospitals are central and structural units of the Health System and that they present and represent great social value (Vaz, 2010), it is normal that, due to their relevance, health policies focus on these institutions.

Therefore, new management models are often sought that, by innovating, are expected to enable the achievement of good results (Casella, 2009; Vaz, 2010). This is a purpose advocated by those responsible for Health in Portugal, in the governmental domain, to the extent that they defend that the public health system should ensure social integration and cohesion by providing well-being to the population through the economic and financial sustainability of the respective institutions (Ministry of Health, 2018).

With regard to health care, the Constitution of the Portuguese Republic itself provides in article 64° n°. 1 that all citizens have the right to health protection and the duty to defend and promote it. It also states in n°. 2 of article 64 that the right to health protection is realized through a national health service that is universal and general and, considering the economic and social conditions of citizens, tends to be free of charge. In this sense, it assumes the requirement of optimizing resources, which are public, and promoting efficiency and effectiveness in the operations carried out by organizations in the public health sector.

This universal access to health care is made concrete by the Central Administration of the Health System (2023) when considering that the activities, objectives, and results to be achieved by the health care providers of the National Health Service (NHS) should ensure timely, quality and efficient access to health care, as well as develop a management culture that is rigorous, accountable, transparent and focused on meeting the health needs of all citizens. However, it is frequent to hear through the media that, given the quality of the information generated, it is not always possible to guarantee compliance with the guiding principles in a useful and timely manner. Likewise, there is not always the possibility of improving the information generated and subsequently analyzed by the Management Bodies.

The assessment of the activities performed in hospitals, in terms of the profitability of the services that are part of it, as well as the quality assurance of the activity, is considered a highly complex task. As a response to this reality, the most recent legal framework (Decree Law, 1988, 1999, 2005, 2017) provides for the creation of Integrated Responsibility Centers (CRIs) as intermediate levels of administration. The purpose of these CRIs is to decentralize and facilitate decision-making based on the grouping of homogeneous units, seeking greater technical and social efficiency, through the organization and development of their activity by responsibility and cost centers. They aim to enhance the results of health care provision, improve the accessibility of users and the quality of services provided, increasing the productivity of the resources applied (Decree Law, 2017). Some of the most relevant characteristics are the following:

- are middle management organic structures, depending on the Board of Directors, with which they establish an internal contractualization process, through which they negotiate their commitment to care and economic-financial performance for periods of three years;
- are made up of multidisciplinary teams that voluntarily propose to adhere to an organizational model guided by negotiated objectives, transparency of processes, and accountability of the parties for a common project, which recognizes and rewards collective and individual performance.
- are provided with the material resources necessary for the exercise of their activity, being responsible for the respective control of the use and rendering of accounts as regards the assistance results achieved and the associated costs and income, the latter being valued according to the approved price lists for the various contracted services.

It is assumed that CRIs should have management tools, particularly in terms of management accounting, which value all transactions with other services, internal or external to the NHS institution where they are located. The CRIs are based on individual and team accountability for the operationalization of the internal reorganization of health care institutions, motivating professionals to work in the NHS, ensuring the development of best clinical practices focused on the needs of users, adapting health institutions to contemporary forms of management that ensure economic and financial efficiency and sustainability.

It is expected that the planned autonomy will allow the use of certain facilitating tools for the strategic management of health units, through the development and implementation of more appropriate management tools, namely what concerns the control of results, increased motivation, and staff performance (van der Kolk et al., 2019). However, there is a serious risk that these CRIs may represent "autonomous islands" within an archipelago submerged by a heavily bureaucratized and centralized context.

4. Objectives and Methodology

Given the fact that the legal framework of CRIs emerged at the end of the 1980s and was established at the end of the 1990s, we now have the opportunity to perform an assessment of this innovation in order to identify the practical results achieved. Considering that this innovation was defined by government decree, the methodology associated with the case study (Yin, 2018) was adopted, and a central hospital in Portugal was chosen where a CRI was implemented.

It is a hospital unit of reference, contextualized in the provision of health care in Portugal and that aggregates a high potential of health resources in the region where it is located, originating opportunities both in terms of complementarity and reorganization of services. Its mission is to provide differentiated health care to all citizens within the scope of its responsibility and capacity, having presented, in the more recent past, several problems associated with the inability to respond to health services due to a breakdown in installed capacity. It has services with high technical differentiation that optimize existing resources, ensuring the provision of health care to a population of about 250 thousand inhabitants.

Considering the integrative nature of these CRIs, we decided to analyze and assess the advantages and benefits obtained from their creation and implementation through the adoption of the focus group methodology (Bloor et al., 2001; Queirós & Lacerda, 2013; Wilkinson, 1998). The choice of members for the focus group aimed at including the persons responsible for the areas/domains in which there was an organizational impact as a result of the creation of the CRIs. This focus group was composed of seven professionals who were responsible for the following areas: Medical; Surgical; Anesthesiology; Complementary Diagnostic Means; Research and Teaching; Financial and Budget area and Management Body.

The study was conducted in two phases. In the first stage, the dimensions that should be subject to assessment were defined. In the second, an objective assessment of the previously identified dimensions was carried out considering the results achieved in the performance of the respective activities and functions.

5. Analysis of the Results

Regarding the first phase of the study, the focus group concluded, after several interactions, that, given the purpose of its creation by the government, the most relevant dimensions for analysis of the benefits and advantages of the CRI should be the following:

- clarification of the CRI in the organic structure;
- degree of autonomy in the definition of specific strategies to meet the objectives set;
- degree of autonomy in internal contractualization;
- degree of autonomy in budget preparation and commitment;
- real capacity to define a goal-oriented organization model;
- degree of influence on the need for urbanization or organizational and IS re-architecture;
- degree of autonomy in the acquisition and management of Human Resources, Equipment, and Infrastructure, necessary for the exercise of its activity;
- evaluation and control of performance (…, productivity, efficiency, …).

In addition to these dimensions, several timely comments were made on the logic followed by the Government in relation to this innovation, and these may constitute opportunities for future studies:

- The proposed reorganization by decree-law, an institutional instrument through which the government defines the legal and functional framework of public institutions, does not seem to be the most appropriate way, especially when there is no proof of concept to validate such a change. Such a definition presupposes an adequate model for any hospital regardless of the specificities that may exist regarding organic, geographical, social, and economic particularities of the regions where they are located. The question arises, is a "tailor-made suit" for all the most adequate solution for the diversity of the existing health problems?
- the form and autonomy in the requisition of resources for the CRI, through internal contracting processes with other areas, may imply constraints in other areas. If the global resources are the same, the eventual transfer of resources to new areas may "strangle" the functioning and productivity of the areas which are more limited. The question arises: will this solution have an impact on overall productivity?
- The voluntary creation of multidisciplinary teams, as a premise for the construction of a goal-oriented organization model, is conditioned to the identification and adherence of human resources to the project. Since the main objective of the CRI is to increase the productivity, efficiency and effectiveness of hospital performance, is volunteering the option that maximizes the acquisition of the necessary skills to achieve the objectives?
- Although the principle of responsibility and budgetary autonomy is present, it is conditioned by the institution's overall budget. Can the CRIs manage the resources necessary for the exercise of their activity? What is the autonomy in defining the price of the services provided?

With regard to the second phase of the study, through the focus group, it was possible to make the following assessment in relation to the dimensions identified:

- The CRI is explained in the organic structure of the respective hospital unit;
- The degree of autonomy of the CRI in the definition of specific strategies to fulfill the defined objectives is very limited and conditioned to the global budget of the hospital unit, insofar as, legally, it is not possible to obtain external resources, either human or financial, to finance the respective CRI activities;
- The degree of autonomy in the internal "contractualization", although based on the employees' voluntary choice to be integrated into this new area, is conditioned by the impacts that their departure may have on the services where they work. In addition, this option and willingness to change may not correspond to the profile required by the CRI;
- The degree of autonomy in budget preparation and commitment is limited to the legal framework for public expenditure;
- The real capacity for orientation by objectives is limited to the approval of several hierarchical levels, from the administration to the guardianship;
- The degree of influence on the need for urbanization or organizational and IS re-architecture presupposes significant investments, with the CRI's activities being

guided by the existing IS. Changes to the IS are subject to the approval of the Board of Directors;
- Performance evaluation and control (…, productivity, efficiency, …) is dependent on the existing outputs made available by the IS.

All these findings represent significant limitations to the aims of improving the productivity, efficiency, and effectiveness of the CRIs. However, it is possible, despite all the limitations, to present a positive balance, having seen an increase of around 40 % in surgeries in one year and a consequent reduction in the surgical waiting list. The impact verified in terms of consultations also allowed a reduction in the median waiting list time for consultation.

6. Conclusions

The main objective of this study was to verify whether the creation of CRIs has improved the operation and performance of the hospital unit under analysis. The improvement in efficiency and effectiveness, especially in health care institutions, by decree is strongly limiting in relation to the defined objectives. Although it is understandable that this is a public health unit and that there is traditionally a centralized perspective on this sector, the indicators of the results obtained often depend on the characteristics and problems of the surrounding community. On the other hand, management models should be defined or given some autonomy by hospital administrations in order to be adjusted to the specificity of the respective institutions.

The results of the focus group, consolidated with the evaluation carried out, show that this new reality provides some autonomy to management, through the adoption of new financing and remuneration rules according to the volume of activity performed. However, given the existing legal and hierarchical limitations, increases in the levels of quality obtained and the associated productivity are limited.

The main reflection of the respective creation results in managerial, administrative, and decision-making autonomy and the creation of a new area (CRI) in the organizational chart. However, the need for organizational architecture, namely at the IS level, is a medium-term project whose results will not be immediate. This constraint also limits the information made available directly related to the CRI.

Limitations and future work:

The creation of CRIs in the Portuguese public health sector still raises many questions due to the lack of existing research. Given the complexity of these organizations, it will be interesting in the future to further study other management dimensions and analyze the experience of other hospital units in the country regarding the creation of CRIs. On the other hand, it will also be important to assess the benefits of this new structure among users and other stakeholders involved.

References

Alves, A. (2014). *Innovation in hospital management—40 years of April in healthcare*. Almedina (in Portuguese).

Anunciação, P. F., & Geada, N. S. (2021). Change management perceptions in Portuguese hospital institutions through ITIL. *International Journal of Healthcare Information Systems and Informatics (IJHISI)*, *16*(4), 1–20. http://doi.org/10.4018/IJHISI.20211001.oa18

Anunciação, P. F., & Zorrinho, C. (2006). *Organizational urbanism—How to manage technological shock*. Sílabo Publishing (in Portuguese).

Assembly of the Republic. (1999). Special edition. *Polymers*, *9*(4). https://doi.org/10.1590/s0104-14281999000400002 (in Portuguese).

Bloor, M., Frankland, J., Thomas, M., & Robson, K. (2001). *Focus groups in social research*. Sage Publications.

Casella, P. (2009). The hospital as a structure—Hospital governance. *Alfragide*, 289–302 (in Portuguese).

Central Administration of the Health System (CAHS). (2023, January 13). *Terms of reference for hospital contracting*. https://www.acss.min-saude.pt/wp-content/uploads/2016/10/Termos-Referencia-Contratualizacao_2023.pdf

Decree-Law nº. 19/1988, January 21, *Government Journal*, 1st Series, https://dre.pt/application/file/a/506334 (in Portuguese).

Decree-Law nº. 374/1999, September 18, *Government Journal*, 1st Series-A, 219, 6489–6493, https://dre.pt/dre/detalhe/decreto-lei/374-1999-569893 (in Portuguese).

Decree-Law nº. 233/2005, December 29, *Electronic Government Journal*, 1–39, https://dre.pt/dre/legislacao-consolidada/decreto-lei/2005-66348268-107599709 (in Portuguese).

Decree-Law nº. 18/2017, February 10, *Health Ministry, Government Journal*, 1st Series-A, 30, 694–720. http://data.dre.pt/eli/dec-lei/18/2017/02/10/p/dre/pt/html (in Portuguese).

Fernandes, A. (2014). *The public-private combination—40 years of April in healthcare*. Almedina (in Portuguese).

Harfouche, A. (2008). *Hospitals transformed into companies—Analysis of the impact on efficiency: A comparative study*. Higher Institute of Social and Political Sciences (in Portuguese).

Jordan, H., Neves, J., & Rodrigues, J. (2015). *Management control at the service of strategy and managers* (10th ed.). Áreas Publishing (in Portuguese).

Kaplan, R. S., & Norton, D. P. (2001). *Organization oriented to the strategy—The strategy-focused organization*. Campus Publishing (in Portuguese).

Mikkola, L., & Stormi, I. (2020). Lecture on change in hospital management groups. *Journal of Change Management, 21*, 287–306. Advanced online. https://doi.org/10.1080/14697017.2020.1775679

Ministry of Health. (2018, January 10). Pre-proposal of law of bases of health. pp. 1–40. https://www.sns.gov.pt/wp-content/uploads/2018/06/LEI_BASES_18062018_pre_proposta_apresentacao_INSA.pdf

Oliveira, A., & Anunciação, P. F. (2023). Information systems governance: Some dimensions to management. In M. V. Kaya (Ed.), *Social and economic studies within the framework of emerging global developments* (Vol. 1, pp. 139–152). Peter Lang.

Queirós, P., & Lacerda, T. (2013). The importance of interview in qualitative research. In I. Mesquita & A. Graça (Eds.), *Qualitative research in sport* (Vol. 2). Porto: Center for Innovation and Intervention Training in Sport, Faculty of Sport. Porto University *(In Portuguese)*

Saltman, R. B., & Duran, A. (2016). Governance, government, and the search for new provider models.International *Journal of Health Policy and Management, 5*(1), 33–42. https://doi.org/10.15171/ijhpm.2015.19826673647

Silva, A. H. N. M. B. (2021). Conceptualization of an integrated responsibility center for the ORL service of the IPO Lisbon (Master's thesis). ISCTE—University Institute of Lisbon. http://hdl.handle.net/10071/23562

van der Kolk, B., van Veen-Dirks, P. M. G., & ter Bogt, H. J. (2019). The impact of management control on employee motivation and performance in the public sector. *The European Accounting Review, 28*(5), 901–928. https://doi.org/10.1080/09638180.2018.1553728

Vaz, A. (2010). Portuguese public hospitals. In *30 years of national health service: A commented path*. Almedina Publishing (in Portuguese).

Vaz, S. C. M. S. (2020). *The role of information management in competitive intelligence: A case study in an average company* (pp. 1–124). https://recipp.ipp.pt/handle/10400.22/17389

Wilkinson, S. (1998). Focus group methodology: A review. *International Journal of Social Research Methodology, I*(3), 181–203. https://doi.org/10.1080/13645579.1998.10846874

Yin, R. (2018). *Case study research, design & methods* (5ª ed). Sage.

Pedro Fernandes da Anunciação, Fernando Miguel Gonçalves, &
Fabio Alexandre Chaves Martins

The Importance of Information Systems Governance: The Case of the Cement Industry

1. Introduction

Building Information Modeling (BIM) is associated with a tool that, based on information modeling, provides digital models for civil construction throughout its life cycle. The models available include several phases, from the initial design to the construction phase or even demolition. BIM, as software, provides a set of features (budgeting, planning, execution, etc.) that ensure the necessary information flows between the various stakeholders, respecting the life cycle of buildings and minimizing the disadvantages of manual treatment or non-integrated automated treatment of information (Borrmann et al., 2018). Although the software constitutes the "most visible part" of the potential of this tool, its information-centered base allows a set of relevant advantages for the construction activity, such as the possibility of projection and documentation of a building, adopting a holistic approach to construction and maintenance projects, among other aspects (Kjartansdóttir et al., 2017). In this sense, BIM should not be limited to only one software. Should stimulate management for a systemic perspective of information systems architecture, able to cover all phases of the development of a given engineering work (Langner et al., 2019).

This architecture, in the field of civil construction, should be based on a shareable collection of data/information on the whole building, including a three-dimensional technology-based perspective that provides information on each of the physical and logical elements, and provide solid knowledge about the reality under analysis. The systemic perspective proposed by BIM challenges the change in construction companies, from the evolution of traditional culture and fragmented nature of information management and information systems (IS) to a systemic or holistic view of their operation. The evolution to a holistic perspective is a necessary, but not sufficient condition for the increase of information sharing, stabilization of documents supporting the construction (architecture, budget, etc.) or to meet the information needs of the various stakeholders involved in construction projects, among other advantages.

Considering the complexity of the projects, the necessary degree of involvement of the various stakeholders, the high degree of integration between the various phases of the projects, and the longevity of the life cycle of the buildings (Ciotta et al., 2021) makes clear the need for a governance perspective to linkage processes, systems, and digital models that facilitate the management of the life cycle of buildings and the transfer of knowledge in an urban framework of information sharing between the various stakeholders involved (Oliveira & Anunciação, 2023). It should be noted that economic activity, in general, is clearly supported by a collaborative perspective (Muñoz-La Rivera, 2019).

In the technological field, BIM solutions facilitate the modeling of construction objects, the specification of their characteristics, the allocation of costs as well as knowing the impacts of any changes to be made over time (Kumanayake & Bandara, 2012). By covering all phases of the life cycle of buildings (design, construction, equipment, operations, repairs, and demolitions) all information respects the architecture supporting the support computer models (architecture, construction, technology, economy, etc.) (Milyutina, 2018), facilitating the integration of information and activities between the various organizational areas. Providing a single repository of information, which can be shared by all stakeholders, allows, from a management perspective, to carry out permanent and updated monitoring of the cost forecast, facilitating the simulation of the evolution of the entire construction process (Azhar et al., 2007).

However, although IT tools facilitate the provision of information and the generation of knowledge, they should also be contextualized from a governance perspective, facilitating their integration into the IS and enabling the assumption of data and information as an organizational asset. Thus, it can be affirmed that the architecture of IS, from the modeling of information, requires new management practices in construction (Milyutina, 2018).

All too often, valuable information is lost in failures associated with information flows that occur throughout the life cycle of building construction. It is therefore important to adapt the processes of collection, documentation, maintenance, and sharing of information assets in a format appropriate to the needs (Boton & Forgues, 2018; Ray, 2020), throughout the life cycle of a building (from its design to demolition), facilitating, in an integrated way, the flow of design and delivery, through the collaborative use of semantically rich 3D digital building models at all phases of the design and construction. This opportunity allows us to foresee a complex process of digital transformation, giving perspective to a challenging process of change management (Gamil & Cwirzen, 2022) and a focus on the analysis of related investments (Howard & Bjork, 2008; Lu et al., 2014).

2. The Importance of Governance

Gamil and Cwirzen (2022) consider that digital transformation in the cement industry should allow savings in time and resources, including finances. To this end, access to information and increased availability and efficiency of IS is essential, to improve business processes through the availability of real-time data and optimization of monitoring and control functions of operational processes. It is in the scope of such need that emerges the role of Governance. The Information Systems European Club (ISGec, 2010) states that the scope of IS Governance should include the definition of policies and strategies related to IS, which are compatible with Corporate Governance; the identification of objectives for investments, with a view to assessing their implementation; the specification of the functional relevance to the IS, through the insertion in the organizational macro-structure; the characterization of an organization and management model for the IS, capable of characterizing the adopted practices, namely at the level of Organizational Urbanism (Anunciação & Zorrinho, 2006), Architecture (Esteves & Anunciação, 2021) and IS planning; the acquisition and implementation of solutions within the IS; the realization of economic and financial analysis associated with investments in IS; forms of organization and exploitation of IS and also control of the performance of IS (Oliveira & Anunciação, 2023).

These are important aspects when seeking to highlight the centrality of IS in the competitive context of the economy. However, often these are characteristics perceived only through technology. Oliveira (2023) and Mansour et al. (2021) consider that information and communication technology (ICT) should find the appropriate place in organizational objectives and strategies. Construction companies are no exception. However, the association of ICT with strategy is often made through the optics of investments and productivity gains, lacking sensitivity to the contextualization of ICT a broader conceptual framework associated with IS (Gonçalves et al., 2019).

Construction companies sometimes experience some difficulties in adopting the BIM model due to the lack of knowledge related to the processes of inclusion of technical concepts and application of technological features (Yahya Al-Ashmori et al., 2019). Companies expect the implementation of BIM to increase productivity and efficiency during the phases of design, programming, acquisition, construction, etc. (Yahya Al-Ashmori et al., 2019), solving existing problems at the level of information and information systems.

The advantage of BIM is that most outputs (e.g., technical drawings) are derived directly from the model and are therefore automatically consistent with each other. In addition, it facilitates the detection of possible conflicts between the different partial models allowing the resolution of conflicts between the various phases of construction (Borrmann et al., 2018). For this reason, Carvalho (2019) states that, in the long term, the benefits of BIM and its productivity will compensate for the investment of the purchase of computer equipment and training of workers, as their use produces a more accurate cost estimate and unforeseen implementation costs can be avoided. The creation of a project developed in BIM allows you to follow its development in real-time and create continuous and updated budgets.

As mentioned above, it is expected that the acquisition of technological solutions will allow the generation, more or less automatically, of the benefits most desired by management, such as, in this specific case, the integration of calculations and simulations, because much input information about the geometry of the building and the material parameters can be taken directly from the model; compliance with codes and regulations, in an automated way, since they are in the model; the generation of budgets, since the tool allows the precise identification of quantities by providing reliable cost estimates and facilitating the preparation of specifications for contractors the subsequent issuance of invoices, among other advantages (Borrmann et al., 2018; Leśniak et al., 2021). However, it should be noted that, apparently, the logic is inverted. As Esteves and Anunciação (2021) points out, the development of IS should be initiated by business and not by technology. Even if this can happen through innovation, organizational and business models should always be adjusted.

This is an adjustment that must be made within the framework of change management. This is evident, for example, when it is found that the implementation of BIM does not modify criteria or design patterns, but restructures the way professionals and processes develop and interact with each other. For example, regarding the teams involved in a construction project, each team member is aware of the importance and objectives of the process, of the associated roles and responsibilities, and acquires knowledge of the skills and competency requirements necessary for the success of the project (Muñoz-La Rivera, 2019). The change may require adjustments, for example, in operation models, processes, operations, and management models, among others (Caeiro, 2021; Góes et al., 2020).

At the IS level, one of the main advantages of BIM lies in the registration of a single repository of all data generated or processed. Assumes data/information as precious assets that become accessible to the organization at any time. This relevance, from a technological perspective, is more evident in the three-dimensional dimension of digital technology by providing information about the entire life cycle of the construction project, providing a detailed representation of the associated information.

This technology enables the extraction of different types of information facilitating the management of the expected situation and the real situation and allows correcting errors and adjusting to achieve the desired objectives (Dong, 2017). The resulting BIM product is a parametric, intelligent, and data-rich digital representation of the construction project, providing a data/information-rich model that enables visualizations suited to the diverse needs of users. Data can be extracted from the model and worked to generate information in order to make decisions and improve the construction process (Sampaio, 2017). By supporting the development of different project components, it allows full interoperability between specific systems, and various types of analysis or simulations, facilitating the tasks of budgeting, construction, maintenance, and management (Sacks et al., 2018; Sampaio & Gomes, 2022; Sampaio et al., 2021).

3. Objectives and Methodology

This study aimed to evaluate the potential contributions of the BIM methodology to the cement industry in Portugal. In Portugal, there are two cement companies, which feed the value chain of civil construction and public works in the country. Given the size of the companies, the analysis was focused on the area of control, innovation, and by its nature, greater impact on the methodologies and technological tools that support the cement activity and what concerns the operation of these companies. The choice of area (control, innovation, and development) is due to the following factors: area of high integration with other organizational areas (exploration, production, quality, etc.), improvement and innovation of products, evaluation and technical communication between stakeholders (internal and external), a specialized center for technical knowledge, technical support for the evaluation of strategic decisions and investments, and B2B and B2C relationship center.

The research technique used was based on the Focus group (Queirós & Lacerda, 2013; Wilkinson, 1998), having joined 15 professionals representing the diversity of specialties present in this organizational area, with their respective functions being the following: technical responsibility of laboratory, laboratory technicians; product research and development technicians, construction technical support and concrete production responsibility.

The study was developed in two phases. The first one aimed to analyze the relevant dimensions for framing and analyzing the governance dimension, and the second, to analyze the advantages of adopting a technological solution associated with BIM in the cement industry.

4. Results Analysis

With regard to the first stage of the study, the Focus group identified as relevant topics in the scope of Governance, the following dimensions: availability of information in real-time, innovation management, organizational planning, investment evaluation, and benefits of a technological solution associated with BIM.

Stabilized these dimensions, as being the most relevant and challenging for the stakeholders in the Focus group in the context of the cement industry, felt the need to specify the impact that each of them may have on the organizational functioning, and the advantages that could be obtained with the possibility of investment associated with the BIM tool.

Regarding the need to provide information in real-time, the participants considered that this possibility would allow a more timely and effective decision on the existing problems. In addition, it would also be expected to improve the efficiency of the teams involved, minimizing the deviations and delays in the execution of the works and reducing the PDCA (Plan-Do-Check-Act) cycle. However, it was recognized that this need would require a new reference for information management and possible adjustments of existing IS, as the associated benefits would only be achieved if all data/ information is updated and available.

Regarding innovation management, they stressed the importance of the area of control, innovation, and development and its activities, considering that they are directly related to competitiveness. Through innovation, economic sustainability is more clearly guaranteed. This area has a relevant role in the design, integration, and dissemination of new materials and products with the various stakeholders, internal and external. It is its responsibility to launch and introduce new materials, conduct tests, justify the relevance of their adoption, disseminate projects, and evaluate results. It also plays an active role in the maintenance of buildings, by improving and updating the materials applied, ensuring adequate levels of performance of buildings and longevity in their use. As a result, it assumes responsibility for customer satisfaction, sharing with them information, and new techniques. Establishes a value co-creation interface with suppliers, partners, and subcontractors, contributing to a competitive time-to-market. It also plays an important role in the monitoring and evaluation of the results of the value chain, as well as the update of the technical specifications of the IS, through the provision of information associated with the products.

Regarding organizational urbanization, the need and relevance of information and knowledge sharing in an integrated way were highlighted, which is dependent on the definition of a competence matrix and a knowledge map defined for the various areas and organizational functions. This need will presuppose a re-architecture of processes and IS in a framework of organizational urbanization, especially in the face of the opportunity to invest in technological tools focused on information. These requirements seem critical, as they allow a faster response to the market, from an organizational reduction of bureaucracy, and functioning based on a culture based on knowledge. These are also conditions for economic sustainability.

Regarding the evaluation of investments and use of information technologies, it was considered to be a relevant element in the strategies at IS level. As in any other type of investment, it is important to evaluate the degree of satisfaction in the use of IS/ IT and analyze the support that is given to the operational and decision requirements in organizations. The multiplicity of IT and, above all, deficiencies in integration significantly limit the management of information as an organizational and economic asset and the generation of knowledge. This leads to increased efforts to manage the technology park and the dispersion of knowledge. The lack of consolidation of IS in the cement industry continues to limit their development, for example in access to new levels associated with industry 4.0, although the cement industry is more likely to adopt new technologies than the construction sector. In this field, projects related to industry 4.0 go beyond the simplification of processes and implementation of computer tools, through the management of information at various levels, from the so-called factory floor to operational and executive directions, facilitating historical analysis, trends, and deviations.

Regarding the second phase of the study, which focused on the analysis of the benefits of the potential adoption of a technological solution associated with BIM, they considered that this could contribute to the optimization of work and to the real-time monitoring of critical processes. It would have the great advantage of unifying the databases and allowing detailed monitoring of the projects, providing immediate intervention in the identification of possible problems. The possibility of creating visual models in 3D facilitates the visualization of results and the management of information about the life cycle of projects.

In this context, the relevance of change management was also highlighted, since it was considered necessary to carry out training activities on the new software, adapt processes, and adopt a new business culture that overlaps the traditionally conservative culture, aged and prone to resistance to change.

5. Conclusions

Technology is profoundly changing all industries and changing the way we work in all sectors, and the cement industry is no exception. However, this sector still shows some resistance to the adoption of digital processes and technological innovation. However, investment in technologies alone is not sufficient for obvious competitive gains. It is important that technologies are contextualized in the scope of information management and IS.

The BIM methodology can be a new approach to organizational functioning for companies, since it focuses on information on the structure of the software available, opening a new functional perspective on economic activities and the different stakeholders involved. This perspective provides a unique image of the phases of the life cycle of buildings and a mutual language between the various specialties, among other aspects.

Thus, this systemic perspective on a multivariate reality (stakeholders, materials, equipment, etc.) requires a governance dimension on systems (e.g., information systems), resources (e.g., data and information), technologies (e.g., information technologies), among others.

With regard to BIM, although it has been found that this technology is still partly unknown to those working in the sector since it is a technological solution with a high cost, the sensitivity of respondents to the expected benefits associated with possible adoption should be noted. These consider that their adoption would imply changes in the organizational modus operandi, information and knowledge management, way of working, and existing processes, among other aspects. In addition, it would involve a rigorous change management program, given that the cement industry is an aging, traditional industry that still proves to be resistant to technological changes. Despite the undeniable advantages that this methodology/solution can provide, a demanding economic and financial analysis associated with the investment decision is recommended.

Limitations and future work:

> The scope of the study limitations highlights the circumscription of the analysis only to an organizational area. Despite its relevance, the possibility of conducting a study involving the remaining organizational areas would allow a more comprehensive and complete analysis of organizational reality. In this sense, it would be interesting to integrate a representative of the various areas for a more complete analysis and a greater awareness of the potential of the methodology analyzed.

On the other hand, it would also be important to involve external stakeholders associated with the construction value chain. The cement industry is upstream of the chain and conducting the study in downstream companies would be relevant for further complementarity of the analysis, particularly as regards the relevance and impact of the methodology/technological tools associated with BIM.

References

Anunciação, P. F., & Zorrinho, C. (2006). *Organizational urbanism—How managing technological shock in companies.* Sílabo Publishing (in Portuguese).

Azhar, S., Hein, M., & Sketo, B. (2007). Building information modeling (BIM): Benefits, risks and challenges. *BIM-benefit*, *18*(9), 11.

Borrmann, A., König, M., Koch, C., & Beetz, J. (2018). Building information modeling: Why? What? How? In *Building Information Modeling* (pp. 1–24). Springer International Publishing.

Boton, C., & Forgues, D. (2018). Practices and processes in BIM projects: An exploratory case study. *Advances in Civil Engineering*, 2018, 1–12. https://doi.org/10.1155/2018/7259659

Caeiro, A. M. V. (2021). *Implementation of BIM methodologies in the development of structural projects* (Masters dissertation). Instituto Superior de Engenharia de Lisboa. Repositório Científico do Instituto Politécnico de Lisboa. http://hdl.handle.net/10400.21/13818

Carvalho, J. R. D. (2019). *Advantages of the BIM system in construction project and management environments.* http://repositorio.unitau.br/jspui/handle/20.500.11874/3632

Ciotta, V., Asprone, D., Manfredi, G., & Cosenza, E. (2021). Building information modelling in structural engineering: A qualitative literature review. *CivilEng*, *2*(3), 765–793. https://doi.org/10.3390/civileng2030042

Dong, R.-R. (2017). The application of BIM technology in building construction quality management and talent training. *Eurasia Journal of Mathematics Science and Technology Education*, *13*(7). https://doi.org/10.12973/eurasia.2017.00860a

Esteves, F. J. M. & Anunciação, P. F. (2021). Architecture—Essential dimension in information systems. In *Information Systems—Paradigms and Solutions for Management.* Plátano Publishing (in Portuguese).

Gamil, Y., & Cwirzen, A. (2022). Digital transformation of concrete technology—A review. *Frontiers in Built Environment*, *8*, 1–14. https://doi.org/10.3389/fbuil.2022.835236

Góes, M. B., Rioga, C. L., Campos, I. L. de A., Freitas, L. D. de, Barbosa, S. J., & Souza, F. T. de. (2020). Benefits of BIM method implementation in the planning and management of construction. *Latin American Journal of Innovation and Production Engineering*, *8*(14), 107. https://doi.org/10.5380/relainep.v8i14.77617

Gonçalves, F. M., Pimenta, J., & Anunciação, P. F. (2019). The information systems governance and the new Paradigms in the industry. In *Information systems governance—Concepts, good practices, and case studies*, Information Systems Governance European Club (ceGSI-Portugal) (pp. 117–133). Chiado Publishing (in Portuguese).

Howard, R., & Björk, B. (2008). Building information modelling—Experts' views on standardisation and industry deployment. *Advanced Engineering Informatics*, *22*(2), 271–280. https://doi.org/10.1016/j.aei.2007.03.001

Information System Governance European Club (ISGec). (2010). *Why the Corporations are asking for an information systems governance?*. http://www.cegsi.org/index.php/documents/telechargement-du-document-la-gouvernance-des-systemes-d-information-pourquoi/la-gouvernance-des-systemes-d-information-pourquoi (In French).

Kjartansdóttir, I. B., Mordue, S., Nowak, P., Philp, D., & Snæbjörnsson, J. T. (2017). *Building information modelling-BIM*. Civil Engineering Faculty of Warsaw University of Technology.

Kumanayake, R., & Bandara, P. (2012). *Building information modelling (BIM); how it improves building performance*. https://www.researchgate.net/publication/322624164_Building_Information_Modelling_BIM_How_it_Improves_Building_Performance

Langner, C., Hermann, L. R., & Radüns, C. D. (2019). Advantages and disadvantages of the BIM concept in the construction area. *Hall of Knowledge*, *5*(5).

Leśniak, A., Górka, M., & Skrzypczak, I. (2021). Barriers to BIM implementation in architecture, construction, and engineering projects—The polish study. *Energies*, *14*(8), 2090. https://doi.org/10.3390/en14082090

Lu, W., Fung, A., Peng, Y., Liang, C., & Rowlinson, S. (2014). Cost-benefit analysis of building information modeling implementation in building projects through demystification of time-effort distribution curves. *Building and Environment*, *82*, 317–327. https://doi.org/10.1016/j.buildenv.2014.08.030

Mansour, A., Qtaishat, H., Samara, E., & Husamie, R. (2021). Information technology practice in cement industry. *Wseas Transactions on Business and Economics*, *18*, 855–864. https://doi.org/10.37394/23207.2021.18.81

Milyutina, M. A. (2018). Introduction of building information modeling (BIM) technologies in construction. *Journal of Physics. Conference Series, 1015*, 042038. https://doi.org/10.1088/1742-6596/1015/4/042038

Muñoz-La Rivera, F., Vielma, J. C., Herrera, R. F., & Carvallo, J. (2019). Methodology for building information modeling (BIM) implementation in structural engineering companies (SECs). *Advances in Civil Engineering, 2019*, 1–16. https://doi.org/10.1155/2019/8452461

Oliveira, A. (2023). *Information & management—Two sides of the same coin*. Sílabo Publishing (in Portuguese).

Oliveira, A., & Anunciação, P. F. (2023). Information systems governance: Some dimensions to management. In M. V. Kaya (Ed.), *Social and economic studies within the framework of emerging global developments* (Vol. 1, pp. 139–152). Peter Lang.

Queirós, P., & Lacerda, T. (2013). The importance of interviews in qualitative research. In I. Mesquita & A. Graça (Eds.), *Qualitative research in sport* (Vol. 2). Center for Innovation and Intervention Training in Sport, Faculty of Sport. Porto University (in Portuguese).

Ray, J. (2020). BIM beyond design guidebook. In *National academies of sciences, engineering, and medicine*. https://doi.org/10.17226/25840

Sacks, R., Eastman, C., Lee, G., & Teicholz, P. (2018). *BIM handbook: A guide to building information modeling for owners, designers, engineers, contractors, and facility managers*. John Wiley & Sons. https://doi.org/10.1002/9781119287568

Sampaio, A. Z. (2017). BIM as a computer-aided design methodology in civil engineering. *Journal of Software Engineering and Applications, 10*(02), 194–210. https://doi.org/10.4236/jsea.2017.102012

Sampaio, A. Z., & Gomes, A. M. (2022). Professional one-day training course in BIM: A practice overview of multi-applicability in construction. *Journal of Software Engineering and Applications, 15*(05), 131–149. https://doi.org/10.4236/jsea.2022.155007

Sampaio, A. Z., Gomes, A. M., & Farinha, T. (2021). BIM methodology applied in structural design: Analysis of interoperability in ArchiCAD/ETABS process. *Journal of Software Engineering and Applications, 14*(06), 189–206.

Wilkinson, S. (1998). Focus group methodology: A review. *International Journal of Social Research Methodology, I*(3), 181–203. https://doi.org/10.1080/13645579.1998.10846874

Yahya Al-Ashmori, Y., Bin Othman, I., Bin Mohamad, H., Rahmawati, Y., & Napiah, M. (2019). Establishing the level of BIM implementation—A case study in Melaka, Malaysia. *IOP ConferenceSeries.MaterialsScienceandEngineering, 601*(1), 012024. https://doi.org/10.1088/1757-899x/601/1/012024

Pedro Fernandes da Anunciação, Vitor Dinis,
Antonio Briones Peñalver, & Francisco Joaquim Madeira Esteves

Main Dimensions of Management Preventive Maintenance in the Industry 4.0 Context

1. Introduction

Industry 4.0 is industrial companies' present challenge. Industry 4.0 is described as the fourth industrial revolution since the first industrial revolution in the late 18th century (Xu et al., 2018). The increasing presence of technologies, like IoT, IA, Robots, and 3D printing, among others, has allowed a deep change in the production systems, challenging industrial companies to a strategic reframing (Watson et al., 2017). Industry 4.0 (I4.0) expresses an unprecedented movement toward the creation of intelligent industrial units (smart factories) (Schwab, 2016) and a convergence of operational and information technologies (Popa et al., 2021). Industrial processes digital transformation presents itself as a key driver for the development of the industrial economy and provides new management contexts in diversified organizational domains (Anunciação et al., 2022).

The relevant technological above mentioned, such as Internet-of-Things (IoT) or Artificial Intelligence, challenges information systems and organizational processes and procedures and generates a need for new perspectives and approaches relative to information systems, such as the urbanistic organizational approach (Anunciação, 2014; Anunciação, 2015; Anunciação & Zorrinho, 2006; Oliveira & Anunciação, 2023) or information systems governance (Gonçalves et al., 2019) to support and improve the relationship between economic organizations.

In Industry 4.0 the excellence of coordination in an "urban" context of a broader economy will be essential (Gonçalves et al., 2019). According to the authors, the main factors that can be highlighted are:

- The coordination of external processes will go beyond the physical limits of factories in the logistics integration of suppliers and other stakeholders;
- The depth of automation and its sophistication will depend even more on advanced external information systems (IBM Watson, Google IoT, and Tensor Flow, etc.) that will blur the respective frontiers;
- Industrial information systems will require the establishment of multidisciplinary teams, with variable geometry over time, requiring more careful management of the knowledge generated and its maintenance in the information systems;

- new economic blocs will compete in the digital dimension: business systems supported on the Internet, manipulated news, mobile devices and applications, encryption, and advanced combat systems.

Production becomes more customized, allowing for a displacement of mass production to unitary productions and presenting higher demands at the management level of resources (materials and equipment). Digital manufacturing and smart, completely customizable product-service systems go hand in hand with each other in what is widely called the fourth industrial revolution (Industry 4.0) (Riel et al., 2017). Custom production provides more adequate answers to market solicitations and consequent productivity gains, which presupposes the market reading capacity of its needs and trends, and requires equipment availability assurances, namely in what regards its availability. Equipment availability demands an accrued focus on the strand of preventive maintenance, as a means of minimizing eventual outages, aggregating skills at the level of mechanical engineering, but also the level of information technologies.

These, among other factors, compose requisites that differ from traditional industry. Equipment reliability is now a critical variable in the sense that it conditions product quality and affects industrial company competitiveness.

Considering that economic activity is supported by logistic chains allowing for a daily market supply, the production chains tend to answer according to these requisites, avoiding, for instance, the production to stock, in the sense that it represents a capital cost which, by itself, compromises competitiveness. So, a trend develops for production in real-time in correspondence with needs, rising in this way the criticality of equipment availability.

In this context, maintenance takes a significant prevalence in an operational environment that is new. This development requires new management models and new tools to ensure production equipment operationality and to allow for complexity and economic risk reduction.

2. The Relevance of Dimensions Associated with Industry 4.0

Industry 4.0 (I4.0) initiative encompasses the digitalization of production processes based on devices autonomously communicating with each other along the value chain. According to the European Union Directorate-General for Internal Policies Report, I4.0 has significant effects in many areas, namely in the economic and monetary affairs, employment and social affairs, the environment, public health, and food safety, the industry, research and energy, and the internal market and consumer protection. This study considers three key dimensions of change relevant to Industry 4.0: technological change, social change, and change in the business paradigm.

In the technological change dimension, digitalization has been the major driver of changes throughout the value chain, and while many businesses recognize the need to adjust, far fewer, especially among SMEs are prepared for it. Digitalization brought significant challenges, with associated costs and risks, for firms, especially in digital security areas such as intellectual property protection, personal data, and privacy; design and operability of systems; environmental protection, and health and safety.

In the social change dimension, there is little awareness of I4.0 outside the key stakeholders—large firms tend to be disposed to accept changes, and unions remain skeptical and very cautious. While a skills gap exists, reinforced by a gap in willingness, the new ways of work will not be incorporated, and, also important, the skills mix now in demand for I4.0 is continuously changing as new technologies are being developed, exposing a true race between education and technologies. In this dimension, we must consider that with the introduction of Industry 4.0 into production, the cooperation between man and machine is becoming increasingly important. Especially in the field of human-robot collaboration, an increase in flexibility and an option for automation even with smaller batch sizes are expected (Gualtieri et al., 2018).

Change in the business paradigm represents another important challenge for SMEs to participate in I4.0 supply chains, which embrace costs, risks, reduced flexibility, and reduced strategic independence. Also, standardization continues to be a major challenge from the perspective of large-scale implementation of I4.0. This aspect also relates to the very important questions about the future of the industrial sector in the EU—will I4.0 strengthen the EU industry's leadership or is it a requirement to maintain its position, or if leadership will inevitably pass to the new emerging economies?

There are several relevant dimensions associated with Industry 4.0 mentioned by several authors, such as functional safety & cyber security (Link et al., 2018); interoperability and Security (Watson et al., 2017); integrated safety/cybersecurity requirements elicitation (Riel et al., 2017). Other authors presuppose other associated dimensions, such as protocols, time-sensitive networking, and unified architecture (Etz et al., 2020).

The different perspectives and dimensions considered by the diversity of authors who have approached the theme of Industry 4.0 led to the development of this work with the objective of, through the consultation of several professionals related to the industry, identifying the dimensions that should be considered in the pragmatic perspective of the challenge associated with this concept.

3. Objectives and Methodology

This work is part of a more in-depth project searching to study, in a short time, maintenance reality in the context of Industry 4.0. However, given a deeper understanding of Industry 4.0 reality, as well as preparation of analysis tools of the associated reality, it was decided to realize an exploratory study searching for the identification and correct usage of the dimensions that, in this scope, condition or might do it for Industry 4.0. Considering the coverage of this theme, as well as the challenges associated, this study will focus on the strand of industrial maintenance.

The choice of this strand is a result of some characteristics and requirements of Industry 4.0, namely, what refers to real-time production, the production customization, among others, which demand particular management care over equipment maintenance. Maintenance presents itself as a critical factor in the industrial digital transformation.

In this scope, and in a more concise form, the research work here presented has as its purpose the identification of the main dimensions which must compose an analysis of production equipment maintenance in the context of Industry 4.0. Considering that information and communication technology brought a set of new paradigms to industrial unities production processes, as well as a trend for the reduction of the production cycle, for customized production, among others, it appears relevant the comprehension of the role that maintenance can and must-have in the assurance of equipment operability. Equipment management and performance depend on the adequacy of maintenance to the utilization demands. Contrary to standardized production, where equipment utilization values and associated maintenance needs appear easy to frame and understand, in the Industry 4.0 context a not contextualized management of the demands associated with equipment may condition the desired flexibility.

For this identification, we appealed to the focus group technique (Queirós & Lacerda, 2013; Wilkinson, 1998). The meeting of several specialists, in the different perspectives associated with the theme of industrial management, will for sure facilitate the analysis of different subjects related to Industry 4.0 and, in particular, to industrial maintenance. Through this methodology we looked for, from the theme of subjectivization of the several stakeholders, to reach objectivity in the reflection based on the knowledge and experience of each of the participant specialists.

The sharing of knowledge, experiences, and different viewpoints and, especially, the need for a consensus, facilitates obtaining integrated solutions for specific problems. The added value of this methodology corresponds to obtaining value from synergies that, otherwise, would be difficult to obtain.

There were eleven (11) participating experts, being:

- four (4) with responsibilities in production in different sectors of economic activity,
- three (3) industrial company information systems managers,
- two (2) information systems teachers,
- one (1) production management teacher, and
- one (1) chief executive officer of a software house, an expert in industrial maintenance software development.

The choice of the different areas was based on the need to include, in the field of information systems, three central stakeholders: the owner, the architect, and the constructor, a reference left by Zachman (1987). In this context, and following a similar logic, specialists in the area of production management were incorporated, as they represent the stakeholders associated with the business and incorporate the challenge of transforming the industry in a 4.0 context. The teachers, for their theoretical knowledge of tools and methodologies that should support organizational development toward digital transformation, and the directors of information systems, given their practical knowledge as privileged actors in the process and projects of digital transformation. The chief executive officer is a representative stakeholder of software development, from the constructor's perspective.

The study was accomplished in two different phases. The first one had as a target to identify the dimensions present in Industry 4.0 and that must be an object of analysis given its comprehension. The second one targeted the identification of the set of elements that, associated with each of the dimensions previously considered, give a more deep and complete characterization of the industrial reality associated with the study subject.

In both several meetings were held, until an understanding and generalized agreement was reached on the analyzed subjects.

4. Analysis of Results

In the first phase of the study, the focus group debated the main dimensions in the context of industry 4.0 that must be considered in the scope of equipment maintenance management. The dimensions are shown here as well as the arguments presented for each one:

- Information systems—information systems (IS) compose central elements in the production and maintenance management in the context of industry 4.0, insofar as

information technologies integrate the production equipment themselves and, as such, support industrial activities.
In addition to technologies, the importance of data must be considered, insofar as the adoption of technologies such as the Internet of Things generates an exponential production of data that presupposes new management requirements at the level of industrial information systems.

- Maintenance management—decision-making data and information available from the production equipment, made available, for instance, by diversified sensors that integrate equipment, demands a greater maintenance management perceptiveness, insofar as they allow for real-time knowledge and the eventual need for an intervention taking in consideration its availability.
  Availability is a critical success factor in real-time production and market distribution.
- Maintenance organization—equipment with incorporated technologies should allow, behind information availability on their state, a more efficient and effective intervention facilitating a more complete and embracing analysis of the equipment, for instance, of the operational conditions and the maintenance associated costs.
- Equipment—is essential to the availability of technical documentation, allowing the understanding of the operational specifications necessary for normal operation, as well as identifying their localization and operational procedures.
- Preventive maintenance plans—for every piece of equipment must exist a preventive maintenance plan, allowing for a correct intervention given its usage and containing the description of the concrete maintenance tasks to accomplish.
- Workload management—equipment workloads must be identified, monitored, and managed. Also, they must allow for intervention planning making use of their history.
- Maintenance work order requisition/execution—maintenance interventions must allow the identification of the operator and the intervention scope, and the registered information must have an evolution analysis, allowing for equipment maintenance plan adjustments.
  Work orders must be managed to optimize costs and intervention types, as well as to ensure their realization in the predicted periods.
  It is also important to develop relational capital in this domain, as a way for, producers and suppliers, to optimize equipment reliability.
- Materials and components management—materials and components stock must be adequate to the maintenance interventions plan. Their packaging in the warehouse must be adequate for their preservation, and their respective references e specificities related to the equipment.
- Human capital—maintenance technical staff must retain the necessary knowledge about the intervening equipment, owing such knowledge to be actual in terms of the equipment's technical specifications.
  Such knowledge must allow for the understanding and justification of the nature of the performed interventions, differentiate wearing situations or undue equipment usage, and support performance evaluation associated with operation and maintenance.

- Management control—management control must support itself in different tools allowing the follow-up of the situations related to maintenance, namely, the existence of budgets that allow the identification of deviations.

Behind these dimensions, the focus group pointed out the importance of framing the relevant factors in the evolution of Industry 4.0. In this scope, they considered that this evolution presupposes the need for a reframing of the information architecture and the information systems, with a special focus on the information and communications technologies and on the development of a governance perspective over the IS. Only the adequacy of the governance perspective, allowing orientation to investments, politics, strategies, etc., could frame and justify new quality requisites at the information level and of information systems or reduce the pressure associated with Big Data or other activities related, such as Analytics, among other aspects.

The second part of the study searched to identify the components associated with each of the previously identified dimensions to realize a complete analysis of each one. So, the focus group considered that in the analysis of each identified dimension the following aspects should be considered:

- Information systems:
  - maintenance management support by the information system area;
  - maintenance information system as a subsystem of the enterprise information system;
  - integration of maintenance information system with other subsystems (for instance, Production, Stocks, etc.);
  - maintenance information systems architecture coverage of all maintenance activities;
  - Equipment identification in maintenance information systems;
  - forecasts and alerts to intervention needs;
  - maintenance information systems performance indicators.

- Maintenance management decision:
  - Technical/operational and economic maintenance decisions;
  - Information Systems based decisions.

- Maintenance organization:
  - maintenance procedures manual;
  - periodic meetings with stakeholders;
  - sharing maintenance results to supplier's;
  - maintenance quality service manual;
  - Previous budget to maintenance interventions.

- Equipment:
  - technical documentation;

- o equipment technical identification;
- o equipment operation description.

- Preventive maintenance plans:
  - o preventive maintenance plans for all maintenance objects;
  - o safety condition definition for equipment;
  - o definition of the maintenance tasks for each equipment;
  - o monitorization of maintenance plans.
- Workload management:
  - o criteria for workloads definition and control analysis;
  - o intervention report, resources used, and utilization time registration;
  - o criteria for maintenance costs and historic analysis.
- Maintenance work order requisition/execution:
  - o characteristics maintenance work order requisition/execution (operator, scope, equipment, period, problem, request status, and so on).
- Materials and components management:
  - o stock management criterion;
  - o inventory articles characterization;
  - o stocks (materials and components) periodic validation.
- Human capital:
  - o technicians and operator opportunity training;
  - o technicians and operator performance assessment;
  - o specificity of instructions to maintenance operations;
  - o cost activity-based affectation to extraordinary maintenance.
- Management control:
  - o budget orientation to maintenance costs management;
  - o standard maintenance costs control procedure;
  - o deviations analysis between budget and real costs associated with maintenance.

Beyond these ten dimensions, it was also analyzed the success conditions for evolution to Industry 4.0. In this scope, the focus group considered that this evolution presupposes:

- Evolution to I4.0:
  - o demand an information architecture and an architecture for the information systems and technologies;
  - o governance perspective over the IS and governance/life-cycle management of information;
  - o demand information systems, data, and information quality requisites;
  - o Big Data and Analytics activities;
  - o new skills human resources level (Human Capital), new dynamics and organizational requisites (Structural Capital), and communication channels (Relational Capital);

- o project management perspective adoption in the transaction to industry 4.0;
- o technological park dimension and maintenance complexity of the industrial information systems;
- o new processual practices and clients relations;
- o quality level, flexibility, and productivity;
- o contingency plans;
- o digital twins for modeling, simulation, and instantaneous follow-up of equipment and their status;
- o forecast from digital twins in the future preventive maintenance planning.

5. Conclusions

We can mention that maintenance management assumes a critical success factor in industrial activities to support a real-time market approach. Economic and productive activity increasingly depends on the operability and reliability of equipment. These incorporate technological components that are connected with organizational information systems, constituting complex technological systems that defy demanding management.

The answers must be given at two levels. At the top management level, through the development of a governance approach, and at an intermediate level, through the development of good governance practices. This study made it possible, through the knowledge and experience of the elements of the focus group, to identify a multidisciplinary diversity of essential dimensions for an adequate framework of maintenance in an Industry 4.0 context, of which the following points stand out:

- the maintenance management should be supported by information systems that must be integrated with enterprise Information systems;
- maintenance demand an information systems architecture, especially for information technologies;
- maintenance requires the development of a governance perspective over the Information systems and technologies;
- the maintenance information system must make available forecasts and alerts for intervention needs, specify the resources involved, register the work requests, and make available performance indicators;
- the maintenance decisions must be based on a technical/operational and economic basis;
- the maintenance activities must be realized in articulation with production;
- the maintenance plans should be monitored;
- the maintenance requires proximity with producers/suppliers.
- the maintenance practice should demand continuous and permanent training for the technicians and operators;

- maintenance demands specific and dedicated budget control;
- maintenance demand for new skills and professional abilities at the level of human resources (Human Capital), new dynamics and organizational requisites (Structural Capital), and communication channels (Relational Capital).

Limitations and future research work:

The main limitation of the study carried out refers to the fact that it constituted an exploratory work to identify, through the focus group technique, the main dimensions that should be considered in the field of maintenance when framed in an evolutionary context for the 4.0 industry.

It is believed that this limitation does not detract from the value and opportunity of the topic addressed and that it can be minimized with the perspective of future research works.

Therefore, it is foreseen in the future the development of two complementary studies. The first one allows the confirmation and consolidation of these dimensions through a survey of a significant sample of production managers from different industrial companies. And a second one that allows assessing the degree of maturity that industrial companies present in this domain in Portugal.

References

Anunciação, P. F. (2014). *Ethics, sustainability and the information and knowledge society*. Chiado Publishing (in Portuguese).

Anunciação, P. F. (2015). Organizational change through information systems: Metavision-project management model in internet banking. In *Handbook of research on effective project management through the integration of knowledge and innovation* (Chapter 23, pp. 450–465). IGI Global.

Anunciação, P. F., Dinis, V. M. L., Briones Peñalver, A. J., & Esteves. F. J. M. (2022). Functional safety as a critical success factor to Industry 4.0. *Procedia Computer Science*, *204*, 45–53. https://doi.org/10.1016/j.procs.2022.08.006

Anunciação, P. F., & Zorrinho, C. (2006). *Organizational urbanism—How to manage technological shock*. Sílabo Publishing (in Portuguese).

Etz, D., Brantner, H., & Kastner, W. (2020). Smart manufacturing retrofit for brownfield systems. *Procedia Manufacturing*, *42*, 327–332. https://doi.org/10.1016/j.promfg.2020.02.085

Gonçalves, F., Pimenta, J., & Anunciação, P. F. (2019). *Information systems governance and new industrial paradigms. Information systems governance—Concepts, best practices, and case studies* (pp. 117–136). Chiado Publishing.

Gualtieri, L., Rauch, E., Rojas, R., Vidoni, R., & Matt, D. T. (2018). Application of axiomatic design for the design of a safe collaborative human-robot assembly workplace. *MATEC Web of Conferences*, *223*, 01003, ICAD 2018. https://doi.org/10.1051/matecconf/201822301003

Link, J., Waedt, K., Zid, I. B., & Lou, X. (2018). Current challenges of the joint consideration of functional safety & cyber security, their interoperability and impact on organizations—How to manage RAMS + S (Reliability availability maintainability safety + security). In *12th International Conference on Reliability, Maintainability, and Safety (ICRMS)*. IEEE. https://doi.org/10.1109/ICRMS.2018.00043

Oliveira, A., & Anunciação, P. F. (2023). Information systems governance: Some dimensions to management. In M. V. Kaya (Ed.), *Social and economic studies within the framework of emerging global developments* (Vol. 1, pp. 139–152). Peter Lang Publishing.

Popa, P., Zarrina, B., Barzegarana, M., Schulteb, S., Punnekkatc, S., Ruhd, J., & Steinerd, W. (2021). The FORA fog computing platform for industrial IoT. *Information Systems*, *98*, 101727.

Queirós, P., & Lacerda, T. (2013). The importance of interviews in qualitative research. In I. Mesquita & A. Graça (Eds.), *Qualitative research in sport* (Vol. 2). Center for Innovation and Intervention Training in Sport, Faculty of Sport. Porto University (in Portuguese).

Riel, A., Kreiner, C., Macher, G., & Messnarz, R. (2017). Integrated design for tackling safety and security challenges of smart products and digital manufacturing. *CIRP Annals—Manufacturing Technology, Elsevier*, *66*(1), 177–180. https://doi.org/10.1016/j.cirp.2017.04.037

Schwab, K. (2016). *The fourth industrial revolution*. World Economic Forum.

Watson, V., Tellabi, A., Sassmannshausen, J., & Lou, X. (2017). *Interoperability and security challenges of Industrie 4.0* (Lecture Notes in Informatics [LNI], p. 973). Gesellschaft für Informatik.

Wilkinson, S. (1998). Focus group methodology: A review, *International Journal of Social Research Methodology*, *1*(3), 181–203. https://doi.org/10.1080/13645579.1998.10846874

Xu, L. D., Xu, E. L., & Li, L. (2018). Industry 4.0: State of the art and future trends. *International Journal of Production Research*, *56*(8), 2941–2962.

Zachman, J. (1987). A framework for information systems architecture. *IBM Systems Journal*, *38*(3), 276–292. https://doi.org/10.1147/sj.263.0276

Pedro Fernandes da Anunciação, Rui Menezes Vaz, Mario Vale, Karollyne Cruvinel de Freitas, & Pedro Rosario da Costa

The Criticality of Information in the Pandemic Context Management: The Case Study of Safe COVID Testing in Portugal

1. Introduction

Society is currently living in the so-called information age. This designation, Information Society, expresses information as the main economic resource and Information Systems and Technologies (IST) as the main platform. The generation of value associated with IST increasingly requires strategic management by organizations and managers toward the development of intelligent organizations (Anunciação, 2014). Information, knowledge, and intelligence constitute three resources that have become part of the universe of business management, thus becoming essential resources for the competitive development of organizations and the efficiency of decision-making (Anunciação et al., 2022). Information is currently a strategic resource in organizations (Oliveira, 2021). Through the adoption of appropriate models of information management, organizations can make appropriate readings of the external environments in which they are involved, adapt response times to economic and social demands, and adapt internal resources and capabilities to the demands of competitiveness (Carujo et al., 2021).

Competing means being able to identify signals from the external environment, interpret them, react to the market, and present value, thus fostering trust among stakeholders and ensuring that everyone can understand the flexibility of the information life cycle by highlighting the transparency of the process and the shared ownership of the solution between business and IST, thereby fueling interdependence (Monteiro et al., 2021).

Accurate and current information has been highlighted around the world as a critical requirement for the response to the COVID-19 pandemic, providing the basis for a preservation and privacy data-sharing platform for other forms of notification about diseases that could be used in future health emergencies (Field et al., 2021). Competing also presupposes the availability of information and achieving more ambitious goals than the competition. If we consider that in the global economy, competitive advantages are associated with the ability to innovate and, above all, differentiate beyond information, knowledge assumes a relevant preponderance. In this context, in the organizational domain, knowledge management presupposes a higher level of demand as it requires a high standard of quality of information and information systems.

Following these aspects, the architecture of IST should be directed to the promotion of knowledge (creation, acquisition, retention, diffusion) in the organizational environment, and should be reflected in the competitive differentiation in the market (Anunciação & Geada, 2021). The development of information has become an essential tool to understand the ever-changing data as was the case with the COVID-19 pandemic. Thus, ensuring the use of information data that really serves the needs of people has become a priority for the development of the IST (Li et al., 2022). Knowledge, in the way it is conceived, shared, used, transformed, and validated, creates value for its characteristics of rarity, imperfect imitation, and irreplaceable. As long as these characteristics prevail, the organization is at a competitive advantage over its competitors. It is in this sense that it can be said that knowledge must be managed and considered a resource for management. The key to fighting the pandemic was to present data in data reports in a transparent way, allowing any decision to control the pandemic to be based on high-quality data (Adrian et al., 2021)

Thus, sustainable competitive advantages presuppose continuous management of organizational knowledge and, with its use, the generation of economic value, reflecting this knowledge in organizational skills. This continuous management should provide organizational learning, which should be an engine for the creation of core competencies in the company. Real competitive advantage is based on faster learning. Only attentive and agile organizations will be able to respond adequately to the needs of the economy and society (Araújo Júnior & Cândido, 2020). The case study associated with the need for responses for management and control of the pandemic situation was only possible due to the association of various stakeholders, such as health institutions, an information technology company, the Portuguese Government, and the European Commission itself, which allowed the development of a value-generating solution to a collective problem.

The pandemic situation accelerated the development of information technology, especially innovation in digital technologies (Wang et al., 2021) due to the obligation of a relational requirement imposed on various economic organizations (health, distribution, security, government, technology, communications, etc.). Some concepts that have come to be highlighted by some researchers in the area of information systems, such as the concept of Organizational Urbanism (Anunciação & Zorrinho, 2006), IST Architecture

(Anunciação, 2016; Esteves & Anunciação, 2021), IS Governance (Oliveira & Anunciação, 2023), Information Governance (Esteves & Anunciação, 2023), among others.

2. The Role of "Safe COVID Testing" Information Systems

The COVID-19 pandemic was an unprecedented and unexpected situation in Portugal. Like most countries, health Portuguese institutions were not prepared to deal with the pandemic situation on this scale. The high spread of this overwhelming virus has given rise to the need for drastic measures in real-time. Faced with the rapid loss of human lives and the difficulty of making resources available, some entities urgently understood the creation of an entity that would facilitate the obtaining of answers, through information and communication technologies (ICT) from a timely diagnosis associated with the various moments of control established.

The Safe COVID Testing Information System (SCTIS) results from a consortium between institutions in the area of health and ICT, with the aim of promoting and facilitating the COVID testing of the population, simultaneously providing tools to testing entities for rapid achievement of results and consequent information to competent entities in the health area. It is an IS based on a digital platform, managed by a consortium that brings together several health service providers. This platform enables the scheduling of COVID tests at the national level, assigns the result to the user, and informs the competent entities of the results obtained. It provides for the safeguarding of data confidentiality, which is protected by the legal framework of the General Regulation on Data Protection (European Union, 2016).

The SCTIS was developed in record time, given the urgency, through the development of software capable of processing the data associated with testing, establishing direct and immediate communication with the health platforms of the Portuguese Government, to systematize quickly and effectively the information obtained through the results diagnosed in the COVID-19 tests. Given the need to monitor the evolution of the number of daily cases in Portugal, the information provided by this system has facilitated the identification and definition of pandemic control measures.

Given the evolutionary characteristics of the pandemic situation and the technical and scientific lack of knowledge of the virus, associated with the manual treatment of information, mainly carried out through the manual release of information directly on digital platforms provided by the State, came to show that the methodology of obtaining data/ information was slow and inadequate to the requirements and gravity of the situation. On the other hand, the need for immediate investments in human resources for the treatment and updating of information generated a significant increase in costs, since, to feed the databases of the various systems, very high time availability was required. The temporal aspect seems to be a critical resource in the control of the situation and in decision-making, quickly the various stakeholders involved understood the system's infeasibility and existing dynamics. In addition to this situation, the fact that much of the data is not reliable, since inconsistencies and duplication of data were detected, increases the risks in decision-making and management of health resources. This situation has often led to difficulties in monitoring the evolution of the spread of the pandemic (Field et al., 2021).

Given the high rate of transmissibility of the virus, which spread at alarming levels and in a short period of time, especially during 2020, and the inability of the National Health Service (NHS) to respond to the diagnosis of the Portuguese population, the opportunity to develop a new technology-based SI that would increase the volume of tests performed, provide an immediate and consistent update of data/information from a single database and facilitate integration with other IS, namely associated with health institutions and the State. The SCTIS solution had in its design base an urban aspect (Anunciação & Zorrinho, 2006), related to the need for integration of the various stakeholders and the need for value generation, both resource management, either the informational or decision perspective (Li et al., 2022). The generation of collective value, for health entities and the population in general, could only be generated through relational dynamics among the various stakeholders involved. This relational aspect, from an operational perspective, was relevant in ensuring the functional viability of the associated conceptual model, in accepting the defined testing network, decision-making of health institutions, and the definition of the general information system that would provide information and knowledge to institutions and the general population. The definition of the mass testing network highlights the important role of pharmacies, which have become testing sites.

The IST also made available the entire life cycle of testing, allowing citizen registration on the digital platform, the treatment of information associated with the collection of material for analysis, and the availability of a result in a short time (about 30 minutes) sending the resulting information directly to the user and other related entities.

The possibility of permanent access to information and the consequent creation of knowledge has become an almost daily reality. The SCTIS allowed, throughout the project, the timely detection of testing needs and identification of gaps in the testing process, such as unrealized scheduling, cancellations, lack of responsiveness by testing centers, late delivery of results, and general discontent of users, among other examples.

Some information that allows characterizing the size and scope of the project are the following: about 750,000 tests performed in a year (2021–2022); 11,250,000 € of associated business volume; about 250 partners (pharmacies, laboratories, clinics, etc.); degree of coverage of the entire continental territory and islands; and issuance of 2,500,000 digital certificates.

This reality allowed a significant flow of information and the generation of increased levels of knowledge, which materialized through the development of manuals of procedures and health guidelines to minimize the impacts of the pandemic.

3. Objectives and Methodology

The objective of the present study was to evaluate the impacts of the development of the SCTIS seeking to obtain a specification of the generation of value for the involved parts. Using the Focus group technique, invitations were addressed to 16 representatives of the various entities involved, namely, the General Directorate of Health (GDS), Shared Services of the Ministry of Health (SSMH), and the National System of Epidemiological Surveillance (NSES), Health Centers, Vaccination Centers, Pharmacies, Laboratory, NHS and users to jointly identify the various aspects the benefits achieved. The use of this technique allows the various individual perceptions to be shared and contextualized in a value chain context, being more easily identified as the individual value and the contribution to the final value obtained.

As a methodology, two steps were proposed: the identification of the impact of the project carried out and the identification of the main dimensions of analysis and evaluation. This sequence allows, firstly, a global knowledge for each of the participants of the overall values associated with the project; and, secondly, to assess, in the context of information and knowledge, the various aspects in which there have been significant improvements in the fight against the pandemic.

4. Analysis of Results

For the first stage, the overall results of the developed system have been identified and are summarized below:

- carrying out more than 750 thousand COVID tests, in the period between June 2021 and December 2022, with the automatic generation of more than 7,000 notifications per day at peak of the pandemic;

- immediate generation (a few seconds) of test results and validation of results by an authorized technician;
- sending the result by email and the possibility of, in 30 minutes, the user being able to download the COVID digital testing certificate, issued by NHS24.

Then, considering the criticality of information and knowledge, we sought to define the main dimensions of analysis to be adopted in the general evaluation of the benefits obtained with the development of SI Safe COVID Testing, and identified the following:

- criticality of information in assessing the daily situation and the evolution of pandemic impacts;
- criticality of knowledge and its management in the administration of the pandemic;
- immediate availability of test results for real-time monitoring of the evolution of the pandemic situation;
- integration of information between the various competent entities (GDS, SSMH, Health Centers, Vaccination Centers, Family Doctors, etc.) and the European Commission (Digital Certificate);
- organizational urbanization among the various stakeholders, supported by the definition of policies, procedures, functions, and manuals guiding the operation in a situation of contingency and specification of functions and competencies, with the definition of minimum qualifications, substitution policies, and the main responsibilities of each function;
- focus on the increase of human capital with the flexibility of the generation of projects and multidisciplinary teams for analysis and decision of the measures to be taken;
- sharing of information and knowledge at the international level, particularly within health institutions;
- improving the conditions for access and availability of information to stakeholders and society in general, allowing a rapid adjustment of measures to the evolution of the pandemic;
- contingent management of society and economy (for example, change of testing conditions, mandatory testing for travel, conditions of access to restaurants and cinemas, or restrictions on movement between municipalities) according to the daily assessment of the evolution of the number of infected;
- strengthening national technological infrastructures for the creation of conditions associated with the requirements of the new legal framework of teleworking conditions;
- centrality of relevant information in NSES and facilitation of access to various health technicians and their availability to the general public;
- definition of a lifecycle for data and information stored in the SCTIS set at six months in accordance with Regulation (EU) No 679/2016 of 27 April (European Union, 2016);
- definitive deletion of information after the stipulated period, in accordance with the legal period required by law, with automatic deletion by the system itself;

- increasing information management requirements in line with new economic and social requirements;
- improvement of the quality of the information processed by the NHS, since it is the user himself who fills the data in the SISCT, which are automatically validated by the NHS;
- integration of information systems, in so far as, once the data was entered on the platform, the user could go to the testing centers, receive the result, and being able to download the respective digital certificate. the information is sent to the NSES platform which makes the statistics available to the Government;
- increased productivity, achieved by reducing redundancy and inconsistency of data, and increased efficiency by minimizing storage costs and needs.

Regarding the relevance of knowledge, we asked the Focus group to indicate the organizational elements where they noticed changes in relation to the pre-pandemic organizational reality. The first element referenced was the organizational culture for innovation. In this, the following were highlighted as being excellent: democratic spirit, public recognition of innovation, the systemic vision of the organization, adaptation to change, and regularity of meetings at various levels of management and employees. The remaining aspects were considered sufficient.

The second element mentioned was the role of top management, having been highlighted as excellent in the following aspects: encouraging team spirit, valuing human resources, proposing new challenges, and stimulating teamwork.

The third element mentioned was the function or organizational aspect. In this context, the main aspects mentioned were: flexibility in forming interdisciplinary groups, the autonomy of working groups, and performance evaluation.

The fourth element addressed was human resources policy. This context referenced knowledge management, the promotion of self-development and critical thinking, actions to promote organizational culture, the identification of internal and external sources of information, and the preparation of management to educate employees and build a shared vision.

The fifth element refers to recruitment and selection. The elements referenced were the rigor of the selection process, increased creativity, and learning ability through hiring.

The sixth element was training. The elements mentioned were collective learning and interrogation environment of routines and processes.

Also mentioned were the information systems: global adequacy of existing information systems to knowledge management, document management tools, and metadata repositories.

5. Conclusion

The SCTIS was a relevant tool in generating critical information for the management and control of the pandemic. The lack of knowledge of the virus, the speed of spread, and the need to generate knowledge about it evidenced the information as a critical resource. The economic and social domains required new IS, as well as the integration of existing ones at the level of the various health entities as an essential resource for the evaluation and control of the pandemic.

The development of the SCTIS provided information about the results of the tests to the population in real-time, allowing prompt action of the authorities and responsible entities, in particular the Government. The information provided allowed the generation of higher levels of knowledge. Although much of the knowledge has gone through the experience that professionals have been obtaining (tacit knowledge), it is also worth highlighting the need to generate scientific knowledge as a way to ensure effective decision-making.

Health institutions have been forced, in good time and as far as possible, to improve their organization and their processes, seeking, in the context of their activities, different solutions according to the demands of the surrounding environment.

The value of information and knowledge appeared critical in the context of the pandemic. It is important that the lived experiences can integrate the field of organizational learning, namely the assumption of information and knowledge as organizational and economic assets, the criticality of IS in improving decision-making processes, and the effectiveness of decision outcomes.

The evolution of IS in health has been marked by the optimization of the most relevant information flows within an organization. Although this evolution is essentially marked by a technological nature, the development of health activities has long understood the relevance of information processing and knowledge generation in decision-making and intervention close to reality. It is clear that one lives in an increasingly turbulent and unpredictable environment, where the benefits and value to society need to be permanently reinvented.

The pandemic was an opportunity for companies to create cycles of value generation through knowledge. The organizational learning and knowledge management projects allowed, by virtue of the situation, the creation of a dynamic of innovation, skills development, creation and testing of new and different ideas, learning from the surrounding environment in which they are inserted and fitness for new challenges. They adopt, as a response, new structures and management processes that trigger new processes at the relational level.

In conclusion, it is important to highlight the key factors in the perception of the value of information and information systems, with a view to strategic objectives: operational excellence; new products, services, and models of operation or relationship with customers/users; new relationship dynamics Customer-supplier; better decision-making; greater sustainability.

In the specific case of the SCTIS, it can be evidenced that the improvement of the quality of the information, resulting from the improvement of the SI, therefore, the improvement of the decision-making. With the most accurate, fast, reliable, and available information, knowledge levels have also increased, and the following aspects have been highlighted in general: better performance than traditional IS; faster responses to system customers, in particular to the Portuguese Government; improved responsiveness to stakeholders in real-time.

Regarding the company that manages the SCTIS, it should be noted that the information provided by the SCTIS was decisive for the various situations in which it was necessary, as it allowed the expansion of the testing network at the national level.

Limitations and future work:

> It would be interesting and pertinent to carry out, in the future, a more comprehensive and statistically significant study on the criticality of knowledge management in the universe of health institutions involved in the pandemic in Portugal.

References

Adrian, V., Sari, I. R., & Hikmahrachim, H. G. (2021). Application of executive information systems for COVID-19 reporting system and management: An example from DKI Jakarta, Indonesia. Application of information system for COVID reporting. In *Proceedings of the 1st virtual conference on implications of information and digital technologies for development*, pp. 387–397.

Anunciação, P. F. (2014). *Ethics, sustainability, and information and knowledge society* (1st ed., Vol. 1). Chiado Publishing (in Portuguese).

Anunciação, P. F. (2016). Organizational urbanism: A value proposal for the generation of organizational intelligence to healthcare institutions—The case of a Portuguese hospital center. In *Handbook of research on information architecture and management in modern organizations* (Chapter 21, pp. 458–486). IGI Global.

Anunciação, P. F., Dinis, V. M. L., Briones Peñalver, A. J., & Esteves. F. J. M. (2022). Functional safety as a critical success factor to Industry 4.0. *Procedia Computer Science, 204*, 45–53. https://doi.org/10.1016/j.procs.2022.08.006

Anunciação, P. F., & Geada, N. S. (2021). Change management perceptions in Portuguese hospital institutions through ITIL. *International Journal of Healthcare Information Systems and Informatics (IJHISI)*, *16*(4), 1–20. http://doi.org/10.4018/IJHISI.20211001.oa18

Anunciação, P. F., & Zorrinho, C. (2006). *Organizational urbanism—How to manage technological shock.* Sílabo Publishing (in Portuguese).

Araújo Júnior, R. H. de, & Cândido, A. C. (2020). Competitive advantage and knowledge management. *InCID: Journal of Information Science and Documentation*, *11*(1), 93–113. https://doi.org/10.11606/issn.2178-2075.v11i1 (in Portuguese).

Carujo, S. J. R., & Anunciação, P. F. (2021). Digital transformation as a competitive factor in supply chain management: Proof of concept in one of the largest editorial groups in Portugal. *Economics and Culture*, *18*(2), 61–72. https://doi.org/10.2478/jec-2021-0015

Esteves, F. J. M., & Anunciação, P. F. (2021). *Architecture—Essential dimension in information systems. Information systems—Paradigms and solutions for management.* Plátano Publishing (in Portuguese).

Esteves, F. J. M., & Anunciação, P. F. (2023). Information governance. A framework proposal for enterprise managers. In M. V. Kaya (Ed.), *Social and economic studies within the framework of emerging global developments* (Vol. 1, pp. 153–168). Peter Lang Publishing.

European Union (2016). GDPR-General Data Protection Regulation (2016), Regulation (EU) 2016/679 of the European Parliament and of the Council of 27 April 2016, EUR-Lex - 32016R0679 - EN - EUR-Lex (europa.eu)

Field, E., Dyda, A., Hewett, M., Weng, H., Shi, J., Curtis, S., Law, C., McHugh, L., Sheel, M., Moore, J., Furuya-Kanamori, L., Pillai, P., Konings, P., Purcell, M., Stocks, N., Williams, G., & Lau, C. L. (2021). Development of the COVID-19 real-time information system for preparedness and epidemic response (CRISPER), Australia. *Frontiers in Public Health*, *9*. https://doi.org/10.3389/fpubh.2021.753493

Li, X., Wang, H., Chen, C., & Grundy, J. (2022). An empirical study on how well do COVID-19 information dashboards service users' information needs. *IEEE Transactions on Services Computing*, *15*(3), 1178–1192. https://doi.org/10.1109/TSC.2021.3114673

Monteiro, W. R., Prado, M. L. do, & Reynoso-Meza, G. (2021). Leveraging data scientists and business expectations during the COVID-19 pandemic. http://arxiv.org/abs/2103.05425

Oliveira, A. (2021). *Information & information systems—Promises, realities & policies.* Sílabo Publishing (in Portuguese).

Oliveira, A. & Anunciação, P. F. (2023). Information systems governance: Some dimensions to management. In M. V. Kaya (Ed.), *Social and economic studies within the framework of emerging global developments* (Vol. 1, pp. 139–152). Peter Lang.

Wang, Q., Su, M., Zhang, M., & Li, R. (2021). Integrating digital technologies and public health to fight COVID-19 pandemic: Key technologies, applications, challenges and outlook of digital healthcare. *International Journal of Environmental Research and Public Health*, *18*(11). https://doi.org/10.3390/ijerph18116053

Theodore Koutroukis, Charis Vlados, & Dimos Chatzinikolaou

Implications of the COVID-19 Pandemic on Human Resource Management and Labor Relations: Social Dialogue for the New Global Era

1. Introduction

The COVID-19 pandemic has had a profound impact on the global economy (Soto-Acosta, 2020), which has been further compounded by the rapid technological advancements of the Fourth Industrial Revolution, leading to the disruption and restructuring of many established professions and industries (Bonilla-Molina, 2020). This has resulted in a significant shift for all socioeconomic entities worldwide (Koutroukis et al., 2022; Marinov & Marinova, 2021), including the labor market, which has been greatly impacted (Dhakal et al., 2021; Eaton & Heckscher, 2021; Pacheco et al., 2022).

In the wake of the COVID-19 pandemic, it has become evident that further research is required to comprehensively understand the profound changes taking place in the workforce. The purpose of this conceptual essay is to examine the alterations that have occurred in human resources and employment relations due to the pandemic (Jaakkola, 2020). It also proposes the concept of social dialogue as a means of facilitating the necessary organizational reforms. With the emergence of structural changes in labor relations, the objective is to establish whether Social Dialogue (SD) is a critical factor for the future growth of all socioeconomic organizations that have been affected by the crisis, and to draw definitive conclusions.

2. Navigating the Impact of COVID-19 on Human Resources: Challenges and Opportunities for HR Management

The COVID-19 pandemic has presented numerous challenges for Human Resource (HR) managers and practitioners, many of whom lack the necessary training and expertise to cope with this complex crisis (Hamouche, 2021). While it is difficult to predict the long-term effects of the pandemic, it is crucial for HR professionals to re-evaluate their roles and responsibilities in guiding organizations through this crisis. This includes developing strategies to boost employee morale, motivation, and engagement in the context of remote work, as well as promoting the development of soft and ICT skills and adapting to innovative workforce practices and digitalization. Failure to prioritize these areas can lead to lower job satisfaction, reduced job performance, and turnover, as well as imbalances between cost reduction and employee productivity (Gonçalves et al., 2021).

To overcome these challenges, HR practitioners have been implementing a range of measures, such as providing frontline workers with training on Occupational Safety and Health (OSH) issues, as well as initiating incentive plans at all levels of the organization to motivate employees (Sulaiman et al., 2020). However, the human resource management processes that have undergone the most significant changes have been related to making small adjustments, improving internal communications, and implementing appropriate OSH standards within organizations. Additionally, factors such as the level of preparedness, the nature of the industry, the availability of resources, and the role of HR professionals have been identified as critical in adapting organizations to the novel working environment.

In the context of the COVID-19 crisis, it is essential for HR practitioners to digitalize recruitment processes, encourage employees and executives to embrace change, prioritize upskilling, build crisis management skills, and establish transparent communication based on trust and discretion (Nutsubidze & Schmidt, 2021; Pouliakas & Wruuck, 2022). HR managers may also face difficult ethical dilemmas related to balancing business priorities with public health and safety measures (Hadjisolomou & Simone, 2021). By taking a proactive and strategic approach, HR professionals can help organizations navigate the challenges of the pandemic and emerge stronger in the long term.

3. Restructuring Labor Relations in the Post-COVID-19 Era through Effective Social Dialogue

3.1. The Impact of COVID-19 on Labor Relations: Analyzing Challenges and Opportunities in the Post-Pandemic World

The COVID-19 pandemic has brought about numerous challenges and difficulties in employee relations, resulting in significant changes in the labor market. The International Labor Organization (ILO) has highlighted that the widespread adoption of teleworking has accelerated the restructuring of the labor market (ILO, 2021c). In Europe, over one-third of employed individuals worked from home after the pandemic, with significantly higher rates in the United States. The pandemic has had varying impacts on different industries, with female workers in retail trade, accommodation, and food services being among the most affected (ILO, 2021b).

In recent years, professional relationships have deteriorated due to fewer meetings and personal contact with colleagues, and the rise of global uncertainty has motivated many businesses to reorient their employment relations toward undertaking and ad hoc agreements to limit social regulations and personnel benefits (ILO, 2021a; Mora Cortez & Johnston, 2020). Remote working has become a regular part of the routine for many workers over the last three years, which has shifted the balance between labor and management in the face of this new socioeconomic environment (ILO, 2021c).

The literature recognizes three main levels of implications regarding the impact of COVID-19 on employment: employer-side, employee-side, and trade-union-wise. In terms of employer-side implications, it is essential for businesses to manage the consequences of the pandemic, which includes taking care of employee stress outside of the workplace, ensuring compliance with OSH standards, monitoring employee performance, modifying work schedules, and supervising employees regardless of their location. Furthermore, businesses that choose to relocate to decentralized low-cost workplaces or abroad may benefit from reduced production costs, although the degree of "telemigration" is affected by the degree to which various professions are conducive to remote work (Sostero et al., 2020).

The lockdown and quarantine have resulted in restrictions on work mobility and an increase in outsourcing and gig workers. There has also been a dispersion of remote work and a reorganization of the working process, requiring contemporary techniques of home-based work and online collaboration. This digital transformation has posed a challenge to employee commitment and engagement due to a lack of effective interpersonal and/or face-to-face communication (Collings et al., 2021).

On the employee-side, remote workers have reported feeling unsatisfied and alienated. While some have found the new working procedures and habits to be beneficial, leading to improved conditions in their work and living environments, there is a risk of creating unsocial schedules for workers, leading to increased psychological pressure, uncertainty, and stress (Eurofound, 2020). Additionally, remote workers may have to pay for their working expenses such as broadband availability and equipment costs. For traditional workplace employees, there is a demand for better OSH standards that adopt social distancing (Schall & Chen, 2021).

Finally, the wide dispersion of decentralized micro-worksites poses a threat to trade union rights, preventing industrial action and suppressing the power of organized labor. National labor regulations and institutions have been designed with typical workplaces in mind, where the physical presence of employees facilitates worker organization and union activity (Markey, 2020).

The COVID-19 pandemic has exacerbated the "digital divide," resulting in disparities in teleworkability and essential wage variations (Stancheva, 2022). This digitalization era has caused a split in the labor class, with the working poor on one side and richer employees on the other, leading to sharper problems of social integration and inclusion (Calderón-Gómez et al., 2020; Sutherland et al., 2020). Older workers have been more likely to follow COVID-19 preventive measures and can use their digital skills, whether they choose remote work or not (Kooij, 2020).

Many enterprises have adopted hybrid models of working, combining face-to-face and virtual work in a fast, turbulent economic and social environment. However, it seems that many workers will face lower wages in the near future, which will probably create more inequalities in the labor market due to the lack of sophistication and intellectual capital among employees (Vlados et al., 2019). Particularly, people belonging to vulnerable groups face significant obstacles in finding new jobs. Low-competitiveness sectors and less-adaptable local business ecosystems will likely suffer the consequences of this trend. It is not clear whether various socioeconomic organizations could address this problem by achieving higher performance (Chatzinikolaou & Vlados, 2022).

To sum up, the COVID-19 pandemic has exacerbated income inequalities and led to a drop in overall labor income, as well as a decrease in informal labor market incomes. Health inequalities have also emerged, with workers in safe remote jobs or at risk outside-of-home jobs facing different health risks (Adams-Prassl et al., 2020). Additionally, workers have often had to pay higher health and care costs to protect themselves from COVID-19. The pandemic has also had a significant negative impact on employment, with an increase in unemployment, a drop in labor force participation, and a rise in the working poor (Palomino et al., 2021). A decline in temporary contracts has also been observed, indicating limited impact of employment protection measures for casual workers. The pandemic has disproportionately impacted lower-wage earners and poorly-capitalized businesses, leading to significant job losses. To promote inclusiveness for vulnerable populations, governments need to enhance their protection measures, such as providing income support, housing security, and addressing structural weaknesses in the labor market. They should also discuss implementing a universal basic income and adopt better policy intelligence. Social partner consensus and support would be beneficial in making these state interventions in the economy more effective (Baldwin & Weder, 2020; Goodhart & Pradhan, 2020).

3.2. Social Dialogue as a Key Strategy for Improving Labor Relations in the Post-COVID-19 Era

SD is an essential prerequisite for promoting and implementing effective economic and social policies. Research suggests that policymakers must take into account the interests and opinions of all concerned parties during the decision-making process in order to achieve success (Koutroukis & Kretsos, 2008).

The ILO defines SD as "all types of negotiation and consultation, or simply the exchange of information between, or among, representatives of governments, employers, and workers on issues of common interest relating to economic and social policy. It is a key tool in the governance of work, for the promotion of sustainable economic growth and social justice" (ILO, 2022, p. 7).

Involvement of social partners in decision-making regarding economic and social policy yields long-term results. Experience in bipartite or tripartite concertation among employees, employers, and/or the government can contribute to avoiding anomalies, deadweight effects, and conflicting information in disseminating guidance on new or amended policy measures. This concept of partnership between social partners may foster more effective policy measures and prevent the worsening of social and labor market inequalities.

Table 1 illustrates the various levels of SD that were observed in EU countries in the early stages of the pandemic. It is evident that different degrees of social partner participation in decision-making and implementation of anti-COVID-19 measures were adopted in each group of countries.

Table 1. Social partner involvement in employment protection measures during the COVID-19 pandemic, 2020

Level of involvement	Countries
Designing/Amending Measures	Austria, Denmark, Finland
Strong Involvement (including through tripartite bodies)	Belgium, Cyprus, Estonia, Germany, Hungary (employers), Ireland, Malta, Netherlands, Spain, Sweden
Consultation and Evaluation (through tripartite bodies)	Portugal
Weak Involvement in Early Phases but Stronger Involvement in Subsequent Design/Amendment of Measures	Czechia, France, Greece, Italy, Lithuania, Slovenia
Information Only (including in tripartite bodies)	Bulgaria, Latvia, Romania
No Involvement	Croatia, Hungary (trade unions), Poland, Slovakia

Source: Eurofound (2021, p. 66)

Such discrepancies in the level of social partner involvement in employment protection measures during the early phases of the pandemic may be attributed to several factors, such as the differing labor relations systems and institutional frameworks in different countries, the level of social partner trust and cooperation, and the urgency and severity of the pandemic's impact. For instance, countries with a tradition of strong social dialogue systems such as Denmark and Finland saw a higher level of involvement in designing or amending measures, while in countries with weaker social partnership systems, such as Croatia, Poland, and Slovakia, the social partners were less involved in decision-making. Additionally, the severity of the pandemic's impact on a country's economy and labor market may have led to a greater need for social dialogue and cooperation in designing effective employment protection measures. Overall, the level of social partner involvement in employment protection measures during the pandemic highlights the importance of effective social dialogue in promoting sustainable economic growth and social justice in the post-COVID-19 era.

The ILO (2022) recently conducted a study that found effective SD to be crucial in achieving positive outcomes during the COVID-19 pandemic. The study analyzed data from 133 countries and found that countries with strong SD systems tended to have higher levels of social partner involvement in designing and amending employment protection measures. Additionally, the study found that trade unions could play a significant role in addressing the negative impacts of the pandemic and building a more inclusive, sustainable, and resilient society (Otieno et al., 2021). However, the study also noted that unions must enhance their policy-making capacity at the national and/or transnational level to achieve these positive outcomes. Previous research has suggested that tripartite concertation among employer organizations, trade unions, and governments can lead to smart win-win strategies that promote employee competitiveness (Koutroukis & Roukanas, 2016). In addition, trade union engagement in SD procedures can motivate firms to avoid redundancies and other negative impacts on employees that have been observed in countries with weaker partnership traditions.

The post-COVID-19 era has presented challenges for businesses across various industries, with many adopting rapid adaptations to survive and thrive. At the industry level, collective agreements have been impacted by management decisions regarding OSH regulations, salaries, benefits, and redundancies. However, the bargaining culture prevalent in some industries facilitates the inclusion of worker concerns in employee relations adjustments. Industry-level negotiations have the potential to promote mutually beneficial targets and actions in response to post-COVID challenges related to the workforce (Fay & Gadimi,

2020). While these negotiations can be effective, businesses could do more to foster resilient social dialogue schemes that add value to employee relations.

Research indicates that labor-management communication regarding OSH issues has increased during the COVID-19 era. In fact, 88 % of employers surveyed reported increasing their communications with personnel on OSH issues (ILO, 2022). To further promote effective social dialogue, businesses could initiate social dialogue fora and employee voice procedures at the business level. By doing so, labor and management can work together to address issues affecting employees and promote sustainable practices.

In conclusion, the impact of the COVID-19 pandemic on labor relations and employment protection measures was significant and varied across different countries, with the level of social partner involvement depending on several factors. However, evidence suggests that effective social dialogue between employer organizations, trade unions, and governments can lead to smart win-win strategies, enhance employee competitiveness, and foster resilient social dialogue schemes. At the industry level, negotiation and communication between labor and management on various issues can help in adapting to the post-COVID challenges and lead to mutually beneficial targets and actions. Ultimately, promoting effective social dialogue is essential for achieving sustainable economic growth and social justice in the post-COVID-19 era, and stakeholders must work together to ensure its implementation.

4. Conclusion and Prospects

In conclusion, the COVID-19 pandemic has brought about significant changes to the labor market, creating challenges and opportunities for workers and organizations alike. The acceleration of digital transformation and the need for new skills and knowledge have amplified the existing labor market inequalities, highlighting the importance of social dialogue as a means of addressing them. While there have been shortcomings in the utilization of social dialogue during the pandemic response, evidence suggests that it can be a powerful tool for promoting cooperation and preventing conflicts at the workplace level.

Looking forward, further research is needed to better understand the role of social dialogue in the post-COVID era, as well as to identify best practices and successful strategies for promoting effective partnerships and employee voice in different industries and regions. There is also a need for policymakers and business leaders to recognize the importance of investing in HR development and social dialogue, as they play a crucial role in enhancing competitiveness and sustainability in the global economy. By creating more inclusive and collaborative working environments, businesses can improve productivity, innovation, and employee well-being, thereby contributing to the long-term success of their organizations and the wider economy.

References

Adams-Prassl, A., Boneva, T., Golin, M., & Rauh, C. (2020). Inequality in the impact of the coronavirus shock: Evidence from real time surveys. *Journal of Public Economics*, *189*, 104245. https://doi.org/10.1016/j.jpubeco.2020.104245

Baldwin, R. E., & Weder, B. (2020). *Economics in the time of COVID-19*. CEPR Press. https://voxeu.org/content/economics-time-covid-19

Bonilla-Molina, L. (2020). COVID-19 on route of the Fourth Industrial Revolution. *Postdigital Science and Education*, *2*(3), 562–568. https://doi.org/10.1007/s42438-020-00179-4

Calderón-Gómez, D., Casas-Mas, B., Urraco-Solanilla, M., & Revilla, J. C. (2020). The labour digital divide: Digital dimensions of labour market segmentation. *Work Organisation, Labour & Globalisation*, *14*(2), 7–30.

Chatzinikolaou, D., & Vlados, C. (2022). Crisis, innovation and change management: A blind spot for micro-firms? *Journal of Entrepreneurship in Emerging Economies* (ahead-of-print). https://doi.org/10.1108/JEEE-07-2022-0210

Collings, D. G., Nyberg, A. J., Wright, P. M., & McMackin, J. (2021). Leading through paradox in a COVID-19 world: Human resources comes of age. *Human Resource Management Journal*, *31*(4), 819–833.

Dhakal, S., Burgess, J., & Connell, J. (2021). COVID-19 crisis, work and employment: Policy and research trends. *Labour & Industry: A Journal of the Social and Economic Relations of Work*, *31*(4), 353–365. https://doi.org/10.1080/10301763.2021.2005758

Eaton, A., & Heckscher, C. (2021). COVID's impacts on the field of labour and employment relations. *Journal of Management Studies*, *58*(1), 275–279. https://doi.org/10.1111/joms.12645

Eurofound. (2020). *Living, working and COVID-19*. Publications Office of the European Union. https://data.europa.eu/doi/10.2806/467608

Eurofound. (2021). *COVID-19: Implications for employment and working life*. Publications Office of the European Union. https://data.europa.eu/doi/10.2806/160624

Fay, D. L., & Ghadimi, A. (2020). Collective bargaining during times of crisis: Recommendations from the COVID-19 pandemic. *Public Administration Review*, *80*(5), 815–819. https://doi.org/10.1111/puar.13233

Gonçalves, S. P., Santos, J. V. dos, Silva, I. S., Veloso, A., Brandão, C., & Moura, R. (2021). COVID-19 and people management: The view of human resource managers. *Administrative Sciences, 11*(3), 69. https://doi.org/10.3390/admsci11030069

Goodhart, C., & Pradhan, M. (2020). *The great demographic reversal: Ageing societies, waning inequality, and an inflation revival.* Springer International Publishing. https://doi.org/10.1007/978-3-030-42657-6

Hadjisolomou, A., & Simone, S. (2021). Profit over people? Evaluating morality on the front line during the COVID-19 crisis: A front-line service manager's confession and regrets. *Work, Employment and Society, 35*(2), 396–405. https://doi.org/10.1177/0950017020971561

Hamouche, S. (2021). Human resource management and the COVID-19 crisis: Implications, challenges, opportunities, and future organizational directions. *Journal of Management & Organization, 19*, 1–16. https://doi.org/10.1017/jmo.2021.15

ILO. (2021a). *A global trend analysis of the role of trade unions in times of COVID-19: A summary of key findings (executive summary).* International Labour Organization.

ILO. (2021b). *Global Wage Report 2020–21: Wages and minimum wages in the time of COVID-19.* International Labour Office.

ILO. (2021c). *Working from home: From invisibility to decent work.* International Labour Office.

ILO. (2022). *Enhancing social dialogue towards a culture of safety and health: What have we learned from the COVID-19 crisis?* [World Day for Safety and Health at Work 2022 Report]. http://www.ilo.org/global/topics/safety-and-health-at-work/resources-library/publications/WCMS_842505/lang--en/index.htm

Jaakkola, E. (2020). Designing conceptual articles: Four approaches. *AMS Review, 10*(1), 18–26. https://doi.org/10.1007/s13162-020-00161-0

Kooij, D. T. (2020). The impact of the COVID-19 pandemic on older workers: The role of self-regulation and organizations. *Work, Aging and Retirement, 6*(4), 233–237.

Koutroukis, T., & Kretsos, L. (2008). Social dialogue in areas and times of depression: Evidence from regional Greece. *African Journal of Business Management, 2*(4), 77–84.

Koutroukis, T., & Roukanas, S. (2016). Social dialogue in the era of memoranda: The consequences of austerity and deregulation measures on the Greek social partnership process. In A. Karasavvoglou, Z. Aranđelović, S. Marinković, & P. Polychronidou (Eds.), *The first decade of living with the global crisis: Economic and social developments in the Balkans and Eastern Europe* (pp. 73–82). Springer International Publishing. https://doi.org/10.1007/978-3-319-24267-5_6

Koutroukis, T., Chatzinikolaou, D., Vlados, C., & Pistikou, V. (2022). The post-COVID-19 era, fourth industrial revolution, and new globalization: Restructured labor relations and organizational adaptation. *Societies*, *12*(6), Article 6. https://doi.org/10.3390/soc12060187

Marinov, M., & Marinova, S. T. (2021). *COVID-19 and international business: Change of era*. Routledge.

Markey, R. (2020). The impact of the COVID-19 virus on industrial relations. *The Impact of the COVID-19 Virus on Industrial Relations*, *85*, 147–154.

Mora Cortez, R., & Johnston, W. J. (2020). The Coronavirus crisis in B2B settings: Crisis uniqueness and managerial implications based on social exchange theory. *Industrial Marketing Management*, *88*, 125–135. https://doi.org/10.1016/j.indmarman.2020.05.004

Nutsubidze, N., & Schmidt, D. A. (2021). Rethinking the role of HRM during COVID-19 pandemic era: Case of Kuwait. *Review of Socio-Economic Perspectives*, *6*(1), 1–12. https://doi.org/10.19275/RSEP103

Otieno, G. O. (2021). Trade union membership dynamics amidst COVID-19: Does social dialogue matter? *International Journal of Labour Research*, *10*(1–2), 1–12.

Pacheco, G., Plum, A., & Tran, L. (2022). *The Pacific workforce and the impact of COVID-19*. New Zealand Work Research Institute, Auckland University of Technology. https://workresearch.aut.ac.nz/__data/assets/pdf_file/0009/674559/Pacific-Labour-Market-Outcomes_final_website.pdf

Palomino, J. C., Rodríguez, J. G., & Sebastian, R. (2022). The COVID-19 shock on the labour market: Poverty and inequality effects across Spanish regions. *Regional Studies*, *57*(5), 814–828. https://doi.org/10.1080/00343404.2022.2110227

Pouliakas, K., & Wruuck, P. (2022). *Corporate training and skill gaps: Did COVID-19 stem EU convergence in training investments?* Institute of Labor Economics (IZA).

Schall, M. C., & Chen, P. (2021). Evidence-based strategies for improving occupational safety and health among teleworkers during and after the coronavirus pandemic. *Human Factors*, 0018720820984583. https://doi.org/10.1177/0018720820984583

Sostero, M., Milasi, S., Hurley, J., Fernandez-Macias, E., & Bisello, M. (2020). *Teleworkability and the COVID-19 crisis: A new digital divide?* European Commission.

Soto-Acosta, P. (2020). COVID-19 pandemic: Shifting digital transformation to a high-speed gear. *Information Systems Management*, *37*(4), 260–266. https://doi.org/10.1080/10580530.2020.1814461

Stantcheva, S. (2022). *Inequalities in the times of a pandemic* (No. w29657; p. w29657). National Bureau of Economic Research. https://doi.org/10.3386/w29657

Sulaiman, M. a. B. A., Ahmed, M. N., & Shabbir, M. S. (2020). COVID-19 challenges and human resource management in organized retail operations. *Utopia y Praxis Latinoamericana*, *25*(Extra 12), 81–92.

Sutherland, W., Jarrahi, M. H., Dunn, M., & Nelson, S. B. (2020). Work precarity and gig literacies in online freelancing. *Work, Employment and Society*, *34*(3), 457–475. https://doi.org/10.1177/0950017019886511

Vlados, C., Katimertzopoulos, F., Chatzinikolaou, D., Deniozos, N., & Koutroukis, T. (2019). Crisis, innovation, and change management in less developed local business ecosystems: The case of Eastern Macedonia and Thrace. *Perspectives of Innovations, Economics and Business*, *19*(2), 114–140.

Zuzana Birknerova & Lucia Zbihlejova

Creation of a Business Competency Model for Managers

1. Introduction

In managerial work, the issue of competencies plays an important and inseparable role. Many types of competencies and competency models are mentioned in the literature. For the purposes of the chapter, we focused on the competencies of managers in the field of business.

A holistic model of managerial competencies with an expanded domain captures the key areas essential for managerial performance: business, intrapersonal, interpersonal, leadership, career and mentoring skills. Managerial competency models examine key generic competency models. There are behavioral models in the literature (Boyatzis, 1982, 2008; McClelland, 1973, 1998); functional (Knasel & Meed, 1994); work (Mansfield & Mathews, 1985); holistic (Cheetham & Chivers, 1998); multidimensional (Le Deist et al., 2005); and domain ones (Hogan & Warrenfeltz, 2003). Asumeng (2014) highlights both the strengths and weaknesses of each model, but emphasizes the need for career and mentoring skills in context with managerial effectiveness.

In the chapter, we rely on all the mentioned competency models from a theoretical, practical and research point of view, with a focus on the field of business. The main goal is the creation of a business competency model for business managers. The objective of the research project is to identify the factors of business competency model creation by business managers.

2. Competency Models

According to Ulrich et al. (2007), among the means of developing the quality of managers it is necessary to include their competencies. The basis for defining them are values, knowledge and abilities in a broader sense. Currently, they also include the ability to use this knowledge in practice. Attention is focused on individuals with special knowledge that improve companies' position on the labor market and increase their price and value. Retaining them requires rewarding the best talent and developing new leaders (Eunjung & Scott You, 2013).

In order to ensure customer expectations, it is necessary to monitor business conditions in addition to the human side. A balance of both aspects is expected so that the manager is appropriately focused on people as well as on the business side. This will bring long-term benefit to the organization (Ulrich et al., 2007). An example of a specific competency model is the model of the Society for Human Resource Management, which was created from the results of a survey on a sample of more than 32,000 respondents (Scott-Jackson & Mayo, 2017). The resulting model includes nine competencies: Human Resource Expertise, Ethical Practice, Leadership & Navigation, Business Acumen, Consultation, Communication, Critical Evaluation, Global & Cultural Effectiveness, and Relationship Management.

The competency model is built so that specialists in the field of human resources are as effective as possible in their work. Competencies form the basis of success for the functioning of the HR (Eunjung & Scott You, 2013). What the mentioned models have in common is that they were created due to the growth and performance of the company for which they were custom-made, but with regard to interpersonal relations, management and globalization.

2.1. Business Competencies

Boyatzis (1982) indicated competencies as skills, characteristics, set of knowledge, motives, social roles, aspect of self-image. He also introduced competencies into managerial practice as the abilities and capabilities of an individual to behave in an adequate manner, in accordance with the requirements of the job position and the company's environment, with an emphasis on achieving desirable results (Boyatzis, 2008).

In the present, according to Krawczyk-Sokołowska (2008), an important aspect of managerial work is to pay attention to problem-solving, creative cooperation, mutual assistance in illustrative activities, motivation for creativity (also in Štefko et al., 2017). Kubeš et al. (2004) characterize the competency approach as focusing on the behavior of managers, on what they do. It is behaviorally anchored. It brings out the essentials in their behavior, which leads to success even in difficult situations. It is directly linked to the effectiveness of the individual as well as the organization as a whole (Tomková et al., 2021). Competencies predict behavior, thinking and expression in specific situations.

2.2. Competency Models in Management

According to Kubeš et al. (2004), a competency model describes a specific combination of knowledge, skills and personality characteristics that are necessary to effectively fulfill company tasks. It is related to a specific managerial position, specific organization and type of business. It shows what behavior needs to be developed, encouraged and rewarded, while making this behavior measurable.

Competency models are used to identify knowledge, abilities, skills and other data needed to hold assigned positions in the organization. The competency model is a suitable tool for hiring and selecting new employees, evaluating existing employees, in case of changes in the company, such as a change in the organizational structure or company culture (Kubeš et al., 2004). It helps in the development of workers, evaluation of their work performance, in their career growth, as well as in planning the advancement of employees. The authors divide competencies into soft, professional general and professional specific competencies. The use of the competency model is most often used for position definition, employee selection and as a tool for manager development.

The holistic model of managerial competency captures six key areas necessary for managerial performance: business, intrapersonal, interpersonal, leadership, career and mentoring skills. Competency models receive due attention in the literature. They are divided into:

- behavioral (Boyatzis, 1982, 2008; McClelland, 1998);
- functional (Knasel & Meed, 1994);
- work competency (Mansfield & Mathews, 1985);
- holistic (Cheetham & Chivers, 1998);
- multidimensional (Le Deist & Winterton, 2005);
- domain model (Hogan & Warrenfeltz, 2003).

The mentioned division provides an overview of the literature and authors who pay due attention to the issue. Close relationships can be seen between career skills, mentoring skills and managerial effectiveness. Each of the mentioned models is based on the individual competencies required for the performance of managerial work.

Rapidly changing conditions and circumstances demand from managers a specific handling of business management work and thus the use of new managerial competencies. The competency management model should therefore contain skills and knowledge that a manager should have, for example, professional competencies (hard skills)—general professional competencies, specific professional competencies, as well as soft skills.

3. Research Project

The main objective of the research project is to identify the factors of creating a business competency model for business managers. The research problem is to find out which of the business management competencies are the most important for business managers and how managers are evaluated. Based on this, we established a hypothesis: "There is an internal factor structure of the business competency model creation questionnaire."

The research sample consisted of 256 respondents—business managers aged between 20 and 65 (M = 36.58 years, SD = 9.856). Business managers reported years of managerial practice from 1 to 39 years (M = 11.89, SD = 8.762) and business experience from 1 to 30 years (M = 8.93 years, SD = 6.977).

3.1. Methodology and Methods

We carried out the research through a questionnaire, which is aimed at creating a business competency model, while we were inspired by the model of the authors Spencer and Spencer (1993). The authors state that their model, which consists of 21 competencies, was created on the basis of long-term research of various competency models containing separate types of behavior. They established criteria and scales for their identification and evaluation. For the purposes of the conducted research, we have created a Business Competency Model Creation Questionnaire (BCMCQ), which consists of items focused on 19 competencies based on the model by Jevšček (2016), who describes the competencies in more detail. For the field of business management, we adapted them and labeled them as presented below. Respondents expressed their opinion on individual items by expressing their degree of personal agreement or disagreement with the statements on a 7-point Likert scale (1 = definitely no, 2 = no, 3 = rather no than yes, 4 = neutral answer, 5 = rather yes than no, 6 = yes, 7 = definitely yes).

To process the research results, we used statistical methods: factor analysis (Principal Component method with Varimax rotation), Cronbach's alpha, t-test for two independent samples, Pearson's correlation coefficient, descriptive statistics in MS Excel and IBM SPSS Statistics 26 statistical software.

3.2. Research Results

Based on the results of Bartlett's test 3481.490 (significance 0.000), we extracted three factors using factor analysis (Principal Component method with Varimax rotation). In Table 1, we present the extracted factors of the creation of the business competency model. We extracted the factors of the competency model on a sample of 256 business managers.

Table 1. Extracted factors of the creation of the competency model of business managers

BCMCQ items	F1	F2	F3
I focus on achieving results and setting challenging goals.	.599		
I create complex plans, analyze problems, have analytical thinking.			.759
I create new concepts and models, I have conceptual thinking.			.595
I introduce new detailed and complex systems to increase order and improve quality.	.593		
I am customer service oriented, I focus on the client's needs and satisfaction.		.616	
I ensure and reward the growth and development of others, I provide them with support.		.629	
I am decisive, I use force, I enforce quality standards, control and discipline.	.729		
I am flexible, adaptable, able to accept change and resilient.		.597	
I use complex influencing strategies adapted to individual situations and cooperation.			.624
When searching for information, I look at things more deeply and can define the problem.	.688		
I am proactive, I try to create new opportunities and prevent problems.	.837		
I understand complex problems, I have an interpersonal diagnostic awareness.	.769		
I understand long-term organizational problems, I have organizational awareness.		.655	
I am mission- and vision-oriented, I have a developed business mindset.		.669	
I build relationships, networks, use resources, develop personal contacts.		.676	
I am independent, willing to take responsibility, I am not afraid of challenging situations.			.699
I can keep calm, I am resistant to stress and have well-developed self-control.			.631
I lead the team responsibly, I am able to present a convincing vision.	.769		
I prefer teamwork, conflict resolution, motivation of others.		.694	

Source: Own elaboration

The extracted factors explain 63.121 % of the variance. In research, the stated percentage is acceptable. Table 2 describes the explained percentage of variance in more detail. We have specified the factors for business managers in terms of content: F1 Result-Oriented Competencies, F2 Others-Oriented Competencies,

F3 Self-Oriented Competencies. The mentioned structure of the factors of the creation of the business competency model is also confirmed by the result of the graphic processing of the used scree plot method (Figure 1).

Table 2. Percentage of the variance explained for BCMCQ

	Rotation sums of squared loadings		
BCMCQ Factors	**Total**	**% of Variance**	**Cumulative %**
F1 Result-Oriented Competencies	5.337	28.092	28.092
F2 Others-Oriented Competencies	3.368	17.725	45.817
F3 Self-Oriented Competencies	3.288	17.304	*63.121*

Source: Own elaboration

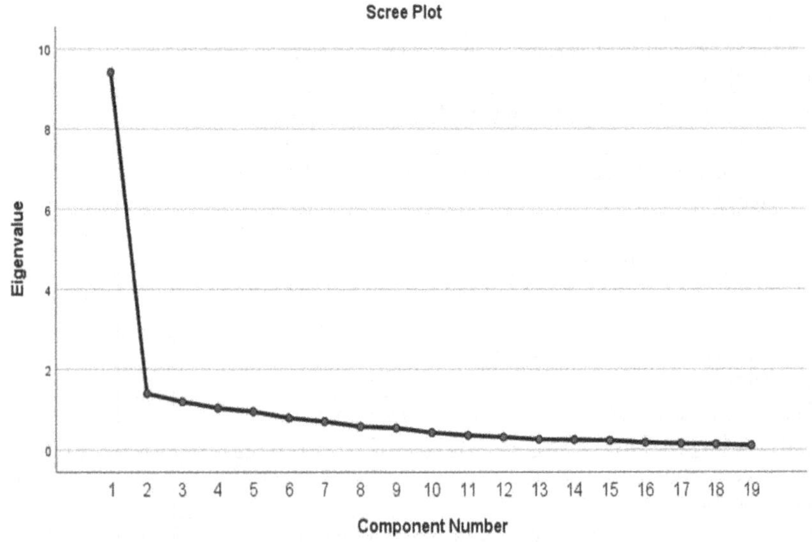

Figure 1. Scree plot of the factors of BCMCQ
Source: Own elaboration

We determined the accuracy and reliability of the research tool by calculating Cronbach's alpha values. The satisfactory values confirm the mentioned structure of the extracted factors. It represents an acceptable level of reliability of the items within the individual factors of the business competency model creation questionnaire. We present reliability values calculated on a sample of business managers.

- F1 Result-Oriented Competencies: Cronbach's alpha = .903
- F2 Others-Oriented Competencies: Cronbach's alpha = .877
- F3 Self-Oriented Competencies: Cronbach's alpha = .846

Based on skewness and kurtosis testing, it is possible to consider the distribution of data in the factors of the BCMCQ as normal, and thus the distribution of frequencies in the statistical set as symmetrical (Table 3).

Table 3. Skewness and kurtosis of the data distribution in the factors of BCMCQ

	Result-oriented competencies	**Others-oriented competencies**	**Self-oriented competencies**
Skewness	-.596	-.475	-.183
Kurtosis	.115	.012	-.583

Source: Own elaboration

We also confirmed the factor structure of the Business Competency Model Creation Questionnaire by analyzing the relationships between individual factors. The appropriateness of the factor structure of the Business Competency Model Creation Questionnaire is also indicated by the calculated values of the intercorrelation coefficients between the extracted factors, which we present in Table 4.

Table 4. Intercorrelation coefficients between the factors of the BCMCQ

	Result-oriented competencies	**Others-oriented competencies**
Others-Oriented Competencies	.783**	
Self-Oriented Competencies	.704**	.684**

** Statistical significance at the level of .01
Source: Own elaboration

In Table 4, we recorded the intercorrelation coefficients between all the factors of the Business Competency Model Creation Questionnaire by calculating the value of the Pearson correlation coefficient. We noted high statistically significant positive correlations. It means that these are factors that describe related areas of the competency model. All assessed business management competencies forming our proposed competency model are related to each other. We confirmed that the questionnaire examines the factors of the same construct with content connections.

As part of the verification of the hypothesis, we focused on the creation of a business competency model. After the validity and reliability tests, we used descriptive statistics to describe in Table 5 the individual competencies that make up the business competency model in terms of the minimum, maximum, average value and standard deviation of the respondents' answers on a 7-point Likert scale (1 = definitely no, 2 = no, 3 = rather no than yes, 4 = neutral answer, 5 = rather yes than no, 6 = yes, 7 = definitely yes).

Table 5. Competencies forming the business competency model

Competencies forming a business competency model	**Minimum**	**Maximum**	**M**	**SD**
10. Finding information.	1	7	5.11	1.575
19. Teamwork and cooperation.	1	7	5.04	1.808
4. Focus on order, quality and accuracy.	2	7	5.01	1.601
17. Self-control.	1	7	4.98	1.452
18. Team leadership, management.	1	7	4.93	1.785
5. Orientation to customer services.	1	7	4.84	1.495
9. Impact and influence.	1	7	4.82	2.063
6. Development of others.	1	7	4.80	1.624
8. Flexibility.	1	6	4.80	.963
3. Conceptual thinking.	1	7	4.77	1.397
13. Organizational awareness.	1	6	4.73	1.495
2. Analytical thinking.	1	6	4.62	1.308
7. Using the position of manager.	1	7	4.41	1.687
1. Orientation toward achieving results.	2	6	4.34	1.243
12. Interpersonal understanding.	1	6	4.10	1.548
15. Building relationships.	1	6	3.99	1.375
11. Initiative.	1	6	3.97	1.194
14. Organizational commitment.	1	6	3.91	1.158
16. Self-confidence.	1	5	3.80	.938

Source: Own elaboration

F1 Result-Oriented Competencies is made up of the competencies presented in Table 6.

Table 6. Competencies forming F1 Result-Oriented Competencies

F1 Result-Oriented Competencies	Minimum	Maximum	M	SD
Finding information	1	7	5.11	1.575
Focus on order, quality and accuracy	2	7	5.01	1.601
Team leadership, management	1	7	4.93	1.785
Using the position of manager	1	7	4.41	1.687
Orientation toward achieving results	2	6	4.34	1.243
Interpersonal understanding	1	6	4.10	1.548
Initiative	1	6	3.97	1.194

Source: Own elaboration

Table 6 shows that within the factor F1 Result-Oriented Competencies, the business managers we approached rated the competencies Finding information, Focus on order, quality and accuracy, and Team leadership, management the highest (on a scale of "yes rather than no"). On the contrary, Interpersonal understanding and Initiative were assessed the lowest (on the "neutral answer" part of the scale).

F2 Others-Oriented Competencies is made up of the competencies presented in Table 7.

Table 7. Competencies forming F2 Others-Oriented Competencies

F2 Others-Oriented Competencies	Minimum	Maximum	M	SD
Teamwork and cooperation	1	7	5.04	1.808
Orientation to customer services	1	7	4.84	1.495
Development of others	1	7	4.80	1.624
Flexibility	1	6	4.80	.963
Organizational awareness	1	6	4.73	1.495
Building relationships	1	6	3.99	1.375
Organizational commitment	1	6	3.91	1.158

Source: Own elaboration

As illustrated in Table 7, within the factor F2 Others-Oriented Competencies, the business managers we approached rated the competency Teamwork and cooperation the highest (on a scale of "yes rather than no"). On the contrary, Building relationships and Organizational commitment were assessed the lowest (on the "neutral answer" part of the scale).

F3 Self-Oriented Competencies is made up of the competencies presented in Table 8.

Table 8. Competencies forming F3 Self-Oriented Competencies

F3 Self-Oriented Competencies	Minimum	Maximum	M	SD
Self-control	1	7	4.98	1.452
Impact and influence	1	7	4.82	2.063
Conceptual thinking	1	7	4.77	1.397
Analytical thinking	1	6	4.62	1.308
Self-confidence	1	5	3.80	.938

Source: Own elaboration

Table 8 shows that within the F3 Self-Oriented Competencies, the business managers we approached rated the competency Self-control the highest (on a scale of "yes rather than no"). On the contrary, Self-confidence was assessed the lowest (on the "neutral answer" part of the scale).

Based on the factor importance categorization method, we determined degrees of importance (Table 9). When compiling the ranking of the importance of business competencies, we were inspired by the results of research by Spencer and Spencer (1993).

Table 9. Categorization and degrees of importance of factors

Degrees of importance	Categorization of importance
>5.0	Very important
>4.5–5.0	Important
>3.5–4.5	Somehow important
>2.0–3.5	Not important
1–2.0	Not important at all

Source: Own elaboration according to Spencer and Spencer (1993)

Based on these degrees of importance and the average values of individual items, we compiled the overall order of competencies in the competency model in Table 10.

Table 10. Order of importance of competency items forming the competency model

Competencies forming the competency model	M	Categorization of importance
When searching for information, I look at things more deeply and can define the problem.	5.11	Very important
I prefer teamwork, conflict resolution, motivation of others.	5.04	Very important
I introduce new detailed and complex systems to increase order and improve quality.	5.01	Very important
I can keep calm, I am resistant to stress and have well-developed self-control.	4.98	Important
I lead the team responsibly, I am able to present a convincing vision.	4.93	Important
I am customer service oriented, I focus on the client's needs and satisfaction.	4.84	Important
I use complex influencing strategies adapted to individual situations and cooperation.	4.82	Important
I ensure and reward the growth and development of others, I provide them with support.	4.80	Important
I am flexible, adaptable, able to accept change and resilient.	4.80	Important
I create new concepts and models, I have conceptual thinking.	4.77	Important
I understand long-term organizational problems, I have organizational awareness.	4.73	Important
I create complex plans, analyze problems, have analytical thinking.	4.62	Important
I am decisive, I use force, I enforce quality standards, control and discipline.	4.41	Somehow important
I focus on achieving results and setting challenging goals.	4.34	Somehow important
I understand complex problems, I have an interpersonal diagnostic awareness.	4.10	Somehow important
I build relationships, networks, use resources, develop personal contacts.	3.99	Somehow important
I am proactive, I try to create new opportunities and prevent problems.	3.97	Somehow important
I am mission- and vision-oriented, I have a developed business mindset.	3.91	Somehow important
I am independent, willing to take responsibility, I am not afraid of challenging situations.	3.80	Somehow important

Source: Own elaboration

From the point of view of the order of importance of the competency items that make up the competency model, the most important for business managers is Finding information (When searching for information, I look at things more deeply and can define the problem.), Teamwork and cooperation (I prefer teamwork, conflict resolution, motivation of others.) and Focus on order, quality and accuracy (I introduce new detailed and complex systems to increase order and improve quality.). Self-confidence (I am independent, willing to take responsibility, I am not afraid of challenging situations.) was rated as the least important, but it was rated at a neutral level of importance, that is, as "somehow important."

Based on the aforementioned analyses, it can be concluded that the *hypothesis* "There is an internal factor structure of the business competency model creation questionnaire." has been *supported.*

4. Conclusion

In the conducted research, we compiled a business competency model based on the categorization of the importance of the extracted factors of the designed verified questionnaire. Its creation was inspired and based on the model by Spencer and Spencer (1993) and the research by Jevšček (2016), whose goal was to find out which competencies influence the performance of managers. Unlike our research sample of business managers, the author addressed a wider sample of managers, regardless of the field of activity. Similarly to our research, Horváthová et al. (2019) were able to create a competency model for the position of a sales manager in a manufacturing industry organization.

Competencies that are used today for the functioning of the organization, which have an important function in it, may later be insufficient after a change in the situation and their meaning will no longer be so important. The organization must therefore monitor the relevance of competencies. The preparation of business managers within the framework of future requirements for business deployment is the greatest asset for the success of the organization (Kubeš et al., 2004). The study of competencies is the subject of current research in many areas with an emphasis on their evaluation. McClelland (1973) studied approaches to testing individuals and proved that success does not depend on the intelligence of the individual, but on their competencies, which are manifested in their behavior.

It is important to determine the abilities, skills and competencies that a business manager should have in order to properly perform their work. Based on the theoretical principles, the research in this chapter was dedicated to verifying the established hypothesis on a sample of business managers. This hypothesis was supported, which means that the internal factor structure of the business competency model creation questionnaire was found to exist.

Acknowledgment

The compilation of this chapter was supported by the research grant project KEGA No. 018PU-4/2023.

References

Asumeng, M. (2014). Managerial competency models: A critical review and proposed holistic-domain model. *Journal of Management Research*, *6*(4), 1–20.

Boyatzis, R. E. (1982). *The competent manager: A model for effective performance*. John Wiley & Sons.

Boyatzis, R. E. (2008). Competencies in the 21st century. *The Journal of Management Development*, *27*, 5–12.

Cheetham, G., & Chivers, G. (1998). The reflective (and competent) practitioner. *Journal of European Industrial Training*, *22*(7), 267–276.

Eunjung, L., & Scott You, K. (2013). How are global HR competency models evolving for the future? [Online]. https://core.ac.uk/download/pdf/17170671.pdf

Hogan, R., & Warrenfeltz, R. (2003). Educating the modern manager. *Academy of Management Learning & Education*, *2*(1), 74–84.

Horváthová, P., Čopíková, A., & Mokrá, K. (2019). Methodology proposal of the creation of competency models and competency model for the position of a sales manager in an industrial organisation using the AHP method and Saaty's method of determining weights. *Economic Research-Ekonomska Istraživanja*, *32*(1), 2594–2613.

Jevšček M. (2016). Competencies of process managers. *Journal of Universal Excellence*, *5*(1), 13–29.

Knasel, E., & Meed, J. (1994). *Becoming competent: Effective learning for occupational competence*. Employment Department.

Krawczyk-Sokołowska, I. (2008). Rola menedżera w przedsiębiorstwie innowacyjnym. In I. Krawczyk-Sokołowska (red.), *Teoretyczne i praktyczne aspekty innowacji w gospodarce polskiej* (pp. 145–155). Sekcja Wydawnictw Wydziału Zarządzania Politechniki Częstochowskiej.

Kubeš, M., Spillerová, D., & Kurnický, R. (2004). *Manažerské kompetence: způsobilosti výjimečných manažerů* (183 p.). Grada Publishing.

Le Deist, F. D., & Winterton, J. (2005). What is competence? *Human Resource Development International*, *8*(1), 27–46.

Mansfield, R., & Mathews, D. (1985). *Job competence: A description for use in vocational education and training*. Further Education College.

McClelland, D. C. (1973). Testing for competence rather than for intelligence. *American Psychologist*, *1*(28), 1–14.

McClelland, D. C. (1998). Identifying competencies with behavioural-event interviews. *Psychological Science*, *9*(5), 331–339.

Scott-Jackson, W., & Mayo, A. (2017). *HR with purpose: Future models of HR*. Henley Business School.

Spencer, L. M., & Spencer, S. M. (1993). *Competence at work: A models for superior performance* (372 p.). Wiley.

Štefko R., Bačík R., Fedorko R., Gavurová B., Horváth J., & Propper M. (2017). Gender differences in the case of work satisfaction and motivation. *Polish Journal of Management Studies*, *16*(1), 215–225.

Tomkova, A., Ondrijova, I., Ratnayake-Kascakova, D., & Nemec, J. (2021). Leaders and Machiavellian manifestations: Workers' innovation development and business performance. *Marketing and Management of Innovations*, 3, 23–31.

Ulrich, D., Brockbank, W., Johnson, D., & Younger, J. (2007). *Human resource competencies: Responding to increased expectations*. Wiley Periodicals.

Mariken Ross & Eneken Titov

Healthcare Leadership Competencies in the Turbulent Times and Trends

1. Introduction

In the times of major changes and need for rapid decision-making it is best to be prepared on the highest possible level. Predicting the future is not possible but we can make justified forecasts based on knowledge and models available. Making use of predicted trends and keeping them in mind is one of the possible ways to prepare for the unknown.

Turbulence in healthcare overall is at all-time high with several contributing factors. In addition to the known or "classical" change triggers in healthcare, such as aging population (Christensen et al., 2009), lack of qualified personnel (WHO, 2022) and inequity in access to medicine (Baeten et al., 2018, WHO, 2022) there are several important new characters on the stage. COVID-19 pandemic has changed the face of medicine tremendously with ongoing aftershocks lasting probably for years to come. In Europe the war in Ukraine has brought additional new types of challenges into medical reality, for example our systems' capability of frontline medicine or accessibility to certain drugs or resources. Equally important is the addition of new data and with that new knowledge—over a decade ago the doubling time of medical knowledge was estimated to be around 3.5 years with predicted value for 2020 being 73 days (Densen, 2011). It remains to be seen how the medical reality will cope with the increase and speed of doubling data. Also significant is the staggering increase in the cost of healthcare, with new drugs prices climbing into unprecedented heights. A recent report states that median launch prices increased from $2115 (IQR, $928–$17 866) per year in 2008 to $180 007 (IQR, $20 236–$409 732) per year in 2021 (Rome et al., 2022). In this light it is not unexpected that the focus for healthcare leadership is also at an all-time high with published articles in databases (PubMed) increasing from 930 in 2010 to 2,118 in 2020.

In the midst of all of this it is more important than ever to understand the challenges faced by the healthcare leaders, to be prepared for the future and to retain the ability to accept and grow together with expected and unexpected changes. The aim of this article is to describe the main trends in the healthcare and healthcare leadership, link them with the expectations and competencies of medical leaders and to define the sub-competencies needed to succeed in the rapidly changing landscape of healthcare leadership.

2. Theoretical Background

Healthcare leadership is a somewhat new concept in the widely known field of organization leadership, constituting a separate entity with its own paradigms and principles. As the pressure for effective and affordable healthcare increases, so does the urgent need for outstanding (exceptional) leaders in medicine.

Depending on whom you ask, the definition of clinical or healthcare or medicine leadership varies on a wide spectrum. The engagement and guiding role of physicians in health system improvement or it can be defined simply as a formal leadership role performed by a physician (Berghout et al., 2017), butut medical leadership can also be an integrated role of an individual physician, being a part of the medical competence and daily work (Baker & Denis, 2011; Edmonstone, 2009). Perhaps the most distinct definition of healthcare leadership is the ability to influence others effectively and ethically for the benefit and sake of patients (Hargett et al., 2017).

There are several different trend sets to look for in healthcare leadership, because a prepared leader should be aware of not only global future work trends but also of leadership trends and healthcare trends (Figure 1). Preparing for the future is based on these brought together with the complexity of it all being a bit easier to comprehend due to several of the aforementioned trends overlapping. Artificial intelligence and its uses, high level of flexibility, increased digitalization—these are interdisciplinary keywords in every aspect (Quantic, 2022) but there are several other factors one needs to keep in mind when preparing for the days ahead.

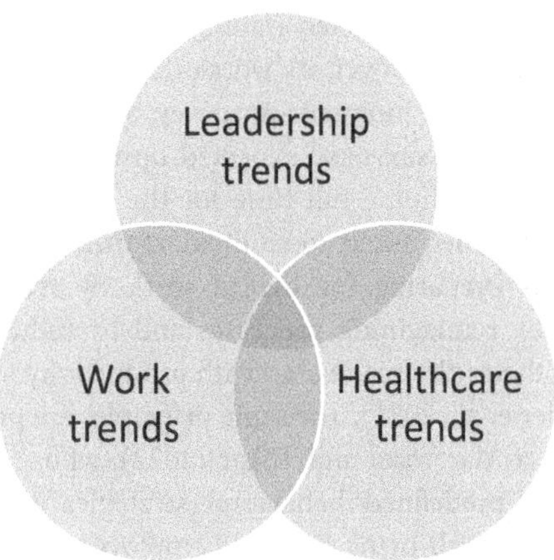

Figure 1. Significant trends in healthcare leadership

Combining the reviews and analyses with predictions done by Forbes, McKinsey, Harvard Business Review and Becker's Hospital Review main trends and future challenges in healthcare leadership can be visualized. According to their predictions we can see emerging leadership trends as increased need and capability to (rapid) change management, skills and knowledge to be prepared for increased digitalization and hybrid teams, and more focus on negotiation, project management and strategic thinking. In healthcare and medicine trends some of the same trends remain true, as artificial intelligence (AI) and digitalization are highly important here as well. In healthcare increased personalization remains as a major topic, but more and more the focus will be on biohacking and datafication, and in European Union a new proposal for regulation, the European Health Data Space is already in action (Directorate-General for Health and Food Safety, 2022). High costs and higher public pressure to gain rapid access to new drugs, especially in high efficacy drugs (e.g., in cancer or rare disease treatment) is also focus point for all healthcare leaders around the world. For work and workplace trends it can be observed that hybrid working, which made its breakthrough during the pandemic remains paramount, as well as flexibility, sustainability and AI integration (Alexander et al., 2021; Bruce, 2022; McRae et al., 2023; Newman, 2022). In particular hybrid work and digitalization are important in all aspects of healthcare leadership as AI integration is seen as specific separate entity within digitalization.

Hybrid work, one of the predicted trends is already partially incorporated into daily work having fully proven its worth during pandemic era and being here to stay, at least for the moment. A survey of Forbes showed that more than half of the companies surveyed expected up to 50 % of their employees to continue working from home full time for the next year and the number slightly dipped to 49 % when asked about the next three to five years (Newman, 2022). Organizations preparing for hybrid work by training managers for remote leadership, by reimagining processes and by rethinking how to help employees thrive in their role are the ones with productivity increases during the pandemic (Alexander et al., 2021). The same principles are proven in healthcare in research by Oleksa-Marewska and Tokar (2022), whose study analyzed the relationship between predefined behavioral strategies and competencies of leaders and the affective well-being of hybrid employees. Their research showed significant correlations between chosen variables and affective well-being, but it is well worth mentioning that in this study the employees' well-being was mainly explained by the adaptability domain in leadership strategy, which in turn was connected with patient orientation, a proactive approach to changes and promoting organizational learning (Oleksa-Marewska & Tokar, 2022). A systematic analysis in 2022 emphasizes on the finding that leaders need to be interactive and cannot be working in an isolated function during crisis, further underlining the need for healthcare leader to demonstrate their ability to focus on the task, while empathizing with individuals' situations and demonstrating nimble adaptability to rapidly changing events. Healthcare and public health leaders should have competencies in people and adaptive competencies in order to face current and future crises (Sriharan et al., 2022). To succeed in combining remote and face-to-face work and leadership organizations need to provide clear guidelines and training for remote work and leadership (Ameel et al., 2022).

Hybrid work goes hand to hand with digitalization—another major trend not only in future work but also in healthcare and healthcare leadership. Further on both trends are very relevant and somewhat overlapping with another influential factor—the use and integration of artificial intelligence (The Economist, 2022; Newman, 2022). Review by Ingebritsen et al. already in 2014 provided evidence that clinical leaders are important for successful IT adoption in healthcare organizations and that the clinical leaders whose aim is to improve the quality of care should develop the required IT competencies, establish good partnership with IT specialists and be proactive in various IT inputs (Ingebritsen et al., 2014). Successful leaders who understand and predict digital technologies that may transform the entire healthcare industry are more likely to be also successful in digital leadership and digital transformation (Alanazi, 2022).

When we look into healthcare leadership theories and main knowledge, skills and values needed for that we can find that there have been numerous authors describing different competencies needed for healthcare leadership, with more or less overlapping results. In the landscape of medical leadership competency models are well established and widely used, with the most recognized models being the National Center for Healthcare Leadership, version 3.0 which is mainly created for use in the United States of America, and the International Hospital Federation model used globally, either in original or slightly modified version (International Hospital Federation, 2015).

In our previous research (Ross & Titov, 2022) we defined and described the main competencies and values needed for present-day healthcare leadership in the Estonian setting. For this we compared main contemporary competency models and conducted research in North Estonia Medical Centre (NEMC). Non-personalized online questionnaires were used to better understand the everyday goals and challenges for mid-level healthcare executives together with their values. The results of that research enabled the creation of the proposed healthcare leadership competency model for NEMC, which consists of core values and six main competency domains with sub-competencies. Main domains include relations and connection, organizational environment and quality orientation, professional and personal development, finance and personnel management, leadership and innovation and clinical skills. Competency domains with their respective sub-competencies are shown in Figure 2 (Ross & Titov, 2022).

Figure 2. NEMC healthcare competency model, competency domains and sub-competencies

Results from previous research also allowed us to formulate the main values and attitudes in the healthcare leadership, as this was part of the research goals. We defined three categories for the values, with honesty, openness and giving and receiving feedback being the first category, self-esteem and inner balance the second and valuing employees the third category.

We will now describe the changes needed to be implemented in the model based on the described trends and predicted challenges in healthcare and leadership.

3. Research Methodology

For the purposes of healthcare leadership research, semi-structured expert interviews with open questions were performed with eight high-level executives and medical leaders, either clinic directors or medical directors. The results from the previous research interviews and anonymous web-based questionnaires were further evaluated with focus on most highly rated activities and their importance in relations to described trends. We also conducted four new semi-structured interviews with medical leaders from NEMC to evaluate new trends and their influence on the domains and sub-competencies described previously in the NECM healthcare leadership competency model.

4. Results and Discussion

The main current and predicted future trends for healthcare leadership are summarized in Figure 3.

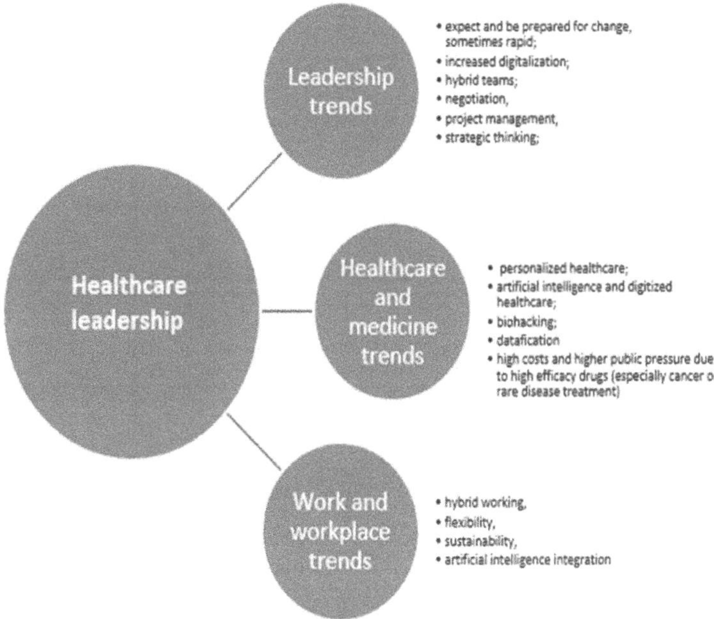

Figure 3. Current and predicted trends in healthcare leadership

Looking deeper into the importance and subjective rating of activities given by the participants we can also visualize 10 specific activities (see Figure 4) which were rated as extremely important (rating higher than 4.5) compared to the others. In addition to clinical work, which has previously been proven to be extremely important by different authors (Quinn & Perelli, 2016; Ross &

Titov, 2022; Witman et al., 2011) there are several activities directly connected to the expectations and trends previously described. The importance of being knowledgeable about national strategies, reimbursement or financial changes and plans is considered to be one of the major factors by all participants. The same is true for personnel management and teamwork with a positive and encouraging work environment being one of the shared goals. The value of creating the vision for the future together with the development plan and action plan and proactively evaluating problem areas was also considered to be extremely important with similar rating among all four (vision, development plan, action plan, problem evaluation) components.

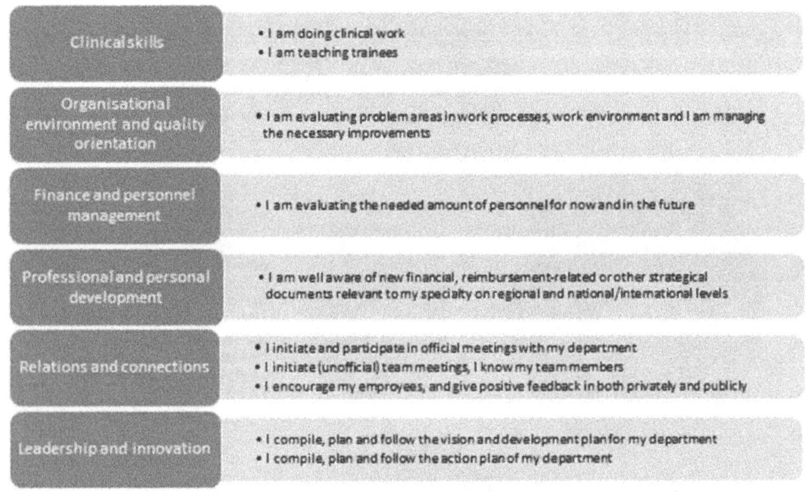

Figure 4. Summary of the main ten most important activities in relation to their respective competency domains in the NEMC healthcare leadership competency model by Ross and Titov (2022)

In expert interviews the domains and also the sub-competencies described within the domains in Figure 2 remain relevant. Driving factor for starting as a medical leader is always the inner need for specialty or healthcare development and improvement with increasing the quality of care. Several interview participants emphasized the wish to improve the healthcare system overall. Competencies required for medical leadership overlap with the ones defined previously in questionnaires with main focus on teamwork, communication and relations, quality management and strategic planning. In higher positions the need for bigger picture, urgency to understand national background and processes, financial thinking, and innovation increases. All participants agree that the need to predict and understand the future needs is increasingly important and the skills and knowledge of the future medical leaders should be taught accordingly. Main attitudes and values for the present medical leaders are defined as honesty, capability to achieve goals, having a vision for the future and power to motivate others.

In the recent expert interviews, we can see that although some trends are adjustable to the existing sub-competencies and action the remaining trends require new activities and sub-competencies to be defined. Remaining trends not presently represented by respective sub-competencies (see Figure 5) are mostly from healthcare and work trends and reflect the need to keep up with the times, with hybrid team management and artificial intelligence and biohacking being repeatedly emphasized in the interviews.

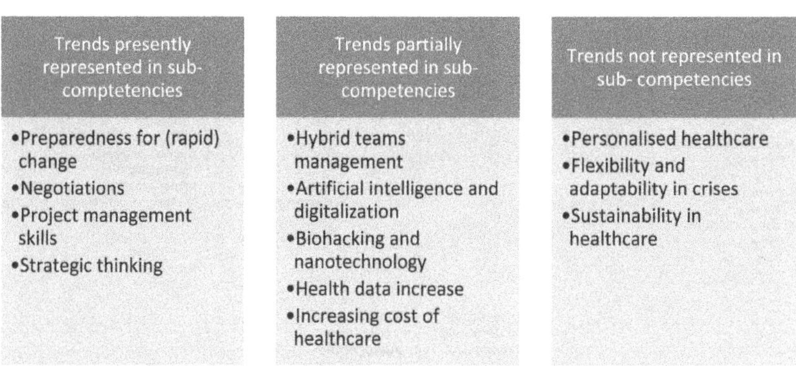

Figure 5. Predicted trends and their respective sub-competencies in NEMC healthcare leadership competency model

Three main trends that are not currently represented in the model are the increasingly personalized healthcare, need for increased flexibility, and adaptability and sustainability. Partially represented are the hybrid teams, artificial intelligence, and digitalization, biohacking, increase in health data production, storage and data types and increasing cost of healthcare. Modifications required in the current model should involve both the unrepresented and partially represented areas, as the present model is not in concordance with described trends and sub-competencies are not created to take those trends into account.

While it is possible to show that main actions from Figure 4, for example: "I am evaluating problem areas in work processes and work environment and I am managing the necessary improvements" could also be used to describe the trends partially represented in the sub-competencies (see Figure 5) and therefore acceptably represent those in the model, it was clearly stated by the participants during the interviews that the actions and activities defined in previous research (and therefore the sub-competencies as well) are not inclusive and detailed enough to consider them as appropriate surrogates for the trends analyzed in current research.

The proposed sub-competencies needed in the context of new trends in leadership and healthcare are shown in Figure 6.

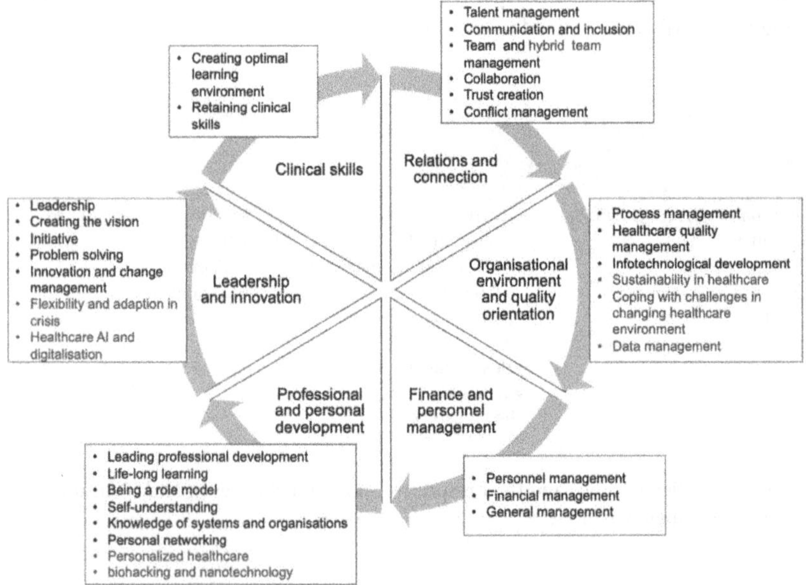

Figure 6. Proposed model update with newly added sub-competencies reflecting important trends in leadership and healthcare

The complexity and intricacy of the proposed competence model increases with each added sub-competency, making it burdensome to use and less convenient for everyday purposes. It is reasonable to propose that the model should be divided into several levels, with first level model being simplified version suitable for beginners and possibly third or fourth level already meant for experts in the field. Practical implementation and validation of this approach should be the topic for future research. However, it is important to continue with model improvements and if needed also with new additions as this is a living model and needs to be constantly updated in concordance with changing environment.

5. Conclusion

The aim of this research was to describe new trends and challenges in healthcare leadership and to use the defined trends for updating the current healthcare leadership model characterized in our previous research. For our research we used leadership, medicine and workplace trends proposed by several renowned reviews and conducted semi-structured interviews with medical leaders in North Estonia Medical Centre. Based on the results we proposed several changes in our previously defined healthcare leadership competency model, with added sub-competencies in accordance to the proposed trends. New sub-competencies were added into the domains of leadership and innovation, professional and personal development, relations and connections and organizational environment and quality orientation.

References

Alanazi, A. T. (2022). Digital leadership: Attributes of modern healthcare leaders. *Cureus, 14*(2), e21969. https://doi.org/10.7759/cureus.21969

Alexander, A., Cracknell, R., De Smet, A., Langstaff, M., Mysore, M., & Ravid, D. (2021). *What executives are saying about the future of hybrid work*. https://www.mckinsey.com/capabilities/people-and-organizational-performance/our-insights/what-executives-are-saying-about-the-future-of-hybrid-work

Ameel, M., Myllynen, M., & Kallakorpi, S. (2022). Exploring hybrid leadership: Experiences of remote leadership in healthcare. *Journal of Nursing Administration, 52*(12):653–658. https://doi.org/10.1097/NNA.0000000000001227

Baeten, R., Spasova, S., Vanhercke, B., & Coster, S. (2018). *Inequalities in access to healthcare. A study of national policies*. European Commission. https://ec.europa.eu/social/BlobServlet?docId=20339&langId=en

Baker, G. R., & Denis, J., L. (2011). Medical leadership in health care systems: From professional authority to organizational leadership. *Public Money & Management, 31*, 355–362.

Berghout, M. A., Fabbricotti, I. N., Buljac-Samardžić, M., & Hilders, C. G. J. M. (2017). Medical leaders or masters?—A systematic review of medical leadership in hospital settings. *PLoS One*, *12*(9), e0184522. https://doi.org/10.1371/journal.pone.0184522

Bruce, G. (2022). The top innovation trends 0f 2022, according to the health system execs. *Becker's Hospital Review*. https://www.beckershospitalreview.com/innovation/the-top-innovation-trends-of-2022-according-to-health-system-execs.html

Christensen, K., Doblhammer, G., Rau, R., & Vaupel, J. W. (2009). Aging populations: The challenges ahead. *Lancet*, *374*(9696), 1196–11208. https://doi.org/10.1016/S0140-6736(09)61460-4

Denis, J. L., & Van Gestel, N. (2015). Leadership and innovation in healthcare governance. In *The Palgrave international handbook of healthcare policy and governance*. Palgrave Macmillan.

Densen, P. (2011). Challenges and opportunities facing medical education. *Transactions of the American Clinical and Climatological Association*, *122*, 48–58.

Directorate-General for Health and Food Safety. (2022). Proposal for a regulation—The European Health Data Space. *COM(2022)*, *197*(2). https://health.ec.europa.eu/publications/proposal-regulation-european-health-data-space_en

Economist, The. (2022). *Ten business trends for 2023, and forecasts for 15 industries*. https://www.economist.com/the-world-ahead/2022/11/21/ten-business-trends-for-2023-and-forecasts-for-15-industries

Edmonstone, J. (2009). Clinical leadership: The elephant in the room. *International Journal of Health Planning and Management*, *24*(4), 290–305. https://doi.org/10.1002/hpm.959

Hargett, C. W., Doty, J. P., Hauck, J. N., Webb, A. M., Cook, S. H., Tsipis, N. E., Neumann, J. A., Andolsek, K. M., & Taylor, D. C. (2017). Developing a model for effective leadership in healthcare: A concept mapping approach. *Journal of Healthcare Leadership*, *9*, 69–78. https://doi.org/10.2147/JHL.S141664

Ingebrigtsen, T., Georgiou, A., Clay-Williams, R., Magrabi, F., Hordern, A., Prgomet, M., Li, J., Westbrook, J., & Braithwaite, J. (2014). The impact of clinical leadership on health information technology adoption: Systematic review. *International Journal of Medical Informatics*, *83*(6), 393–405. https://doi.org/10.1016/j.ijmedinf.2014.02.005

International Hospital Federation. (2015). *Leadership competencies for healthcare services managers*. International Hospital Federation (IHF). https://www.ihf-fih.org/download_doc_file.php?doc=dfff684f5fd4854ad43566085950b8a8

McRae, E. R., Aykens, P., Lowmaster, K., & Shepp, J. (2023). 9 trends that will shape work in 2023 and beyond. *Harvard Business Review*. https://hbr.org/2023/01/9-trends-that-will-shape-work-in-2023-and-beyond

National Center for HealthCare Leadership. (2018). *NCHL health leadership competency model*. https://nchl.member365.org/publicFr/store/item/19

Newman, D. (2022). *The future of work: More hybrid, more collaborative, more automated*. https://www.forbes.com/sites/danielnewman/2022/07/31/the-future-of-work-more-hybrid-more-collaborative-more-automated/?sh=2c7dc4cb9c46

Oleksa-Marewska, K., & Tokar, J. (2022). Facing the post-pandemic challenges: The role of leadership effectiveness in shaping the affective well-being of healthcare providers working in a hybrid work mode. *International Journal of Environmental Research and Public Health*, *19*(21), 14388. https://doi.org/10.3390/ijerph192114388

Quantic. (2022). *The future of leadership in 2030: 6 new disruptive trends*. https://quantic.edu/blog/2022/08/05/the-future-of-leadership-in-2030-6-new-disruptive-trends/

Quinn, J. F., & Perelli, S. (2016). First and foremost, physicians: The clinical versus leadership identities of physician leaders. *Journal of Health Organization and Management*, *30*, 711–728. https://doi.org/10.1108/JHOM-05-2015-0079

Rome, B. N., Egilman, A. C., & Kesselheim, A. S. (2022). Trends in prescription drug launch prices, 2008–2021. *JAMA*, *327*(21), 2145–2147. https://doi.org/10.1001/jama.2022.5542

Ross, M., & Titov, E. (2022). Necessary leadership competences in changing healthcare systems. In *Economic and social development: Book of proceedings; Varazdin development and entrepreneurship agency (April 1/April 2, 2022)*. ProQuest.

Sriharan, A., Hertelendy, A. J., Banaszak-Holl, J., Fleig-Palmer, M. M., Mitchell, C., Nigam, A., Gutberg, J., Rapp, D. J., & Singer, S. J. (2022). Public health and health sector crisis leadership during pandemics: A review of the medical and business literature. *Medical Care Research and Review*, *79*(4), 475–486. https://doi.org/10.1177/10775587211039201

WHO. (2022). *Health workforce*. https://www.who.int/health-topics/health-workforce#tab=tab_1

Witman, Y., Smid, G. A. C., Meurs, P. L., & Willems, D. L. (2011). Doctor in the lead: Balancing between two worlds. *Organization*, *18*, 477–495.

Khamdamov Shoh-Jakhon

Theoretical and Methodological Aspects of Intensive Economic Growth in Ensuring Sustainable Economic Development

1. Introduction

Relevance and necessity of the book. According to world experience, the contribution of intensive (intensive) factors dominates economic growth in developed countries, while the contribution of extensive factors dominates in developing countries. In 2015, UN member states adopted the Sustainable Development Program until 2030. In this program, special attention is paid to the task of achieving an increase in efficiency in the economy. Today, in this respect, in order to ensure sustainable economic development, the activation of accelerated factors of economic growth is considered as one of the urgent problems.

The chapter about Theoretical and methodological aspects of intensive economic growth in ensuring sustainable economic development. Also you readers can learn factors of intensive economic growth, growth indicators and theur calculation methods (Diewert, 2000).

Targeted scientific research has been organized to provide a scientific solution to a number of problems in achieving sustainable economic growth in the world. In this regard, to develop the social aspects of economic growth based on the growth of the gross domestic product (GDP) and the optimal and rational use of its factors, increase the level of employment and labor productivity, increase its effectiveness, and improve the methodological approaches to increase the quality of sustainable economic growth by applying appropriate macroeconomic policy levers special attention is paid.

2. Theoretical Aspect of Sustainable Development and Intensive Economic Growth

Factors of intensive economic growth refer to all factors affecting productivity, economy, and quality of production.

Factors of intensive economic growth at the national level include: introduction of innovations;

1) workforce qualification;
2) favorable conditions for market economy;
3) infrastructure;
4) efficiency of state administration;
5) alternative and cheap energy sources;
6) corruption;
7) health;
8) rule of law;
9) cultural factors and others.

As a general index for determining intensive economic growth, we can cite the Total factor productivity indicator.

Total factor productivity is an economic concept that refers to the set of factors affecting production, in addition to labor and capital costs.

Factors of intensive economic growth (productivity factors) are grouped as follows:

Group I—main capital (investment) factors. Their role is determined by the quality, level of development and utilization of investments and long-term material assets. These factors are related to the mechanization and automation of work, the introduction of advanced technologies and, accordingly, the use of high-quality and efficient materials.

But the growth of materialized labor should not exceed the increase in the volume of work achieved due to the influence of these factors, at the same time, since any type of activity is closely related to fixed assets, their structure and the technologies used, it is almost difficult to accurately determine the increase in the volume of work achieved only by increasing the fixed capital.

Group II—socioeconomic factors. These are the composition and qualifications of employees, working conditions, health of the nation, attitude of employees to work, etc. In this group, the composition of employees and the quality of work have a special place. Moreover, the contribution of each person to the total labor is not the same: in the team, some always have more than the average value, and others less than the average value (Zhou et.al., 2020). However, current collective methods of calculating labor productivity do not take this into account. The productivity of an individual employee depends on his abilities, skills, knowledge, age, health and a number of other factors. From the point of view of labor productivity, it is important for the employer to find "his" employee, whose work ability and labor productivity are potentially above average values. This selection of employees is supported by the system of job quality assessment and career selection.

In this group of factors, it is necessary to note the spending of the country on education and health care, that is, the spending of the society on the social sphere. There is no doubt that the professional training of employees depends on the level of school and vocational education, including higher education, and the health of the nation and each employee, in particular, depends on the state of medical care of the population. The complete composition and reasonable structure of food products, the availability of consumer goods, including competitive products, the level of development of the service sector and housing and communal services are necessary components of the quality of life, and the quick and timely restoration of human activity affects his mood. and creates a sense of comfort and reliability. Among the socioeconomic factors, it is necessary to include the mechanism of redistribution of society's income between different layers of the population.

Group III—organizational factors. They cover a set of measures on labor and management organization, personnel management. With the development of the economy, the role of this group of factors increases. The concept of labor organization and management includes choosing the size and location of the enterprise, cooperation, specialization and combination as a form of production organization, the scheme, structure and style of enterprise management, and determining the tasks of its divisions. A special group consists of factors affecting team relations and work discipline.

They are, firstly, the system of values of employees and the principles of mutual relations that affect the goals of employees, the behavior of employees and the microclimate in the team: econdly, measures to activate and encourage employees; and thirdly, management decisions, work defect and error control and warning measures. The effect of these factors of labor productivity results from objective, including natural and social, activity conditions. Among them, it is necessary to note the climatic conditions and the availability of natural wealth of the country, its social development, political life and the level of well-being of the population.

In the analysis of economic growth, the quantitative and qualitative changes of production factors are divided into two groups: intensive (active, qualitative) and extensive (extensive, quantitative). In individual enterprises, these two types of economic growth may exist in their pure form in separate periods (Charnes, 1978).

As for the national economy, active and extensive types of economic growth usually exist at the same time, but one of them is the leader, so the national economy is distinguished by the "mainly intensive" or "mainly extensive" type of economic growth.

A wide variety is achieved due to an increase in the amount of use of one or more factors of production. With a wide range of economic growth, there is an increase in GDP, in addition to an increase in the use of factors of production. Therefore, this type of economic growth is characterized by the level of continuous use of equipment, technology, personnel skills and labor productivity. The main disadvantage of broad-based economic growth is that as their use increases, the rate of economic growth declines. If the volume of use of one of the three factors increases at a faster rate, its share in the gross product will increase. As a result, broad economic growth itself can be divided into the following three types:

- capital-intensive (requires capital);
- labor-intensive;
- resource intensive.

With an intensive type of economic growth, the growth of the gross product is achieved by improving the quality of production factors.

First, through the use of advanced and efficient machines and equipment, labor tools, secondly, by using more economical labor goods, thirdly, by reducing the consumption of raw materials per product unit, fourth, by improving the quality of manufactured goods, and fifth, by using a more skilled workforce (Khamdamov, 2019a).

It can be concluded that the intensive type of economic growth is characterized by technological progress and, as a result, an increase in labor productivity.

Extensive and intensive types of economic growth are interrelated, so they cannot be contrasted. An increase in labor productivity is a characteristic feature of intensification of production, but generally, labor productivity increases due to the use of new technology, and this is a characteristic feature of broad economic growth (an increase in the share of capital).

Depending on the decrease in the share of one of the factors of production, economic growth can be divided into three types:

capital saver;
labor saving;
resource saver.

PhD. Khamdamov and Prof. A. Usmanov, we have developed the following definition, having studied the economic term "Sustainable Development" in depth.

Sustainable development is quantitative and qualitative growth of GDP provided by renewable natural, production and labor factors of development. In this case, it is necessary to consider the stability of development in time periods—current, medium and long-term periods of development. In the current period, it is possible to achieve high rates of GDP growth based on the tasks of economic growth.

However, taking into account the medium- and long-term perspectives of economic development and ensuring its sustainable development, the growth rate of GDP should be based mainly on the opportunities for rapid economic development, that is, more intensive factors of development (TFP).

3. Intensive Economic Growth Indicators and Their Calculation Methods

Factors of intensive economic growth refer to all productivity factors that affect productivity, economy, and quality of production. As a general index for determining intensive economic growth, we can cite the Total Factor Productivity indicator.

Total factor productivity (Total Factor Productivity) is an economic concept, which means a set of productivity factors affecting production, in addition to labor and capital costs.

Labor productivity is one of the most important quality indicators of the enterprise and represents the efficiency of labor costs (Khamdamov, 2021b).

As a result of labor activity, goods and services are produced, which are characterized, firstly, by production costs, and secondly by market value. For each type of goods and services, the ratio of these two values multiplied by their volume determines the profitability of production.

Production efficiency can also be measured by comparing its volume with the value of the main assets of the enterprise engaged in the production of these products. This indicator is called fund return.

They are distinguished by labor productivity at the level of the country, region, industry, labor productivity at the enterprise, and individual labor productivity of an individual employee.

The work of people involved in production is called labor force. At each stage of production, labor is not used, that is, the means of production—raw materials, energy, equipment, tools, etc. are used. This part of labor is called reified (Reified), or past labor (Past Labor).

Each enterprise has a certain level of labor productivity, which can increase or decrease depending on various factors. A necessary condition for the development of production is the increase in labor productivity. Increasing labor productivity means saving material and life labor and is one of the most important factors for increasing production efficiency. The growth of labor productivity is an expression of a universal economic law, an economic necessity for the development of society, regardless of the current economic system.

An increase in labor productivity leads to a decrease in the total amount of labor in each unit of output. The level of labor productivity is influenced by the amount of extensive use of labor, labor intensity, and the technical and technological state of production.

Productivity in its broadest sense is the mental tendency of a person to always look for opportunities to improve what is already there. It is based on the belief that a person can do better today than yesterday and tomorrow can do better than today. It requires continuous improvement of economic activity.

The purpose of labor activity is to obtain the product of labor, that is, the production and sale of a specific product, the sale of goods or the provision of services. The productivity of this labor is important for the employee and the labor team, and is expressed by the level of the amount of work received per labor unit, including time unit. And the higher this level, the lower the costs per unit of time, because the increase in the volume of work leads to an increase in labor productivity, which reduces fixed costs. An increase in labor productivity leads to an increase in the volume of work performed by the labor force in a given unit of time, and a decrease in the time spent on a unit of work.

Labor productivity (P) is measured by the amount of output produced by one employee per unit of time (hour, shift, week, month, year) and is calculated using:

$$P = O/N$$

Here,

P is labor productivity,
O is the amount of work per time unit, and
N is the number of workers.

The general trend of labor productivity growth is manifested by the decrease of the share of living labor in the product, the increase of the share of materialized labor (raw materials, materials), but the decrease of the total amount of labor available in the production unit. This is the essence of increasing labor productivity (Jones, 1997).

The change in the ratio between living and material labor can occur in different ways, depending on the level of development of the productive forces. At the highest stage of scientific and technical development, with the growth of mechanization and automation of production, the cost of live and material labor per unit of production decreases, but the cost of live labor is much lower than the previous wages, so the share of live labor in the product decreases. Therefore, the higher the level of mechanization and automation of labor, the greater the role it plays in its economy due to the reduction of materialized labor costs. The essence of scientific and technical progress is to reduce labor costs, which is the essence of increasing labor productivity (Khamdamov, 2020a).

As the productive forces of society develop in general labor, with a corresponding increase in the share of materialized labor, the share of living labor naturally decreases.

4. Labor Productivity

Labor productivity factors can be grouped as follows:

1. growth factors of living and material labor. This differentiation of factors is related to measures to increase the share of intensification reserves and fixed capital within the framework of normal labor intensity;
2. *factors of labor productivity growth based on movement time. In this group a) current factors related to organizational and technical measures that do not require significant investment; b) there are promising factors related to fundamental changes in technique and technology. Their effect is considered for a long time (usually more than a year);*
3. *factors grouped according to their place in the economy:*

   (a) general economic;
   (b) network and industry;
   (c) within the company;
   (g) workplace.

The influence of general economic factors is related to the social division of labor, including international labor, the availability and use of labor resources, and the structure of production (Khamdamov, 2021b). Sectoral and sectoral factors of labor productivity growth are related to the specific features of production organization—its specialization, concentration and harmony, and mutual cooperation of production. Factors of labor productivity growth in the workplace include, first of all, a set of measures to eliminate the loss of working time and its rational use. All factors of labor productivity discussed above should be checked in the process of analytical work in the enterprise to determine their importance and impact on the future. Factor analysis of labor productivity examines indicators that have a direct impact on its change. For example, it is possible to study the influence of the percentage of workers employed in production, the number of working days, the length of the working day, and the hourly productivity of labor on changes in employee productivity over a certain period. Calculation of the impact of these factors on the change in the level of the average annual output of industrial and production workers is carried out by the method of absolute differences.

Reserves are potential, real opportunities to reduce labor costs per unit of production, as well as working time losses and economically unequal labor costs.

Reserves for improving the use of live labor (workforce) include reserves related to the organization and working conditions, the structure and placement of personnel, creating organizational conditions for continuous work, and ensuring high material and moral interest of employees in the results of work.

Reserves for more efficient use of material labor (fixed and current assets) include reserves for more economical and full use of the main production assets, as well as raw materials, materials, components, fuel, energy and other circulating funds. Current reserves can be implemented very quickly without additional capital investments and without significant changes in the technological process.

According to signs of utilization, it is necessary to separate the stocks of tools—equipment, which are inefficiently used for capacity or shift work; learned, but not yet used, advanced labor methods, as well as damage reserves—product defects, fuel overruns, loss of working hours (Jones, 1997).

In addition to reserves for reducing labor intensity and improving the use of working time in the fields of use, reserves for more rational use of company employees are of great importance. This direction is primarily related to improving the organizational structure—reducing the cost of the management scheme and increasing the efficiency of personnel management. In addition, reserves of rational placement of personnel, taking into account experience and qualifications, the system of selection and development of personnel in the enterprise, and official growth programs of employees play a large role (Khamdamov, 2019b).

Ways to increase labor productivity are the main areas that can be used to save labor costs, that is, ways to reduce the cost of live labor. Sources of growth of labor productivity are specific types of labor, thanks to which these labor costs are saved (Diewert, 2000).

Reserves of labor productivity growth can be national economy, industry, domestic production. *Internal production reserves are created by efficient use of equipment, working time, and reduction of labor costs for the production of a unit of production (labor intensity) in industrial enterprises. According to time, they are divided into current and prospective.*

National economic reserves are formed as a result of organizational and technical activities such as creation of new labor tools and facilities, rational placement of production.Industrial reserves contribute to the growth of labor productivity due to economically reasonable division of labor, improvement of the technical base, etc.

The number of labor-producing reserves includes improving the use of the working time fund and increasing labor intensity to a moderate level by compacting working hours.

Labor-saving reserves should include all reserves associated with reducing the labor intensity of production.

All internal production reserves of labor productivity growth should be further divided into two types: labor-producing and labor-saving.

Stocks within production for a group of labor-generating factors are usually estimated by indicators of the use of a working day and a working year (Denison, 1962).

4.1. Methods of Measuring Total Factor Productivity

Total factor productivity is a measure of productivity calculated by dividing total output in the economy by the average of labor and capital (Charnes, 1978). Represents growth in real output, excluding growth in inputs such as labor and capital.

The most commonly used production function is the Cobba-Douglas function, which is:

$$Q = A * K^{\alpha} * L^{\beta}$$

Here,

Q is the total product (production volume),
A is total factor productivity,
K is capital,
α is output elasticity of capital,
L is work, and
b is output elasticity of labor.

If we rearrange the Cobb-Douglas function, we get the following formula for total factor productivity: YaOU (TFP) = A = Total Product / Average Income(WAI) =

$$Q/(Ka * Lb)$$

TFP means an increase in total output, which leads to an increase in income. Technological change is driven by intangible factors such as education, research and development, synergy, etc. Table 1

Table 1. Methods of measuring labor productivity

Natural method	It is used to express the production efficiency of similar products
Value method	Used to express the productivity of production of non-current goods, the value is measured in monetary units
Work method	Represents the ratio of the produced product to the unit of time spent on it

There are three natural, value and labor methods of measuring labor productivity. Their advantages and disadvantages can be found in Table 1 (Zhou, 2020).

The following growth accounting equation tells us the relationship between growth in total output, growth in labor and capital, and growth in GDP:

$$\frac{\Delta Q}{Q} = \alpha \times \frac{\Delta K}{K} + \beta \times \frac{\Delta L}{L} + \frac{\Delta A}{A}$$

- In the new economic environment, the problem of improving the development of a plan to significantly improve quality and increase labor productivity is especially urgent. This is an important condition for ensuring an economically correct balance between labor productivity and the growth rate of wages. Two indicators are usually considered in productivity improvement plans: production volume—the number of products produced per unit of work time
- labor intensity—the amount of working time spent per unit of production.

5. Conclusion

The volume of production is the most common indicator of the level of labor productivity. There are several ways to calculate output based on the amount of work done and time spent.

In short, the Gross Productivity Factors (GRP) indicator is considered as a general index for determining intensive economic growth. Gross productivity factors is an economic concept that refers to the set of productivity factors that affect production, in addition to labor and capital costs.

References

Bing Zhou, Xiaoyan Zeng, Lu Jiang, and Bing Xue (2020). High-quality economic growth under the influence of technological innovation preference in China: A numerical simulation from the government financial perspective. *Structural Change and Economic Dynamics*, *54*, 163–172.

Charnes, A. (1978). Measuring the efficiency of decision making units. *European Journal of Operational Research*, *2*, 429–444.

Denison, E. F. (1962). The sources of economic growth in the United States and the alternatives before us. *New York: Committee for Economic Development*, 297–308.

Diewert, E. (2000). The challenge of total factor productivity measurement. *International Productivity Monitor*, *1*, 45–52.

Jones, C. I. (1997). *Introduction to economic growth* (pp. 1–200). Stanford University.

Khamdamov, Sh. (2019a). Analysis of the history of economic growth and its prospects. In *Problems and prospects of national economic development: Trends, growth reserves and strategies, a collection of scientific articles*, pp. 14–24.

Khamdamov, Sh. (2019b). Indicators and conditions for sustainable development. In *13th RSEP International Conference on Business, Economics & Finance*, pp. 37–43.

Khamdamov, Sh. (2020a). Analysis of international indicators of innovative development and inclusive growth in the Republic of Uzbekistan. In *19th RSEP international economics, finance & business conference. Proceedings full papers*, pp. 282–288.

Khamdamov, Sh. (2020b). Analysis of the state of the green economy in Uzbekistan. *Journal of Innovation in Economics*, *2*, 107–114.

Khamdamov, Sh. (2021b). Calculating share of factors of intensive economic growths in Uzbekistan. In *First International workshop on communication management, soft computing and digital economy. Proceedings full papers*, pp. 282–288.

Camelia Cercel (Zamfirache)

Competitive Rural Economy in the Emerging Countries of the European Union

1. Introduction: The Concept of Rural Area

Several definitions have been given for the concept of rural area and we can make multiple descriptions of the countryside. The concept of rural areas is particularly complex, which has a variety of opinions on its definition and components.

The rural and rurality are also the object of study for a multitude of social sciences, history, geography, sociology, etc., each of these approaches them through the prism of specificity of their conceptual system. Defining the concept of the rural in a clear-cut, straightforward way is an extremely difficult scientific endeavor, its characteristic dimensions being of an economic, social, ecological and other natures, placing the rural in a permanent contradictory dispute. The term rural is often opposed to urban and it is characterized by physical, economic, social and cultural dimensions. Generic, the rural expresses extreme relations. It is a multi-purpose, interdisciplinary and interactive concept. Consequently, the rural concept is presented by specialists in different fields of social sciences in a diverse range of formulations, which essentially comprise: an assembly different from the urban one, characterized by the predominance of agricultural activities and manufacturing industry, respectively the specific function of rural areas being agricultural production (Mathieu, 1969); sociologically, the rural is characterized by a specific way of life, behavior and system distinct from the urban; geographically, the rural is differentiated by the way it occupies space, grouped or dispersed. These are the ideas that underlie research into rural areas in economic, sociological and geographical aspects.

In terms of the functions performed, the countryside comprises the following areas, which may change the structure of their activities according to the needs and development of the economy at a given time (Gavrilescu & Giurcă, 2000):

- rural areas with complex functions specific to mountain and foothill areas; livestock farming is the main activity, but these areas create the conditions for a diversified rural economy;
- areas with mixed functions, where agricultural activities are combined with tourist activities, industrial, forestry and fisheries activities in varying proportions;
- rural areas with predominantly agricultural functions, where the cultivation of crops and livestock is the economic base.

Over time, the countryside has evolved, undergoing certain transformations which are designated by concept of rural development, which has undergone various interpretations, linked to The European Charter for Rural Areas also specifies the functions of this environment, which refer to the economic, ecological and cultural-social fields.

The economic function of the rural, at the same time as its basic function, is the activity agricultural activity. Alongside this economic activity, other branches of the economy are also expanding in the agricultural activities. In the modern view, the rural is no longer seen as a predominantly agricultural area. If the structure in rural areas is more diversified, the social consequences are more advantageous: employment opportunities increase, the population is more stable, young people remain in rural communities, more efficient use of part-time work of employees in private family farms.

The ecological function refers to the protection and preservation of the rural, which can provide a healthy environment for the population. Uncontrolled, excessive industrialization in some rural areas, harsh exploitation in some areas, over-industrialization of the livestock sector, indiscriminate logging in some forest areas have led to significant imbalances, pollution of the countryside, deterioration of the agricultural landscape etc.

The social-cultural function aims to form, develop and improve social relations between members of village communities and within various educational institutions, including associative activities of an economic, social and cultural nature. In terms of human ties activities within communities, the rural is essentially a social space.

In my opinion, looking at these functions of the rural, I believe that in the European Union agriculture is not only an important sector, but above all a way of life. The rural is not just a setting for organizing and carrying out various economic and social activities in which agriculture plays a central role, but it is also an important social and spiritual space with profound implications for the development and progress of rural communities.

The agricultural definition of the rural is given by Recommendation No 1296/ 1996 of the Parliamentary Assembly of the Council of Europe with reference to the European Charter for Rural Areas. In this sense, the rural area has in its structure an inner area comprising villages and small towns for: agriculture, forestry, aquaculture, fishing; economic and cultural activities of those living in these areas; non-urban leisure and recreation areas; and others.

There are other definitions for rural areas[1]:

- In France, the rural is the territory where agricultural production is predominant and the elements of space are found in their pure state;
- In Belgium, the rural defines a kind of landscape and territory that is cultivated by man;
- In Germany, "rural" is considered to be all areas located outside high-density areas;
- In the USA, the terms "rural-farm" and a "rural non-farm" are used.

In rural areas the exchange of matter and energy with the environment is closer to natural. In rural areas, agriculture usually dominates. In mountain areas forestry, wood processing and crafts dominate. In mountain, coastal and delta areas, the following also predominate: agro-tourism, hunting and fishing. In rural areas, practical, manual and multi-skilled professions predominate. The characteristic of the rural population is to work simultaneously in agricultural and non-agricultural sectors.

The natural landscape of the countryside is a true diamond of humanity. The airy landscape through flora and fauna is unrivaled in terms of human health. Peace and quiet, the climate, the clean air, the soothing landscape, the social calm, cannot be quantified to measure rural habitat.

The rural way of life, traditions and customs constitute the local or regional popular culture. The true value of the rural is given by its social, cultural, economic and ecological life of these areas.

In the process of developing the rural, greater attention must be paid to the components that characterize the authentic rural and give it: individuality, specificity and originality, which are at the heart of the protection and development of the rural, and must be developed and used sustainably in order to maintain them unchanged as long as possible.

The Organization for Economic Co-operation and Development (OECD) uses the number of inhabitants per square kilometer for the concept of rural areas. Thus, only places with a population density not exceeding 150 inhabitants/km^2 are considered rural settlements and constitute rural areas. In recent decades, EU countries have used different definitions of rural/urban areas. In the context of a European Union, which brings together quite a large number of countries, it is essential to standardize the criteria for defining rural areas. All this is necessary in order to create a common and uniform database, which will be the starting point for all European Commission reports and publications.

---

1 https://www.gazetadeagricultura.info/dezvoltare-rurala/1439-descrierea-spatiului-rural.html.

Thus, in 2010, the European Union adopted a revised classification of urban/rural areas, which establishes three categories of regions: predominantly rural regions, intermediate regions and predominantly urban regions. The basis for this division is a modified version of the OECD typology previously used by the European Commission. The important elements taken into account are population density and the presence of large urban centers (including their share of the region's total population).

Romania has not yet adopted this typology, as it still has its own methodology of defining rural areas.

Romania's territory is administratively structured into villages, communes, towns, municipalities and counties. Out of all these, the village and the commune are specific to rural areas. The village is the smallest territorial unit, which has the characteristics of a rural settlement, and the commune is the administrative-territorial unit which is made up of the rural population united by the same interests and customs, being composed of one or more villages. As regards the administrative side, the Romanian rural area has 2,861 communes comprising 12,957 villages.[2]

2. Comparative Analysis of the Competitive Rural Economy in Rural Areas of the European Union

In the emerging countries of the EU, agriculture has undergone multiple transformations in economic and social structure over time. I believe that we can phase its modernization as follows: a first phase when small production was the majority, a period in which the modernization of agriculture promoted by national agricultural policies practically begins, the second phase which is marked by economic integration, the establishment of the European Economic Community (EEC) and the increase in agricultural production and the third phase which corresponds to the current period when the Common Agricultural Policy (CAP) measures are being implemented. In the EU countries the family type of agriculture is predominant and is made up of small and medium-sized family farms.

The Food and Agriculture Organization of the United Nations (FAO) defines a family farm as "...an agricultural holding that is managed and operated by a household and where the agricultural labor force is largely supplied by that

---

2 https://www.madr.ro/docs/dezvoltare-rurala/programare-2014-2020/studiu-potential-socio-economic-dedezvoltare-zone-rurale-ver-10.04.2015.pdf.

household" (European Commission, Eurostat, Statistics-explained, Agriculture statistics—family farming in the EU access data 10 Jan 2023) Family farms are by far the most common type of farm in the European Union (EU).

In the European Union, currently made up of 27 Member States, there were 10.3 million farms farming 156.7 million hectares of land in 2016. Out of these, a third (33.3 %) of the EU's agricultural holdings (referred to as "farms") were in Romania and a cumulative quarter in Poland (13.7 %) and Italy (11.1 %) (European Commission, Eurostat, Statistics-explained, From farm to_fork—a statistical journey, access date 10 Jan 2023).

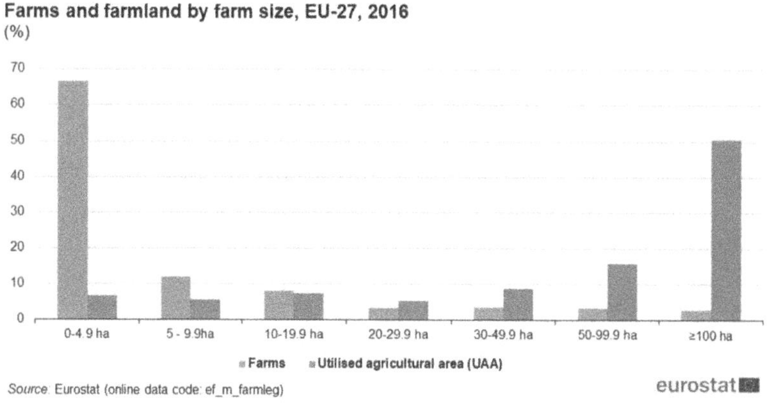

Figure 1. Classification of farms and agricultural land by area, EU-27, 2016 (%)

Source: Eurostat (ef_m_farmleg) https://ec.europa.eu/eurostat/statistics-explained/index.php?title=From_farm_to_fork_-_a_statistical_journey/ro&oldid=501261

Also, as can be seen in Figure 1, farms in EU countries are small in size.

Organic farming is the new type of agriculture promoted in the EU by regulations and policies.

Agriculture occupies an important place in Romania's economy and has major development prospects in the European context, thanks to favorable soil and climate conditions and potential in the sphere of organic production. Between 1995 and 2016, the contribution of agriculture to the national GDP decreased from 14.7 % in 1995 to 4.7 % in 2016, while the share of the labor force employed in agriculture was close to that of 1995. In 2015, the share of the workforce in agriculture in Romania was 25.9 %, representing the highest share in the EU, whose average was 4.4 %. 84 % of workers in agriculture in

Romania were part of the unsalaried staff category, while the average share of unsalaried workers in the agricultural sector in the EU was 72 %, the gross value added generated at the worker level being about 50 % lower than the EU average (National Strategy for the SUSTAINABLE DEVELOPMENT of Romania 2030, access date 12 Jan 2023).

Organic farming is a dynamic system in Romania, and lately it is on an upward trend. In 2010, the total area cultivated by organic production method was 182,706 ha (about 1.4 % of the total agricultural area used), and at the end of 2017 it was 258,470,927 ha, with a total number of about 8,434 operators certified in the organic farming system, an increase of about 41.5 %.

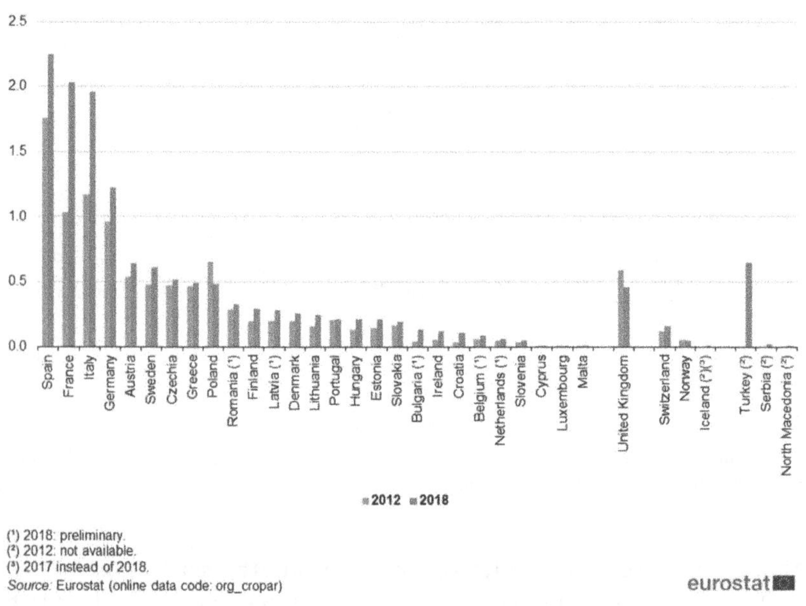

Figure 2. Total organic area (fully converted and in conversion), 2012 and 2018 (million ha)

Source: Eurostat (org_cropar) https://ec.europa.eu/eurostat/statistics-explained/index.php?title=From_farm_to_fork_-_a_statistical_journey/ro&oldid=501261

In 2018, organic farming covered approximately 13.0 million hectares of land in the EU, representing an estimated 8.3 % of the total utilized agricultural area. According to what can be seen in Figure 2, a large part of the total EU organic area was in only four Member States: Spain (17.3 %), France (15.7 %), Italy (15.1 %) and Germany (9.4 %) (European Commission, Eurostat, Statistics-explained, From farm to_fork—a statistical journey, access date 10 Jan 2023).

Looking at the developed EU countries on organic farming, I consider France and Germany as an example for the emerging countries of Central and Eastern Europe (Romania, Hungary, Bulgaria, Estonia, Poland, Lithuania, Latvia, Czech Republic, Slovenia, Slovakia, Croatia).

From Figure 2, we can see that France is the second largest country in the EU in terms of area devoted to organic farming, namely 2,035,024 hectares (2018), according to FIBL. Practically, France has 13 % of the organic farming area in Europe. France recorded the highest increase in land devoted to organic farming in 2018, with 290,604 hectares. Also, organic producers in France, 41,632 in number, represent 10 % of the total continent-wide. The market for organic products in France stands at a turnover of €9.1 billion (2018), 2nd place in Europe (Ecoferma, Organic farming in the EU case study France, access date January 12, 2023).

Also from Figure 2, we see that Germany is one of the leaders in terms of area devoted to organic farming. At EU level, Germany ranks 4th, 1,521,314 ha, which is 10 % of the total European area devoted to organic farming (Ecoferma, Organic Farming in the EU case study Germany, access date 12 Jan 2023).

The same cannot be said for the emerging EU countries of Central and Eastern Europe. In Romania only 2.4 % of the agricultural area is occupied by organic farming, which is a rather low percentage, below 8 % of the EU average and well below the 25 % threshold, which is foreseen by the Green Pact. Bulgaria is also in the same situation as Romania with a rather small share of organic farming in the total agricultural area, namely 162,332 ha in 2018 out of a total of 4.5 million ha.

An important aspect I consider is the growth potential in the emerging countries of Central and Eastern Europe (Romania, Hungary, Bulgaria, Estonia, Poland, Lithuania, Latvia, Czech Republic, Slovenia, Slovakia, Croatia). The basis of a competitive rural economy is sustainable economic growth. As an indicator to measure sustainable economic growth we can use GDP. Also, the circular economy can be considered to have positive effects on competitive economic growth.

At the same time, in order to increase resilience in the face of crises, I believe that a better prioritization of public spending and allocations to important areas in crisis situations, such as health, education, investments in infrastructure, is necessary in Romania and in the rest of the EU member states. In this way we can better overcome crisis situations. In my opinion, for a sustainable growth of rural economies in emerging EU countries, a very important role is played by European funds.

A positive impact on Romania is also brought by the resources allocated from the National Recovery and Resilience Plan (NRRP). It is very important how this program is implemented, which represents for Romania a grant of 14.2 billion euros from the European Union, as well as a loan of 14.9 billion euros in the framework of the recovery program. At European level the recovery program is estimated at 800 billion euros. The Romanian plan is part of a global logic that aims to improve the EU's competitiveness. This amount targets very specific aspects of economy such as the adoption of digital and ecological transition and also the consolidation of cohesion in the single market. In the context of the COVID-19 pandemic, which has had negative consequences for our country, Europe and the whole world, the NRP through the Recovery and Resilience Mechanism (RRM) brings the necessary reforms for the real development of a European country in the green and digital age, ensuring a balance between the priorities of the European Union and the development needs of Romania.

EU and national policies are largely responsible for the development of the rural economy in the emerging EU countries.

To address the challenges in rural areas, the EU has created and implemented the Common Agricultural Policy (CAP).

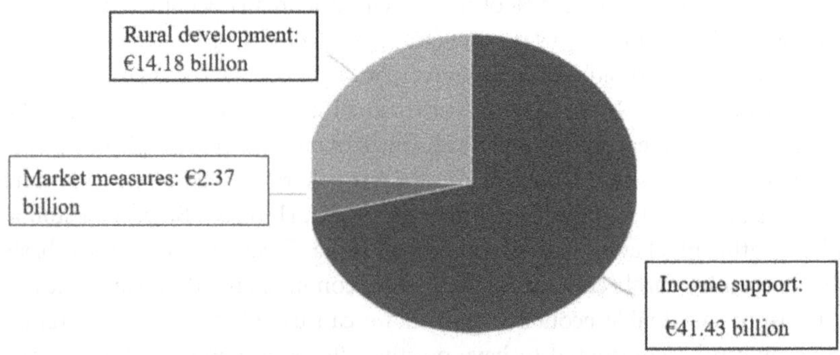

Figure 3. CAP financing

Source: https://agriculture.ec.europa.eu/common-agricultural-policy/cap-overview/cap-glance_ro

Figure 3 shows that most of the EU funding goes to farmers. The CAP is financed by two funds within the EU budget, the European Agricultural Guarantee Fund (EAGF) and the European Agricultural Fund for Rural Development (EAFRD).

The National Rural Development Program (NRDP) is the program through which non-reimbursable funds are granted by the European Union and the Romanian Government for the economic and social development of rural areas in Romania. In the NRDP are presented funding lines to achieve the priority objectives of Romania.

CAP expenditure by Member State in 2020

EU Member States	Direct payments	Market measures	Rural development	Total
	1 000 EUR	1 000 EUR	1 000 EUR	1 000 EUR
Belgium	481 836	60 758	102 723	**645 317**
Bulgaria	781 855	18 386	338 990	**1 139 231**
Czechia	855 832	16 537	321 615	**1 193 984**
Denmark	814 070	12 212	151 589	**977 871**
Germany	4 768 123	117 256	1 394 589	**6 279 967**
Estonia	142 536	1 476	129 177	**273 189**
Ireland	1 201 194	59 338	312 570	**1 573 102**
Greece	1 982 609	59 445	698 261	**2 740 315**
Spain	5 125 093	599 856	1 183 394	**6 908 343**
France	6 909 823	550 551	1 987 740	**9 448 114**
Croatia	317 338	13 061	282 343	**612 741**
Italy	3 599 133	677 514	1 501 763	**5 778 411**
Cyprus	48 125	5 922	18 881	**72 929**
Latvia	277 306	3 048	161 492	**441 846**
Lithuania	480 492	3 344	264 151	**747 987**
Luxembourg	32 841	556	14 511	**47 909**
Hungary	1 266 719	40 211	486 663	**1 793 593**
Malta	5 117	344	13 859	**19 320**
Netherlands	666 190	22 583	147 976	**836 749**
Austria	691 597	22 298	567 266	**1 281 161**
Poland	3 402 201	25 553	1 187 301	**4 615 055**
Portugal	680 228	107 898	582 456	**1 370 581**
Romania	1 912 461	65 671	1 139 927	**3 118 059**
Slovenia	133 869	7 022	120 721	**261 611**
Slovakia	447 758	11 255	214 525	**673 538**
Finland	523 450	6 473	344 777	**874 699**
Sweden	686 818	11 875	249 819	**948 511**
EU27_2020	38 234 612	2 520 441	13 919 080	**54 674 132**

Note: Expenditure in commitments for direct payments and market measures; ceilings of support for rural development from EU budget only.

Sources: European Commission, Directorate General for Agriculture and Rural Development. Updated: June 2021

Table 1. CAP expenditure by Member State in 2020

Source: https://agriculture.ec.europa.eu/system/files/2022-01/agri-statistical-factsheet-eu_en_0.pdf

As shown in Table 1, the developed EU countries account for 72.80 % of the EU's CAP expenditure in 2020, unlike the emerging countries of Central and Eastern Europe and (Romania, Hungary, Bulgaria, Estonia, Poland, Lithuania, Latvia, Czech Republic, Slovenia, Slovakia, Croatia) whose CAP expenditure amounts to 14.870.834 (thousand EURO), representing 27.20 % of total CAP expenditure at EU level. These data convince us that we must follow the rural development model of the developed EU countries.

Through the two programs NRDP and NRRP funds are allocated, in which money allocated to environmental protection have a large share.

The provision of accessible and quality infrastructure and its efficient use are key priorities, particularly in emerging market economies. Achieving these priorities in a cost-effectively will not only stimulate economic growth, but will also improve inclusiveness and, in some cases, environmental performance. The agricultural sector has historically played an important role in emerging markets.

The European model of agriculture is based on a competitive sector, market oriented, fulfilling also other public functions such as environment protection, offering more convenient residential settlements for rural population and integration of agriculture with the environment and forestry. The Common Agricultural Policy is shifting from direct subsidies granted to agriculture (pillar 1 of PAC) to the integrated development of rural economy and to environment protection (pillar 2 of PAC). The Romanian rural economy, dominated by agriculture in most parts of the country, is still poorly integrated into the market economy. In the actual context of the agricultural economy, the well-being of rural and urban farmers, as well as the well-being of agricultural producers, depends on the way in which marketing techniques are understood and applied.

The Romanian producer must act in accordance with the existing economic situation, to apply technical and economical methods which offer him stability and economic efficiency. The producer is required to produce in accordance with what is required on the domestic and international market, to react promptly to the needs of the consumer.

The Romanian farmer and those of the European Union Member States must adapt to the existing economic reality at European and world level and adopt technical and economic methods that will provide stability and economic efficiency. The products obtained must also comply with European and world market standards.

In the current context, for economic and social recovery following the impact of the COVID-19 pandemic on the economy of each country, a recovery plan for Europe is necessary. In this regard, the European Commission is proposing a reinforcement of the funds available to support farmers and rural areas, and which aims to meet the objectives of the European Green Pact.

Organic farming is a promising direction and increasingly in demand by the greening of farming, which has great potential thanks to natural technologies of production.

Agriculture can be the main source of growth for countries where it is the backbone of the economy, as well as contributing to poverty reduction and environmental improvement in countries in all three groups, albeit in different ways. This requires improving the competitiveness and resilience of smallholder farmers by diversifying sources of income through labor markets and non-agricultural sectors of the rural economy and facilitating the successful migration of those previously employed in agriculture.

I believe that studies in this field need to be expanded and massive research is needed in order to follow the implementation of the established guidelines and the transition to sustainability. Basically, there is a need for so-called indicators to measure sustainability, instead of measuring growth in the economy, which does not express the level of a country's well-being, nor the negative effects on the environment. An example of this is the German research institute ZOE, where indicators have been developed under the name "Doughnut Economics" (ZOE-Institute ZOE Report Towards Europe, Accessed January 15, 2023).

Emphasis on the need to develop indicators for measuring access to goods such as food, housing and mobility. These indicators can be considered as true measuring progress toward achieving the EU's priority objectives in Green Pact and resilience and sustainability targets.

3. Conclusions

Competitive rural economy is a priority need of our days when we bring into discussion rural areas. The negative impact of the COVID-19 pandemic, the war in Ukraine, the energy crisis and the multiple climate changes are the clear motivation for the need of sustainable economic growth that will underpin the functioning of a competitive rural economy in the emerging and developed EU countries.

In my opinion, if we want to leave future generations a cleaner planet, we need to rethink the way we exploit natural resources, we need to gradually move to ecological agriculture, to the circular economy, which ensures a rational use of natural resources.

References

Gavrilescu, D., & Giurcă, D. (2000). *Agro-food economy* (pp. 10–30). Expert Publishing House, Bio terra. https://ec.europa.eu/eurostat/statisticsexplained/index.php?title=Agriculture_statistics_-_family_farming_in_the_EU

https://agriculture.ec.europa.eu/sustainability_ro

https://ec.europa.eu/eurostat/statistics-explained/index.php?title=From_farm_to_fork_-_a_statistical_journey/ro&oldid=501261

https://ecoferma.ro/agricultura-ecologica-in-ue-studiu-de-caz-franta-cooperativele-calea-spre-succes/

https://ecoferma.ro/agricultura-ecologica-in-ue-studiu-de-caz-germania-sprijin-financiar-pentru-fermierii-ecologici/

https://ecoferma.ro/agricultura-ecologica-in-ue-studiu-de-caz-germania-sprijin-financiar-pentru-fermierii-ecologici/

https://agriculture.ec.europa.eu/system/files/2022-01/agri-statistical-factsheet-eu_en_0.pdf

https://zoe-institut.de/wp-content/uploads/2021/11/ZOE_Report_Towards-Europe.pdf

https://www.gazetadeagricultura.info/dezvoltare-rurala/1439-descrierea-spatiului-rural.html

https://www.madr.ro/docs/dezvoltare-rurala/programare-2014-2020/studiu-potential-socio-economic-de-dezvoltare-zone-rurale-ver-10.04.2015.pdf

https://www.edu.ro/sites/default/files/Strategia-nationala-pentru-dezvoltarea-durabila-a-Rom%C3%A2niei-2030.pdf

Mathieu, N. (1969). *Planning issues of French rural regions, in geography and regional planning* (pp. 105–115). Institute of Geographical Research of the Academy of Sciences of Hungary.

Ligia Nascimento & Manuela Faia Correia

Evolution Drivers for the Higher Education Teacher

1. Introduction

More than a core human right, education represents the main driver of progress, cutting across the 17 Sustainable Development Goals, and providing a structural basis for just, egalitarian, and inclusive societies (United Nations, 2020). Therefore, education and training converge a fundamental vector of social prosperity, being able to underpin the quality of life, productivity, and sustainable development. Higher education is strategically contributing to the development of scientific and technological systems. Accordingly, the higher education teacher (HET) has a great responsibility for society's development (M. Ferreira, 2009).

For many years, universities' meaning of existence was research (Barbato et al., 2019). Given the pressure generated by the social, cultural, and economic changes, the role of higher education institutions (HEIs) has been rethought to privilege the teaching dimension, both in the contents of the courses and the learning methods (Barbato et al., 2019). One of the expectations placed on HEIs is their contribution to economic and social transformation, through the corresponding empowerment of the population to perform in a global labor market (Behari-Leak, 2017). Higher education changed its political, economic, and social settings, which has implications for the universities' organization and management (Santos et al., 2016).

The exponential increase in demand for higher education took place in the 1960s since a much broader set of citizens has begun to seek the training that would equip them with skills for a professional career. The higher education student is an adult who deliberately chooses the desired profession, as well as the program and HEI. Therefore, HEI students expect their teachers to be quite experienced and knowledgeable about the various issues of the work-related context (V. Ferreira, 2010).

2. Role Reorientation

In this new reality of greater massification of education, the teacher-student relationship began to take on the shape of a professional-client relationship. Accordingly, HET's role has transformed, moving from the focus on training to providing professional skills to customers, thus, given employability concerns, selling an educational product and attracting students "consumers" (Barbato et al., 2019; Santos et al., 2016).

As a condition for success, the pedagogical project of each higher education program and the assessment methods should be aligned with each profession's profile, if the teacher has in-depth knowledge of the work area for which students are qualifying. Being embedded in these contexts, whether through work or research, is a specificity and a condition for practicing teaching (V. Ferreira, 2010).

In developed societies, what is most valuable is not what is known, but what that knowledge enables one to perform. The future is envisioned as complex and, more than acquiring a set of knowledge accumulated over time, people need to be prepared to deal with unknown, unforeseen, and uncertain contexts. That is, basic knowledge is important, but motivation and the so-called "soft skills" are even more precious. Among these skills are proactivity and innovation (curiosity, persistence, ability to take risks), teamwork, communication, leadership, decision-making, and problem-solving. The very employability of citizens dictates this: what is valued at the entrance into the labor market are, more than information and technical expertise, the mastery of intellectual tools (e.g., reasoning and analysis) and interdisciplinary integration, critical thinking, and the ability to continue learning. Hence, the role of education systems and HEIs become fundamental.

Another changing factor is the need to articulate the educational offer with the student's uniqueness. Since comprehension and the ability to apply knowledge are strongly individual, so is the teaching-learning process, thus the student became an active subject of learning (M. Ferreira, 2009; Nóvoa, 2009). Moreover, several higher education students are professionals who enter or re-enter higher education at different stages of their life and thus vary in the background they bring to the learning process (Cendon, 2018). This fact has led, on the one hand, to experimentation with different curricula and electives and the combination of classes with distance learning components, leading to greater flexibility in the student's training pathway and favoring their employability. On the other hand, it highlighted the individualization of teaching and that students should be directly involved in the learning processes.

Concepts such as interactive and cooperative education emerged (Barbato et al., 2019; M. Ferreira, 2009), moving from a teacher-centered process to a student's learning process. Direct student collaborative engagement in higher education curriculum design has been advocated as fostering shared responsibility, gaining skills that help them adapt to an ever-changing, complex world (Lubicz-Nawrocka, 2018), and has evidenced improved feedback, attendance, and marks (Brooman et al., 2015; Stoller, 2015).

As part of the plan to create a European higher education area that allows comparability, compatibility, and mobility of citizens in the European Community and, therefore, ensures Europe's competitiveness in the world, the Bologna Declaration had a great influence on the reorientation of teaching toward an integral training student-centered model, as a user and transformer of the acquired learning according to the challenges faced.

The recognition that academic performance is higher when associated with participatory learning has led to the development of active learning methodologies, which aim at overcoming goals both in the cognitive sphere (knowledge), practical application (know-how), and socio-affective dimension (how to be, that is, behaviors and attitudes). Thus, the development of the critical, participative, and creative student is achieved with active, non-inert methodologies (Lázaro et al., 2018). A more interactive classroom model, in which students are questioned, forces teachers to be prepared to redirect the lesson plans to the student's attitudes and interests, which asks a constant need for adaptation (M. Ferreira, 2009; Nóvoa, 2009).

The preparation of citizens committed to values such as justice and social inclusion is starting to draw attention as an integral part of the role of HEIs, requiring additional preparation to enable HETs, not only in teaching these issues but also in the relationship established with very diverse groups of students (Behari-Leak, 2017; Nóvoa, 2009).

This citizens' holistic education beyond the knowledge of a profession is associated with Humboldt's model of the university, for whom HEIs also had a "moral education of the nation" mission (M. Ferreira, 2009). HETs are mediators between generations, acting as guardians and communicators of national heritage, then being a moral ideal that students should look at and follow (Ilaltdinova et al., 2018).

The higher education students' revealed, as the criteria for a good teacher, knowledge mastery, pedagogical skills, and diversified methodologies that encourage critical thinking, easy and clear language accompanied by practical and relevant examples, dynamism, and the establishment of good interpersonal relationships and respect for students (Figueiredo, 2018; Morrison & Evans, 2018; Soriano & Aquino, 2017).

HEI's reform process depends on how HETs perceive and accept those new ideas. Some findings indicate that most teachers are indifferent to the changes (e.g., Gutsu et al., 2020). Thus, the future of higher education entails innovation and the transformation of mindsets and HETs' practice. In the new approach, where students are required to behave more actively, HET becomes a mentor who encourages reflection, and self-study and provides high-value interactions with students (Cendon, 2018), by sharing expertise in a designer of knowledge role (Trinidad, 2020).

3. Role Preparedness and Challenges

For the desired transformation, part of the solution could be effective teacher training programs focused on the new role, how to perform it successfully, and considering the educational context specificities of each subject area. Academic degrees legitimate HETs' knowledge in the respective scientific field, but often there is no initial psycho-pedagogical preparation training. HETs have high levels of cognitive thinking skills, but pedagogical and transformative thinking are not at the same level (Karjalainen & Nissilä, 2022). If specific structuring training for teaching and learning processes lacks, HETs do not scientifically know the elements that constitute the teaching action itself, such as planning, class organization, methodologies, didactic strategies, assessment, and the teacher-student interaction peculiarities (Lourenço et al., 2016). Some compulsory higher education training has been implemented worldwide with gains in HET's perceptions of pedagogy and practices and student learning (Nguyen & Laws, 2019).

Global-wide comparative analysis showed the need for pre-service and in-service training programs that balance methodological preparation with the development of personal qualities (Ilaltdinova et al., 2018), being advocated a "pedagogy of kindness" to increase feelings of connection and inclusion and improve both student learning and well-being (Rawle, 2021).

Nonetheless, learning to be a teacher does not end with formal programs. Lourenço et al. (2016) add that this training can be integrated into the doctoral program and evaluation, but as a foundation for a lifelong and autonomous learning process, since, as with the scientific *habitus*, the development of the pedagogical *habitus* is also continuous for and in the teaching practice.

HET's new challenges lie beyond the acquisition and evidence of pedagogical skills that allow conducting learning situations in a relevant and innovative way and, thus, enabling their mission of developing and preparing the next generations.

Higher education has been characterized by a marked level of institutionalized individualism, in the sense that the HET, sponsored by the respective academic community, has become accustomed to great freedom of originality and intellectual quality, in a safe space and largely independent from the respective

HEI (Barbato et al., 2019). This autonomy and status were enhanced by international and transdisciplinary networks, which allowed HETs to build their unique path in research. It is as if HETs had the monopoly to determine the goals and guidelines of academic work (Santos et al., 2016), illustrating the HEIs' "professional bureaucracy" (Mintzberg, 1979).

Globalization's pressure and socioeconomic trends have imposed changes associated with neoliberal policies, which constrain HEIs to competitiveness and, therefore, are regulated by the economy and controlled by market mechanisms. Integrating a European higher education area implies decentralization of the educational process, not only for students but also for institutions and governments (M. Ferreira, 2009). If, on the one hand, cost containment measures and possible funds reduction lead HEIs to adopt management models of organizations operating in the global market (Behari-Leak, 2017), on the other hand, the expectations placed on them, to "produce" professionally competent graduates for the competitive market, are reflected in a growing system of norms and procedures that academics have to obey and, consequently, cause erosion in their autonomy degree within their institutions (Barbato et al., 2019; Santos et al., 2016).

V. Ferreira (2010) warns about the "trivialization" of the HET's practice, due to the precarious nature of some contractual conditions, which induce to work in several HEIs or accumulate teaching with another paid activity and, thus, viewing teaching not as a career, but as a job in "educational corporations" that follow international policies. This author argues that HET should not be considered a mere employee, nor be submitted to economic criteria and corporate management practices, labeled as having a utilitarian logic, which not only is contrary to the conception of the Human as a knowledge generator and its history builder but also enhancing a decline in teaching programs quality.

From our perspective, the key lies in a compromise. On the one hand, financial issues should not condition knowledge growth and the quality of its transference to the community, because it evolves the economy and the world. On the other hand, the quest for knowledge and total freedom/independence regarding teaching should not happen at any cost, because it may preclude other economic critical aspects and, thus, hinder allocating the necessary resources to HEIs. We believe that only a mutually accepted virtuous circle can lead HEIs and HETs to fulfill their purposes of contributing to social and human progress. In the current knowledge society, as the economy is based on knowledge and knowledge is based on the economy, the aim will be to develop both in parallel to obtain synergies and mutual gains (Santos et al., 2016).

We previously envisioned the historical evolution of the university's role, migrating from a research orientation to a focus on knowledge transfer. However, teaching has not become the sole function of HETs, which accumulate with scientific investigation. This means that, to the challenges brought about by changes in teaching purposes and methods, efforts on research activities, from which HETs cannot resign, must be added. This binomial is actually inseparable (M. Ferreira, 2009), since not only is needed for a society in transformation, but also contributes to instilling in students a critical analysis attitude, continuous questioning, and enthusiasm for knowledge that equip them with the desired intellectual autonomy, that is, the ability to learn how to learn. In other words, research can integrate the educational strategy. Yet, HET's work was intensified by great pressure to publish, not contemporizing with adequate time for reflection and scientific output, and leading to a context marked by publication duty, in an immediatism and urgency culture (Santos et al., 2016).

Contemporary job descriptions have begun to place greater emphasis on the teaching component, while still requiring active scientific research responsibilities, participation in community liaison, as well as management and administrative skills (Behari-Leak, 2017). These are the institutional dimensions that have reoriented academic identity, but even though bureaucratic tasks expanded, leaving less time to dedicate to the quality of teaching, the academic identity's essence is still based on the relationship with knowledge, its generation, and dissemination (Santos et al., 2016).

4. Role and Technology

The digital era's importance and impact on HET activity should be highlighted. In fact, the new demands that socioeconomic transformations have brought to HET's role and work were accompanied by the imperatives inherent to the 4.0 revolution. The advances in Information and Communication Technologies (ICT) have affected the way human beings think, act, and learn, so their integration into the teaching process is an added challenge for the teacher (Lázaro et al., 2018).

If at a certain time, teachers felt little support regarding the classrooms' physical and technological structure in higher education courses, nowadays they are faced with a technological arsenal that emerges and changes at great speed and that requires differentiated knowledge. Simultaneously, HETs must be competent in illustrating content with appropriate and meaningful multimedia resources, preparing dynamic classes, addressing academic plagiarism issues, and knowing how to deal with learning platforms and discussion forums (V. Ferreira, 2010).

With ICTs, distance learning has become an alternative in higher education settings. In this case, the lack of face-to-face contact limits the extent to which the teacher can establish a relationship with students, hampering knowing who the students are, their pace, and degree of involvement, and frustrating the desire for full individualized monitoring. Due to the COVID-19 pandemic-imposed transformations, that triggered the greatest disruption of educational systems in history (United Nations, 2020), full remote teaching was a reality that teachers have dealt with over a period. An international study during pandemic constraints confirmed HETs' struggles with online teaching (unpreparedness, ICT access, and reliability, reduced relationality), quality of teaching, and workload (Philips et al., 2021), highlighting the challenges of connecting emotionally with students at a distance (Cain et al., 2022). Some aspects of the teaching digital evolution and certain contingencies of contemporary times seem to contradict some paradigm shift prerogatives and recommendations of the Bologna Declaration.

In face-to-face teaching, however, the traditional approach evolution and suitability to the current learning needs can reap great help from ICT, using blended/hybrid teaching resources as the basis of active methodologies, such as flipped classroom, peer work, gamification, and project-based and problem-solving learning. These are some proposals that grant the student an active role in the learning process (Lázaro et al., 2018). This implies that HETs must act on multiple fronts, with technology-based activities in both face-to-face and virtual environments that help students to seek and build knowledge, select, and interpret different information, as well as share knowledge with their peers.

Efforts have been made to identify trends and innovations in higher education regarding online, blended, and lifelong learning contexts, with a particular focus on pedagogical aspects (Witthaus et al., 2016). The project offered a framework for a next-generation pedagogy and corresponding practices was proposed, consisting of five orientations under the acronym IDEAS: (1) Intelligent pedagogy—using technology to optimize the learning experience; (2) Distributed pedagogy—sharing ownership by different stakeholders of the learning pathways; (3) Engaging pedagogy—curriculum design and delivery aiming encouraging students' active participation in the learning process; (4) Agile pedagogy—making curricular pathways flexible and customizable, attending to student experience and needs; and (5) Situated pedagogy—emphasizing the relevance of contextualizing learning in the real world. This proposal addresses most of the concerns previously mentioned.

Despite all the possible benefits that ICTs can bring to higher education, additional digital literacy efforts are required from HETs, regarding knowledge, handling, experimentation, and monitoring of new technological tools to be integrated into an instructional strategy. Some universities have made investments in teaching platforms that enable ICT use as the basis of active methodologies. However, as Lázaro et al. (2018) recognize, many teachers are not prepared to adopt a new posture and make use of these resources with pedagogical intentionality. We resume here the formerly raised mindset and specific training concerns, placing them in a future scenario, progressive or disruptive, where a pivot to remote teaching will likely occur.

5. Conclusion

HET's role has expanded, comprises a variety of tasks to accomplish under time pressure, and work seems to be constantly lagging and unsatisfactory. Dealing with all these challenges has increased HET's vulnerability to frustration and dissatisfaction, physical and mental fatigue, and anxiety and stress reactions, raising concerns about their mental health (V. Ferreira, 2010; Philips et al., 2021; Santos et al., 2016), which is not alien to the unpreparedness for new ways of work, increasingly based on the digital.

The future of HETs is challenging, to say the least. The changes in HEI's role and dynamics determine transformations in teachers' work and imply rethinking their identity. Their responsibilities will remain that of creating and transferring knowledge, albeit no longer as mere "transmission." Instead, a pedagogical shift focused on active methods is associated with the development of agile competencies in the search for and application of knowledge specific to each situation, which students will face in the workplace. Only in this way can teaching practice create value, for students, society, and the economy. Nevertheless, to achieve this, HETs must take the initiative to get a set of theoretical, practical, and socio-affective psycho-pedagogical knowledge, which the pathway to the academic degree that officially qualifies for teaching at higher education did not require. And they are urged to do so in a rapidly changing world, adapting to the innovations, demands, and vicissitudes brought about by the digitalization of education, while at the same time, in line with their career progress, ensuring additional management and administrative tasks, which include, in regulated contexts of budget restraint, concerns for competitiveness and the reputation of their HEIs and subject area.

References

Barbato, G., Moscati, R., & Turri, M. (2019). Is the role of academics as teachers changing? An exploratory analysis in Italian universities. *Tuning Journal for Higher Education*, *6*(2), 97–126. https://doi.org/10.18543/tjhe-6(2)-2019pp97-126

Behari-Leak, K. (2017). New academics, new higher education contexts: A critical perspective on professional development. *Teaching in Higher Education*, *22*(5), 485–500. https://doi.org/10.1080/13562517.2016.1273215

Brooman, S., Darwent, S., & Pimor, A. (2015). The student voice in higher education curriculum design: Is there value in listening? *Innovations in Education and Teaching International*, *52*(6), 663–674. https://doi.org/10.1080/14703297.2014.910128

Cain, M., Campbell, C., & Coleman, K. (2022). "Kindness and empathy beyond all else": Challenges to professional identities of Higher Education teachers during COVID-19 times. *Australian Educational Researcher*. https://doi.org/10.1007/s13384-022-00552-1

Cendon, E. (2018). Lifelong learning at universities: Future perspectives for teaching and learning. *Journal of New Approaches in Educational Research*, *7*(2), 81–87. https://doi.org/10.7821/naer.2018.7.320

Ferreira, M. (2009). O professor do ensino superior na era da globalização [The Higher Education Teacher in the age of globalization]. *Revista Iberoamericana de Educación*, *50*(5), 1–10. https://doi.org/10.35362/rie5051908

Ferreira, V. (2010). As especificidades da docência do ensino superior [The specificities of teaching in higher education]. *Revista Diálogo Educacional*, *10*(29), 85–99. http://www.redalyc.org/pdf/1891/189114444006.pdf

Figueiredo, M. L. (2018). Características de um bom professor na percepção de universitários [Characteristics of a good teacher as perceived by university students]. *Humanas Sociais & Aplicadas*, *8*(22), 37–51. https://doi.org/10.25242/887682220181386

Gutsu, E. G., Demeneva, N. N., Mayasova, T. V., Kolesova, O. V., Kochetova, E. V., & Tivikova, S. K. (2020). Current problem of education management: Subjective attitude of university teachers to changes in higher education. *Universal Journal of Educational Research*, *8*(11B), 6036–6041. https://doi.org/10.13189/ujer.2020.082239

Ilaltdinova, E. Y., Frolova, S. V., & Lebedeva, I., V. (2018). Top qualities of great teachers: National and universal. *Advances in Intelligent Systems and Computing*, *677*(199379), 45–52. http://link.springer.com/10.1007/978-3-319-67843-6

Karjalainen, A., & Nissilä, S.-P. (2022). Higher Education Teachers' conceptions of professional development and change: A longitudinal case study of university pedagogy prospects. *International Journal of Educational Methodology, 8*(3), 609–623. https://doi.org/10.12973/ijem.8.3.609

Lourenço, C. D. da S., Lima, M. C., & Narciso, E. R. P. (2016). Formação pedagógica no ensino superior: O que diz a legislação e a literatura em Educação e Administração? [Pedagogical training in higher education: What do the legislation and literature say in Education and Administration?]. *Revista Da Avaliação Da Educação Superior, 21*(3), 691–718. https://doi.org/10.1590/s1414-40772016000300003

Lubicz-Nawrocka, T. M. (2018). From partnership to self-authorship: The benefits of co-creation of the curriculum. *International Journal for Students as Partners, 2*(1), 47–63. https://doi.org/10.15173/ijsap.v2i1.3207

Lazaro, A., Sato, M., & Tezani, T. (2018). Metodologias ativas no ensino superior: O papel do docente no ensino presencial [Active methodologies in higher education: The role of the teacher in face- to-face teaching]. *Congresso Internacional de Educacao e Tecnologias*, 1–12. https://cietenped.ufscar.br/submissao/index.php/2018/article/view/234

Mintzberg, H. (1979). *The structuring of organizations*. Prentice-Hall.

Morrison, B., & Evans, S. (2018). University students' conceptions of the good teacher: A Hong Kong perspective. *Journal of Further and Higher Education, 42*(3), 352–365. https://doi.org/10.1080/0309877X.2016.1261096

Nguyen, T. V. S., & Laws, K. (2019). Changes in higher education teachers' perceptions of curriculum. *Journal of Applied Research in Higher Education, 11*(1), 76–89. https://doi.org/10.1108/JARHE-06-2018-0097

Nóvoa, A. (2009). *Professores: Imagens do futuro presente* [*Teachers: Images of the future today*]. Educa.

Philips, L., Cain, M., Ritchie, J., Campbell, C., Davis, S., Brock, C., Burke, G., Coleman, K., & Joosa, E. (2021). Surveying and resonating with teacher concerns during COVID-19 pandemic. *Teachers and Teaching, Theory and Practice*, 1–18.

Rawle, F. (2021). *A pedagogy of kindness: The cornerstone for student learning and wellness*. The Campus. https://www.timeshighereducation.com/campus/pedagogy-kindness-cornerstone-student-learning-and-wellness

Santos, C. D. C., Pereira, F., & Lopes, A. (2016). Efeitos da intensificação do trabalho no ensino superior: Da fragmentação à articulação entre investigação, ensino, gestão académica e transferência de conhecimento [Effects of work intensification in higher education: From fragmentation to the articulati].

Revista Portuguesa de Educação, 29(1), 295–321. https://doi.org/10.21814/rpe.6820

Soriano, G. P., & Aquino, M. G. B. (2017). Characteristics of a good clinical teacher as perceived by nursing students and faculty members in a Philippine university college of nursing. *International Journal of Nursing Science, 7*(4), 96–101. https://doi.org/10.5923/j.nursing.20170704.04

Stoller, A. (2015). Taylorism and the logic of learning outcomes. *Journal of Curriculum Studies, 47*(3), 317–333. https://doi.org/10.1080/00220272.2015.1018328

Trinidad, J. E. (2020). Understanding student-centred learning in higher education: Students' and teachers' perceptions, challenges, and cognitive gaps. *Journal of Further and Higher Education, 44*(8), 1013–1023. https://doi.org/10.1080/0309877X.2019.1636214

United Nations. (2020). *Policy brief: Education during COVID-19 and beyond.* https://doi.org/10.24215/18509959.26.e12

Witthaus, G., Rodriguez, B. C. P., Guardia, L., & Campillo, C. G. (2016). *Next generation pedagogy: IDEAS for online and blended higher education.* Final report of the FUTURA project. http://hdl.handle.net/10609/51441

Kristaps Lesinskis, Inese Mavlutova, Janis Hermanis,
Aivars Spilbergs, & Liga Peiseniece

The Impact of Using a Digital Tool KABADA on Entrepreneurial Intension on Generation Z Higher Education Students in Central, Eastern and Southern Europe

1. Introduction

Recent research identified a total of 2,185 indexed research publications on trends in entrepreneurship education in prominent journals (Sreenivasan & Suresh, 2023). According to the findings, a significant number of publications have been published on the growth of entrepreneurship education research. The major themes developed out of the co-occurrence network are determinants of entrepreneurship education for building an entrepreneurial intention among students in higher education, entrepreneurship in the classroom, and innovation and entrepreneurship education.

Asimakopoulos et al. (2019) findings indicate that entrepreneurial education is positively associated with the intention to undertake entrepreneurial activity, in addition to demonstrating a positive moderation effect role of social norms on the relationship between entrepreneurial self-efficacy and entrepreneurial intention. According to findings of Reissová et al. (2020) there are some other factors, such as the country of origin and gender—the ones that are also statistically significant.

The major characteristic of the Generation Z is the global perspective of their views and thinking, tolerance to diversity thanks to the development of the Internet, social platforms and digital opinion leaders (Schawbel, 2014). According to Scholz and Rennig (2019), significant differences exist in the profile of Generation Z representatives in different parts of the world, among different European countries, or even within a single country, but the most important characteristic of Generation Z is the usage of IT tools.

The abovementioned reasons challenged the authors to conduct a study with a purpose to examine and analyze the effects of using an educational digital tool KABADA on entrepreneurial intention among Generation Z in CEE countries and SE countries, as well as to analyze the impact of subjective norms and beliefs on entrepreneurial intention.

The research and its results capture novelty as the training method itself with the digital tool KABADA is unique since the tool was developed and put into use only in 2022.

The results and discussion of the research found statistically significant impact of the use of digital tool in entrepreneurship education on entrepreneurial intention, statistically significant differences between CEE and SE countries in Generation Z and discovered how different beliefs and norms impact entrepreneurial intention in the sample researched. Most of the research results confirm the conclusions of other researchers in the field.

2. Educational, Behavioral and Regional Factors Influencing Entrepreneurial Intention

By conducting an in-depth review of the literature in this topic, it can be concluded that the results of the research so far in the scientific literature show a controversial picture regarding the impact of entrepreneurship education on entrepreneurial intention.

Maheshwari et al. (2022) identify the factors which have been most studied in the literature and determine which factors are less explored to measure the entrepreneurial intention of students. The analysis of the papers clearly demonstrated that the Ajzen's Theory of Planned Behavior (TPB) model and cognitive factors dominate this area of research.

Many researchers have found positive impact of entrepreneurial education on entrepreneurial intention, as well as strong relation between behavioral factors and entrepreneurial intention. Asimakopoulos et al. (2019) indicates that entrepreneurial education is positively associated with the intention to undertake entrepreneurial activity, in addition to demonstrating a positive moderation effect role of social norms of behavior on the relationship between entrepreneurial self-efficacy and entrepreneurial intention. Cera et al. (2020) investigated the relationship between entrepreneurship education and entrepreneurial intention in a Balkan countries. Iwu et al. (2021) explored factors that may influence student entrepreneurial intention and found that the respondent group strongly accede to the usefulness of entrepreneurship education for economic development which reveals that they are well-versed with the role and gains of entrepreneurship at a macro level. Significant positive entrepreneurship education impact on entrepreneurial intentions was found also by Wang et al. (2023).

Wibowo and Narmaditya (2022), investigated how the direct effect of digital entrepreneurship education on digital entrepreneurship intentions. His study provided insights related to psychological and behavioral aspects in the form of entrepreneurial inspiration as one of the predictor variables and mediators for increasing digital entrepreneurship intentions. The importance of digital entrepreneurship education is stressed also by Carvalho et al. (2021).

Mónico et al. (2021) evaluated the students' perception of the entrepreneurial education level of higher education institutions (HEIs) and its impact on their entrepreneurial intention in Portugal. The results pointed indirect effects of the entrepreneurial universities on entrepreneurial intention by the entrepreneurial motivations of the students to become an entrepreneur. Oropallo et al. (2007) noted the professional condition of the entrepreneur is important for business success in Italy.

On the contrary, there are also several studies that question or limit the positive effect of entrepreneurial education on entrepreneurial intention. Reissová et al. (2020) finds that if the monitored variables (e.g., personal characteristics) are not considered, it is possible that education aimed at starting and developing a business is less effective. Draksler and Sirec (2021) examined the impact of entrepreneurship education on entrepreneurial intentions and entrepreneurial competencies of university students in Slovenia from a socio-psychological perspective using a conceptual research model based on Ajzen's TPB and the competency approach. Research by Martínez-Gregorio et al. (2021) examined the efficacy of the entrepreneurship education in student samples, attending to studies with a pre-post test design and a control group. The results showed small effect sizes for EE in increasing Entrepreneurship Intention and self-efficacy.

Several authors indicate on regional differences. One of the main conclusions of new theoretical and empirical approaches is that entrepreneurship and entrepreneurial intentions are heavily determined by place (Acs et al., 2015; Audretsch, 2015; Fritsch & Mueller, 2004). According to findings of Reissová et al. (2020), there are three the most significant factors for the willingness to run the business, the most important being ability to accept risk, but there are some other factors, such as the country of origin and gender—the ones that are also statistically significant.

3. The First Digital Natives: Generation Z

The focus of the authors' research is Generation Z, from whom the research sample is made. Right now, Generation Z is actively entering higher education studies and choosing a professional career.

The word "generation" can be defined and explained in different ways. Eyerman and Turner (1998) call a generation a group of people who are united by a similar culture, providing them with a collective consciousness, and try to integrate this group in a certain period of time. Howe (2014) describes a generation as the totality of all people born in more than 20 years, or roughly at one stage of a person's life: childhood, youth, middle age, and old age. Pichler et al. (2021) define this concept as people in a particular group who experience the same significant events over a period of time.

While some authors include in Generation Z those born between 1997 and the second decade of the twenty-first century, other scholars believe that Generation Z are people born after 1995. Some other scientists believe that Generation Z was born between 1996 and 2010 (Chillakuri & Mahanandia, 2018). The point on which there is a consensus among experts: the Generation Z does not know the world without the internet and virtual reality has become as real as the physical world in their lives. Another characteristic of the Generation Z is the global perspective of their views and thinking, tolerance to diversity thanks to the development of the Internet, social platforms and digital opinion leaders (Schawbel, 2014). Scholz and Rennig (2019) indicate that significant differences exist in the profile of Generation Z representatives in different parts of the world, among different European countries, or even within a single country, but the important characteristic of Generation Z is the usage of IT tools.

According to Iftode (2019), Generation Z has a number of characteristics that are not typical to the previous generations—ability to operate in both real and virtual worlds, good ability to quickly obtain and disseminate information and to communicate via social media.

4. Digital Tool KABADA and Description of the Experiment

KABADA (2023) (stands for Knowledge Alliance of Business Idea Assessment: Digital Approach) is a structured, Web-based platform or digital tool that allows business plan development. Informed by theoretical research, relevant statistics, and artificial intelligence (AI) insights, the tool guides new entrepreneurs through every step of the way, helping them understand where they stand, where and how they might consider going, and what challenges and opportunities lie ahead (KABADA Consortium, 2023; Lesinskis et al., 2022). In the digital age, automated software with machine learning and artificial intelligence is widely used in both business and everyday life; therefore, it has to be used in education and other areas of societal life (Lesinskis et al., 2021; Mavlutova et al., 2020).

In the period from September to December 2022, the authors of the research conducted an experiment, providing 14 educational sessions for three hours for representatives of the Z generation in universities in Latvia, Lithuania, the Czech Republic (CEE countries) and Portugal, Spain and Italy (SE countries) using KABADA tool. In each session, its participants were surveyed both before and after (pre-post) the session.

The total number of respondents who participated in the sessions was 248. All of them filled out the questionnaires before the session, and 193 of them after. The use of appropriate statistical methodology made it possible to obtain a statistically correct comparison of the results before and after the educational session. CEE countries were represented by 123 respondents, and SE countries by 125 respondents.

Before starting the research, the following hypotheses were developed:

H1: The positive effect of the use of a digital tool KABADA in entrepreneurship education on the entrepreneurial intention of Generation Z representatives is not statistically significantly different in CEE and SE countries.
H2: The subjective norms and behavioral control have a statistically significant effect on the entrepreneurial intention of representatives of the Generation Z.

To test the hypotheses, specific tests (Mann-Whitney U test and Wilcoxon signed-rank test) were performed that check the statistical significance for changes or differences in results.

5. Results and Discussion

In general, the results obtained during the experiment showed a positive effect of the educational session with KABADA tool on the respondents' entrepreneurial intention (see Table 1).

Table 1. Entrepreneurial intention of all respondents before and after the educational session (Likert scale 1–7; 1 = very low, 7 = very high), 95 % confidence interval mean

		Valid answers	Mean	Upper	Lower	Std. deviation
Q: How high is your intention to become an entrepreneur?	Before	248	4.79	4.991	4.59	1.614
Q: How high is your intention to become an entrepreneur?	After	193	5.176	5.369	4.984	1.366

Source: Authors, computed with JASP Team (2023). JASP (Version 0.17)

In order to test H1, entrepreneurial intention and its change were separately analyzed in respondent groups representing CEE countries and SE countries. The results are shown in Table 2.

Table 2. Entrepreneurial intention of all respondents before and after the educational session (Likert scale 1–7; 1 = very low, 7 = very high), 95 % confidence interval mean

	Mean	Upper	Lower	Confidence interval
CEE—Before (n = 123)	5.23	5.50	4.96	0.27
CEE—After (n = 94)	5.57	5.80	5.35	0.23
SE—Before (n = 125)	4.36	4.64	4.08	0.28
SE—After (n = 99)	4.80	5.09	4.51	0.29

Source: Authors, computed with JASP Team (2023). JASP (Version 0.17)

Although the increase in entrepreneurial intention can be observed in all sample and in both groups of countries, when performing the Mann-Whitney U test (checks if the mean values of the two samples differ significantly, used for an ordinal scale of values to which a Likert scale 1–7 corresponds, p value should be less than 0.05 to show statistically significant difference), it is possible to obtain the following results with regard to statistical significance:

1) There are significant differences between answers before and after sessions in all sample (p = 0.019)
2) There are significant differences between answers before and after sessions in SE countries (p = 0.046)
3) There are no significant differences between answers before and after sessions in CEE countries (p = 0.212)

Thus H1 is rejected—the positive effect of the use of a digital tool KABADA in entrepreneurship education on the entrepreneurial intention of Generation Z representatives is statistically significantly different in CEE and SE countries.

Table 3. Evaluation of statements containing subjective norms and behavioral control by respondents of all sample (n = 248) (Likert scale 1–7; 1 = strongly disagree, 7 = strongly agree), 95 % confidence interval mean

able	Mean	Upper	Lower	Confidence Interval
1. My interest in entrepreneurship is affected by society in general	3.86	4.07	3.64	0.21
2. My interest in entrepreneurship is affected by opinion leaders	3.83	4.05	3.61	0.22

Table 3. Continued

able	Mean	Upper	Lower	Confidence Interval
3. My interest in entrepreneurship is affected by close relatives	3.61	3.83	3.38	0.22
4. My interest in entrepreneurship is affected by teachers	3.48	3.69	3.27	0.21
5. My interest in entrepreneurship is affected by my friends	3.47	3.68	3.26	0.21
6. I would be able to become an entrepreneur if I believed that I should become one	4.86	5.07	4.65	0.21
7. I would be ready to become an entrepreneur if I thought I should become one	4.86	5.05	4.66	0.20

Source: Authors, computed with JASP Team (2023). JASP (Version 0.17)

For the respondents answers on Likert scale where they had to evaluate agreement with seven statements (see Table 3), Wilcoxon signed-rank test was conducted. This test checks whether the mean values of two samples (columns) differ significantly, and is used for an ordinal scale of values to which a Likert scale 1–7 corresponds. It allowed to conclude that for the set of first five statements related to the subjective norms of respondents, it is possible to divide them in two statistically significantly different sets depending on impact factor:

1) Intention affected by society in general and by opinion leaders
2) Intention affected by close relatives, teachers and friends

The first set is statistically significantly more important than the second set. The p value of Wilcoxon signed-rank test is 0.043 between the 2nd and 3rd strongest agreement for the statements on subjective norms thus making statistically significant difference between mentioned sets of factors. There was no statistically significant difference between factors inside each of those two sets.

However, the mean agreement levels with the statements are very close but still below the midpoint of 4 on a Likert scale from 1 to 7.

The level of agreement with the 6th and 7th statement which are related to behavioral control turns out to be very high, being close to 5 on average.

Thus H2 is rejected regarding the impact of subjective norms on the entrepreneurial intention, while confirmed regarding the behavioral control which shows significant impact on entrepreneurial intention.

The results obtained from this research confirm the revelations of Asimakopoulos et al. (2019), Cera et al. (2020), Iwu et al. (2021), Wang et al. (2023) and many others stating that entrepreneurial education has a positive effect on entrepreneurial intention. At the same time literature review revealed also some doubts about the impact of entrepreneurial education on entrepreneurial intention—it was expressed by Draksler and Sirec (2021), Martínez-Gregorio et al. (2021) and Reissowa et al. (2020). This opinion also gets some support from the research conducted by the authors, as it shows that in one of the studied regions of the European countries (CEE countries) this effect is indeed minimal and statistically insignificant.

This research strongly supports the previous research results by Acs et al. (2015), Audretsch (2015), Fritsch and Mueller (2004) that entrepreneurial intentions are heavily determined by environmental factor place. Both the level of entrepreneurial intentions and impact on it from educational sessions with KABADA tool proved to be significantly different in CEE and SE countries.

6. Conclusions

The overall conclusion of the study is that the use of the entrepreneurship education digital tool KABADA has a positive effect on entrepreneurial intention in Generation Z. However, significant differences can be observed between the positive effects in CEE countries and SE countries, as a result of which the hypothesis that such differences do not exist had to be rejected. A statistically significant positive effect can be observed only in SE countries. At the same time, it should be noted that this is achieved at a lower base level of entrepreneurial intention compared to CEE countries. These findings support most of the previous studies stating that even though mostly entrepreneurship education brings positive effects on entrepreneurial intentions, there are certain limitations and not always effects are obvious. This study reinforces the aforementioned doubts when the research is carried out on a regional scale.

The study rejected part of the second hypothesis that stated that the subjective norms of Generation Z members significantly influence their entrepreneurial intention. This turned out to be a false claim, with research showing that rather these norms have a neutral effect.

Another part of that hypothesis, which stated that behavioral control has a significant effect on the entrepreneurial intention of Generation Z, turned out to be true and was confirmed. Indeed, belief of respondents in ability and readiness to become an entrepreneur if they thought and believed they should become one, turned out to be strong.

This study was largely focused on analyzing regional differences in the impact of using a digital tool in entrepreneurship education on Generation Z entrepreneurial intention. However, such a study has the limitation of covering only two of several European regions.

Acknowledgment

The authors acknowledge to KABADA—Erasmus+ KA2 Knowledge Alliances program (project number: 612542-EPP-1-2019-1-LV-EPPKA2-KA).

References

Acs, Z., Szerb, L., Ortega-Argilés, R., Aidis, R., & Coduras, A. (2015). The regional application of the global entrepreneurship and development index (gedi): The case of Spain. *Regional Studies*, *49*(12), 1977–1994.

Asimakopoulos, G., Hernández, V., & Peña Miguel, J. (2019). Entrepreneurial intention of engineering students: The role of social norms and entrepreneurial self-efficacy. *Sustainability*, *11*(16), 4314. https://doi.org/10.3390/su11164314

Audretsch, D. B. (2015). *Everything in its place: Entrepreneurship and the strategic management of cities, regions, and states*. Oxford University Press.

Carvalho, L., Mavlutova, I., Lesinskis, K., & Dias, R. (2021). Entrepreneurial perceptions of students regarding business professional career: The study on gender differences in Latvia. *Economics and Sociology*, *14*(3), 217–238. https://doi.org/10.14254/2071-789X.2021/14-3/12

Cera, G., Mlouk, A., Cera, E., & Shumeli, A. (2020). The impact of entrepreneurship education on entrepreneurial intention. A quasi-experimental research design. *Journal of Competitiveness*, *12*(1), 39–56. https://doi.org/10.7441/joc.2020.01.03

Chillakuri, B., & Mahanandia, R. (2018). Generation Z entering the workforce: The need for sustainable strategies in maximizing their talent. *Human Resource Management International Digest*, *26*(4), 34–38. https://doi.org/10.1108/HRMID-01-2018-0006

Draksler, T. Z., & Sirec, K. (2021). The study of entrepreneurial intentions and entrepreneurial competencies of business vs. non-business students. *Journal of Competitiveness*, *13*(2), 171–188. https://doi.org/10.7441/joc.2021.02.10

Eyerman, R., & Turner, B. S. (1998). Outline of a theory of generations. *European Journal of Social Theory*, *1*(1), 91–106. https://doi.org/10.1177/13684319800 1001007

Fritsch, M., & Mueller, P. (2004). Effects of new business formation on regional development over time. *Regional Studies*, *38*(8), 961–975.

Howe, N. (2014, October 27). Introducing the homeland generation (Part 1 of 2). *Forbes.*

Iftode, D. (2019). Genertion Z and learning styles. *SEA—Practical Application of Science, 7*(21), 255–262.

Iwu, C. G., Opute, P. A., Nchu, R., Eresia-Eke, C., Tengeh, R. K., Jaiyeoba, O., & Aliyu, O. A. (2021). Entrepreneurship education, curriculum and lecturer-competency as antecedents of student entrepreneurial intention. *The International Journal of Management Education, 19*(1), 100295. https://doi.org/10.1016/j.ijme.2019.03.007

KABADA Consortium. (2023). Start off your business on the right foot. http://kabada.ba.lv/#/

Lesinskis, K., Carvalho, L., Mavlutova, I., & Dias, R. (2022). Comparative analysis of students' entrepreneurial intentions in Latvia and other CEE countries. *WSEAS Transactions on Business and Economics, 19*, Art. #147, pp. 1633–1642. ISSN / E-ISSN: 1109-9526 / 2224-2899. https://doi.org/10.37394/23207.2022.19.147 SCOPUS

Lesinskis, K., Mavlutova, I., Peiseniece, L., Hermanis, J., Peiseniece, E., & Pokatayeva, O. (2021). Modern business teaching: The stable market provisions for emerging generations. *Journal Studies of Applied Economics (Estudios de Economía Aplicada) Exploring Sustainable Urban Transformation Concepts for Economic Development, 39*(5). http://dx.doi.org/10.25115/eea.v39i5.5202

Maheshwari, G., Kha, K. L., & Arokiasamy, A. R. A. (2022). Factors affecting students' entrepreneurial intentions: A systematic review (2005–2022) for future directions in theory and practice. *Management Review Quarterly*, 1–68. https://doi.org/10.1007/s11301-022-00289-2

Martínez-Gregorio, S., Badenes-Ribera, L., & Oliver, A. (2021). Effect of entrepreneurship education on entrepreneurship intention and related outcomes in educational contexts: A meta-analysis. *The International Journal of Management Education, 19*(3), 100545. https://doi.org/10.1016/j.ijme.2021.100545

Mavlutova, I., Lesinskis, K., Liogys, M., & Hermanis, J. (2020). The role of innovative methods in teaching entrepreneurship in higher education: Multidisciplinary approach. In I. Kabashkin, I. Jatskiv, & O. Prentkovskis (Eds.), *Reliability and statistics in transportation and communication* (pp. 684–693). Springer. https://doi.org/10.1007/978-3-030-44610-9_66

Mónico, L., Carvalho, C., Nejati, S., Arraya, M., & Parreira, P. (2021). Entrepreneurship education and its influence on higher education students' entrepreneurial intentions and motivation in Portugal. *BAR-Brazilian*

Administration Review, *18*, e190088. https://doi.org/10.1590/1807-7692bar2021190088

Oropallo F., Biggeri, L., & Calza, M. (2007). Factors affecting the success of new entrepreneurs in Italy: A multivariate statistical model approach conference. Entrepreneuriat: Nouveaux défis, Paris, 11.06.2007 nouveaux Volume: Cahier de la Recherche de l'ISC Paris CRISC N° 17.

Pichler, S., Chiranjeev, K., & Granitz, N. (2021). DITTO for Gen Z: A framework for leveraging the uniqueness of the new generation. *Business Horizons*, *64*(5), 599–610. https://doi.org/10.1016/j.bushor.2021.02.021

Reissová, A., Šimsová, J., Sonntag, R., & Kučerová, K. (2020). The influence of personal characteristics on entrepreneurial intentions: International comparison. *Entrepreneurial Business and Economics Review*, *8*(4), 29–46. https://doi.org/10.15678/EBER.2020.080402

Schawbel, D. (2014). Gen Z employees: The 5 attributes you need to know. *Entrepreneur Europe*. https://www.entrepreneur.com/article/236560

Scholz, C., & Rennig, A. (2019). *Generations Z in Europe: Inputs, insights and implications* (Changing context of managing people). Emerald Publishing. ISBN 10 1789734924.

Sreenivasan, A., & Suresh, M. (2023). Twenty years of entrepreneurship education: a bibliometric analysis. *Entrepreneurship Education*, 1–24. https://doi.org/10.1007/s41959-023-00089-z

Wang, X.-H., You, X., Wang, H.-P., Wang, B., Lai, W.-Y., & Su, N. (2023). The effect of entrepreneurship education on entrepreneurial intention: Mediation of entrepreneurial self-efficacy and moderating model of psychological capital. *Sustainability*, *15*, 2562. https://doi.org/10.3390/su15032562

Wibowo, A., & Narmaditya, B. S. (2022). Predicting students' digital entrepreneurial intention: The mediating role of knowledge and inspiration. *Dinamika Pendidikan*, *17*(1), 25–36. https://doi.org/10.15294/dp.v17i1.36161

Sonia Massari & Sara Roversi

Mutualism, Integral Ecology and Regenerative Mindset: The Paideia Campus as an Innovative Pedagogical Practice Model

1. Introduction: New Mutualism Forging the Job Market

Compared to the past, the traditional way of conceiving and experiencing the professional sphere is undergoing profound and sudden changes. New patterns such as Great Resignation (Kuzior et al., 2022; Serenko, 2022), Quiet Quitting (Formica & Sfodera, 2022; Scheyett, 2023), Hustle Culture (Burgess et al., 2022; Yuningsih & Prasetya, 2022), carried out by the so-called Generation YOLO (You Only Live Once), are the symptoms of a reshaping of the professional working context.

With reference to the Quiet Quitting phenomenon, new needs are arising. These include the need to lead a balanced lifestyle and to prevent the dangers of burning out, just as to define the value of a person going beyond the exclusive reference of their professional performances (Scheyett, 2023). These phenomena, triggered by the global COVID-19 pandemic, not only have reversed the course from the extractive logic of exploiting the human capital (Hofrichter, 2000), but have also accelerated the path toward new business organizational models. In fact, the labor market represents the area in which the evolution of individual lifestyles, social arrangements, economic and financial aspects, and human needs are reflected.

The labor market appears to be increasingly oriented toward new forms of mutualism (Venturi & Zandonai, 2022). The concept of mutualism consists in the equal cooperation between several parties to ensure mutual benefit of all parties involved (Boucher et al., 1982). Mutualism could relocate humans back into a truly harmonious relationship within society and the entire natural ecosystem, as natural cycles represent its highest manifestation.

In this sense and applied to business models, a new mutualism is bringing the logic of work back toward service models. This could result in shortening the distance between interpersonal and inter-organizational relationships and skills, between human needs and those of the planet, making companies and businesses more social and inclusive.

The continuous depletions of natural ecosystem that have been redefining this era as the "Anthropocene" (Crutzen & Stoermer, 2021) resulted in the urgency to deal with "poly-crises" (Homer-Dixon et al., 2022; Zeitlin et al., 2019). This era is also pushing businesses to measure their impact with ESG (Environmental, Social, and Governance) indicators, including ethics and sustainability criteria into their business strategies.

These business models grounded on mutualism have always existed. Cooperatives have been defined by the Italian Census report (Confcooperative, 2022) as "social chains" of the territory. This is especially visible with agribusinesses, which have proven to be capable of sustaining the pivotal sector of *Made in Italy*, including the primary sector, which embraces the designation of origin, small-scale manufacturing, the economy of the local landscape, and Mediterranean models. These models appear to be resilient to global challenges, while supporting the national economy and employing more than 1.2 million people in Italy alone (World Cooperative Monitor, 2022). Another confirmation from the Italian context also comes from the Italian Small and Medium Enterprises (SME) Welfare Index Report (Welfare Index PMI, 2022) which has recognized the direct connection between enterprise solidity and resilience with their ability to provide collective welfare. The reference is not only to welfare and protection activities, economic support for families, and human capital development, but also to support services for workers' families, suppliers, and local citizens.

According to the report in fact focusing on community welfare is also rewarding for companies in economic terms. This aspect is recently confirmed by the Transitions Performance Index (TPI), a composite indicator to measure countries' performance and assess economic, social, environmental and governance transition.

These elements are preparatory to understanding how much the current change in business models are interlinked with the need for changing the mindset. The mindset is defined by Bosman and Fernhaber (2017) as the fil rouge connecting the cognitive sphere, intended as the set of competencies and skills acquired in life, and behaviors, which are the concrete manifestation and externalization of those competencies. The mindset is by definition not standardizable (Cannon & Elford, 2017) but must be able to adapt and cope in the best possible way with the different situations in which we find ourselves acting (and reacting). What is most urgent nowadays is therefore not training people a "new" mindset, but rather how to develop a mindset open for change and able to implement the urgent request for an integral ecology.

There is no doubt that the actions of humankind have consequences on the world around us, and professionals, of all types and sectors, should take responsibility for paving the way for the construction of a new paradigm of consumption, dictating its new rules. In the current scenario of work and mutualism described above, a collaborative effort between designers, researchers, engineers, mentors and storytellers needs to be fostered to positively influence people's production and behavioral systems: to ensure that products, services and systems are well-analyzed, well-designed and well- constructed in a way that provides lasting value to people with the least impact on the planet, creating a more equitable and regenerative economic system.

2. Learning from the Mediterranean Framework of Integral Ecology

Integral ecology (Pope Francis, 2015) needs investing in acts of human generosity and creating the enabling environment for actions of courage and love that are often not codified, not always codifiable, and not even standardizable. The current social fluidity, which has prompted sociologists to define it as liquid (Bauman, 2013a, 2017), is grounded on uncertainty, ambiguity and high volatility (Mack et al., 2016), widespread nomadism which affects everyone and at all levels, from digital to climate nomadism, and a profound loss and emptying of values (Bauman, 2013b). Scholars have been defining our society as already at the dawn of the fourth industrial revolution—the cognitive revolution, underpinned by a profound change of mindset and an enhancement of Human Capital (Sakhapov & Absalyamova, 2018). These aspects, symptoms of a collective and integral malaise, call for new mindsets, new methodologies, new pedagogical models and approaches. It is from here that our society, can start again to patch up the current fragmentations.

The cultural framework of the Mediterranean Basin, from which the Mediterranean Diet originates, is grounded on a holistic concept of education: Paideia, which perfectly reflects the idea of integral ecology. Coming from the conception of pedagogical development in force in ancient Greece, παιδεία (paideia) refers to integral human education, a process of long-life learning which intimately places man's role in relation to his surroundings and engages Man and Environment in a relationship of absolute communion and co-creation of value. A confirmation of this statement comes from the wide application of physics in the ancient Greece, where physikḗ was employed in reference to all aspects of the study of Nature and not just what we now call "physics." In fact, in one of Aristotle's most important works, Physics, questions relating to time, space, infinity and causality are all considered as relevant aspects of the discipline. Similarly, also according Parmenidies, one of the most famous philosophers in the Ancient Mediterranean Basin, the Salerno medical school, the first and most important medical institution in Europe in the Middle Ages, and Galeno, one of the most important Mediterranean preventive medicine scholars, science cannot be separated by philosophy. Both literature (Annan-Diab & Molinari, 2017; Spring, 2000; Vladimirova & Le Blanc, 2016) and several international declarations recognize that education is a universal right capable of uniting all Sustainable Development Goals.

In this contribution, the authors will debate the importance to restart from these models of mutualism and integral ecology, which are perfectly encapsulated in the traditional educational model at the heart of the Mediterranean culture designed and applied in Pollica (located in the Cilento region—Italy), through the Pedagogical Method of Paideia Campus.

The Pedagogical model applied in Pollica has responded to the needs presented in the introduction of this paper, and has introduced and supported new paradigms of territorial regeneration based on the principles of the UNESCO Intangible Heritage of the Mediterranean Diet, as a real tool capable of driving development policies that aim to protect resources, enhance biodiversity, implement circular models, and use food as a tool for inclusion and diplomacy. This path is leading to a rationalization of energy production and use, but it is also a way through which to defend the weak and those who need it most. A regeneration process that is requiring flexible, creative mindsets, and above all awareness and active participation and that cannot be lasting without being permeated through local territories and their communities.

3. Case Study: Paideia Campus in Pollica

The Future Food Institute (FFI) is an Italian-based ecosystem focusing on food to facilitate exponential positive change to sustainably improve life on earth through education and innovation. FFI has concretely applied this model of paideia into one of its Living Laboratories (hereafter Living Lab) (ENoLL, 2023) located in Pollica.

Pollica is a rural village located in the Cilento Region (Italy), in the heart of the Mediterranean and is officially recognized by UNESCO as one of the Seven Emblematic Communities of the Mediterranean Diet. The Paideia Campus Living Lab in Pollica is the result of the collaboration between the Future Food Institute and the Municipality and community of Pollica and is conceived as an experimental hub and open-air laboratory of education and co-creation with the local community to design, prototype, and co-create together a model of integral ecological regeneration, starting from shared human values.

To achieve this goal, the Paideia Campus Living Lab applies the Paideia Educational model that society has inherited from millennia of history, culture, science, encounters in the Mediterranean area by adapting and updating the Mediterranean interpretation of integral ecology to current challenges and contexts. The Mediterranean Basin can be defined as the symbol of integral ecology *ante litteram,* as direct synergies have now been evidenced between the Mediterranean Diet approach and the more recent One Health Approach (Tangredi, 2022). Evidence also confirms that the Mediterranean model of integral ecological regeneration respects the principles of harmony that also govern Nature (Altomonte et al., 2013; Keys & Keys, 1959), supports examples of organizational and mutualistic models, often family models (Da Roit & Sabatinelli, 2005) and reunite together six dimensions of life: the political, social, individual, environmental, cultural and economic dimensions.

The need to apply new, more harmonious and holistic approaches that can bring together the different dimensions of life, bring together the different stakeholders who are directly and indirectly involved in the agribusiness system, and facilitate virtuous connections and activities that can accommodate diversity is imperative to enhance skills and perspectives and foster collective prosperity.

The Pedagogical Model/Method applied by the Paideia Campus can be identified in six pillars. The 6-S that reflect the Mediterranean approach and lifestyle: Senses, Savoir Faire, Sustain, Solidity, Sensitivity, Sighting.

More in details:

1. Senses: Education, also intended as the road towards new working professions, should be able to engage not only mental activities and logical processes, but also stimulate all five senses. Education can overcome the limitations of passive theoretical learning (Al-Juboury, 2007) and become immersive experiences able to support in-the-field activities, active discoveries, engagement, creativity, and fun.
2. Savoir Faire: Competences and professionalism should be taught, learnt and also experienced. Nature can be seen as a master teacher in the field of science, biology, chemical reactions, and interconnections. The Cilento region where Pollica is located and many cities in the Mediterranean emerge as of the areas in the world with a high number of centenarians, representing living educating communities, just as learning the application of regenerative processes in the fields with local regenerative farmers and sustainable fishermen. Learning from them and with them is crucial to train not only to train critical thinking and empathy, but also both hard and soft skills, which are incredibly in need in the professional market (Dixon et al., 2010; Winstead et al., 2009).

3. Sustain: knowledge for its own sake is not useful and not applicable. It is only when knowledge can be directly applied in problem-solving that education systems will be able to train the citizens (and not just professionals) of tomorrow, foster their sense of agency and directly support local communities and economies. The Paideia Campus model teaches that the educational approach can only be participatory and challenge-based: educate to include, participate, co-create, contribute, regenerate.
4. Solidity: the educational model must be solid and concrete, replicable over time and resilient, able to adapt to difficulties and changes. That is why it cannot rest on the concept of immutability, but rather in that of impermanence (Kaufman, 2017), to be able to train young minds to change, to "dance in ambiguity" (Leifer & Steinert, 2011). This includes an adaptation component, fostering adaptability to build resilience, recognizing challenges but also looking at their hidden potential related to any dormant resources.
5. Sensitivity: the Paideia Campus model trains for self-connection but also reframes education as the art of listening to each other. Being rooted on common human values, education becomes intimately linked with the Golden Rule, or the rule of reciprocity: treat others the way you wish others to treat you (Singer, 1963). This is what can lead to a complete regeneration of the minds.
6. Sighting the future: education is not talking about the present, nor vertically presenting existing situations but providing students with the tools to see, reshape, and co-create the future. Youth should regain their ability to envision, which is a crucial component of allowing others to see a brighter future and act consequently to make it possible. If properly empowered and prepared with design thinking techniques and prosperity design, youth can envision solutions and cultivate a positive sense of possibility. This is the basis for radical collaborative creativity, which directly triggers innovation.

This pedagogical model is the evolution of the educational model "Learning to Empower," a three-stage model composed of Inspiration, Aspiration, and Perspiration (Figure 1), already used by the Future Food Institute in the last years with great results (from 2014).

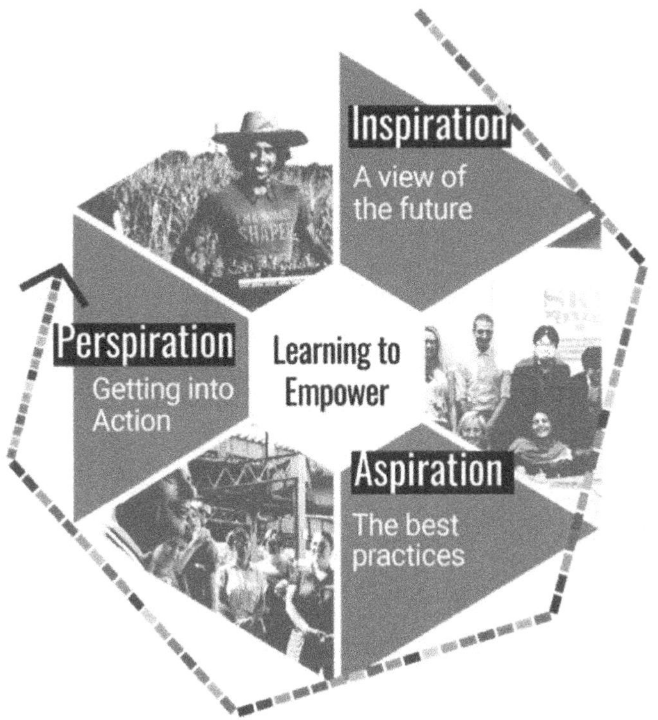

Figure 1. Inspiration, aspiration, perspiration model
Source: By Future Food Institute

According to this model, Inspiration is designed as the phase of discovery and listening; Aspiration is the phase of involvement and knowledge in the field, that brings participants to directly engage with the territory and the local stakeholders actors; Perspiration (then changed in Action) is the experimentation phase, in which individuals can become agents of change capable of generating prosperity for the community (Figure 1).

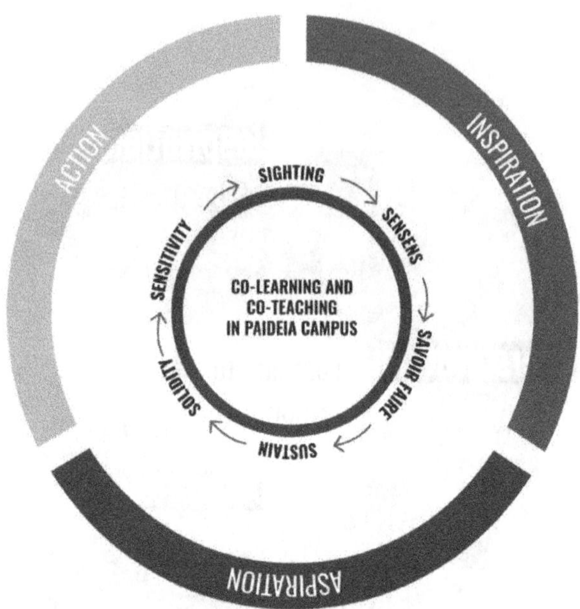

Figure 2. 6-S Paideia campus pedagogical method-model
Source: By the authors

4. Discussion: The Circular Model of Regenerative Education

The approach underlying the Pedagogical Method of Paideia Campus can be presented as a Circular Model of Regenerative Education (Figure 3).

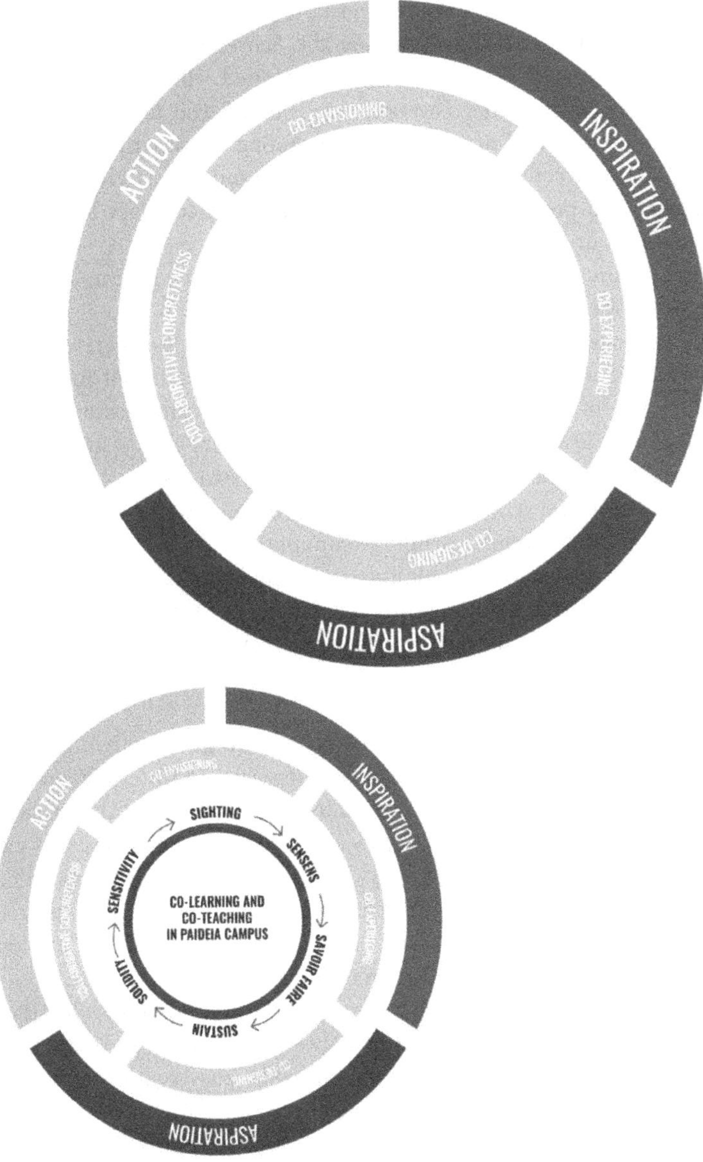

Figure 3. Circular model of regenerative education

Source: By the authors

Starting with the last element mentioned, the more the Sighting the future is trained, the more both the mind and the Senses will be nurtured through experiential activities in which the skills acquired will be an integral part of an immersive Savoire faire. The reference is to a Savoir faire which is capable of enriching both hard and soft skills, including Sensitivity, which is needed to Support local communities and economies and this is crucial to provide the educational process with the Solidity necessary to adapt to the constant challenges of our era.

Three main additional benefits can be highlighted from the Circular Pedagogical Method of Paideia Campus.

The first one consists in the role of the territory as a concrete contributor of knowledge. As described above, the method proved to self-fuel a constant virtuous circle of collective prosperity, where the sense of the possible regenerates the desire for learning, and where learning triggers direct support to local territories, from which knowledge is concretely drawn.

The second aspect is the central role of the community. By supporting integral ecology, the model helps learning communities discover the roots of their successes and challenges. By building deeper understanding through dialogue, identifying practical solutions to adaptation challenges, and redesigning scenarios for equitable and sustainable justice, educators can become agents for collective prosperity, and the community can maximize their educating role to ensure win-win processes for everyone.

The third aspect is the value of diversity applied by the collectivity. The Circular Pedagogical Method of Paideia Campus embraces and fosters the potential of transdisciplinary applied in educational models (Massari, 2021) by enriching the traditional educational model with new skills, new methodologies, new content, and new languages.

All these aspects amplify the benefits that the method can play in the pedagogical system and, especially if replicated, can become a model of sustainable development grounded on the idea of co-learning.

This also implies recognizing a central role of the mindset, which is the result of continuous and constant interaction between the internal and external world. The 6-S pedagogical model, already supported by phases aimed at training the cognitive, emotional, and interactive sphere, must evolve to meet the need to form a flexible mindset, open to impermanence, capable of forging itself through continuous collaboration to create real change.

5. Conclusion

Professionals and the labor market must quickly equip themselves to face unprecedented scenarios. An unstable economy, policies fail to provide prospects for growth, and people need to rethink their consumption patterns with well-being as the sole focus. Communities of practice are essential, but their thematic fields (domain), which create the common context and a common sense of identity, must be re-defined. The community also needs to be strong and encourage interaction and relationships based on mutual respect and trust. Finally, the practice must consist of the set of ideas, tools, information, styles and stories that community members develop, share and maintain.

New narratives are needed. having the capacity to imagine new scenarios, preferably regenerative and no longer just sustainable. This requires integral education: paideia.

At Paideia Campus, education is a shared construction, participation in a practice and not a mere transmission of codified knowledge. Therefore, the model emphasizes the collaborative nature of the process: co-experience, co-designing, co-creating, co-envisioning (Figure 4). Moreover, context plays a key role in developing the skills of individuals and the community. These reflections relate well to the idea of situated and therefore sustainable innovation, which arises from a contextual dimension that includes physical, social and productive space.

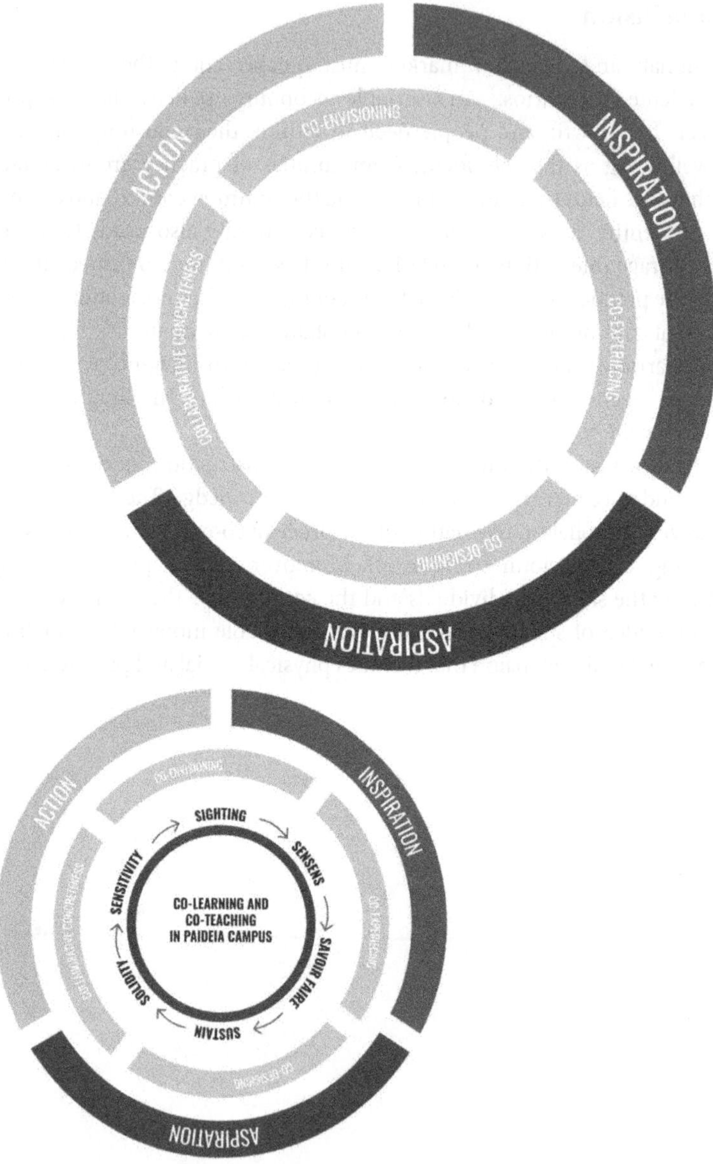

Figure 4. Collaborative Paideia campus pedagogical model
Source: By the authors

The urgency of a profound renewal of the current educational model constitutes the central issue of our times. Paideia Campus model for integral ecological regeneration can become a pivotal tool to bring the Italian school system back to our roots, the pillars of our own culture, the heart of essential human values This would entail reconnecting science, history, philosophy, active citizenship, ecology to human education.

The cultural framework of the Mediterranean Diet is co-teaching and co-learning the importance of quality living, the value of togetherness and of living (and respecting) places, people, territory, and food. This is a universal right and not a privilege for the few and it inevitably is connected to education.

Mindset is a key lever for improving the educational system and the sustainable development. The 6-S model can be translated into an important strategic tool for the educational model to support sustainable innovations. Rather than focusing efforts on defining the "right mindset" and training in the skills "needed for the future," the authors believe in prioritizing the creation of enabling environments for people to train their mindsets, to be ready to deal with life's unpredictability in a resilient way. Holding together the complexities of today's world should not be a matter for improvised equilibrists, but for wise observers of Nature, careful seekers of the balance between mind, body, heart and emotions.

Finally, the community dimension, offers fertile ground for the identification and implementation of innovative ideas based on the sharing of common visions (sights), know-how and practices. A systemic approach such as the one proposed by the 6-S Model of the Paideia Campus, can certainly contribute to the consolidation of this different vision of innovation, which gives an important role to the multi actors present in Cilento and to the problems before the possible innovative content. The idea, therefore, is not to transfer innovations, but to contextualize them, that is, to adapt them to the specific context (the Mediterranean area), to the needs of local producers and identified territories.

Acknowledgment

Special thanks to Erika Solimeo for editing an earlier draft of this manuscript, to Sofia Cavalleri and Stefania Petruzzelli for proofreading the final versions of the paper and to Camilla Carioli *for drawing the graphs* of the Paideia Circular Pedagogical Model. Thanks to the Pollica Municipality and Stefano Pisani (Mayor of Pollica).

References

Al-Juboury, N. (2007). From passive learning to critical thinking. *Journal of College of Education for Women*, *18*(1). https://www.iasj.net/iasj/download/5c4d66bfbf0f52af

Altomare, R., Cacciabaudo, F., Damiano, G., Palumbo, V. C., Gioviale, M. C., Bellavia, M., Tomasello, G., & Lo Monte, A. I. (2013). The Mediterranean diet: A history of health. *The Iranian Journal of Public Health*, *42*(5), 449–457. https://www.ncbi.nlm.nih.gov/pmc/articles/PMC3684452/

Annan-Diab, F., & Molinari, C. (2017). Interdisciplinarity: Practical approach to advancing education for sustainability and for the Sustainable Development Goals. *The International Journal of Management Education*, *15*(2, Part B), 73–83. https://doi.org/10.1016/j.ijme.2017.03.006

Bauman, Z. (2013a). *Communitas. Uguali e diversi nella società liquida*. Aliberti Editore.

Bauman, Z. (2013b). *Liquid life*. John Wiley & Sons.

Bauman, Z. (2017). *Liquid fear*. Polity Press.

Bosman, L., & Fernhaber, S. (2017). Defining the entrepreneurial mindset. *Teaching the Entrepreneurial Mindset to Engineers*. https://doi.org/10.1007/978-3-319-61412-0_2

Boucher, D. H., James, S., & Keeler, K. H. (1982). The ecology of mutualism. *Annual Review of Ecology and Systematics*, *13*(1), 315–347. https://doi.org/10.1146/annurev.es.13.110182.001531

Burgess, A., Yeomans, H., & Fenton, L. (2022). "More options … less time" in the "hustle culture" of "generation sensible": Individualization and drinking decline among twenty-first-century young adults. *The British Journal of Sociology*, *73*(4), 903–918. https://doi.org/10.1111/1468-4446.12964

Cannon, F., & Elford, N. (2017). *The agility mindset: How reframing flexible working delivers competitive advantage*. Springer Nature.

Confcooperative. (2022). Un paese da ricucire. *Focus Censis Confcooperative*. https://www.confcooperative.it/LInformazione/Primo-Piano/festa-della-repubblica-festa-della-cooperazione-cooperative-catena-sociale-del-valore

Crutzen, P. J., & Stoermer, E. F. (2021). The "Anthropocene" (2000). In S. Benner, G. Lax, P. J. Crutzen, U. Pöschl, J. Lelieveld, H. G. Brauch (Eds.), *Paul J. Crutzen and the Anthropocene: A New Epoch in earth's history*. The Anthropocene: Politik—Economics—Society—Science (Vol. 1). Springer.

Da Roit, B., & Sabatinelli, S. (2005). Il modello mediterraneo di welfare tra famiglia e mercato. *Stato e mercato, Rivista quadrimestrale*, *2*, 267–290. https://www.rivisteweb.it/doi/10.1425/20483

Dixon, J., Belnap, C., Albrecht, C., & Lee, K. (2010). The importance of soft skills. *Corporate Finance Review, 14*(6), 35–39. https://www.proquest.com/openview/aa5f345bde23cacbf99574378aeef44b/1?pq-origsite=gscholar&cbl=46775

European Network of Living Labs (ENoLL). (2023). https://enoll.org/about-us/

Formica, S., & Sfodera, F. (2022). The Great Resignation and Quiet Quitting paradigm shifts: An overview of current situation and future research directions. *Journal of Hospitality Marketing & Management, 31*(8), 899–907. https://doi.org/10.1080/19368623.2022.2136601

Hofrichter, R. (2000). *Reclaiming the environmental debate: The politics of health in a toxic culture* (R. Hofrichter, Eds.). The MIT Press.

Homer-Dixon, T., Renn, O., Rockstrom, Donges, J. F., & Janzwood, S. (2022). *A call for an international research program on the risk of a global polycrisis.* http://dx.doi.org/10.2139/ssrn.4058592

Kaufman, P. (2017). Critical contemplative pedagogy. *Radical Pedagogy, 14*(1), 1–20. https://www.academia.edu/31097956/Critical_Contemplative_Pedagogy

Keys, A., & Keys, M. (1959). *Eat well and stay well.* Doubleday & Company.

Kuzior, A., Kettler, K., & Rąb, L. (2022). Great resignation—Ethical, cultural, relational, and personal dimensions of Generation Y and Z employees' engagement. *Sustainability, 14*(11), 6764. https://doi.org/10.3390/su14116764

Leifer, L. J., & Steinert, M. (2011). Dancing with ambiguity: Causality behavior, design thinking, and triple-loop-learning. *Information Knowledge Systems Management, 10*(1–4), 151–173. 10.3233/IKS-2012-0191

Mack, O., Anshuman, K., Krämer, A., & Burgartz, T. (Eds.). (2016). *Managing in a VUCA world.* Springer.

Massari, S. (2021). Transforming research and innovation for sustainability: Transdisciplinary design for future pathways in agri-food sector. In S. Massari (Eds.), *Transdisciplinary case studies on design for food and sustainability* (pp. 315–326). Woodhead Publishing.

Pope Francis. (2015). *Lettera Enciclica Laudato Si' Del Santo Padre Francesco Sulla Cura Della Casa Comune.* https://www.vatican.va/content/francesco/it/encyclicals/documents/papa-francesco_20150524_enciclica-laudato-si.html

Sakhapov, R., & Absalyamova, S. (2018). Fourth industrial revolution and the paradigm change in engineering education. *MATEC Web Conference, 245*(12003), 1–6. https://doi.org/10.1051/matecconf/201824512003

Scheyett, A. (2023). Quiet quitting. *Social Work, 68*(1), 5–7. https://doi.org/10.1093/sw/swac051

Serenko, A. (2022). The Great Resignation: The great knowledge exodus or the onset of the Great Knowledge Revolution? *Journal of Knowledge*

Management. https://www.researchgate.net/publication/360978837_The_Great_Resignation_The_Great_Knowledge_Exodus_or_the_Onset_of_the_Great_Knowledge_Revolution

Singer, M. (1963). The golden rule. *Philosophy*, *38*(146), 293–314. https://doi.org/10.1017/S0031819100058290

Spring, J. (2000). *The universal right to education: Justification, definition, and guidelines*. Routledge.

Tangredi, B. P. (2022). *The Mediterranean diet and one health: A study in synergies. CABI one health*. CABI International. https://doi.org/10.1079/cabionehealth.2022.0012

Venturi, P., & Zandonai, F. (2022). *Neomutualismo, Ridisegnare dal basso competitività e welfare*. EGEA Editore.

Vladimirova, K., & Le Blanc, D. (2016). Exploring links between education and sustainable development goals through the lens of UN flagship reports. *Sustainable Development*, *24*(4), 254–271. https://doi.org/10.1002/sd.1626

Welfare Index PMI. (2022). Welfare aziendale: un patto sociale per il Paese. https://www.welfareindexpmi.it/wp-content/uploads/2022/12/Rapporto-WIPMI-_2022.pdf

Winstead, A. S., Adams, B. L., & Rogers Sillah, M. (2009). Teaching the soft skills: A professional development curriculum to enhance the employability skills of business graduates. *American Journal of Business Education*, *2*(5), 35–44. https://doi.org/10.19030/ajbe.v2i5.4068

World Cooperative Monitor. (2022). Exploring the cooperative economy—Report 2022. https://monitor.coop/sites/default/files/2022-11/WCM_2022.pdf

Yuningsih, Y., & Prasetya, M. D. (2022). Technology makes hustle culture still happened in pandemic COVID- 19. In D. Napitupulu & T. Sutabri (Eds.), *ICEBE 2021: Proceedings of the 4th international conference of economics, business, and entrepreneurship*. EAI.

Zeitlin, J., Nicoli, F., & Laffan, B. (2019). Introduction: The European Union beyond the polycrisis? Integration and politicization in an age of shifting cleavages. *Journal of European Public Policy*, *26*(7), 963–976. https://doi.org/10.1080/13501763.2019.1619803

Daniela Antonescu

Romania's Tourism Offer and Demand in the COVID-19 Pandemic: A Statistical Overview

1. Introduction

Considered one of the main contributors to the service industry, tourism represents one of the most dynamic sectors globally. During the pandemic with the COVID-19 virus, this sector, along with other important economic sectors, was heavily affected by the restrictive measures imposed to stop the spread of infections. These measures stopped or reduced the flow of tourists, causing significant losses in the field of tourism and the economy as a whole. At the same time, most of the employees lost their jobs, as most of the work was done from home and telework was resorted to, in order to limit social interaction.

During the period when restrictions were relaxed, tourism managers adopted new, more flexible strategies adapted to the conditions imposed by the pandemic period. Making decisions under conditions of uncertainty, promoting tourist destinations, adopting new technologies, ensuring a safe stay and well-being for tourists were the main problems that managers had to face and find solutions for (Agovina & Musella, 2022).

The year 2020 was the most difficult year, an atypical year for tourism, after a glorious period when there was a continuous upward trend in tourist arrivals, overnight stays and income, both globally and in the European Union.

The statistic showed that international arrivals in 2021 decreased by 73 %, while in 2021 they decreased by 72 %. At the end of the year, a slight global recovery was beginning to be seen, which brought hope for this sector. Currently, there is still a gap of 63 % compared to 2019. In Europe, tourism has started to recover slightly, already seeing an increase of 18 % in 2021 compared to 2019. Considering the fact that people like to travel, the conditions are favorable for this sector to recover quickly.

Romania also faced difficulties in the tourism sector, especially in the first part of the pandemic. The program entitled "Rediscover Romania" secured approximately 48 % of the total number of arrivals (accommodation places) from tourist units in 2019. The main destinations where tourism activities took place were: seaside resorts (during the summer season), mountain resorts and spa tourism units. Regarding the location, the majority of tourists oriented themselves both toward the seaside hotels, which ensured the sanitary safety conditions imposed by the pandemic, and toward the small hotels, villas, cabins and agro-tourism guesthouses located in isolated areas (Cretu et al., 2021). The year 2021 brought relaxation measures that led to the partial resumption of tourism services, and in 2022, tourism resumed its slightly upward trend, but on a larger scale.

Considering the above, the article aims to present a relevant picture of the tourism sector in Romania, from the perspective of tourism demand and supply in 2022 compared to 2020, and also a comparative analysis with 2019 (considered a successful year for tourism).

2. Literature Review

From the point of view of its economic and social character, tourism is facing a series of profound transformations at the global level, being closely linked to the development of other sectors and activities that are influenced by it, both from the point of view of evolution and from the perspective of specific characteristics, concepts and factors, etc.

Therefore, due to the beneficial effects it propagates throughout the economy, tourism is considered a main "tool" of economic growth, as (Baretje & Defert, 1972; Snak, 1976): it generates significant income for the countries' economies and stimulates the necessary investments to finance some sectors, being a multiplier factor of economic growth and development; it contributes to the increase of labor force supply by capitalizing on the cultural and natural heritage; it creates opportunities to diversify local economies by capitalizing on resources of any kind; it encourages the emergence and development of local businesses, transforming areas with a low level of economic competitiveness into attractive areas for different categories of investors; it contributes to diversifying the demand for goods and services of other economic sectors (e.g., construction, food industry, crafts, etc.); supports cooperation between local companies, between economic sectors and between different categories of organizations and institutions; contributes to the creation of clusters, where tourism is the main pillar; it has an impact on the reduction of territorial inequalities in terms of gender structure, unemployment differences through the predominant use of female labor.

Through the analyzes and assessments carried out at international level, the World Tourism Organization has identified and clustered the economic effects of tourism into three categories, presented in Table 1.

Table 1. The effects of tourism on the economy

Types of effects	General objectives on which they act	Effects
Global	1. Development strategies	The national economy
		External dependence, international economy
	2. Growth in manufacturing sectors	(Stimulating) production
		(Use of) labor force
Partial	3. Stability of the external sector and external balance	Balancing the balance of payments
		The exchange rate level and the real exchange rate
		Money and money circulation
	4. Public sector and the degree of state intervention	Public revenues Public spending
	5. Prices	Inflation level
		Speculative activities on land
	6. Capital	Ways to distribute income
	7. Spatial planning	Regional development
		Rural area
		Demographic trends
External	8. Protection of human and natural resources	Environmental quality
		Professional training
	9. Sociocultural aspects	The consumption pattern
		Education
		Social & cultural

Source: Minciu (2000) and UNWTO (2022)

3. Materials and Methods

The methodology used in the article is based on the following indicators:

- the number of tourist units (with accommodation functions);
- accommodation capacity (number of seats);
- the number of tourist arrivals, overnight stays;
- the net usage capacity index;
- national and international tourism.

The data analyzed in 2022 (2021) were compared with those obtained in 2020 and also with the highest performance of the tourism sector in Romania obtained in 2019.

The statistical data was collected from the Tempo-online Database (National Institute of Statistics) for the years 2019, 2020 and 2022 (2021). The data were processed in their dynamics, emphasizing the values of the fixed base indices and the structural ones, accordingly interpreting the differences from one year to another.

The performance in tourism was analyzed both at the national and regional (county) level.

The results were illustrated graphically and depending on the case and the specifics of the results were interpreted and the main trends highlighted.

At the end of the paper, in the conclusions, the main ideas were synthesized and it was identified what needs to be done for the next period, so that tourism resumes its upward trend.

3.1. The Touristic Offer

Number of Tourist Reception Units with Accommodation Functions

In 2022, in the Romanian tourism sector, the capacity of tourist accommodation was 9,120 units with touristic function, with a slight decrease, compared to 2021, of 26 accommodation units (-0.28 %) (from 9,120 units to 9,146 accommodation units). Compared to the pandemic year 2020, the number of tourist units was 510 units more (+5.92 %) and 718 accommodation units more compared to 2019 (+8.54 %) (Table 2).

Table 2. Tourist accommodation capacity in Romania, 2019–2022 (no., %)

	2019	**2020**	**2021**	**2022**	**2021/ 2019**	**2021/ 2020**	**2020/ 2019**	**2022/ 2019**	**2022/ 2020**	**2022/ 2021**
No. of units	8,402	8,610	9,146	9,120	108.85	*106.2*	*102.4*	*108.54*	*105.92*	*99.72*
No. of place	356,562	358,119	364,507	367,386	102.2	*101.7*	*100.4*	*103.04*	*102.59*	*100.8*

Source: Own computations based on Tempo-online, http://statistici.insse.ro:8077/tempo-online/#/pages/tables/insse-table, 2023

This increase in 2022 compared to 2020 and decrease compared to 2021 is further analyzed by types of accommodation units, as there are differences determined by the types of challenges and restrictions that have arisen during the COVID-19 pandemic period.

Hotels, which hold an important part of the accommodation capacity compared to the other categories of tourist structures, faced the biggest problems due to the almost non-existent tourist flow during the COVID-19 pandemic.

The most difficult year was 2020, when, starting in March, total movement restrictions were imposed for the entire population. No one was allowed to leave the house or practice different activities (sports, tourism, leisure and relaxation, etc.) that involved direct contact with other people. Schools, universities, companies, sectors that had fields of activity dependent on some forms of human contact were closed. Flights were canceled, trains no longer moved to any location and hospitals no longer received other categories of patients, except those contaminated with the SARS-CoV-2 virus.

In the tourism sector, the most affected service supply structures were hotels. Thus, most hotels were forced to close their activity during the pandemic, and their employees were left without a job.

The share of hotels in total accommodation structures was 18.36 % in 2020, down from 2019, when it registered 19.1 %. The trend of reducing the importance of hotels in the total tourist accommodation capacity continued in 2022, when it reached the value of 17.57 % of the total.

Between 2019 and 2021, 25 hotel units were closed in Romania, leaving 1,583 tourist units available (year 2021), representing 98 % of the 1,608 existing units in 2019 (-2 %). In 2022, the restrictions were gradually canceled from March, which led to the reopening of hotels, but not to the same number as in 2019 (with a minus of 6 hotels). So, in the case of hotels, resilience has not fully occurred. The same downward trend was observed in the case of hostels, motels, tourist cabins, bungalows, holiday villages, tourist stops, student camps. Instead, tourists turned their attention to agritourism guesthouses, which offered safer social distancing conditions. Tourist cottages were also searched, along with campsites, which have increased numerically during the analyzed period (2020–2022).

The reopening of accommodation units came late both for hotels with balneo functions and for other accommodation units, which, at first, opened at a limited capacity. The restaurants were forced to create open terraces and to ensure an appropriate distance between the tables inside. Strict hygiene rules have been imposed, with tourism units having to provide disinfection materials and staff to wear masks, etc.

The summer season brought a breath of fresh air to the hotel industry (the months of June, July, August and September were favorable for improving occupancy).

Number of Places in the Accommodation Units with Function for Tourist Reception

Regarding the tourist capacity represented by the accommodation places in the touristic structures, it registered a good resilience, their total number being higher in 2022 compared to the pre-pandemic year (from 356,562 places to 367,386 places, an increase of 10,824 seats). Even if the number of hotels decreased in total, the number of accommodation places in these structures in 2022 was higher than in 2019 (with an increase of 2,984 places).

The number of accommodation places (beds) increased by 2.2 % in 2021 compared to 2019. In 2022, hotels—apartments, inns, tourist villas recorded increases in the number of accommodation places compared to the year before the health crisis, tourist cabins, tourist cottages, agri-tourism guesthouses.

For the trends recorded in the evolution of the structures with touristic functions, the comparisons being made between 2022 and 2019, in order to identify if their activity has resumed after the crisis and to what extent. Overall, tourist structures increased their number in 2022 compared to 2019, with a percentage of 8.5 %. Thus, there are some categories of touristic structures that have progressed compared to the situation existing before the pandemic crisis, as follows: apartment hotels (+58.8 %), inns (+33.3 %), tourist villages (+6.9 %), campsites (+22.4 %), tourist houses (+54.9 %), guest houses (+1.6 %) and agro-tourism guesthouses (+24.4 %). Important reductions in tourist structures were recorded in the tourist stops (-17 %), holiday villages (-11.1 %), and scholar camps (-14.5 %). By category of structures (year 2022), the largest share is held by agro-tourist guesthouses (38.2 %), followed by touristic guesthouses (18.6 %) and hotels (17.57 %).

Regarding the situation of existing places (beds) in tourist structures, they also registered a total increase of 3 % (2022 vs. 2019). The biggest increases were registered in: hotel-apartments (+66.2 %), tourist cottages (+40.6 %), agro-tourism guesthouses (+15.9 %), inns (+12.5 %) and bungalows (+5.6 %). The most important decreases were at tourist stops (-37 %) and school tables (-19.3 %). The structure analysis shows that hotels own more than 54 % of accommodation places (beds), followed by agro-tourist guesthouses (15.47 %) (Table 3).

Table 3. Structure of units with function for tourists' accommodation, by type of units and the growth rate of their number in 2022 versus 2019 (%)

	Units with function for tourists' accommodation		**Places in units with function for tourist accommodation**	
	Structure by unit type (%), 2022	**Growth rate 2022/ 2019 (%)**	**Structure by unit type (%), 2022**	**Growth rate 2022/ 2019 (%)**
Total	*9.120*	*108.5*	*367.386*	*103.0*
Hotels	17.57	99.6	54.78	101.5
Hostels	3.43	96.9	3.69	98.8
Hotel-apartments	0.30	158.8	0.74	166.2
Motels	2.27	94.5	2.27	97.0
Inns	0.04	133.3	0.02	112.5
Tourist villages	8.31	106.9	4.75	104.8
Chalets	2.41	99.1	1.70	100.6
Bungalows	5.41	88.5	1.08	105.6
Holiday villages	0.09	88.9	0.12	95.6
Camping	0.78	122.4	2.91	101.6
Tourist stops	0.43	83.0	0.44	63.0
Tourist houses	1.39	154.9	0.96	140.6
Scholar camps	0.52	85.5	1.41	80.7
Tourist guesthouses	18.60	101.6	9.41	98.3
Agro-tourism guesthouses	38.20	124.4	15.47	115.9
Accommodation spaces on fluvial and maritime boats	0.26	100.0	0.22	99.2

Source: Own computations based on Tempo-online, http://statistici.insse.ro:8077/tempo-online/#/pages/tables/insse-table, 2023

It can be seen that small accommodation units such as villas, apartments, guesthouses and cabins were very attractive to tourists, they were chosen because they could offer a safe and private stay in a less crowded location. Tourists were aware that during the pandemic a safe stay was needed and they looked for locations where the imposed requirements were respected (masks, disinfection materials, terraces and outside tables, etc.).

In 2021 and after that year, as tourists increasingly used the Internet and mobile phones for online booking, the digitization process in tourism also intensified. Thus, tourists accessed tourist platforms or travel agencies' websites, and providers of tourist offers became more flexible and adapted to tourists' requirements.

Tourist Arrivals

The year 2019 represented the peak of tourism in Romania, the country being visited by 13.37 million tourists, of which 20 % were foreign tourists. 2020 was an atypical year for tourism, being the weakest year in the history of world and Romanian tourism. The movement of people has faced periods characterized by restrictions imposed to stop the spread of the virus and protect the population. Moreover, not only tourism was affected, but also other economic sectors. As a result, people were reluctant to travel anymore, choosing to stay at home (work and spend their holidays). In terms of tourism, the preferences were for domestic tourism, in isolated locations as well as in family guesthouses and hotels—apartments, villas, all of which led to a new way of thinking about free time in the pandemic. Even though inbound tourism suffered during the pandemic, domestic tourism "flourished" under the slogan "Rediscover my own country." Therefore, in the year 2020, the tourism sector was very affected registering only 6.39 million tourists, representing 47.8 % of the number of visitors in the year 2019.

Domestic tourism was dominated by Romanians with a share of 92.9 %. In 2021, when the vaccination process started, people became more confident to travel. Thus, in 2021, the number of arrivals increased to 9.27 million, being 44.9 % higher than in 2020, but 30.7 % lower than in 2019. Romanians represented 90.9 % of the total visitors (only a small part of decided to travel abroad) (Figure 1).

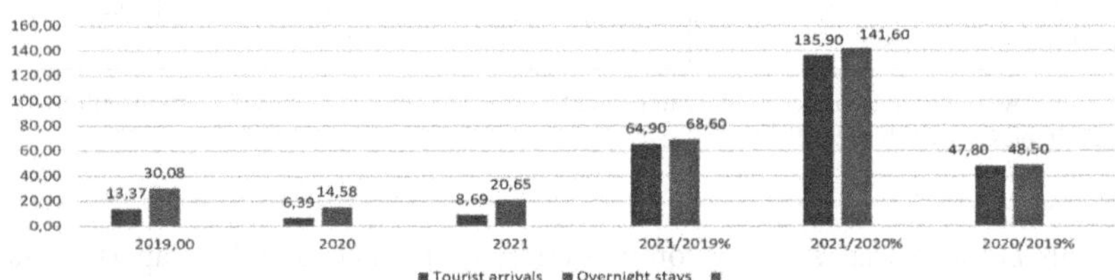

Figure 1. Tourist arrivals and overnight stays in Romania's tourism in the period 2019–2022 (Million)

Source: Own calculation based on the data from NIS, 2022

During the pandemic, tourists' preferences experienced important changes for various destinations. One-third of the visitors preferred to visit Bucharest and the county seat cities. The mountain area was in 2nd place, with 1/5 of the total arrivals. The Black Sea coast held the third position with over 1.14 million tourists (year 2021). Also, the spa resorts received up to 10 % of the total tourist arrivals, and the Danube Delta and the city of Tulcea recorded the lowest percentages.

Compared to the distribution of tourists by destination in 2019, there is an increase in 2021 in spa resorts, the coast and the mountain area, the Danube Delta. As a reflection of the desire to spend holidays in less crowded areas, Bucharest and the county seat cities have recorded a reduction in the number of visitors.

Number of Overnight Stays

In 2021, 20.65 million overnight stays were recorded, 41.7 % more than in 2020, and 31.4 % less than in 2019. In close relation to tourist arrivals, overnight stays were dominated by Romanian tourists: 82.4 % in 2019, 93.2 % in 2020 and 91.1 % in 2021.

The number of overnight stays is strongly correlated with the number of tourist arrivals in the category of tourist accommodation units, but also depending on the destination, the seasonality of the holidays and the measures imposed by the authorities.

The Index of Net Use of Accommodation Capacity

At the national level in 2019, the average of this index was 33.9 %, with variations from one type of accommodation unit to another. The highest degree of use was recorded in apartment hotels (48.2 %), followed by hotels (42.8 %) and hostels (25.2 %).

During the first year of the pandemic (2020), the lowest average value of accommodation capacity utilization was recorded, at 22.8 %. On accommodation structures, the lowest value was at student and preschool camps (4.4 %), followed by inns (6.4 %) and holiday villages (10.8 %).

In 2021, this average rose slightly compared to 2021, to an average value of 26.5 %. In rural tourism, in 2021, the index was much lower: 20 % in 2019, 16.5 % in 2020 and 17.3 %. On touristic structures, the highest value was recorded at apartment hotels (40.2 %) and the lowest value at inns (6.6 %). The comparative analysis of resilience by structure category in 2021 and 2019 shows that there were two types that recorded a value higher than the one obtained before the start of the health crisis: holiday villages (+8.4 %) and tourist cottages (+4.1 %). Student camps had the lowest resilience, which did not reach a little more than half of the value recorded in 2019 (Figure 2).

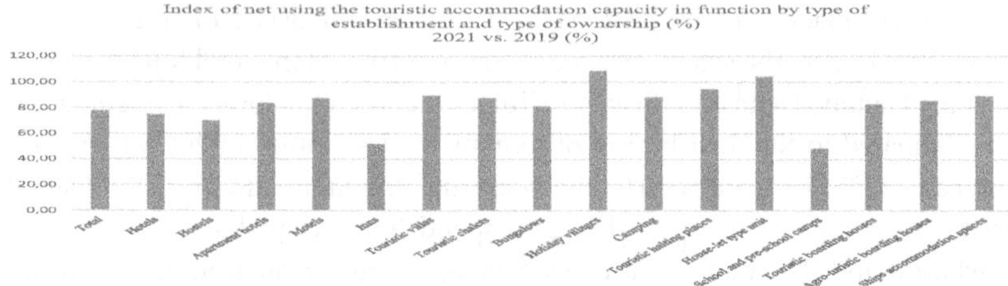

Figure 2. Index of net using the touristic accommodation capacity in function by type of establishment and type of ownership (%)

Source: Own calculation based on the data from NIS, 2022

An analysis by region of the index of net use of tourist capacity (January 2023—January 2019), shows that the North East region recovered slightly (+0.8 %), followed by the South East (+1.2 %), Bucharest Ilfov (+ 4 %) and South West (+ 0.2 %). At the same time, at county level, some managed to reach the value of the index before the start of the health crisis: Satu Mare, Covasna, Harghita, Bacău, Iaşi, Neamţ, Vaslui, Brăila, Constanţa, Galaţi, Argeş.

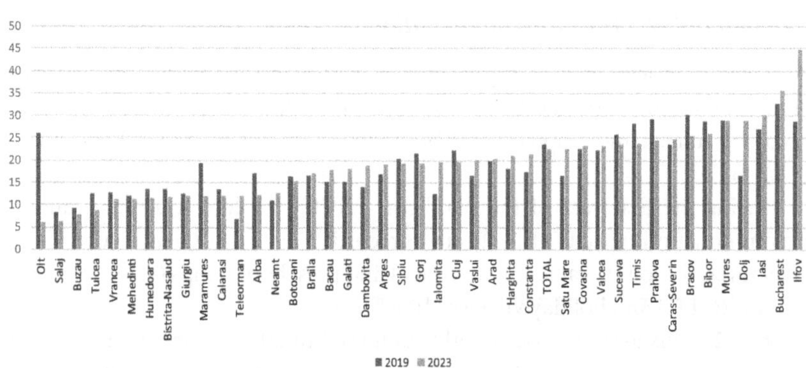

Figure 3. Index of touristic net using accommodation capacity in function by development regions and counties, monthly (January 2019, 2023, %)

Source: Own calculation based on the data from NIS, 2022

Inbound Tourism

The arrivals of foreign tourists in 2019 were 12.81 million, while in 2020 they dropped to only 5 million. The year 2021 brought an increase in this indicator to 6.78 million people registered at Romania's borders.

The most preferred forms of transport were those with a personal car, with a share of 74.5 % in total arrivals in 2019, 82.6 % in 2020 and 79.1 % in 2021. In second place was transport by plane, which had the following rates: 22.9 % in 2019, 14.5 % in 2020 and 17 % in 2021.

Outbound Tourism

In 2019, more than 23 million Romanian tourists traveled outside the country. In 2020, their number dropped to 9.5 million, and later, in 2021, the number began to increase, reaching 11.6 million trips. The main travel destinations were: Bulgaria, Greece and Turkey for the summer period, and in the fall of 2020 exotic destinations (Maldives, etc.) were especially sought after. In 2021, new destinations appeared that were in demand from Romanian tourists, such as Egypt or the Dominican Republic.

Romanians preferred to travel abroad, especially with their own car. In 2019, about 68.4 % of road trips were recorded, while in 2020 there was an increase to 71 %, which will decrease to 66.5 % in 2021. Also, part of the Romanian tourists traveled by plane, abroad, representing around 30.9 % in 2019, 28.3 % in 2020 and 33 % in 2021.

4. Conclusion

Due to the restrictive measures taken by the authorities and the existing feeling of fear among people, both in Romania and internationally, the tourism sector has been severely affected by the COVID-19 pandemic crisis.

Thus, the year 2020 was an atypical year for the tourism sector, which was almost completely paralyzed in terms of the flow of tourists, in the use of accommodation capacities in tourist structures, employees in the sector, related salaries, loss of profit and reduced profitability.

The preference for holiday bookings has mainly focused on small accommodation units, able to ensure distance, privacy, relaxation with family or friends, far from crowded places. The preference for travel turned toward own car, less often by plane, and mainly in locations relatively far from the country.

The holiday vouchers represented an important opportunity to spend the holidays in the country and, at the same time, contributed to supporting the managers and owners of tourist establishments.

The offer of travel agencies has been adapted to the needs of tourists, needs that concerned facilities such as: no cash advance for booking, free cancellation in case of illness, "last minute offers," "early booking offers" at low prices, refunds if lockdown restrictions would be reintroduced etc.

Seaside holidays were the most sought during the summer, weekend tourism was also practiced in the mountain resorts (winter 2020 and 2021). State aid provided as grants to the tourism and hospitality industry helped a lot to cover the losses from the pandemic period. Given that the health alert was canceled on March 9, 2022, tourism began to return slightly (but not completely) to the situation existing in 2019, and, in some situations, to register an increase above pre-crisis values.

References

Baretje, R., & Defert, P. (1972). *Aspects economiques du tourism* (*Economic Aspects of Tourism*). Edition Berger-Levroult.

Cretu, R. C., Stefan, P., & Alecu, I. (2021). Has tourism gone on holiday? Analysis of the effects of the COVID-19 pandemic on tourism and post-pandemic tourism behavior. *Scientific Papers Series Management, Economic Engineering in Agriculture and Rural Development*, *21*(2), 191–197.

Minciu, R. (2000). *Tourism economy*. Uranus Publishing House.

Snak, O. (1976). *Economia şi organizarea turismului* (*Economy and Organization of Tourism*). Sport-Turism Publishing House.

Tempo-online. (2023). *National Institute of Statistic*. http://statistici.insse.ro:8077/tempo-online/#/pages/tables/insse-table

UNWTO. (2022). *Impact assessment of the COVID-19 outbreak on international tourism, Tourism grows 4% but remains far below pre-pandemic levels*. http://www.untwo.org/impact-assessment-of-the-covid19-outbreak-on-international-tourism

Waqas Shair, Saem Hussain, Asma Halim, & Abdul Ghani

Household's Coping Strategies and Food Insecurity Level Amid Global Economic Crisis: The Case of Pakistan

1. Introduction: An Overview of Coping Strategies

Households in developing nations are exposed to various hazards, such as those posed by natural disasters, climate change, and macroeconomic shocks. Some of the risks are individual-specific in nature and faced in their daily life. The household's vulnerability to risk causes instabilities in the household's well-being, which can be evaluated by the household's income or consumption. A household will implement the most appropriate coping strategies for mitigating, lowering, and controlling risk and smoothing consumption following the severity and nature of the risk. The range of coping methods households employ depends on various factors, most notably the crises they experience and the opportunities available. Households make strategic plans to smooth consumption in the case of income shocks.

Erosive and non-erosive coping devices are categorized for strategic household responses for consumption smoothing purposes. The erosive coping strategy is subject to selling an asset to deal with a crisis, which means that the household may never recover the asset or its equivalent. On the other hand, if the household borrows money to deal with the crisis, which is a non-erosive strategy, the household will expectantly be able to repay the debt someday and survive the crisis without having to deplete the asset base. Non-erosive coping strategies are assumed to be preferable to erosive ones. A household's ability to provide "sold assets" in the future may be put at risk by erosive strategies since they reduce the asset base. The household's ability to maintain its standard of living needs to be improved due to a reduced asset base.

On the other hand, if a household can save enough to repay its debts, then it should also be able to save over time to recover the assets sold. This is because the difference between borrowing and selling assets is more definite than it seems. In that scenario, an eroding strategy can benefit one's future standard of living more than an alternative strategy.

2. Various Types of Economic Shocks

Poor people in an economy struggling to smooth consumption in the face of various economic shocks. Rural life in an economy is typically buffeted by many economic shocks, ranging from the whims of nature and the unpredictability of the market to a wide variety of unforeseen personal tragedies. It is typical in the academic literature on crisis and coping with establishing a distinction between the so-called "covariate" or "systemic" shocks and the "idiosyncratic" shocks. This distinction is used to differentiate the two types of shocks. "Covariate" shocks are defined as those that, by their very nature, tend to affect a large number of persons who have some common features, such as the place where they reside or the kind of work they do. Examples of this include natural disasters such as floods, cyclones, and other storms, as well as the unexpected decline in yield or price of a staple crop, which can be attributed either to nature or the market. In contrast, "idiosyncratic" shocks are specific to an individual or a household due to the special circumstances it finds; for instance, the death or prolonged illness of the family's primary income earner or a person losing their job. Idiosyncratic shocks are not as common as "systemic" shocks, but they can still significantly impact.

Based on these considerations, some research proposes separating economic shocks into three categories: asset, income, and spending. Shocks to assets can include the loss of livestock, while income shocks can include job loss and expenditure loss subject to medical care expenditure. The analysis of these shocks requires putting them under broad categories.

Table 1. Typology of shocks

Asset shocks	Income shocks	Expenditure shocks
River erosion	Flood/excessive rainfall	Accident/death of earning member
Death of livestock	Cyclone/tornado/tidal wave	Maternity care
Death of poultry	Drought	Other health
Death/Loss of fish stock	Crop disease	Litigation
Unexpected loss in business	Loss of job	Dowry
Fire/arson	Loss of domestic remittance	
Theft/burglary/robbery	Loss of foreign remittance	
Sequestration of assets	Accident/death of earning member	
Loss of assets by other means		

Source: Osmani and Ahmed (2013)

3. Global Economic Crisis and Food Insecurity

The global economies striving to progress toward pre-existing adverse global economic trends, including rising inflation, extreme poverty, the prevalence of conflicts and wars, increasing food insecurity, deglobalization, and worsening environmental degradation. Given the prior challenges, it asserts that the COVID-19 pandemic has delivered an enormous global economic shock, leading to steep recessions.

From the first decade and a half of the current century, the prevalence of hunger (severe food insecurity) has reduced from 15 % to 11 %. While people suffering from hunger soared from 790 million in 2016 to 828 million in 2021. It implies that 1 in 10 people worldwide suffers from hunger gone a day without eating (SDGs report, 2022).[1] The situation is more vulnerable when looking into moderately or severely food-insecure people. Almost 1 in 3 (nearly 2.3 billion) people worldwide are moderately or severely food insecure, and an additional 350 million have been food insecure since the beginning of the pandemic. This surge is due to climate variability, pandemic, conflicts, economic shocks, growing inequalities, and food price hikes. The role of food price hikes is inescapable because global food prices surged almost 30 % in 2022 (SDGs report, 2022). These potential sources of rising food insecurity would keep the world off track of achieving zero hunger by 2030.

Globally, a 3.8 % increase in food insecurity from 2019 to 2020 added 320 million more people in one year (FAO, IFAD, UNICEF, WFP and WHO, 2021). The increase in food insecurity from 2019 to 2020 is 9 % in Latin America and the Caribbean, 5.4 points in Africa, 3.1 points in Asia, and 1.1 points in Northern America and Europe. The situation of food insecurity is worst in Africa due to the highest prevalence of food insecurity, 59.6 % of the population. Among these, almost 26 % are severely food insecure. The prevalence of food insecurity is relatively lower in Asia; nearly 25.8 % of people are food insecure. Nevertheless, it accounts for almost half the severely or moderately people of the world due to the larger population. It is important to note that the surge in food-insecure people in 2020 is due to the COVID-19 pandemic, which disrupted the supply chain globally and lowered purchasing power by raising food prices. Moreover, job losses due to COVID-19 also worsen the purchasing power of the individual, which in turn, limits access to adequate food. The economic

1 See: https://unstats.un.org/sdgs/report/2022/.

downturn followed by COVID-19 soared the number of unemployed people to 220 million, with more than 33 million jobs lost in 2020.[2]

4. Various Coping Strategies Amid Global Economic Crisis

Mostly a household used erosive and non-erosive strategies subject to the nature of the shock. However, for the global shock, coping strategies is imperative. For this purpose, the Pakistan Bureau of Statistics designed the questionnaire on the "survey for evaluating the socio-economic impact of covid-19." The questionnaire added a separate section on how severely COVID-19 affected Pakistan's households using a 5 Likert scale. Moreover, a particular question on "What the household did to cope with the economic situation during COVID-19." Considering the household's local characteristics, these coping strategies were designed amid the global economic crisis.

The coping strategies to soften global crises' effects are divided into erosive, non-erosive, expenditure-related, public/private assistance and support, and others. The erosive coping strategies (6 items) are related to the sale of assets, while non-erosive coping strategies are related to borrowing (3 items). However, expenditure-related coping strategies (4 items) comprise either compromising the quantity or quality of the goods consumed as a whole. Moreover, public/private assistance and other supports (4 items) are related to deferring utility payments and loans and financial support by the community. Apart from the prior coping strategies, temporary migration due to job loss is also recognized to cope with the economic situation during COVID-19.

The role of coping strategy in softening poverty is widely recognized in the literature; however, its impact on household food insecurity has yet to be explored. Given the importance of food insecurity, the 2nd SDG is related to "Zero Hunger" by the end of 2030. The second SDGs' primary targets are the prevalence of undernourishment, moderate or severe food insecurity, stunting, malnutrition, and anemia. The SDGs were designed to be a "blueprint for achieving a better and more sustainable future for all" with an intent to protect planets, end poverty, and economic prosperity.

2 See: https://unstats.un.org/sdgs/report/2021/goal-08/.

Table 2. Typology of coping strategies

Erosive	**Non-erosive**	**Expenditure related**	**Public or private assistance and support**
Spent savings or investments	Loans from relatives/friends	Reduced non-food expenses, that is, health and education, clothing/shoes etc.	Asked and received help/gift assistance from others in the community (not loan)
Sold productive assets or means of transport (sewing machine, wheel barrow, grain mill, agricultural tools, farm machinery, bicycle, car etc.)	Loans from employer/ moneylenders/ traders	Switched to lower quality or cheaper food	Non-payment of electricity bills
Sold household assets/ goods (radio, furniture, refrigerator, television, jewelry etc.)	Loans from formal sources (/ NGOs/banks)	Reduced quantity of food intake	Non-payment of gas bills
Sold last productive/ female animal	Temporary Migration due to loss of job/ Migrated to look for livelihood opportunities	Discontinuation of education of children due to non-availability of monthly fee	Delayed payment of loans
Consumed seed stock held for the next season			
Sold house/land/plot			

Source: Authors' own categorization based on survey evaluating socioeconomic impact of COVID-19 on well-being of people

5. Food Insecurity Methodology

As a measure of indicator, food insecurity refers to limited access to food, at the level of individuals or households, due to a lack of money or other resources. The severity of food insecurity can measure using data collected with the food insecurity experience scale survey module (FIES-SM) erected by Food and Agriculture Organization (FAO). The FIES-SM consists of eight questions asking to self-report conditions and experiences typically associated with limited access to food.[3]

The FIES consider the individual/household mildly food insecure if he/she responds the compromising on food quality and quantity. For instance, "worried about not having enough food," "ate unhealthy food," and "ate few kinds of food." If the household responds "yes" to any of the previous questions, the said household will be considered mild food insecure. The three questions of moderate food insecurity are related to "skip a meal," "ate less," and "ran out of food." Severely food insecure, for example, is experiencing hunger or going a day without eating. A household/individual is considered food secure if they respond "no" to all eight questions. Mild food insecurity is when a household responds to "yes" for any of Q1–Q3, moderate food insecurity for responding to "yes" for any of Q4–Q6, and severe food insecurity for responding to "yes" for any of Q7–Q8.

6. Severity of Global Economic Shock and Food Insecurity

The global economic shock of 2019 affects the developing economies more strikingly than the developed ones due to a higher share of the vulnerable segment. The shock effect is not identical to all households, but there may be differences in the severity of the shock. Based on personal experience, individuals respond to the severity of shock from "not at all affected" to "severely affected." The severity of shock affects the household is categorized into five (see Figure 1). The facts depict that in Pakistan, 28 % of the households responded that COVID-19 did affect their economic position (see Figure 1). The survey found that 72 % of households are affected by shock. Among these, 28 % reported being mildly affected by COVID-19, and severely affected are 4 %. In a nutshell, the affected household is more in Pakistan, and these households are more vulnerable to the crisis.

3 See for eight questions: https://www.fao.org/in-action/voices-of-the-hungry/fies/en/.

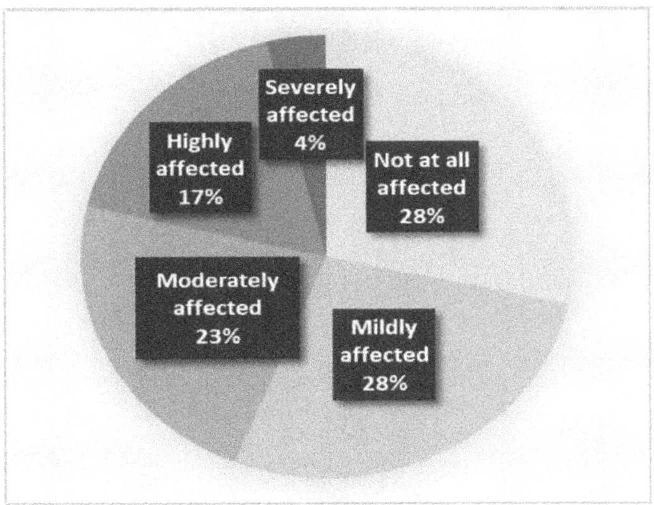

Figure 1. Distribution of severity of shock

Source: Authors' own calculation based on survey evaluating socioeconomic impact of COVID-19 on well-being of people

Although one in four households responded that COVID-19 did not affect them, descriptive statistics confirm the presence of food insecurity in their household. Twenty-three percent of the household are food insecure in the unaffected category, while this figure is relatively low compared to the other household category affected by shock. In the sample, in the mildly affected household, 70 % are food insecure, while more than 90 % of food-insecure households are highly or severely affected by the shock.

It is important to note that households that reported not at all effects from shock are also facing food insecurity, and 43 % of them are mild food insecure, while 69 % of mild food insecurity is in the mildly affected household. Moreover, the proportion of severely food-insecure households increases as the severity of the affected move from "mildly affected" to "severely affected." It implies that the severity of shock is important in influencing the degree of food insecurity.

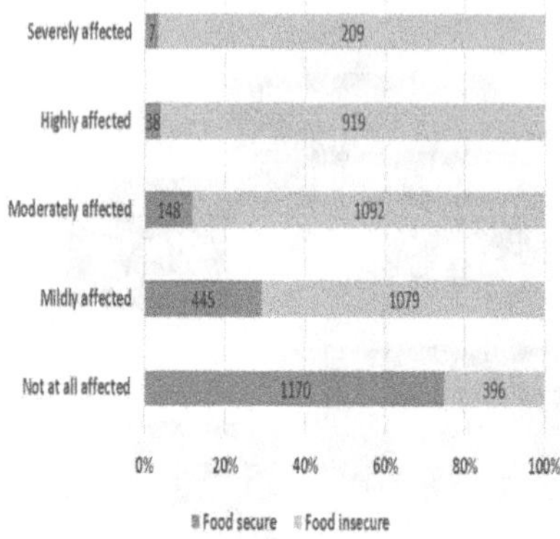

Figure 2a. Severity of shock and food insecurity

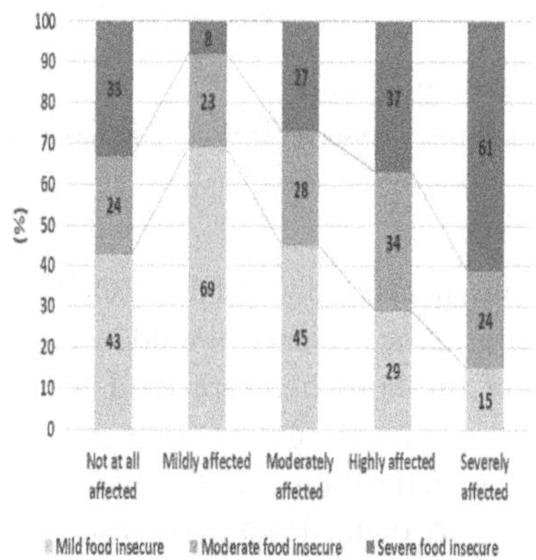

Figure 2b. Severity of shock and degree of food insecurity

Source: Authors' own calculation based on survey evaluating socioeconomic impact of COVID-19 on well-being of people

7. Severity of Shock and Coping Strategies

We have discussed that the effect of a shock on a household is different. A household using various coping strategies in response to the heterogeneous shock effect. The strategies are erosive, non-erosive, public/private assistance and support, and expenditure reduction. Among the available strategies, more than 70 % of the household responded either to reduce the food and non-food expenditure or switch to low-quality food (see Figure 3). Almost 72 % of respondents used their savings/investments from the erosive strategies to cope with the shock. While only a percentage of households sold household/land/plot to cope with the shock. Erosive strategies users are low (less than 9 %, except for saving/investment). In the non-erosive strategies, a higher proportion of households (45 %) received a loan from the informal sector—relative or friend—while a lesser proportion of households (5 %) received one from the formal sector (bank/NGOs). Public/private assistance or support is important in coping with the shock. Almost 43 % of households responded they defer the payment of utilities, while 14 % of the household received assistance or help from public/private actors.

In a nutshell, the distribution of coping strategies across the household suggests that reducing expenditure, either food and non-food, or switching to lower-quality food is a major strategy most households use.

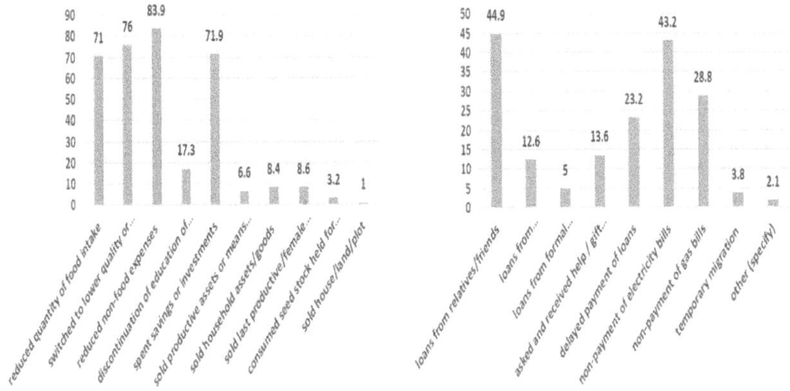

Figure 3. Distribution of coping strategies among the household

Source: Authors' own calculation based on survey evaluating socioeconomic impact of COVID-19 on well-being of people

Although we have discussed that households used strategies in response to an economic shock, strategies with the severity of shock are untapped. We presented Figure 4, which depicts different coping strategies household use against the severity of shock. The severely affected household are more proportional using the erosive strategy, which is subject to the sale of assets. 15 out of 100 severely affected households responded to the sale of household assets to cope with the income shock due to the crisis and smooth the consumption. Moreover, more than 10 % of the severely affected households reported deferring the loan payment, asking for financial assistance, and taking loans from employers or relatives. Among the different coping strategies, the most prominent strategy (use of saving/investment) is used by mildly affected households (46.3 %). On the other hand, 5 out of 100 severely affected household respond using the saving/investment to cope with the shock.

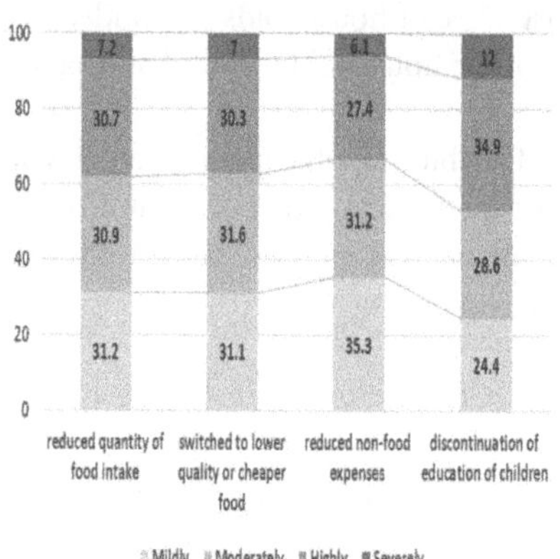

Figure 4a. Severity of shock and expenditure reduction coping strategies

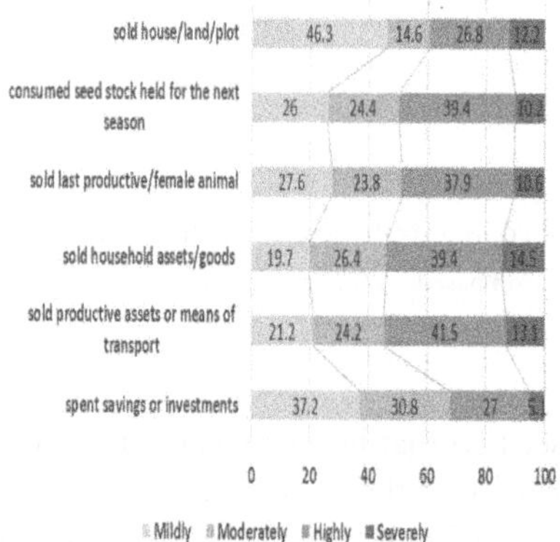

Figure 4b. Severity of shock and erosive coping strategies

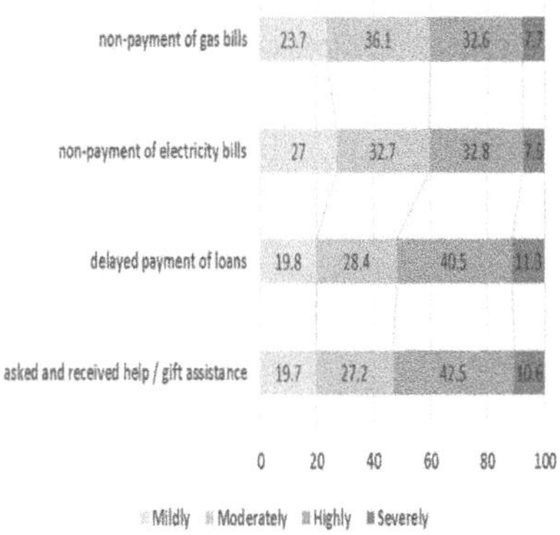

Figure 4c. Severity of shock and public/private support coping strategies

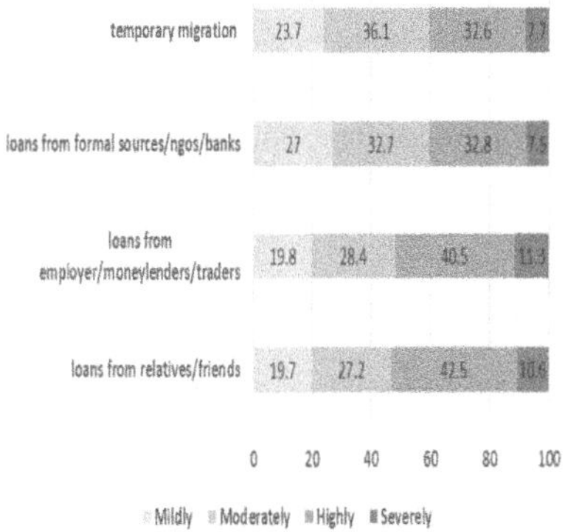

Figure 4d. Severity of shock and non-erosive coping strategies

Source: Authors' own calculation based on survey evaluating socioeconomic impact of COVID-19 on well-being of people

8. Food Insecurity and Coping Strategies

The literature has widely recognized that a household using coping strategies is more vulnerable to shock vis-à-vis a household not using coping strategies. The household with no coping strategies holds a more stable source of income and observed the consumption smoothing pattern. However, the descriptive statistics suggest that 16 % of the household that is food insecure did not use any coping strategies (see Figure 5). It followed that a household without coping strategies is not vulnerable to shock. On the other hand, three of the four households are food insecure, which indicates the presence of an unstable source of income in the household used strategies to cope with the shock.

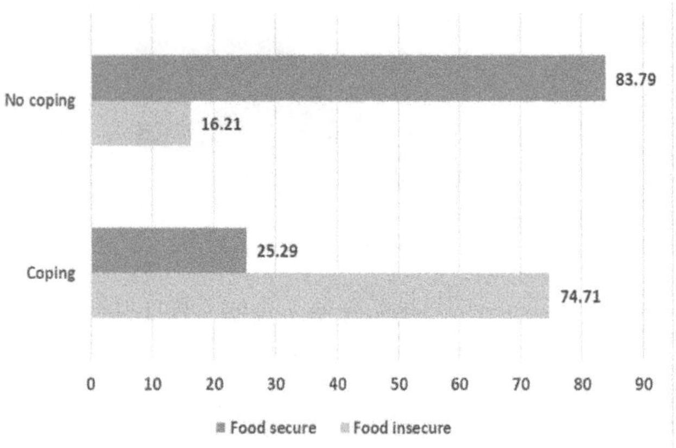

Figure 5. Prevalence of food insecurity in household using coping strategies and no coping

Source: Authors' own calculation based on survey evaluating socioeconomic impact of COVID-19 on well-being of people

We presented the prevalence of food insecurity over the different coping strategies used by the household to hedge against the economic shock (see Figure 6). The household sold house/land/plot is relatively less food insecure than those using other coping strategies. 7 out of 10 households are food insecure in a household using the prior strategy, and this prevalence is lower when compared with other strategies. The prevalence of food insecurity in households using other than (house/land/plot) strategies varied from 89.3 % to 94.2 %. It implies that households using the coping strategies provide food security to a few households (ranging from 11 to 6 out of 100).

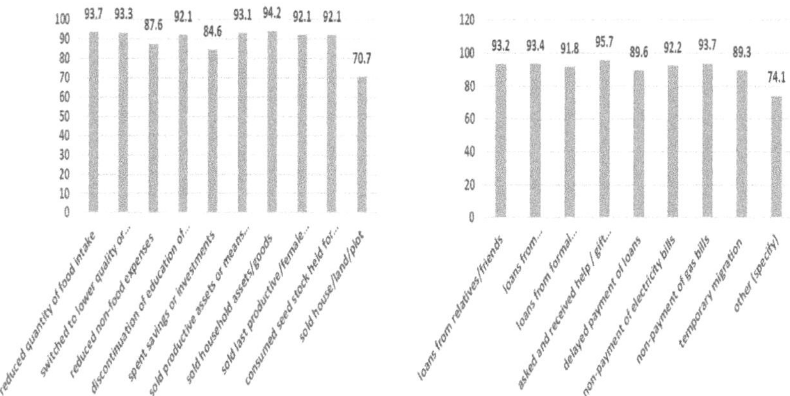

Figure 6. Prevalence of food insecurity by coping strategies

Source: Authors' own calculation based on survey evaluating socioeconomic impact of COVID-19 on well-being of people

It is important to note that households can use multiple strategies to cope with the crisis. We presented Figure 7a to show the frequency distribution of households using the coping strategies. The right-skewed distribution indicates that most households used lower coping strategies than the higher ones. Most households responded with 4 and 5 coping strategies, while 263 used one strategy to cope with the shock. Interestingly, a household with a higher level of coping strategies is proportionately more food insecure vis-à-vis households using lower coping strategies. For instance, the proportion of food-insecure households in the household using one strategy is 41 % (see Figure 7b). While the proportion of food-insecure household in the household using 18 strategies is 86 %. It implies that the lower coping strategy is a more stable source of cop up than the higher strategies.

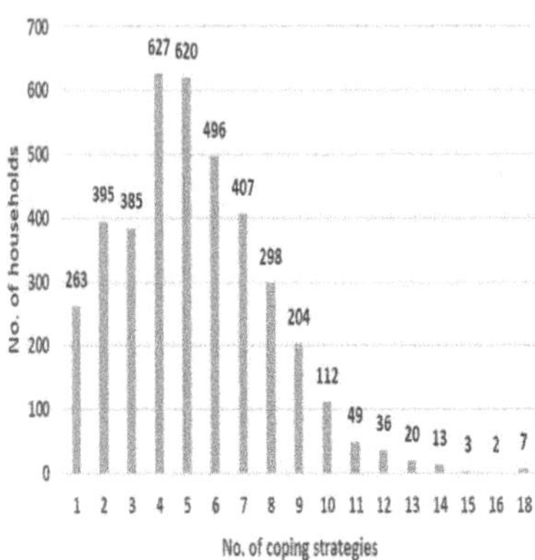

Figure 7a. Frequency distribution of coping strategies

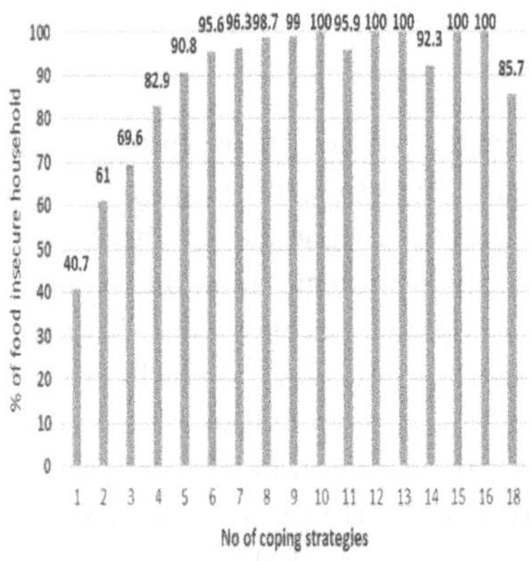

Figure 7b . Frequency of coping strategies and food insecurity

Source: Authors' own calculation based on survey evaluating socioeconomic impact of COVID-19 on well-being of people

9. Coping Strategies and Degree of Food Insecurity

The economic crisis is a pull factor in the transition of households from food security to food insecurity. However, a household can soften the effect of a crisis by using various coping strategies. In the previous section, we discussed that food-insecure households are more in proportion to using coping strategies than households not using coping strategies. Among the household using coping strategies, it is required to tap the use of coping strategies across the degree of household food insecurity.

The severely food-insecure household is relatively more in proportion among the household using the non-erosive coping strategies vis-à-vis mildly or moderately food-insecure households (ranging from 29 % to 43 %). On the other hand, among the food-insecure households using coping strategies, the mild insecure household is more in proportion using the expenditure reduction strategies. Almost 41 % to 45 % of mild food-insecure households used expenditure reduction strategies to cope with the crisis (see Figure 8b). More than 30 % of mild food-insecure households use erosive coping strategies, while more than 23 % of severe food-insecure households use erosive coping strategies (see Figure 8c). However, moderate food-insecure households are lesser in proportion using the erosive coping strategy. The distribution of households using public/private assistance as a coping strategy is identical across the food-insecure household.

We have observed that food insecurity is lower for household categories using the "sale of house/plot/land" as a coping strategy. Almost 48 % and 45 % of the mild and severe households used prior coping strategies, whereas only 7 % of moderately food-insecure households used prior coping strategies. On the other hand, households reported that the "use of saving/investment" as a coping strategy is 48 % mild, 28 % moderate, and 24 % severe food insecure.

Figure 8a. Food insecurity level and non-erosive coping strategies

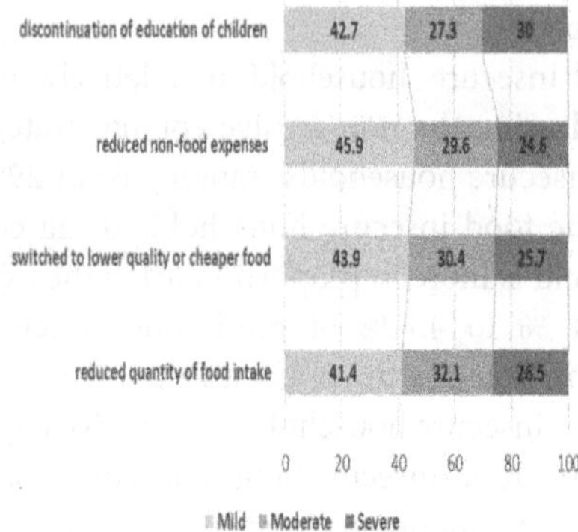

Figure 8b. Food insecurity level and expenditure reduction coping strategies

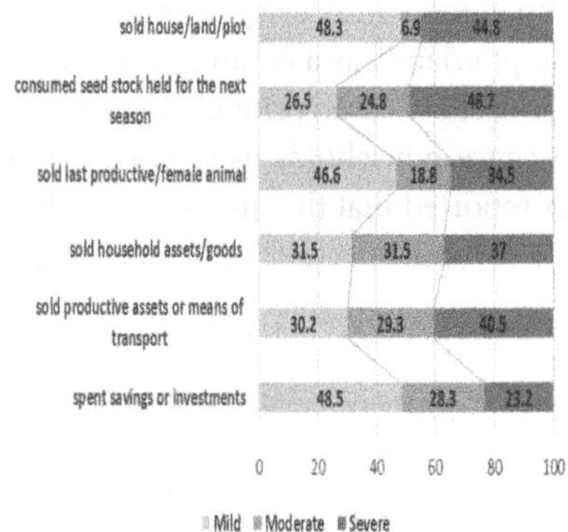

Figure 8c. Food insecurity level and erosive coping strategies

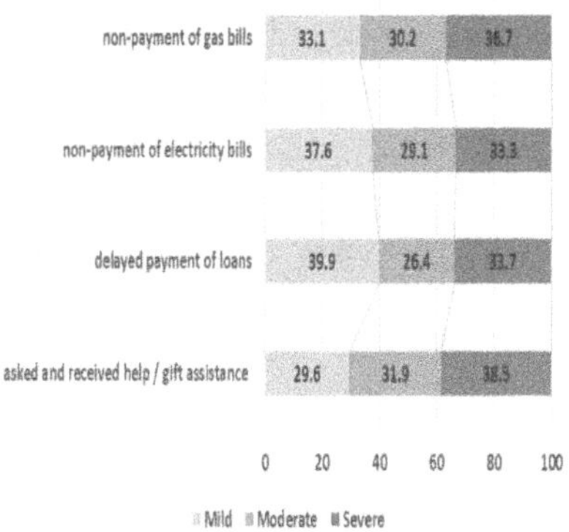

Figure 8d. Food insecurity level and public/private support coping strategies

Source: Authors' own calculation based on survey evaluating socioeconomic impact of COVID-19 on well-being of people

10. Conclusion

This study has analyzed the household's coping strategies and food insecurity amid a global economic crisis. The study's findings are that the prevalence of food insecurity amid the global crisis is more in the household using coping strategies than the household not using any coping strategies. Most households using coping strategies hold unstable income sources and are more vulnerable to an economic shock. The study figured out that almost 72 % of the households in Pakistan responded that the crisis affected their economic position. These prior households used coping strategies to hedge against the crisis. We found that households using "sale plot/house/land" and "spent saving/investment" strategies are proportionately less food insecure when compared with the household using other strategies. We found that a single household use 1 to 18 strategies to cope with the crises. However, a household with more coping strategies is more food insecure than one with one or low strategy.

The study propounds some effective policy measures to ease the prevalence of food insecurity amid global economic shock by providing life insurance subjects to hedge against the crisis. Moreover, targeted disproportional cash transfers from the government can also soften the severity of the shock. Public/private assistance also helped the household cope with the shock. The initiative by the government to defer the payment of utilities and outstanding loans restricts the household to remain mild or moderate than severe. It implies that the lack of assistance by the government and the prevalence of severe food insecurity may be further widespread. Our study found that different coping strategies soften the severe effect of economic shock and restrict some households from being severely food insecure.

References

FAO, IFAD, UNICEF, WFP, & WHO. (2021). *The state of food security and nutrition in the world 2021. Transforming food systems for food security, improved nutrition and affordable healthy diets for all.* FAO. https://doi.org/10.4060/cb4474en

Osmani, S. R., & Ahmed, M. (2013). *Vulnerability to shocks and coping strategies in rural Bangladesh.* Institute of Microfinance.

Ileana Hamburg & Emma O Brien

Inclusive, Digital-Supported Approaches in Entrepreneurship Education

1. Introduction

The European Pillar of Social Rights is underpinned by equity for all regardless of age, gender, ethnicity and disability regarding the participation in education and work (European Commission 2021). To enable full participation in society, all individuals need to be supported to proactively identify opportunities for innovation, to manage change and innovation and solve problems as they emerge (OECD, 2017; Puncreobutr, 2016). Entrepreneurship education (EE) serves as the basis for developing citizens who create value and adapt to change. An entrepreneurial attitude supports resilience and an ability to cope with uncertainty, disruptions and be innovative. It is particularly important post-COVID as digital business models have become more prevalent and so individuals need to be provided with digital skills to succeed in a contemporary society. Digital learning provides inclusive opportunities for participation in education and supports all potential entrepreneurs to develop their digital skills in parallel to entrepreneurial competence. However digital entrepreneurial education has not been widely adopted to date because pedagogical models associated with successful entrepreneurship, for example, practice, real-world immersion, and experiential approaches are difficult to design and implement in an online space (Kassen et al., 2019; Liquori & Winkler, 2020).

It is estimated that about 37 % of the workforce in the EU do not have basic digital skills, digital skills are now seen as a basic literacy that all citizens must have (European Commission, 2013). To increase digital capacity digital and inclusive approaches to entrepreneurship education are required so that all students have equal access. The lack of digital skills currently limits an entrepreneur's ability to identify technology-enabled business opportunities, or exploit digital technologies in their business models (Hamburg, 2020b).

Digital entrepreneurship training programs need to be developed to include potential entrepreneurs, particular underrepresented and disadvantaged groups. Experiential and interdisciplinary pedagogical approaches that enable learners to work in groups with people of different ages, gender and disciplines provide optimal entrepreneurial learning environments. Furthermore, entrepreneurs often feel isolated, inclusive participation though peer support and learning can build confidence and reduce isolation. In addition, learning that involves cooperation with industry is necessary and this requires a different approach for learners and educators. Pedagogical approaches such as problem and project-based learning can provide opportunities for students to collaborate with industry and other learners, conducting themselves in a professional manner and engage in negotiations. This can facilitate the development of networking skills which are key to developing opportunities to start up a business and leverage from resources (Bacigalupo et al., 2016).

This paper explores the need for inclusive entrepreneurship education in a post-pandemic society, the role of digital learning in supporting such and how it can connect formal and informal learning contexts.

2. Digital Entrepreneurship

Digital entrepreneurship can be defined as entrepreneurial opportunities created and pursued through the use of technological platforms and other information-communicating equipment (Saut et al., 2021; Hamburg, 2021). Digital entrepreneurship is an evolving concept that involves "the reconciliation of traditional entrepreneurship with new was of creating and doing business in the digital era" (Le Dinh et al., 2018). It includes the use of technology to market products and service customers, designing and offering products, and services, and reducing cost as well as new opportunities to collaborate with others.

Digital entrepreneurship requires technical and business-related knowledge and skills, which is not easily acquired. Beyond learning new practical skills, digital entrepreneurship is also about new ways of thinking about entrepreneurship itself, it offers new theories of entrepreneurship.

Digital technology has altered the way businesses work and how entrepreneurs set up a business and so the acquisition and adoption of new knowledge and skills are the key. This transformation is driven by digital technologies such as the Internet-of-Things, Blockchain, Artificial Intelligence, Big Data, Cloud Computing, Next-generation Wireless Networks. Such technologies can provide opportunities to reduce costs, access a wider base of customers, and operate on a "green," sustainable basis with low set up costs as they do not require physical spaces to exist (Gocke & Weinger, 2021; Martinez et al., 2018). Some of these technologies have been integrated into daily life and promise for driving innovation, improving productivity, stimulating economic growth, as well as enhancing individual well-being and quality of life (OECD, 2019).

Despite low barriers to entry, digital entrepreneurship has been associated with higher failure rates due to the rapid pace technology evolves and the requirement to continuously adapt to change (Gocke & Weinger, 2021). Therefore, it requires continuous lifelong learning (Butschan et al., 2019). Furthermore, it requires entrepreneurs to operate in an open manner leveraging from external knowledge and new technologies. This requires organizations to develop their absorptive capacity in which they can identify relevant new knowledge, information and technologies and adapt these to meet their individual business context. To support this Brunetti et al. (2020) advocate the need for the development of a digital culture in Lifelong learning whereby there is a "need to create an open and positive mental attitude toward future technological challenge."

3. Digital Entrepreneurship and Inclusion

It is expected that the creation of digital-based businesses could make entrepreneurship more inclusive and also provide products and services which are more inclusive and accessible for marginalized groups. International surveys indicate that women, immigrants, youth and seniors are greatly underrepresented among entrepreneurs in the EU. For example, it is estimated that women accounted for only 15.6 % of digital start-ups in 2018 (OECD, 2019).

The inclusion of marginalized groups in entrepreneurship will enrich the innovation and economic ecosystem. Many researchers highlight the importance of diversity and non-traditional thinking to support creativity and entrepreneurship (Hunt et al., 2022; Moore et al., 2021). Traditionally the focus of entrepreneurial education was on developing entrepreneurial intent, competence and behavior (Jones & Murtola, 2012). Originally research considered entrepreneurial traits and how they can be nurtured (Harrison & Klein, 2007). Recently the discourse has shifted from the "traditional entrepreneur" to consider how non-traditional attributes support entrepreneurial behavior, in particular the role of neurodiversity and neurodiverse characteristics and how they influence entrepreneurial intent. Many studies have found that neurodiverse traits are "overrepresented ... in those active in business venturing" (Hunt et al., 2022; Lerner et al., 2018; Moore et al., 2021). This is often due to the ability of the neurodiverse person to think creatively and outside the box. Ridley (2015) highlighted that neurodiversity is key to innovation and economic evolution, drawing comparisons between biodiversity and neurodiversity. In particular neurodiverse individuals provide potential for innovation to cater for diverse stakeholders and audiences as they have first-hand experiences of engaging with services and products and are aware of the limitations and potential posed by those designed by neurotypical individuals (Roberson et al., 2021).

Extending the concept of diversity, beyond neurodiversity to age, race, gender and sexuality, digital technologies provide potential to empower minority groups to engage in entrepreneurial ventures (Leahy & Broin, 2009). Many have argued of the emancipatory potential of digital technologies in terms of leveling the entrepreneurial playing field (Bruton et al., 2013; Tedmanson et al., 2012), however there is little empirical research to support these claims (Giones & Brem, 2017). Åstebro and Chen (2014) argue that access to resources still remains an issue for marginalized groups regardless of the capacity of digital technologies to reduce the need for significant resource investment such as finance and skills development. However, entrepreneurship is a complex concept that not only requires resources but attributes to support one to leverage from their own talents of resourcefulness, creativity and ability to network (Bacigalupo et al., 2016). McAdam et al. (2020) found that digital technologies empowered women to engage in entrepreneurial behavior as it reduced the barriers associated with participating in male-dominated working environments, and other cultural contexts. Although digital entrepreneurship may not be a complete solution it may reduce the barriers for some groups, for example, for some neurodiverse individuals' social skills are underdeveloped and so digital technologies may enable them to communicate with potential customers and suppliers in a more fluid and seamless manner that would be difficult for them in a face-to-face environment. Similarly, customers may have preconceived biases about a person with a disability or of those from a particular, gender, race or age and so digital entrepreneurship may reduce the potential for bias and discriminations associated with physically meeting people of minority groups.

The OECD argue that there is the potential for 9 million additional people to start a business if inclusive entrepreneurial educational supports were provided. Diverse populations are an untapped resource and are known as the "missing" entrepreneurs (Fletcher, 2021). Neurodiversity is often posed as a deficit (Houdek, 2022) rather than a strength to be leveraged. However, in the entrepreneurial context where creativity and innovation are neurodiversity is a key strength. Entrepreneurs, are individuals who identify business ideas, leverage from resources and invest in these to create value. The entrepreneur is commonly seen as an innovator, a source of new ideas, goods, services, and business/or procedures. But research has illustrated that many entrepreneurs fail in the first five years of start-up (Hamilton, 2011). Corbett (2005) underlined that entrepreneur's knowledge is the main determiner of success or failure that may be realized from exploring a venture. Whether entrepreneurs learn or acquire new knowledge can influence the chances of business success. In particular neurodiverse individuals often struggle with routine and mundane tasks required to sustain a business (Houdek, 2022; Wiklund et al., 2018) and so need to engage in entrepreneurship education to support them to address such constraints.

Furthermore, due to the lack of flexibility of our society neurodiverse individuals often struggle to identify how the "fit in," they lack confidence in terms of their ability which can act as an inhibiting factor. However, holistic approaches to entrepreneurship education can support self-efficacy of such individuals and develop transversal skills regarding how to leverage technology to run businesses more efficiently (Tucker et al., 2021).

In addition to building digital and entrepreneurship skills, it is important to help entrepreneurs from underrepresented and disadvantaged groups build stronger networks so that they can improve their access to funds, opportunities, clients, partners and suppliers.

4. Inclusive Approaches in Entrepreneurship Education Supported by Digital Technology

Inclusive entrepreneurship education involves developing a universal approach to learning that removes barriers to access for all groups of learners (Smith et al., 2017). In particular educators must look at the barriers to entry, participation, engagement and recognition of learning for diverse and marginalized groups. They must provide a safe space to foster positive attitudes to technology in a critical manner and experiment with and evaluate new digital business models. McQuillan and Gavigan (2022) advocate the use of universal design for learning (UDL) when developing an inclusive entrepreneurial education learning environment. However, many marginalized learners have low self-efficacy and self-esteem (Cook et al., 2014; McQuillan & Gavigan, 2022; Wilmshurst et al., 2011) and so inclusive digital entrepreneurship education should be nurturing and supportive as well as challenging highly creative and innovative thinkers. Providing real-world experience is key and providing safe spaces to bridge theory and practice, support for experimentation and reasoned failure (Cordea, 2014). Practical, experiential, reflective learning (Fayolle & Gailly, 2008; Mahmood et al., 2020; Rae et al., 2010) as well as problem-based learning (PBL) and project-based learning (PjBL) (O'Brien et al., 2019) in interdisciplinary groups are well suited for development of entrepreneurial skills (Hamburg, 2021). This hands-on, practical experience is well suited to neurodiverse students who find traditional academic learning environments difficult to navigate. It supports these students to construct and develop their own knowledge in a scaffolded manner rather than passively listening to lecture material. Encouraging learners to theorize what entrepreneurship means in a digital world, requires experiential approaches to learning bridging formal and non-formal learning environments (Nambisan, 2017). Opening the academic environment through the use of digital technologies provide the opportunity to integrate non-formal and formal learning environments and model digital innovation. A digital-oriented entrepreneurship education curriculum is critical, and more research must be conducted into digital entrepreneurship education (Sarma, 2020).

The use of digital approaches in entrepreneurship education prepares students for technological change, which are a prevalent part of society today. A lack of basic digital skills significantly hinders an individual's ability to successfully identify business opportunities, create digital businesses or use digital technologies as self-employed (European Commission, 2017; van Welsum, 2016). Although many people use digital technologies daily, they lack the skills regarding the critical use of digital technology. Therefore, entrepreneurship education programs need to support students to acquire critical digital skills in parallel with entrepreneurship skills and to understand how these skills can be integrated to create innovative businesses (European Commission, 2018; Jones, 2019; Ratten, 2020).

A pedagogical model that highlights diverse digital entrepreneurship role models, develops digital skills, and provides opportunities for mentoring and to network can support inclusive education practices and to support diverse groups to leverage from their talents and resourcefulness. Providing opportunities to develop networks and peer support fosters inclusion and belongingness in a group that often feel excluded and othered (Ignatow & Robinson, 2017).

This requires educational institutes to revise their current models of entrepreneurship and digital education provision to be more accessible and inclusive. Current models of education are often developed by a homogeneous group of individuals, they do not consider underrepresented cohorts (McQuillan & Gavigan, 2022). There is a need to broaden entrepreneurial education models to support those from marginalized communities to actively and inclusively participate in skills development to enable them to leverage from their multiple talents which naturally lend themselves to entrepreneurial behavior and intent. Digital learning has potential to transform and be more inclusive—meeting the needs of not only neuro-diverse entrepreneurs but neuro-typical. The next section will explore models of digital education which can provide the potential to include marginalized learners in entrepreneurial education while simultaneously developing digital skills in digital literacy, digital communication and digital innovation. Most entrepreneurial education is focused on traditional models of doing business, there is a dearth of research in the area of digital entrepreneurship education and if providing entrepreneurial education through digital formats supports digital entrepreneurship (Kraus et al., 2018). However, entrepreneurship education must consider that digital entrepreneurship brings with it many complexities including legislation concerning operating a digital business internationally.

5. Principles of Digital Learning for Inclusive Entrepreneurship Education

A digital pedagogical model is required to support inclusive entrepreneurship. However digital pedagogy is under theorized. Many pedagogical principles are "borrowed" from the 1900s, little research has been conducted to modernize these concepts in a new digital era, for example, experimental learning, constructivism etc. A digital pedagogical model for entrepreneurship education should provide learning spaces that support neurodiverse and diverse learners to stimulate their creativity and inquiry in a scaffolded and safe space while at the same time building self-efficacy and agency (Hamburg, 2021). It should create a facilitate belonging, and holistic development whereby marginalized learners can identify how they fit in, what they bring to society and how they can leverage from their strengths. Below are some principles of digital learning for inclusive education.

Table 1. Principles for an inclusive digital entrepreneurship education learning environment

Principle	
Self-awareness	Provide opportunities for reflection supporting students to become self-aware of their individual learning needs and how they can be supported through digital entrepreneurship education. Competence frameworks such as Digi Comp, Entre Comp and pedagogical frameworks such as Universal design for learning provide opportunities for learners to reflect on their individual competencies and preferences. Self-awareness and self-efficacy are key components of the ENTRECOMP framework. This also supports the development of self-efficacy and confidence that many marginalised and neurodiverse individuals experience (McQuillan and Gavigan, 2022; Cook et al., 2014; Wilmshurst et al., 2011)
Personalised pathways	Enable easy access to resources and provide these in multiple formats to ensure it meets the needs of a wide variety of learner enabling personalised paths to competence development. This aligns to the expert learner dimension of the UDL framework and providing multiple means of engagement, expression and representation.
Participatory Pedagogies	Provide opportunities for learners to co-construct resources and develop media and material through a variety of formats further developing their digital skills and confidences. Marginalised and Neurodiverse students are creative and innovative and have a significant amount of experience, providing opportunities for them to play an active role in shaping their learning is key to support creativity and inclusive approaches to education (Moore et al., 2021; Hunt et al., 2022)
Flexibility	Provides opportunities for flexible delivery including considering those with limited digital infrastructure and skills, through asynchronous, synchronous
Networking and Dialogical learning	Engage learners in dialog with each other, their teacher and with existing entrepreneurs and businesses building networking skills through open models of learning and participative pedagogical approaches. Networking and collaboration underpin several facets of the ENTRECOMP framework. (Bacigalupo et al., 2016)
Supported risk taking	Provide a safe space for collaborative exploration and inquiry with digital technologies through the development of sandboxes and the adoption of pedagogies such as inquiry and problem-based learning. This aligns to coping with the theme uncertainty and risk in the ENTRECOMP framework.
Developing confidence and recognising learning and progression	Nurture learners' confidence through opportunities for collaborative learning and reflection on their progress- assessment literacy can facilitate this as can portfolio development which can provide opportunities for recognition. This is key to building self-efficacy and confidence in neurodiverse individuals.
Critical digital skills	Develop a digital culture and critical digital skills by appreciating the advantages and limitations of technology in a business environment through reflection and questioning and encouraging learners to critically evaluate technologies and develop decision matrices and frameworks to support them in choosing different types of technologies based on their needs. (Brunetti et al., 2020.)
Transfer to practice	Learners engage in pilot projects to investigate how digital models can be transferred to real world scenarios

A proposed digital learning environment to implement this model is outlined in Figure 1. The environment provides spaces for direct teaching, individual reflection and practice-based and collaborative learning as summarized in Table 2.

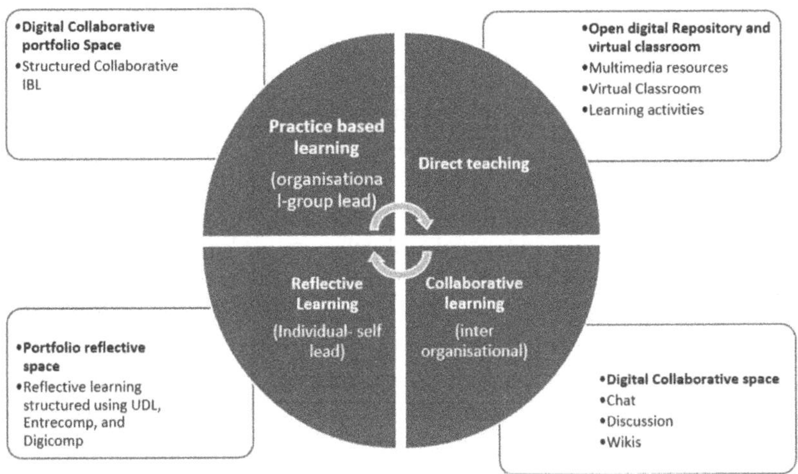

Figure 1. The inclusive digital entrepreneurship learning environment: Principles applied

Table 2. Digital spaces to support principles

Direct Teaching	Collaborative Space	Reflective Space
The classroom provides a repository of direct teaching resources in multiple media catering for all learning preferences making it more inclusive. A digital classroom provides a space for synchronous. Accessible software such as Microsoft Teams is proposed due to its accessibility and functionality for closed capturing, recording and the translation of material.	Practice based learning where learners can work in their groups on their simulated business idea through practice-based pedagogy. This contains a collaborative portfolio to prompt learners through the collaborative IBL model. The portfolio enables multiple forms of representation of knowledge providing a more inclusive learning environment. The provision of a sandbox area to support learners to experiment with different types of technology and record their thoughts is key to practice-based learning	A reflective space for individual learning. This is proposed to be in the form of an individual learning portfolio whereby learners can reflect and demonstrate their learning in a variety of means. The portfolio is proposed to be portable so that the learning can be recognised and accredited for the learners
	Networking and Dialog- where learners can chat, host discussion and share information via wikis with academic mentors, entrepreneurship mentors and their peer learners	

The model is inclusive in that it aligns to the UDL framework providing opportunities for learners to engage with content in a way that meets their needs (multiple forms of representation). In particular, the direct teaching space will provide learning resources in multiple media. Furthermore, learners can engage in multiple forms of learning individual learning, peer learning (organizational) and interorganizational learning. Learners also have individualized support with an academic and entrepreneurial mentor helping to bridge theory and practice. The portfolio structures individual and collaborative learning and empowers the learners to express themselves in a format that meets their individual needs reducing barriers to learning associated with traditional learning environments

The learning environment also provides opportunities for students to build networks internal and external to their learning. In addition, learners can contribute to direct teaching resources by co-creating and construct their own learning paths through reflection and dialogue (self, peer and expert dialogue).

6. Conclusions

This paper explored how digital learning can facilitate inclusive approaches to entrepreneurship education. In particular, we considered the challenges faced by neurodiverse and marginalized groups in the context of employment, entrepreneurship and education. It is clear that current models of education and business do not support marginalized individuals to succeed to their full potential. Although entrepreneurship education has adopted contemporary pedagogical approaches such as experiential and project-based learning this largely been face to face and through traditional mediums. This often excludes those from marginalized groups who have difficulty in returning full time to education or physically attending on campus. Furthermore, the focus of such programs does not consider the holistic needs of marginalized groups who often struggle within academic systems and lack confidence to navigate such. Despite the fact that such learners have a wealth of experience that can enrichen the learning experience for all they often feel inferior to learners who come from more privileged backgrounds.

Inclusive models of entrepreneurship education are required to support such individuals to develop digital skills and engage in education in a flexible manner that supports marginalized groups to recognize their strengths, build self-efficacy and collaborate with peers, academics and entrepreneurs to enable them to develop and sustain business ideas. Not only is this key to the continued evolution of society but achieving the EU aims of increased digital skills, employment and access to quality education and training. Successful pedagogical models to support inclusive digital entrepreneurship equally focus on the individual and their self-awareness in a digital environment, it should nurture self-confidence that many of these individuals lack. Furthermore, it should challenge such individuals by providing opportunities for creativity and innovation through inquiry so learners can investigate a business idea in a safe space with the support of a digital peer and industry network. This will support the development of digital skills in particular digital communication, digital problem-solving and digital networking that supports those from disadvantaged and underrepresented groups to engage in lifelong learning and entrepreneurial activities so they can actively participate in education and work (European Commission, 2021).

References

Åstebro, T., & Chen, J. (2014). The entrepreneurial earnings puzzle: Mismeasurement or real?. *Journal of Business Venturing*, *29*(1), 88–105.

Bacigalupo, M., Kampylis, P., Punie, Y., & Van den Brande, G. (2016). EntreComp: *The entrepreneurship competence framework*. Publication Office of the European Union.

Brunetti, F., Matt, D. T., Bonfanti, A., De Longhi, A., Pedrini, G., & Orzes, G. (2020). Digital transformation challenges: Strategies emerging from a multi-stakeholder approach. *The TQM Journal*, *32*(4), 697–724.

Bruton, G. D., Ketchen, D. J., & Ireland, R. D. (2013). Entrepreneurship as a solution to poverty. *Journal of Business Venturing*, *28*(6), 683–689.

Butschan, J., Heidenreich, S., Weber, B., & Kraemer, T. (2019). Tackling hurdles to digital transformation. The role of competences for successful Industrial Internet of Things (IIoT) implementation. *International Journal of Innovation Management*, *23*(4), 1950036.

Cook, J., Knight, E., Hume, I., & Qureshi, A. (2014). The self-esteem of adults diagnosed with attention-deficit/hyperactivity disorder (ADHD): A systematic review of the literature. *ADHD Attention Deficity and Hyperactivity Disorders*, *6*(4), 249–268.

Corbett, A. C. (2005). Experiential learning within the process of opportunity identification and exploitation. *Entrepreneurship Theory and Practice*, *29*(4), 473–491.

Cordea, C. (2014). The role of extracurricular activities and their impact on learning process. *Annals of the University of Oradea, Economic Science Series*, *23*(1), 1143–1148.

European Commission. (2017). *Digital opportunities for Europe—Digital skills and jobs coalition conference.*

European Commission. (2018a). *Digital education action plan.*

European Commisssion. (2021). *The European pillar of social rights in 20 principles.*

Fayolle, A., & Gailly, B. (2008). From craft to science: Teaching models and learning processes in entrepreneurship education. *Journal of European Industrial Training, 32*(7), 569–593.

Fletcher, D. E. (2021). *OECD report. The missing entrepreneurs 2021: Policies for inclusive entrepreneurship and self-employment* (No. 2021). OECD and European Commission.

Gocke, L., & Weninger, R. (2021). Business model development and validation in digital entrepreneurship. *Digital Entrepreneurship*, p. 71.

Giones, F., & Brem, A. (2017). Digital technology entrepreneurship: A definition and research agenda. *Technology Innovation Management Review, 7*(5), 44–51.

Hamburg, I. (2020b). Facilitating lifelong learning in SMEs towards SDG4. *Advances in Social Sciences Research Journal, 7*(9), 262–272.

Hamburg, I. (2021). Social measures and disruptive innovations in entrepreneurship education to cope with COVID-19. *Advances in Social Sciences Research Journal, 8*(1), 70–80.

Hamilton, E. (2011). Entrepreneurial learning in family business: A situated learning perspective. *Journal of Small Business and Enterprise Development, 18*(1), 8–26.

Harrison, D. A., & Klein, K. J. (2007). What's the difference? Diversity constructs as separation, variety, or disparity in organizations. *Academy of Management Review, 32*(4), 1199–1228.

Houdek, P. (2022). Neurodiversity in (not only) public organizations: An untapped opportunity? *Administration & Society, 54*(9), 1848–1871.

Hunt, R. A., Lerner, D. A., Johnson, S. L., Badal, S., & Freeman, M. A. (2022). Cracks in the wall: Entrepreneurial action theory and the weakening presumption of intended rationality. *Journal of Business Venturing, 37*(3), 106190.

Ignatow, G., & Robinson, L. (2017). Pierre Bourdieu: Theorizing the digital. *Information Communication and Society, 20*(7), 950–966.

Jones, C. (2019). A signature pedagogy for entrepreneurship education. *Journal of Small Business and Enterprise Development, 26*(2), 243–254.

Jones, C., & Murtola, A. M. (2012). Entrepreneurship and expropriation. *Organization, 19*(5), 635–657.

Kassean, H., Vanevenhoven, J., Liguori, E., & Winkel, D. (2019). Entrepreneurship education: A need for reflection, real-world experience and action. *International Journal of Entrepreneurial Behavior & Research*, *21*(5), 690–708.

Kraus, S., Palmer, C., Kailer, N., Kallinger, F. L., & Spitzer, J. (2018). Digital entrepreneurship: A research agenda on new business models for the twenty-first century. *International Journal of Entrepreneurial Behavior & Research*, *25*(2), 353–375.

Leahy, D., & Broin, U. O. (2009). Social networking sites and equal opportunity: The impact of accessibility. In *22nd bled eConference eEnablement: Facilitating an open, effective and representative eSociety*.

Le Dinh, T., Vu, M. C., & Ayayi, A. (2018). Towards a living lab for promoting the digital entrepreneurship process. *International Journal of Entrepreneurship*, *22*(1), 1–17.

Lerner, D., Verheul, I., & Thurik, R. (2018). Entrepreneurship and attention deficit/hyperactivity disorder: A large-scale study involving the clinical condition of ADHD. *Small Business Economics*, *50*(1), 1–12.

Liguori, E., & Winkler, C. (2020). From offline to online: Challenges and opportunities for entrepreneurship education following the COVID-19 pandemic. *Entrepreneurship Education and Pedagogy*, *3*(4).

Mahmood, N., Elahi, R. M., Mukhtar, B., Khan, M. M., Javaid, O., & Hyder, I., 2020. Bottom-up framework for experiential & project-based 4-year BS entrepreneurship program: An intrapreneurial conceptualization at Institute of Business Management (IOBM). *Journal of Entrepreneurship Education*, *23*(5).

Martinez Dy, A., Martin, L., & Marlow, S. (2018). Emancipation through digital entrepreneurship? A critical realist analysis. *Organization*, *25*(5), 585–608.

McAdam, M., Crowley, C., & Harrison, R. T. (2020). Digital girl: Cyberfeminism and the emancipatory potential of digital entrepreneurship in emerging economies. *Small Business Economics*, *55*(2), 349–362.

McQuillan, D., & Gavigan, S. (2022). *Educator handbook for designing inclusive entrepreneurship courses in higher education* (Chapter 4). Technological University Dublin.

Moore, C. B., McIntyre, N. H., & Lanivich, S. E. (2021). ADHD-related neurodiversity and the entrepreneurial mindset. *Entrepreneurship Theory and Practice*, *45*(1), 64–91.

Nambisan, S. (2017). Digital entrepreneurship: Toward a digital technology perspective of entrepreneurship. *Entrepreneurship Theory and Practice*, *41*(6), 1029–1055.

O'Brien, E., McCarthy, J., Hamburg, I., & Delaney, Y. (2019). Problem-based learning in the Irish SME workplace. *Journal of Workplace Learning, 31*(6), 391–407.

OECD. (2017). *Future of work and skills*. Paper presented at the 2nd Meeting of the G20 Employment Working Group 15–17 February 2017, Hamburg.

OECD. (2019). *Measuring the digital transformation: A roadmap for the future.*

Puncreobutr, V. (2016b). Education 4.0: New challenge of learning. *St. Theresa Journal of Humanities and Social Sciences, 2*, 92–97.

Rae, D. (2017). Entrepreneurial learning: peripherality and connectedness. *International Journal of Entrepreneurial Behavior & Research 7*, 214–129.

Ratten, V. (2020). Coronavirus (COVID-19) and the entrepreneurship education community. *Journal of Enterprising Communities: People and Places in the Global Economy, 14*, 753–764.

Ridley, M. (2015). *The evolution of everything: How new ideas emerge.* HarperCollins.

Roberson, Q., Quigley, N. R., Vickers, K., & Bruck, I. (2021). Reconceptualizing leadership from a neurodiverse perspective. *Group & Organization Management, 46*, 399–423.

Sahut, J. M., Iandoli, L., & Teulon, F. (2021). The age of digital entrepreneurship. *Small Business Economics, 56*, 1159–1169.

Sarma, S. E. (2020). Returning to the classroom is a chance to rethink its purpose. *World Economic Forum*. https://www.weforum.org/agenda/2020/07/returning-to-the-classroom-will-be-a-chanceto-rethink-its-purpose/?utm_source=J-WEL+Higher+Education

Smith, A., Jones, D., & Stadler, A. (2017). Designing and delivering inclusive and accessible entrepreneurship education. *Entrepreneurship Education: New Perspectives on Entrepreneurship Education Contemporary Issues in Entrepreneurship Research, 7*, 329–352.

Tedmanson, D., Verduyn, K., Essers, C., & Gartner, W. B. (2012). Critical perspectives in entrepreneurship research. *Organization, 19*(5), 531–541.

Tucker, R., Zuo, L., Marino, L. D., Lowman, G. H., & Sleptsov, A. (2021). ADHD and entrepreneurship: Beyond person-entrepreneurship fit. *Journal of Business Venturing Insights, 15*.

Wilmshurst, L., Peele, M., & Wilmshurst, L. (2011). Resilience and well-being in college students with and without a diagnosis of ADHD. *Journal of Attention Disorders, 15*(1), 11–17.

Hye-Jin Cho

Sorting in Credit Rationing and Monetary Transmission

1. Introduction: The Analytical Framework

1.1. The Credit Rationing Model

Credit rationing matters to market imperfection. There are several arguments to define credit rationing. Most of all, which one is, "rationed" when excess demand for loans in the market is greater than the supply of loans, for example, Jaffee and Modigliani (1969). Also, some borrowers can be. The reason is if the interest rate changes, some receive a loan and others do not. Possibly, the rejected borrower is willing to pay a higher interest rate, for example, Stiglitz and Weiss (1981). Hence, some borrowers are completely "rationed" out of the market. Those arguments focus on the supply side of the market.

In this, we consider a loan market equilibrium model with credit rationing at the firm level with many banks and many potential borrowers.

A central bank meets to set the rate of interest $r \in R \subseteq \mathcal{R}$. In a sense of mean preserving spreads of Rothschild-Stiglitz (1970), we assume that the bank is able to identify a high-return project $\overline{\theta}$ and a low-return project $\underline{\theta}$. The bank has a concave function f (R-R*, r-r*) where R denotes the return to the bank, r denotes the rate of interest, and stars denote target levels. The central bank controls collaterals C and borrowing amount B via the interest rate r* related to the return to the bank $\rho\left(R,\check{r}\right)$ = min (C+R; B(1+r*)) and the first claim on (C+R) where (C+R) may be defaults including bankruptcy costs or partial liquidation that the expected return exceeds liquidity shocks as seen in Holmstrom and Tirole (1998).

At the firm level, the target rate of interest as the ceiling rate of interest $\check{r}$ screens defaults on the borrowing amount B for each individual according to

$$C+R \leq B\left(1+\check{r}\right) \tag{1}$$

if the collateral C plus the return R is insufficient to pay back the promised amount. The borrower must pay back either the promised amount or the maximum he can pay back (C+R).

There is a closed economy in the ten-year discrete time horizon t = 0, 1, 2, …, 10. Two countries negotiate the loan with an international lender. Each borrower puts collateral C at t = 0 and gives back borrowings B and its interest rB at t = 10 to an international lender. The wealth W is given at the initial date such as cash-in-advance. Every year t, the lender has to choose [(ρ, r) ≡ (liquidity, interest rate)] among income Y of return R and makes the decision of the loan contract. The interest rate is a one-year fixed rate and at any time, an international lender measures the income of those two loan projects for adjusting the policy rate. The income Y of an international lender at t is

$$Y_t = \max\left(W + \rho_t R_t — r_t B, W\text{-}C\right) \quad (2)$$

If the default on a loan occurs, the wealth of a borrower is

$$Y_t = W - C \quad (3)$$

If the loan contract continues, the wealth of a borrower is

$$Y_t = W + \rho_t R_t - r_t B \quad (4)$$

1.2. Rationed Inequality

The following assumption is necessary to ensure that each loan fulfills the pledgeability. The liquid asset is not able to be collateral as the whole.

Assumption 1. (pledgeability) Loans can be partially collaterals such that $B > C > 0$.

The following assumption will guarantee that each borrower is risk-averse. The collateral C and ceiling interest rate r are concave. Its indifference curve is up to the ceiling interest rate within the collateral. In other words, there exists an interest rate which maximizes the expected return to the bank (Theorem 3; Stiglitz-Weiss, 1981).

Assumption 2. (bank returns) $f(C,\check{r})$ is concave.

We assume the low-interest rate environment without contraction of credit supply. Borrowings B such as paper wealth is greater than and equal to collateral

C. A low-interest environment occurs when the risk-free rate of interest, typically set by a central bank, is lower than historical average. Then, the parameter of partial liquidation will be at or greater than 0. It implies that the supply of liquidity increases.

Proposition 1.1. For R > 0, if $\check{r} \leq 0$, then $\rho > 0$.

Proof.

$$C + \rho \times R = B(1+\check{r}) \text{ (by the assumption 2: bank returns),}$$

$$\text{We get } \rho = \frac{B(1+\check{r}) - C}{R}$$

If R > 0, then $\rho > 0$ and if R < 0, then $\rho < 0$

(by the assumption 1: pledgeability)

In case of r < 0, remark that B $\check{r}$ < 0.

$$\text{Assumed that } \rho < 0, \frac{B - C + B\check{r}}{R} < 0$$

B-C+B$\check{r}$ < 0 (because of R > 0)

B + B$\check{r}$ < C (contradicted by the assumption 1: pledgeability)

If R > 0, then $\rho > 0$ and if R < 0, then $\rho < 0$

(by the assumption 1: pledgeability)

Proposition 1.2. The mismatch of returns and liquidation value: (1) Excess liquidity: R > 0 and $\rho < 0$
(2) The worst scenario: R < 0 and $\rho > 0$, expected utility decreases.

Proof.

$$E(U) = U(Y_1)p + U(Y_0)(1 - p)$$

In equation (4), Y_t decreases as ρR, then E(U) decreases.

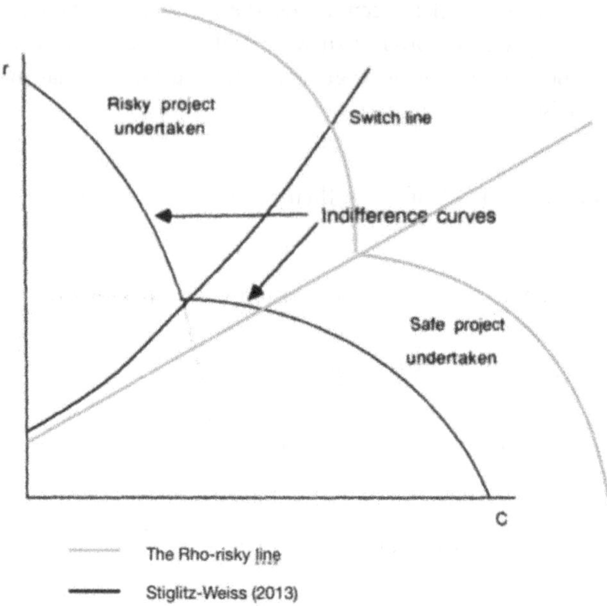

Figure 1. Decreases of the safe expected utility

Definition 1.1. In the plane (interest rate, collateral) of Figure 1, the switch line (Stiglitz-Weiss, 1992) is upward sloping at which the borrower is indifferent between undertaking safe and risky projects.

Proof.

$$\frac{dr}{dc}\Big|_{EU^r = EU^s} = \left(U'(Y_0)(p^s - p^r)\right) \div \left(\left(U'(Y_1^s)p^s - U'(Y_1^s)p^r\right)\right) > 0$$

Proposition 1.3. Risky expected utility decreases, then safe expected utility decrease.

Proof.

$$EU^r \equiv U(Y_1^r)p^r + U(Y_0)(1 - p^r) = U(Y_1^s)p^s + U(Y_0)(1 - p^s) \equiv EU^s$$

Is the interest rate rationed? At this stage, the interest rate is not able to explain why it forms the low interest-rate environment and why it's fixed in the worst economic scenario. Narrowly, limiting the ceiling rate of interest is debatable.

1.3. Rationed Inequality Trap in a Monetary Transmission Model with Two Countries

The model has two types of agents: a credit-rationed country, a non-credit-rationed country and the principal as the international lender. There are ten periods after the post-crisis period. In the first period, the loan contract is signed between an agent and the principal. From the second period, the principal wants to evaluate whether additional loan claims are acceptable. Two agents are risk-neutral with a non-negative liquidity position.

1.4. The Banking Sector

There is a continuum of banks. There are two indices of credit rationing. One is "demand deposit index" which measures by how much demand deposits are larger than total reserves; another one is a "required reserve index," which measures the ratio of excess reserves to total reserves or excess reserves to total reserves. The underlying assumption is that as banks hold more liquidity, they increase credit supply and are less likely to be credit-rationed.

For simplicity, we design the money-in-advance assumption. In detail, the aggregate amount of bank capital is reserved equal to or greater than money by a money multiplier in the market. The first-period inside money in the loan market can be the loan market value M. The distribution of inside money across banks has a money multiplier m such as $1/m$ M. The optimal capital value K is credit-rationed by a reserve requirement rr, $1/m \times M \times rr = K$.

Each country has different demand deposits (DD). For each country, withdrawals of demand deposits (DD) are costly to be liquid in a period 1.

1.5. An International Lender

The lender is big such as the international financial institution (IFI). I refer it as the informed principal who monitors the liquidity position and offers the loan contract. If demand deposits (DD) < reserves (R), the capital value K is over than the optimum. The bank intends to save the precautionary fund, reserves (R)—demand deposits (DD).

Conventionally, the money creation is possible when reserves are less than total deposits. If demand deposits (DD) > reserves (R), the capital value K is reduced than the optimum. The difference of demand deposits (DD) and reserves (R) ought to be rationed.

1.6. Interest-Rate Risk

As is well known in literatures, interest-rate risk carries two origins, according by whom it's born, firstly by banks (Bernanke & Gertler, 1995; Jiménez et al., 2012) or secondly by households and firms (Auclert, 2017; Di Maggio et al., 2017; Ippolito et al., 2018). Eventually, two conjectures say supply of loans in the monetary transmission. By the way, during this pandemic, there can be little doubt if we assume that world economy has only one policy rate which is low and not moved according to decreases of GDP. Let's assume that one homogeneous rate as of 1 % can tell everything about monetary policy. To say the least, the interval of rates may explain more about demand that it goes together with economic growth.

The central bank must predict the policy rate r*. The objective function of return ρ has the belief z by a probability measure μ on Z. This implies the policy rate with a catch-all variable z such that

$$\mu_r(A) = \mu(z \in Z : g(z) \in A) \tag{5}$$

where A is any Borel set in R and g: Z → R is the central bank's policy function.

The bank prefers to set higher interest-rate decision and economic outputs achieve the target rate of interest such that

$$G(z) = argmax_{\check{r}} \rho(\check{r}, z), \check{r} \in R \tag{6}$$

For example, in the low interest environment, the central bank sets the policy rate in a very low level, for example, μ_r (A) = 0.1 %. Likewise, adding a catch-all variable z explains the interval between 0.1 % and 0.12 % where μ_r (0.1, 0.12) $\in$ (0,1).

1.7. Two Indices of Credit Channels

Let $DD^s_{it}(k)$ denote an indicator variable for bank I's reported changes in credit standards for loan category k in quarter t. It supplies credits for the ongoing banking business and credit-worthy agents can decide intermediately. Additionally, let $R^s_{it}(k)$ denote the corresponding change on credit demand.

During the overnight, the amount of reserves ought to meet required reserves in a sense of collateral-in-advance. Possible situations are as follows:

- Demand deposits $DD^s_{it}(k)$ are greater than reserves and are either positive or negative.
- Reserves $R^s_{it}(k)$ are greater than required reserves and have only the positive value.

Central banks are likely to characterize their country's standards of required reserves and reserves as having positively changed. We have four possible answers by those variables than above two categories. Accordingly, four categorical variables $DD^s_{it}(k)$ and $R^s_{it}(k)$ are as follows:

$$DD^s_{it}(k)\begin{cases}\dfrac{DD-R}{R}\\[2ex]\dfrac{DD-R}{DD}\end{cases}$$
$$\text{and} \tag{7}$$
$$R^s_{it}(k)\begin{cases}\dfrac{R-RR}{RR}\\[2ex]\dfrac{R-RR}{R}\end{cases}$$

The timing of credit rationing is ambiguous. For example, firstly, credit supply may be rationed before supply contraction occurs. Secondly, credit supply ought to be rationed after credit supply contraction. As a rule, if the $DD^s_{it}(k)$ index is positive, then the bank should be rationed. On the other hand, if the $DD^s_{it}(k)$ index is negative, then the bank is already rationed.

At the country level, two indices are calculated with the weighted average:

$$\Delta DD^s c^t_n = \Sigma_k \omega_{it}(k) \times DD^s_{it}(k)$$
$$\text{and} \tag{8}$$
$$\Delta R^s c^t_n = \Sigma_k \omega_{it}(k) \times R^s_{it}(k)$$

where the risky status $0 \le \omega_{it}(k) \le 1$ denotes the fraction of the country n's core credit facilities that are accounted for economic figures in category k, as reported at the end of year. The liquidity composition of two indices depicts changes in lending standards and loan demand $\Delta DD^s c_n^{\,t}$ and $\Delta R^s c_n^{\,t}$ of country n = (1, 2, 3,

… $\mathcal{R}^+$). Related to two credit channels, the lending-specific index $\Delta DD^s c_n^t$ can be interpreted in the supply of intermediate credits for check-holders of demand deposits, that is, households or firms, at the country level. The credit facility index $\Delta R^s c_n^t$ represents the response to the fixed policy line of required reserves.

Table 1. Two indices of credit channels

(1) The demand deposit (DD) Index	$\frac{DD-R}{R}$	$\frac{DD-R}{DD}$
(2) The required reserve (RR) Index	$\frac{R-RR}{RR}$	$\frac{R-RR}{R}$

For (1), in Table 1, the behavior of credit-worthy agents is depicted as demand deposits (DD) above reserves (R). There are two sub-categories in which one is greater between DD and R. For (2), required reserves (RR) are fixed per country. The financial distress is possible to be measured by plugging excess reserves R-RR into two different criteria, the regulated rate RR and a real banking variable R. Therefore, credit rationing can be interpreted in two situations. Firstly, when DD is greater than R, the possibility of bank runs is crucial to know how much savings can be withdrawn in the worst scenario. Secondly, when DD is less than R, it may have excess liquidity. Excess liquidity is equated to the quantity of reserves deposited with the central bank by deposit money banks plus cash in vaults in excess of the required or statutory level. In other words, excess liquidity reflects the holding of liquidity (Saxegaard, 2006) for precautionary purposes. It concludes checking reserves above required reserves is crucial.

The country-specific indices in the above equation (8) can be aggregated across countries n in the economic and monetary union such as the European Union according to:

$$\Delta DD_t = \Sigma_n\, \omega_{nt}\, \Delta \times DD_{nt} \text{ and } \Delta R_t = \Sigma_n\, \omega_{it} \times R_{nt}$$

where ω_{nt} is commonly accorded in the economic and monetary union. The heterogeneity of the policy line for credits of each country is possibly considered since even though required reserves are same; reserve amounts are various.

There are two credit channels: the bank lending channel and the balance-sheet channel. (1) The bank lending channel shifts the supply of intermediate credit and screens credit-worthy agents. (2) The balance-sheet channel screens the demand of the borrower according to a "collateral-in-advance" constraint. Rich agents may have more collateral compared to borrowings. To sum it up, the expansionary monetary policy increases bank reserves and bank deposits—available bank loans. The increase in loans will cause investment and consumer spending to rise.

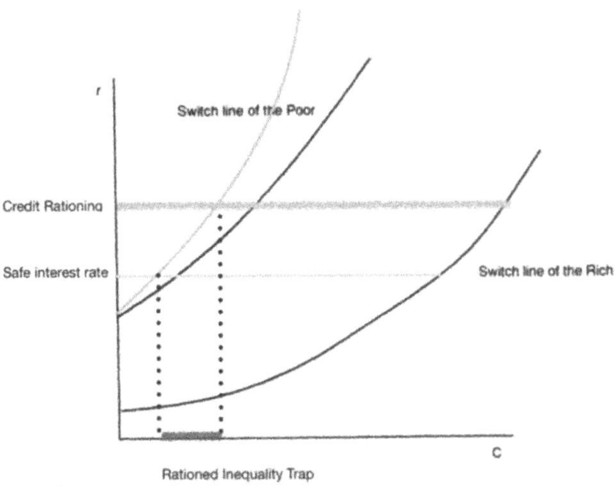

Figure 2. The rationed inequality trap

2. Empirical Findings

Consider three arguments of economic behaviors in the low interest environment. First, the saving behavior is, regulation-induced or precautionary? The policy to lower interest has the aim to stimulate investment. Limiting by lenders such as credit rationing may hamper the monetary transmission. Even though borrowers are willing to pay higher interest rates, the supply of additional credit is constrained. Is this saving related to financial intermediation? McKinnon (1973) and Shaw (1973) depict the risky demand of developing countries in the long-run growth such as high inflation, high zero-interest reserve requirements and government-mandated loan allocations to borrowers. Then, it may be regulated by the establishment of higher interest rates, then it will lead to increased savings.

Otherwise, in the safety trap of Caballero and Farhi (2017), it shows the shortage of safe assets, as opposed to a general shortage of assets, is the fundamental driving force. Money is dominated by non-monetary safe assets as a safe store value having a real rate of return. As same in Holmstrom and Tirole (1997, 1998) and Kiyotaki and Moore (2019), money as outside liquidity supports the value of inside liquidity within the market.

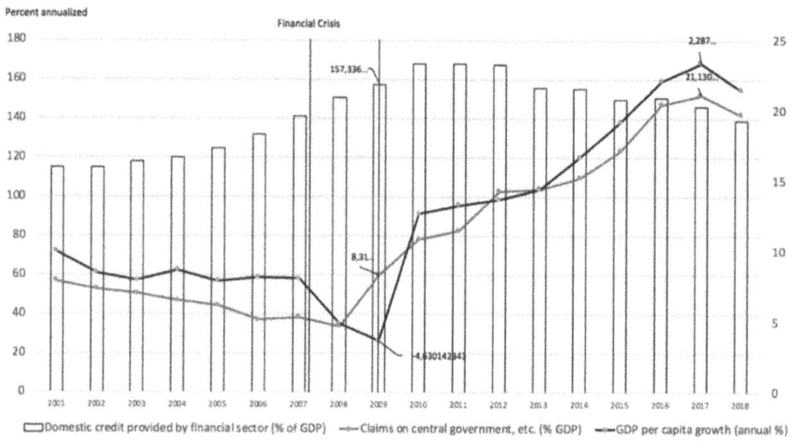

Figure 3. Euro Area (EMU) macroeconomic statistics (2001–2018, % of GDP, World Bank)

Notes: Domestic Credit of the World Development Indicator provided by financial sector is 116 % in 2001 and going up to 170 % in 2011 and smoothing down between 157 % and 144 % for 2013–2018 according to the y-axis (left). The graphs for Claims on central government according to the y-axis (right) and the GDP per capital growth 1/10-scaled show marked similarities, each maximum value: 25, 2.5. Claims on central government are macroeconomic demand deposits, denoted as credits in the asset of the central bank account. It implies the withdrawal is immediately possible and balanced with reserve money in the liability of the central bank account. The gap of domestic credits and claims on central government is 161 % in 2009.

Figure 3 suggests that, on average, GDP per capital growth has been increasing over the post-crisis period in the Euro Area countries. This is true since 2015 for 18 countries (Austria, Belgium, Cyprus, Estonia, Finland, France, Germany, Greece, Ireland, Italy, Latvia, Lithuania, Luxembourg, Malta, Netherlands, Portugal, Slovakia, Slovenia and Spain). GDP per capital growth is positive except for Luxembourg: -0.89 in 2017. The increase of demand deposits over the sample period has been overally pronounced as claims on central government, mainly due to the increase in Austria, Finland, France, Italy, Portugal and Spain from 7.41 to 11.06 % of GDP for 2015–2018. Those demand deposits are not lent out from banks' reserves. The decrease of domestic credits provided by financial sector in Cyprus, Estonia, Greece, Ireland, Malta, Netherlands, Portugal, Slovenia and Spain is coordinated to reduce domestic credit expansion after the crisis. Slowing the pace of the reserve circulation plays a role in dampening credit expansion.

Table 2. 2020 GDP estimates for 2020 of 7 advanced countries compared to 2019, GDP, percentage change, National Statistics Office, published in the IMF World Economics Outlook

Countries	2019	Projection 2020
Canada	1.6	-6.2
France	1.3	-7.1
Germany	0.5	-6.9
Italy	0.3	-9.1
Japan	0.6	-5.1
United Kingdom	1.4	-6.5
United States	2.3	-5.9

Second, the investment behavior: Lenders may agree to lend borrowers funds only "overnight" in the money market. What if the central bank sets a target level of the interest rate close to the overnight rate. For example, in Canada, eight dates per year are fixed for the overnight rate. Historically, the overnight rate has been fixed at the minimum during the period of 1935–1956, 1962–1980. For the floating rate, the overnight interest rate can be above the 3-month treasury bills. Since 1996, the central bank influences on the overnight rate than on 3-month treasury bill rates. As a whole, the interest-rate cut by the central bank is one target to deviate the credit-rationed situation for banks since the target interest rate affects to economic factors such as consumer loans, mortgages.

As time goes by, it becomes the official policy rate which is useful to compare internationally, for example, the federal fund rate in the United States and the two-week repurchase agreement (repo) rate in the United Kingdom, the marginal lending facility rate in the Euro Area: USA 1.75–2 %, UK 0.75 %, EU 0.25 %. It implies that the baseline projection for the economy will be reflected for the interest rate.

Third, the long-term excess liquidity behavior: Not surprising, the definition of long-term liquidity should be defined for economic factors. Liquidity risk is measured for the liquidity shortage mainly in the short term. On the other hand, rational expectation has the great role to react differently in the short-term horizon and the long-term one through the interest-rate channel. The interest-rate channel is the standard Keynesian channel of monetary transmission. A fall in real interest rates lowers the cost of capital and boosts investment spending. What if the low-interest rate cannot imbue the rise of investment? One reason can be price rigidities which differently react in the short-term horizon and the long-term one according to rational expectation.

More specifically, in the investment horizon, Holmstrom and Tirole (2013) show the fixed investment scale which is inherently rationed for firms. If investment decisions depend on the continuation of social values rather than the negative expected return, then initial investments and continuous investments may be credit-rationed.

Incorporating credit-rationed investment into macro-financial decisions, the following phase of the article is analyzing macroeconomic implications of credit supply and demand at the country level. The market imperfection demonstrates the mismatch between credit supply and demand. What can be a certain extent of credit rationing caused by market imperfection? Credit rationing is the denial to access the credit market which affects to the credit growth. Some have attempted to address the credit growth and GDP. Ramcharan et al. (2016) explain shocks in the US economy from market losses of the asset-backed securities (ABS) and the supply of credit: new lending per year fell from an average of around 40 billions before the crisis to about -1.5 billions a year after 2008. Eighty billions in loans over 2009–2010 may depress credit demand, as the US entered into a recession around the same time, that is, U.S. GDP in 14.96 trillion USD (Ayhan et al., 2020). By the end, the argument of mismatch between credit supply and demand, as will be argued later, moves on the type of borrowers in bank credit demand.

On the one hand, Aghion et al. (2010) claim credit rationing may lead to both higher volatility and lower mean growth according to the cyclical composition of investment. Here, we assume that investment is not a continuous decision but rather occasionally triggered when opportunity is given.

2.1. Interest-Rate Risk

Two different estimates of economic growth, respectively on January and April, 2020, need more explanation. In detail, on January 9, 2020, by the World Economic Outlook, IMF projected global economic growth was to rise from an estimated 2.9 % in 2019 to 3.3 % in 2020 and 3.4 % for 2021. Table 3 shows growth slowdown by steady decrease of GDP. It was already a downward revision compared to those in the previous year.

Table 3. Growth slowdown on January 2020 (2018–2020, GDP, percentage change, International Monetary Fund, World Economics Outlook)

Country	Year 2018	Year 2019	Year 2020
World output	3.7	3.5	3.6
Advanced Economics	2.3	2.0	1.7
Euro Area	1.9	1.2	1.3
Japan	0.3	1.0	0.7
United States	2.9	2.3	2.0

Notes: Although Euro area and Japan showed weaker performances, Global growth for 2018 is estimated at 3.7 %, as in the October 2018 World Economic Outlook (WEO) forecast. The global growth forecast for 2019 and 2020 had already been revised downward because of the negative effects of Trump tariff. The time line of Trump tariff is on specific commodities such as solar panels and washing machine (January 2018) and steel and aluminum (March 2018). Especially, goods imported from China were leading to a trade war. Data description: Gross domestic product is based on constant prices. Inflation is according to average consumer prices. Values are rounded to first decimal. For World Output, the quarterly estimates and projections account for approximately 90 % of annual world GDP measured at purchasing-power-parity weights.

In early 2020, the pandemic brings systemic risk to economy. It implies that the "great lockdown" of the entire economic system than a financial crisis in 2008. It affects the supply and demand system systemically. Compared to asymmetric shocks of COVID 19, "very sharp" fall of predicted economic growth rate has been announced and it was not estimated in advance.

On April 6, 2020, as seen in Table 4, the global economy is projected to contract sharply by -3 % in 2020, much worse than during the 2008 financial crisis. Obviously, the stability for economic growth is suspended.

Table 4. The great lockdown shock, shown in GDP estimates of seven advanced countries on April 2020 (2018–2020, GDP, percentage change, National statistics office, published in the IMF World Economics Outlook)

Country	Estimates after	Year 2018	Year 2019	Year 2020
Canada	2019	2.0	1.6	-6.2
France	2018	1.7	1.3	-7.1
Germany	2019	1.5	0.5	-6.9
Italy	2019	0.7	0.3	-9.1
Japan	2019	0.3	0.6	-5.1
United Kingdom	2019	1.3	1.4	-6.5
United States	2019	2.9	2.3	-5.9

In the field of credit rationing, the supply contraction has been adjusted as price normally moves to stability. For example, in a Stigliz-Weiss model, interest rates as an incentive mechanism manipulate the bank's expected return perfectly since the interest is able to sort borrowers. Precisely, this contraction is induced by firms rationing their own credits who perceive the probability of bankruptcy in their normal times. Hence, the expected return to the bank is lowered by an increase in the interest regardless of crisis.

On the contrary, there is no general statement for the opposite direction that a decrease in the interest brings the expected return to the bank is raised. Moreover, already in the low interest environment, we may be at the lower bound of policy interest rate. For example, according to *Financial Times*, the Bank of England on May 7, 2020 held its benchmark interest rate at 0.1 %. To put it plainly, volatility of interest rates is halted compared to "very sharp" fall of predicted economic growth rate during asymmetric shocks of COVID-19.

The primary contribution of this article is to structurally analyze the interest-rate risk. This is achieved by extending a credit rationing model from the country level with intensive pandemic shocks. At a standard firm-level solution with a bank, the interest rate is used to be the screening device for the good type. When interest-rate risk is higher, a bank may become more cautious to screen the type in responding to shocks. The remedy solution for firms is neither firing or disinvest.

2.2. The Excess Liquidity Effect in the Euro Area

A negative interest-rate environment exists when the nominal overnight interest rate falls below zero percent for a particular economic zone. This means that banks and other financial institutions would have to pay to keep their excess reserves stored at the central bank rather than making positive interest income. The evidence will address excess liquidity is highly correlated with time-series data in the financial sector of the Euro Area for the period between 1998 and 2019.

Rows 1–6 of the following table use three reserve maintenance variables such as required reserves, excess reserves, reserves and two selected liquidities, deposit and demand deposit, among the liability variables of banks as the singly explanatory variable in the single linear regression, taken from the monthly accounts of 5,232 banks including 19 national central banks (Belgium, Spain, Lithuania, Portugal, Germany, France, Luxembourg, Slovenia, Estonia, Italy, Malta, Slovakia, Ireland, Cyprus, Netherlands, Finland, Greece, Latvia and Austria) and the European Central Bank (ECB) in the Euro Area. Reserve base at the end of period is applied as the dependent variable in all models.

Liability-absorbing is defined in the 1.4.3 Liquidity of the ECB monthly data. Period averages of daily positions. Liquidity-absorbing factors are deposit facility, other liquidity-absorbing operations, banknotes in circulation and other factors (net). Liquidity-providing factors are main refinancing operations, longer-term refinancing operations, marginal lending facility and other liquidity-providing operations.

As can be seen from row-1 time-series required reserve in bank assets is correlated with the time-series excess liquidity as the dependent variable. On the one hand, row-2 time-series demand deposit is strongly correlated with the time-series excess liquidity. On the other hand, row-3 time-series deposit is not. All variables in following table Table 5 have been normalized by their standard deviations (SD).

Concerning row 1 and 4 time-series, each regulatory control with excess liquidity from them is correlated to the fundamental as reserves and the credit-rationed as required reserves, respectively 7 %, 26 % of R-square. In the comparison of row 2 and 3 times series variables, the single regression model with the time-series demand deposit has much higher R-square than one with the time-series deposits (46.5 % for a row-2 model, 0.14 % for a row-3 model). Finally, row 5 and 6 time-series re-estimates two indices of credit channels: demand deposits minus reserves and reserves minus required reserves.

Probably, liquidity shocks may be driven by deposits or demand deposits in reserves. Row 3 and Row 5 show the different result of excess-liquidity relevant shocks. Once again, excess liquidity is significantly correlated with two indices of credit channels in the post-crisis period of Europe in the low interest environment.

Table 5. The Euro Area financial sector variable on longitudinal measures of excess liquidity (12/1998–09/2019)

Explanatory variable standard deviation of	**Deposit**	**Demand deposit**	**Required reserves**	**Reserves**	**R-Square (p value)**
1			0.5636 (-2.435)		7 % (0.00 %)
2		0.007 (0.116)			46.5 % (0.00 %)

(*continued on next page*)

Table 5. Continued

Explanatory variable standard deviation of	**Deposit**	**Demand deposit**	**Required reserves**	**Reserves**	**R-Square (p value)**
3	0.050 (0.029)				0.14 % (55.36 %)
4				0.005 (0.052)	26 % (0.00 %)
5		0.017 (0.534)		0.010 (-0.262)	84.93 % (0.00 %)
6			0.453 (-4.32)	0.005 (0.06)	45.96 % (0.00 %)

Table 6. Summary of data

250 observables in the post-crisis period. Existing missing 22–23 values filled in the interpolation function. Calculated from 5,232 banks in the European Central Bank (ECB) data.
Dependent variable is excess liquidity. Excess reserve measures excess liquidity and is plotted in Figure 1. The monthly value is calculated by averages of daily positions in the Euro Area banks. Total excess reserves of credit institutions subject to minimum reserve requirements such as 1 % in the Euro Area. 1,252 EUR billions in 2018.
Each row reports standard deviation (SD). The coefficient is given in italics with parentheses below. The time-series of the monetary financial institutions (MFIs) are from linearly regressing on the standard deviation (SD) of explanatory variables. All variables normalized to a SD of 1. So, for example, row 1 reports that a negative sign indicates if required reserve variable increases, then excess liquidity variable decreases.
Deposits with an agreed maturity or notice period over two years held by credit institutions subject to minimum reserve requirement in Euro Area. End of period. Monthly.
Overnight deposits and deposits with an agreed maturity or notice period of up to 2 years held by credit institutions subject to minimum reserve requirements in Euro Area. Banknotes in circulation 1,202 EUR billions excluded. End of period. Monthly. 12,276 EUR billions in 2018.
Required reserve ratios (RRRs) 1 %. Effective January 18, 2012. Down from 2 % between January 1999 and January 2012. 126.8 EUR billions in 2018.

2.3. Excess Liquidity as Cyclical Investment

Does credit rationing play a role in the monetary transmission? The low interest environment implies that banks are not lending much. It doesn't shortly conclude that loan pricing sufficiently changes credit. Specifically, there is no evidence whether poor credit demand excludes non-prime borrowers or not.

For the monetary transmission, the number of continuous players is not the focal point. For example, the number of the national bank is 0 % among total banks. In detail, according to European Central Bank (ECB) data of the Euro Area monetary aggregates, the number of national central banks is 20 among 5,286 monetary financial institutions (MFIs) at the end of May 2019. The calculation is simply done: 20 ÷ 5,286 = 0.00378. Also, credit rationing doesn't have the economic value at the Nash equilibrium. No credit rationing may be the first-best optimum investment (Piketty, 1997) or low investment is the first-best case for everybody. Regardless of continuous players, the interest rate indicates monetary decisions such as the aggregate bank lending volume in Bernanke and Blinder (1992) or liquidity of smaller banks, that is, the bottom 95 % of the size distribution such as Kashyap and Stein (2000). Hence, further investigation about fundamentals and investment goes how the interest channel works.

Separating monetary decision from economic activity has been analyzed with macro data in Bernanke and Blinder (1992) and bank-level data in Kashyap and Stein (2000). Mentioned in Jiménez et al. (2012), that's problematic because of a Taylor rule—determined short-term interest rate changes. Credit rationing is a useful tool to understand monetary decision since it's non-pricing rationing, independent from economic activities. Compared to comparative statics, shown in the theory of consumer and incentives based on microeconomic foundations, credit rationing is deducted in the opposite sense. As a comparative-statics analysis, investment is the largest component of economic fundamentals. Credit rationing is started with investment to address fundamentals.

2.4. The VAR Estimation and Forecasting

To evaluate the impact of two credit channel indices on excess liquidity, I estimate a range of VAR on monthly data from December 1998 to September 2019. The first model is estimated on time-series variables of excess liquidity and the demand deposit (DD) index and the second model is estimated on time-series variables of excess liquidity and the required reserve (RR) index. The assumption is based on the stability of credit channel indices that those indices in the VAR are shortly fluctuated and controlled after several months. Credit channel indices go back to the constant estimation at the end of those models.

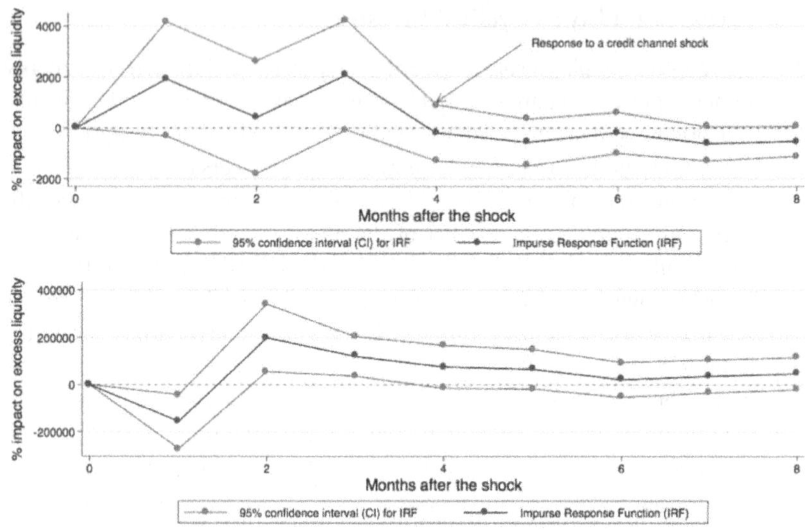

Figure 4. VAR estimation on the impact of a credit channel index concerning excess liquidity

3. Conclusion: The Impact of Untightening Credits

Recognizing credit needs and constraints is important across the economic population and along the healthy life cycle of firms and households. Untightening credits may support the facility of financing sources. The lack of an access to finance is limiting loan entry, for example, no measurement in advance and renegotiation enforcement at the country level. By removing supply-side hurdles, such as the overall opacity of the credit market, the awareness may promote financial sources.

Two different measures of loan demand were obtained for continuous investment categorized into two stages according to precautionary and risk-loving levels. The investment in the credit channel of the transmission mechanism here is of particular importance. Investment is relevant to an interest ceiling constraint which is the specific loan model for banks. We were trying to describe investment for the country-level decision by the international lender in the monetary transmission mechanism.

As the analytic framework of two countries shows, even though no transaction fee for getting loans do not precise the international monetary market, the result can eventually specify key variables and effects of the low interest environment.

When considering possibilities and policies of loans that would generalize the situation for decision-making of the international lender, we need to compare two countries. A credit-rationing country may have excess liquidity as excess reserves.

Thus, the monetary policy of the low interest environment intends to decrease the contraction of loan supply and increase the growth of investment. In conclusion, the importance to understand the liquidity position is crucial to explore new ideas about potential monetary policy and lending.

References

Aghion, P., Angeletos, G. M., Banerjee, A., & Manova, K. (2010). Volatility and growth: Credit constraints and the composition of investment. *Journal of Monetary Economics*, *57*(3), 246–265.

Auclert, A. (2019). Monetary policy and the redistribution channel, *American Economic Review.*

Ayhan, K., Sugawana, N., Terrones, M. (2020). Global Recessions, *World Bank Group.*

Bernanke, B. S., & Blinder, A. S. (1992). The federal funds rate and the channels of monetary transmission. *American Review*, *82*(4), 901–921.

Bernanke, B. S., & Gerler, M. (1995). Inside the black box: the credit channel of monetary policy transmission, *Journal of Economic Perspectives*, 9 (4), 27–48.

Caballero, R., & Farhi, E. (2017). The safety trap. *Review of Economic Studies*, *85*(1), 223–274.

Di Maggio, M., Kermani, A., Keys, B., Piskorski, T., Ramcharan, R., Seru, A. & Yao, V. (2017). Interest rate pass-through mortgage rates, household consumption, and voluntary deleveraging, *American Economic Review*, 107(11), 3550–3588.

Ippolito, F., Ozdagli, A., & Perez-Orive A. (2018). The Transmission of Monetary Policy through Bank Lending: The Floating Rate Channel, *Journal of Monetary Economics*, 95, 49–71.

Holmstrom, B., & Tirole, J. (1997). Financial intermediation, loanable funds, and the real sector. *Quarterly Journal of Economics*, *112*(3), 663–691.

Holmstrom, B., & Tirole, J. (1998). Private and public supply of liquidity. *Journal of Political Economy*, *106*(1), 1–40.

Holmstrom, B., & Tirole, J. (2013). *Inside and outside liquidity*. MIT Press.

Jaffee, D., & Modigliani, F. (1969). A theory and test of credit rationing. *The American Economic Review*, *59*(5), 850–872.

Jiménez, G., Ongena, S., Peydro J. L., & Saurina, J. (2012). Credit supply and monetary policy: Identifying the bank balance-sheet channel with loan applications. *The American Economic Review, 102*(5), 2301–2326.

Kashyap, A. K., & Stein, J. C. (2000). What do a million observations on banks say about the transmission of monetary policy?. *The American Economic Review, 90*(3), 407–428.

Kiyotaki, N., & Moore, J. (2019). Liquidity, business cycles, and monetary policy. *Journal of Political Economy, 127*(6), 2926–2966.

McKinnon, R. I. (1973). *Money and capital in economic development.* The Brookings Institution.

Piketty, T. (1997). The dynamics of the wealth distribution and the interest rate with credit rationing. *The Review of Economic Studies, 64*(2), 173–189.

Ramcharan, R., Verani, S., & Van den Heuvel, S. J. (2016). From Wall Street to main street: The impact of the financial crisis on consumer credit supply. *The Journal of Finance, 71*(3), 1323–1356.

Rothschild, M., & Stiglitz, J. E. (1970). Increasing risk. *Journal of Economic Theory*, 2(3), 225–243.

Saxegaard, M. (2006). *Excess liquidity and the effectiveness of monetary policy: Evidence from sub-Saharan Africa* (IMF Working Papers).

Shaw, E. S. (1973). *Financial deepening in economic development.* Oxford University Press.

Stiglitz, J. E., & Weiss, A. (1981). Credit rationing in markets with imperfect information. *The American Economic Review, 71*(3), 393–410.